American Absolutism

The Psychological Origins of Conspiracism, Cultural War, and the Rise of Dictators

Gary A. Freitas

First Edition

Fulton Books
Meadville, PA

Published by Fulton Books 2023

ISBN 979-8-88982-665-1 (paperback)
ISBN 979-8-89221-298-4 (hardcover)
ISBN 979-8-88982-666-8 (digital)

Printed in the United States of America

Contents

Introduction

We are all sufferers from history.

—R. Hofstadter, *The Paranoid Style of American Politics*

It appears America has arrived at a pivotal juncture in its history, one that is not only challenging the viability of our democratic institutions but also questioning who we are as a nation. Over the past four decades, the Republican Party has incrementally abandoned conservative principles for a power grab that is being supported by a significant percentage of the electorate. And equally alarming, White evangelical America appears to be at war with a multicultural, biracial, feminist, LGBTQ America. It's as if all of us are looking at America for the first time through a kaleidoscope.

Political scientists, economists, and journalists, among many, are struggling to describe a dysfunctional and maladaptive sociopolitical phenomenon referred to today as the Trump MAGA movement. The roots of this movement were present at America's founding and have episodically risen and fallen in significance throughout history. Beginning mid-twentieth century, scholars have variously termed supporters of these social movements as "true believers," "paranoid type," "authoritarian personality," and the "conservative mind." The term *absolute-minded*, as used here, encompasses all these types, focusing on the psychological dynamics that underly populist intrigue throughout our history.

American Absolutism is a psychological examination of the violent undercurrents roiling America today. It applies psychological theory to discern the forces sowing social and political discontent across our political landscape. And what is most startling, at this moment in time, is the obvious transparency with which all of this is taking place. And most bewildering are the outrageous claims of a stolen 2020 election and an attempted coup of the US government. Equally puzzling has been the characterization of public health measures to combat COVID-19 as a hoax and civil rights violation. This is all enveloped in the disturbing embrace of paranoid conspiracies by tens of millions of Americans.

In recent decades, dozens of academic works have attempted to discern the origins of authoritarianism and all its conspiratorial and populist impulses that abound today. And they reveal many fundamental truths about our world: technology and globalization have fueled rapid social change and discontent; rising economic inequality is stress-testing our political system; social, economic, and political turbulence have resulted in a return to tribal identities and herd immunity; anomie and alienation have arisen because of the breakdown of communities and challenges to traditions, beliefs, and norms. Their focus is typically on the political turmoil resulting from rapid change and challenges to people's beliefs and identity in challenging times. But if we are candid, this wealth of scholarship doesn't fully explain what is taking place at ground level.

Understanding what triggers populist discontent has largely been an intellectual exercise comprised of big picture theories as outlined above, but always with the goal of discerning what drives and motivates this behavior. Efforts at measuring and quantifying social discontent and making it more predictable have lagged far behind. And along this theoretical continuum, from macro to micro, many gaps are being filled in by massive efforts at nationwide data collection—surveys, polls, troves of electronic data gathering, and limited but profuse academic research.

American Absolutism is an effort to connect macro and micro theories into a coherent picture of the underlying psychological factors driving the emergence of an authoritarian response and populist discontent. It is not enough to be content with identifying the triggers. We need to better understand how absolutism came to preexist in the minds of so many individuals to begin with. The time has come for us to move beyond defaulting to the idea of it being a predisposition or reducing it to personality type to more fully understanding how it actually comes about and is sustained. What we are slowly coming to understand is that absolutism is not a random condition but one that developmentally arises because of a unique set of personal and social dynamics.

As a psychologist, I have yet to encounter a satisfactory explanation as to why normal people are suddenly expressing delusional ideation in their daily discourse and appear consumed by paranoid ideas and reality-bending conspiracies. The majority are not bending under economic stress or even personal duress in most instances but are all acting like the QAnon Shaman is the new normal. Why are millions of people defying common sense and their own best interests? Why are all the anger and rage directed at medical professionals and school boards? All the while shouting at the world it can go to hell! Really, who would mount an insurrection against the US government based on tweets? There has to be more to this story than meets the eye. Part of the answer lies in the psychology of those raised in absolutist dynamics, making disbelief the default norm in times of crisis.

An unshakeable belief in conspiracies by large numbers of people requires a unique alignment of triggering events, including many people experiencing a deep mistrust fueled by their fear and anger, but also by the presence of an emotional and cognitive predisposition toward conspiratorial thinking. But the question that continually confronts us is why would anyone believe in reality-bending conspiracies? The aim here is to demonstrate exactly how conspiracies become formed in the minds of individuals. It is also important to clarify that absolutism, as is discussed here, is not a personality trait, mental disorder, or a social psychopathology. Rather, it is an archaic trust adaptation confronting a rapidly changing world in an intense struggle to define who we are as a people and a nation. Social theorists and journalists are struggling to understand why so many have come to embrace conspiracies and alternative facts. *American Absolutism* sets out to shed light on the invisible dimension of conspiracism and its social and political impact.

Social Trust

For the past seventy years, social theorists have understood that the default bottom line for our current political unrest lies with the disruption of trust early in life. But this is where the narrative typically ends—the parents were harsh and demanding, and the child was overconforming. We are told the answer to a disruptive conspiratorial world, where millions currently reside, is somewhere near this parent-child fault line. And if this is true, we are truly without a roadmap or schematic, and the origin of absolutism continues to remain vaguely impervious to intervention.

This book offers a theoretical model of social behavior based on extensive social science research. The urgency to publish this work comes from the growing social and political crises America currently faces, where the definition of reality is being tested, and the ability to discern fact from fiction is being challenged by many Americans. Most disturbingly, it is being distorted by political leadership on the right. This failure of reality testing has been a persistent issue in American history, one that has again crossed a violent threshold.

The core issue has always been social trust. The ability of any one person to trust is what holds communities of people together. It is the fabric of our social contract. When this bond is broken, civil discord inevitably ensues. But most significantly, this bond is individually formed at birth and shaped throughout infancy and childhood. And from there, it is rerouted by family, friends, and a lifetime of experiences. But once it is disrupted, it opens the door to a myriad of consequential psychological possibilities that are explored here.

As you read this book, you will immediately begin to think he's talking about "us" versus "them" or red states versus blue states. And on the surface, that will appear to be true. But here is the larger reality. What is presented here is true for all of us, but only if we are enmeshed in the right circumstances, which can trigger failed reality testing in each of us. There is no perfect developmental experience of trust; that is not the real world. In the real world, naïve trust will be continually tested until abandoned for a reality that can be maintained in the face of hardships and oppressive circumstances. Think of trust in these terms. If life was waterboarding us, we would all eventually come to believe in conspiracies if that would make it stop. And if this is not your current reality, feel thankful.

We are all vulnerable to mistrust, but some more than others. The absolute-minded are the most vulnerable and the focus of this book. They began their lives with a significant distortion in the ability to trust. And the potential consequences for a community are forever at play as a result. And distorted trust can only be understood by the fact that it is passed down generationally. While it's easy to rationalize that the absolute-minded are a canary in a coal mine and that we should all be paying more attention, in many instances, they are the problem itself. While their triggers can be highly individualistic, their shared discontent can rapidly spread, much like the transmission of a virus during a pandemic, forcing everyone to confront a community in crisis.

It is equally important to realize that modern conspiracy is not an isolated event that spontaneously pops up in the mind of millions of people. Yes, the emergence of a conspiracy coincides in times of social unrest, but it also requires leaders who are actively sowing discontent and aligning the individual's disbelief and mistrust with the conspiracy. Today's conspiracy requires planning, financial backing, support from many individuals and groups, influential voices and media access, and the ability to strike the right chord with the public.

Activating Authoritarianism

In an exceptionally dense academic book comes a dire and prescient warning to America. *The Authoritarian Dynamic* (2005) by Karen Stenner offers any number of troubling conclusions that we should all be paying attention to. While her work essentially focuses on developing a measure of authoritarianism, her conclusions are significant for understanding the absolute-minded. First and foremost, she emphasizes that social turmoil is key to activating an authoritarian response. She doesn't know why some people are more authoritarian than others, terming it a "predisposition." But she then goes on to note that the "authoritarian predisposition seems to be a relatively innate and enduring individual trait" and that "politics provide the critical inputs that fundamentally alter the behavior of citizens of varying disposition." The key factors are collective and normative threats, which play a substantial role in provoking their "characteristic attitudes and behaviors," particularly the propensity to "express racist, intolerant, and punitive attitudes." We should all be paying attention here. This is a vivid portrait of absolutism.

While Stenner only sees a modest relationship between an authoritarian predisposition and a conservative one, she adds this caveat: "the relationship between the two [is] highly contingent on political and social conditions." I would add that the connection between the two is significant right now, as the Republican Party is continually dog whistling conspiracy theories and distrust in government to its base. Stenner adds that a politics of fear and a "steady diet of negative campaigning, media obsession with political scandals, and the constant ringing of alarm bells regarding society's moral decay" are all triggers for an authoritarian response.

But Stenner's conclusions lead to an even darker realization.

> Exposure to differences, talking about differences and applauding differences—the hallmark of liberal democracy—are the surest ways to aggravate those who are innately intolerant, and to guarantee the increased expression of their predispositions in manifestly intolerant attitudes and behaviors.

Stenner adds:

> Nothing is more certain to provoke increased expression of their latent predisposition than the likes of multicultural education, bilingual policies, and non-assimilation.

The reality of the American political process is that it's pretty much wired to amplify conflict, with endless debate on cable news and online media airing opinions and disagreements 24-7. The result has been polarization and escalating expression of intolerance. America, it turns out, is a hotbed of authoritarian activation and expression. While this has never really been in doubt, it is also clear that social media saturation is turning up the heat.

Powerful Forces are Everywhere

The forces shaping our world are complex and multifaceted. While some see these forces as conspiracies, it is important to recognize that there are many factors at play. The rise of absolute-mindedness can be contextualized by several key constructs, including the divide between rationalists and those with a more absolute mindset. This divide can be seen as a potential source of conflict, both in the United States and around the world. At the heart of this divide are those who are moving toward the future and those who are clinging to the past, to the old ways of power and authority that are being disrupted.

While it may be tempting to view these conflicts through the lens of the "clash of civilizations," as proposed by political scientist Samuel P. Huntington, it is important to recognize that a new paradigm may be emerging. This new paradigm recognizes the complexity and interconnectedness of the forces at play and offers a more nuanced and holistic view of the challenges and opportunities facing our world. Outlined below are the large-scale social factors actively triggering the absolute-minded.

Dynamical social networks. The slow ascent of the contemporary world after nearly six thousand years of civilization-building has resulted in most humans residing in a simulated world of our own design. This insulation from the unpredictable natural world has had enormous repercussions for the absolute-minded and the future. As of 2018, there were 548 cities worldwide with a population over one million, with Tokyo and its surrounding metro area topping the list at over thirty-eight million. While densely clustering people has many social and economic advantages, it has also led to greater social division. Ultimately, this reflects a speeding up of social-cultural change, which is a constant trigger for absolutism.

Human identity formation. The central psychological construct underlying the human condition has always been identity, both individual and group. Traditionally, identity was formed around race, ethnicity, language, faith, tradition, nationality, and culture. It is also what defines humans from all other species on earth. Only humans have the imagination to create their own identity. Any process or event that disrupts identity formation almost always has dramatic consequences and has historically been the basis for conflict. As the modern world engages in the wholesale disruption of identity, it is creating a psychological void for conspiratorial ideation to enter.

E-identity. A 5G network and smartphone now give us an electronic identity that overrides all previous forms of identity. It electronically connects 90 percent of the human race in real time, without considering factors such as race, ethnicity, beliefs, history, or cultural traditions. Language translation is now a simple app. The only thing that matters and distinguishes us is the reliability of our electronic credit. The race is on between data warlords (tech companies) and governments to control our reach into the world and capture our data (and by extension, us). Going forward, this will define the conflict between rationalists and the absolute-minded. The invisibility of technology (algorithmic black boxes, hidden data exploitation, and the ability to manipulate and surveil us) is now imploding on the world, making it ripe for conspiracies to give coherence to all the mysterious and invisible forces controlling and defining us.

Capitalism and globalization. The modern world greatly impacts how we network and how identity is formed. We are quickly being overtaken by electronic networks and e-identities, further disrupting identity formation and the organization of political and economic power. In the past, contact between cultures typically ended in conflict and the formation or collapse of empires. More recently, economic and political conquests have been typical of colonialism and imperialism. We are now entering the age of electronic imperialism, whose parameters are completely unknown to us. Nevertheless, it is shaping identity, surveilling us, and broadly manipulating our thinking and behavior. Throughout the world, it is being used to predict and intervene in our thoughts and actions.

Electronic networking. Richard Hofstadter documents a long history of conspiratorial thinking in America in his seminal article "The Paranoid Style in American Politics," but he notes that something new was propelling this process forward in 1964: "the effects of mass media." Today, it goes without saying that conspiratorial ideation has been amplified at levels never previously experienced, thanks to the advent of TV, computers, internet, smartphones, and social media platforms. Online media can instantaneously silo people and insulate them by their beliefs then continuously reinforce those beliefs with alert algorithms, forever linking them to their fears and prejudices. All of this is done without exposing them to counterfactual information. This echo chamber effect has given rise to what is being termed conspiracism—conspiracy as a system of belief. George Orwell, author of the dystopian novel *1984*, would have perfectly understood what is taking place today. It's as if thought control spontaneously appears straight from the individual mind.

Within our simulated reality, our electronic networking is the equivalent of what Huntington describes as a "clash of civilizations," not dissimilar to five hundred years of European colonization and its impact on identity throughout the world and unending conflict and violence. Today, our simulated reality is quickly evolving, with astonishing and disruptive impacts on the environment, markets, and identity. This has given rise to populism and the anomie of the human condition, what Hannah Arendt and Eric Hoffer described as the antecedents of totalitarianism.

Environment and human population growth. For all its undeniable success over the past five hundred years, capitalism is a voracious creature that is consuming the earth and all of us on it. We are in a race against time that can only be described as a death spiral requiring continued population growth to drive market expansion. Let's get straight to the point. The options for ensuring the survival of human civilization are limited. We can reduce the number of people and slow market expansion; develop cheap and renewable energy sources, which would likely lead to continued human expansion and resource depletion; or learn to live within our means and become less materialistic and more ecologically conscious. In short, we are in serious trouble. As you read this, the impact of this reality is already provoking a global wave of discontent.

The Clash of Minds

A review of the academic history of civilizations reveals that the rise of rational thought has been slow, difficult, and fraught with setbacks. It has been less a clash of civilizations than a battle between the rational and the absolute-minded. Rationality has shone brightly in various periods and places, such as ancient Athens and Rome, the Arab Golden Age, the Italian city-states of the Renaissance, and the European Enlightenment. Today, it is prevalent in about one-third of the world's nations, including the United States, Western Europe, Canada, Australia, New Zealand, Japan, South Korea, and Taiwan. Another third of the world's nations are a mix of rational and absolute-minded cultures, such as India, Turkey, Brazil, Southeast Asia, and Latin America. The remaining one-third is firmly authoritarian and absolute-minded, including China, Russia, Central Asia, the Middle East, and Sub-Saharan Africa.

At first glance, it seems that power struggles between governments, religious leaders, ethnic and racial groups, and cultural elites are the driving force behind conflicts in the world. However, beneath the surface, there is a deeper and more primal motivation—the need to keep people divided by their fears, anxieties, and differences. This has been a fundamental aspect of human identity and the ongoing struggle to survive and assert our identities. Glenn Robinson provides a detailed analysis of the rise of jihad in the Muslim world beginning in the 1980s in his book *Global Jihad: A Brief History*. He offers a bleak conclusion that jihad is a "movement of rage," a rejection of secular reality, scientific knowledge, and Enlightenment values. This aligns with Huntington's theories about the clash of civilizations being a fundamental aspect of the modern world order in his book *The Clash of Civilizations and the Remaking of World Order*.

The argument being made here is that the root of our divisions and ongoing conflicts lies in a simple psychological construct—a structural defect in the ability to trust that impairs identity formation and limits the range of trust. This dynamic is rooted in something as fundamental to our existence as the mother-infant bond and the ability of a community to nurture it. It is also shaped over time by the surrounding social and cultural community. It has taken thousands of years of cultural development to build trust and support the growth of enough rational-minded individuals to begin the slow evolution of human social and cultural progress. This has allowed us to trust not only each other but also the future and to replace the mystical and religious worlds based on absolutism with a more rational reality.

Today, all nations are based on rationalism, a concept that has rarely existed in human history. Our reliance on technology and our interconnected world makes us more rational, even if we are not necessarily more liberated or enlightened. Despite our differences, we are now more dependent than ever on a rational reality. For example, even terrorists like those in ISIS use online recruitment, celebrate their AK-47s, and prefer to drive Toyota pickup trucks to assert their identities in the world.

The world is no longer divided by civilizations, cultures, religions, and languages but rather by political interests that seek to suppress populations and those who either comply or resist. However, the widespread adoption of electronic technology across all nations, cultures, and civilizations has not been accounted for in these divisions. In many ways, we are already electronically "one," even if we do not fully realize or accept it yet. Autocratic states exist only to monopolize power and authority in society, and this is not a cultural, identity, or civilizational issue but rather a "power thing."

Huntington argues for what he calls a "civilizational paradigm" as a guide to future international relations, and he makes a strong case that in the 1990s, the world was on the brink of anarchy and in the midst of a "chaos paradigm." He also maintains that civilizations are the "broadest cultural entity" by which cultural identity is defined and are the "most enduring of human associations" that can be used to understand history and the current world from a geopolitical perspective. He then goes on to describe seven current civilizations (Asian, Indian, Islamic, Western, Orthodox, African, and Latin American). While nation-states are still the primary actors in this model, one of his most valuable insights is that "no paradigm is eternally valid." He suggests that the civilization paradigm may well be obsolete within a few decades. His book was published in 1996.

It might be more useful to think of the world of nation-states as existing along axes of trust and power relationships within and between each other. Authoritarian states are characterized by low trust and highly centralized authority, and this is where absolute-mindedness is most prevalent. On the other hand, democratic or rational-minded states have higher trust and decentralized authority. Every nation falls somewhere in between these two poles to varying degrees, and the influence of culture, ethnicity, and religion on these norms is significant but not fixed. The truth is that there are no traditional communities or societies left on our planet, only authoritarian leaders desperately clinging to power as a hedge against the future, which is already here.

The coming conflicts will not be civilizational but between low-trust and high-trust communities—and those most likely to strike out violently will be the low-trust and absolute-minded. Their paranoia and need to feel in control and identify the threatening "other" is obsessive and, not coincidentally, helps elites maintain power. (Russia's recent invasion of Ukraine is an example of this low-trust dynamic, as are China's threats to Taiwan.)

Politically, the end of history is not in sight; rather, we are undergoing a rapid technological evolution that is transforming our world from the inside out. It is important to understand that corporate capitalism, a relatively low-trust model of human behavior, is driving much of this process. It is a hierarchical and absolutist model that seeks to centralize power (break unions, track and manipulate consumers, maximize profits, and monopolize markets). As we can see, it functions just as well in China as it does in the United States. It is a separate civilizational reality in the world today, along with the seven current civilizations that Huntington outlined. It is a cultural force with its own faith and followers, and much like the early Vatican, it is economically and politically more powerful than most nations on earth.

The most powerful forces shaping the world today may no longer be nation-states (and the degree of absolute-mindedness versus rational-mindedness within them) but rather corporate globalization. However, there is now a third powerful force in the world: the rise of artificial intelligence. This is a force that is just beginning to stand alone and apart from both the civilizational and capitalist models. The reality is that there are too many actors jostling for power within each civilization model for the nation-state to be the only relevant player.

While technology currently appears to be primarily a tool for existing models of human behavior, it is a paradigm-shifting force in all human social organization and stands apart from all that has come before. As knowledge becomes an infinite source of power and authority in the future, the ability of elites to monopolize data and information will define the coming struggles. Data is the power of the future, and the need to collect and control it will be driven by our primal instincts. The conflicts to come will be asymmetrical and will involve nation-states, globalization, human population growth, environmental health, and technological advancement. Huntington's civilizational model is still relevant, but it is only a thin veil for the challenges ahead. The key question is, how will identities hold up in the face of these challenges?

Final Notes

The case put forward here is that one of the primeval sources of our division and eternal conflict begins with a single psychological construct—an early life impairment in our ability to trust that disrupts identity formation. Distrust opens a portal to reality-bending beliefs and conspiracies. It is a woman dying of COVID-19 in a hospital's ICU bed, denying it's the virus and refusing treatment. And it is the parents of school-age children raging at school boards and teachers for mandating masks in classrooms as grandparents are dying and teachers are quitting.

What we are seeing today with the absolute-minded has always been here, always waiting to be triggered. What makes this conspiratorial view of the world so difficult to confront is there really are dark forces all about, manipulating the political process and our economic livelihoods. America did not accidentally arrive at where it is today. Our current reality has been playing out in full view since the end of the Second World War, finally metastasizing and aligning desperate social forces on a significant scale for one of the few times in our history. In short, powerful social forces have triggered the absolute-minded into paranoid fantasies and disbelief.

At the epicenter of our rising absolutism resides White America, on its way to becoming the largest minority as opposed to an absolute majority. And to confirm this change of status, it has become the subject of its own conspiracy, one echoed by White nationalists and Republican leadership, termed "replacement conspiracy theory." It contends that dark-skinned immigrants are numerically and culturally replacing White Americans. The purpose of this allegedly faux-genocidal policy is less clear.

Currently, Republicans and Democrats are undergoing a demographic transition or what might better be termed a cultural mitosis (in biology, this refers to cellular division). An evolutionary, multigenerational social and political speciation is taking place. What Richard Hofstadter had earlier termed "status" politics now fully aligns with "interest" politics for many White Americans. In effect, economic status now formally aligns with cultural values for one of the few times in our history. And it is driving us toward a more illiberal America.

The hope here is to extend the ideas and theories put forward by many outstanding researchers and writers on the topic of the authoritarian-conservative mind, including the seminal works in American politics: *The Authoritarian Personality* by Theodor Adorno (1950), *The True Believers* by Eric Hoffer (1951), and *The Paranoid Style in American Politics* by Richard Hofstadter (1964), but also the commanding insights of Hannah Arendt's *The Origins of Totalitarianism*

(1951). Each of them attempts to address underlying psychological factors driving populism, mass movements, and autocratic politics. This book is an attempt to explore their psychology in greater depth.

We are taking a psychological dive into the depths of an adaptive evolutionary process that has become increasingly dysfunctional in our modern simulated tech reality. Our current culture war and political instability are the culmination of an America that has been at war with itself for six hundred years. Its origins derive from a harsh world that demanded a harsh response—one that inhibited the arrival of the modern world for thousands of years. While absolutism is surprisingly adaptative and normative in relative terms, today it has become an underlying impediment distorting the world for many and potentially threatening the future.

It is important we step back for a moment when discussing our contemporary model of "conservatism" and keep in mind that conservatism is a primal human adaptation. It is a set point for survival that comes to us as an unremitting need for routine and predictability at every level of our social interaction, from our personal need for routine, guiding our social interactions, assuring our physical safety, or anticipating the rising sun and the changing seasons. The requirements for routine and predictability dominate the human experience.

And the most important factor driving our conservative adaptation is a world that fundamentally changes and alters its shape and direction in time frames far beyond our ability to anticipate and control (entropy constant). The result has been an open-ended emotional and cognitive conflict since the spark of human consciousness. From the outset, our biological and social-cultural adaptations have been driven by a conflict between *predictability* and *change*, literally shaping what it means to be human. And from this derives the source of a natural cautiousness when confronted by unanticipated challenges and life-threatening risks. This caution comes not only to each of us but extends to those close to us and the community we live in.

All of us, collectively, proceed with prudence in the face of potentially life-threatening challenges, weighing the pros and cons, conducting cost-analyses, creating redundancy for vital services and system complexity, and adhering to the wisdom of the past and the assurances derived from faith. We want to believe that what has preceded us is part of a shared, if not universal wisdom that can be trusted to guide us when altering the course of our collective lives.

We are all naturally conservative. This book is the story of what happens when human adaptation loses viability as it comes face-to-face with an exponentially evolving complexity—the modern human condition. For generations, we have been outsourcing predictability and routine to rapidly evolving and dynamic social networks. And our failure to continue to adapt in the face of accelerating social-cultural and environmental change is now a threat to human viability, whether that is nuclear conflict, social upheaval, viral pandemics, or habitat collapse. We have created complexity and outsourced agency. We now live in the balance.

We are on a journey to open a psychological black box and reveal the origins of absolute-mindedness, or what has been variously termed the conservative-authoritarian-paranoid mind. Most of the ideas presented here derive from existing research that has been in plain sight for many years. What is unique here is putting this puzzle together, not unlike the parable of the blind men trying to discern an elephant but only able to describe limited parts of the whole. *American Absolutism* is an attempt to present a high-resolution MRI of the psychological forces generating discord and disrupting the American democratic experiment.

Chapter 1

The Absolute-Minded

They aren't just infected with conspiracy; they appear to be inoculated against rationality.

—C. Alter, *Down the Rabbit Hole*

Conformity

Powerful social forces are eternally loose upon the world. That has been our history for over six thousand years. But what is at the beating heart of this process? The enduring source of our division and the deadly conflict that inevitably results? And can we find our way through this in our e-tech interactions and arising machine intelligence? Is technology a network game changer or a sophisticated tool for furthering division and conflict in the coming years?

The two most powerful social forces at work in human cultural adaptation are *conformity of behavior* and *absolutism of thinking*. Broadly, *conformity of behavior* is "going along to get along," participating in the rituals and traditions that have been handed down. But it is also allegiance to the existing social and cultural norms and aligning with the forces of political order and the exercise of authority that governs a community. The *absolutism of thought* is the cognitive analog to the conformity of behavior. In this instance, one's thoughts and ideas must broadly conform to and confirm the social and cultural norms and shared beliefs, myths, and values—"your head is in the game." Together, these two processes confer a broad psychological herd immunity—suppress fear and anxiety, reduce internal conflict, and form the basis of shared belief, assuring the community's generational survival. But have they?

The herd survival strategy turns out to be remarkably rigid and unyielding and was likely a more successful adaption during our prehistory than it is today. Conformity is a coercive demand for acquiescence of the *self* to the *we*, as evidenced in fascist, theocratic, and authoritarian states, which is pretty much all of human history. The expected sacrifices were often extreme as a way of emphasizing their significance. It must be true or right if the cost is so high. Why else would there have been so much human sacrifice? In an extreme form, absolutism is intolerant of any deviation in thinking, no matter how irrational the demand. One must believe whatever they are told. The medieval Roman Catholic Church exercised highly repressive measures for a thousand years by excommunicating, torturing, and burning people at the stake. Everyone else paid a 10 percent tithe to the church. The supposed heresy by the rationally minded included Luther, Kepler, Galileo, Copernicus, and Darwin.

Our social-cultural baseline is highly repressive and focused on ritual conformity to authority. And herein lies a peculiar paradox. The result is the creation of a cognitive bubble where paranoia and conspiratorial thinking are allowed to gestate and grow. And just to be clear, distrust in authority moves in both directions, from the bottom up and from the top down. In the face of frantically changing social realities, the irrationality of unyielding demands for conformity and absolutism is often expressed in conspiratorial delusions, typically directed at the forces of change. What else could it be, given all the other rational options are off the table and might engender a violent response? It's as if we cannot see beyond our most recent successes and do things differently the next time around. Confronted by cracks in the underlying reality, anxious distrust and suspicion arise. Powerful forces must be at play. What other explanation could there be when rational thinking and action are limited?

If any of the above is true, it raises a profound question about how human culture ever evolved. If it was always adhering to conformity and absolutism. It also might explain why change has been slow at every turn in our social-cultural history. Any brief accounting of known past civilizations comes to about ninety splendid mini universes, give or take a few. Maybe we should wonder more about why they all disappeared and have become mostly forgotten. Their devolution likely came in many forms, including violent contact with other cultures, turbulent climatic events, and technological innovation (fire, wheel, metallurgy, agriculture). But primarily from a failure to adapt to changing circumstances. All the ancient civilizations were rigid and absolutist. Heck, if it has been successful for 350 years, why change now? Wrong answer! The two most contiguous models of long-term social adaption today are the Indo-European (by way of the Levant) and the Asian model. Only in the European model did rationality fully evolve adaptive nonauthoritarian communities. But just to be clear, the violent upending of authority has been continuous throughout all cultures for thousands of years.

The question we are confronted with is, What happens in times of profound social-cultural change? Historically, it likely meant the end of a culture—either regressing to a simpler adaptation, absorption by a more vibrant culture, or its outright disappearance. The more dynamic a culture is with change, the greater is its chance of transformation. The case could be made that the invention of America was itself a transformational moment in human cultural history. But it is also evident, looking back, that all significant cultural change imposes a high degree of social conflict and cultural upheaval. And with coming artificial intelligence, it will be no different. Profound change and turbulent upheaval are coming our way and already exist on our laptops and smartphones. The struggle between absolutists and rationalists over how to adapt to artificial intelligence will determine which future we endure.

The Political Origins of Authoritarianism

The three seminal works on the nature of absolutism in American politics are *The Authoritarian Personality* by Theodor Adorno (1950), *The True Believers* by Eric Hoffer (1951), and *The*

Paranoid Style in American Politics by Richard Hofstadter (1964). All three authors were searching for the commonality of extremist and populist dysfunction in the American political process. Hoffer, writing soon after WWII, attempted to understand the dynamics of mass movements such as fascism and communism. He particularly noted the surrender of the "distinct self" and social movements becoming the primary source of identity, with faith elevated above reason. But also noting the projected hatred of "the other" and the primacy of "self-loathing." On the other hand, Hofstadter was attempting to reveal something more subtle by examining conspiratorial thinking in American political life, or what he termed the "paranoid style of mind." Here, the political archetype casts the world in terms of good and evil, emphasizing the immorality of the "other." The critical element of this process was also the projection of self-loathing.

At the time of his writing, Hofstadter focused on what he perceived as an evolving paranoid style of thinking within the Republican Party. Beginning in the 1930s, Republicans came to believe there was a Freemasonry conspiracy behind the implementation of federal income tax, and later, a socialist plot driving the New Deal and social security legislation. In the 1950s, there was the prominence of Senator Joe McCarthy and a widely shared belief among Republicans that communists and communist sympathizers had infiltrated the US government. Among the most outlandish delusions was that the chlorination of public drinking water was a communist plot to weaken us from within. In the 1960s, the conservative John Birch Society and patron saint Barry Goldwater were haranguing that the civil rights movement and the ERA were communist conspiracies seeking to instigate a civil war. In the 1990s, it was conservative Christian orthodoxy that the Federal Reserve, Wall Street, and the Council on Foreign Relations were attempting to create a New World Order.

Today, the Christian Right proselytizes that we are heading toward a civil war if their faith continues to be suppressed by the government, while the Republican Party has fabricated a "deep state" conspiracy comprised of Washington insiders and the federal bureaucracy. This all gets an attempted putsch from the rise of conservative talk radio, cable news, and social media, driven by the paranoid and conspiratorial spouting of right-wing absolutist dogma to the faithful by the likes of Fox News, Breitbart, Newsmax, One America, Parler, Alex Jones, and previously by Rush Limbaugh.

Theodore Adorno dove deeper than Hoffer and Hofstadter and developed the "F-scale." This was an attempt to directly measure the personality traits of fascism. Later studies concluded it was a better overall measure of authoritarianism. To be clear, both authoritarianism and fascism are examples of absolute-mindedness. The predicate was a harsh and punitive family environment leading to a submissive child wanting approval. Self-loathing is present in a highly repressed form, along with anti-intellectualism and preoccupation with superstitious and stereotypical thinking. The world is cast in "we" versus "them" terms, good versus evil, strong versus weak, with a fundamental distrust of elites and a proneness to conspiratorial thinking. There is also a resilient projective identification with authority figures. The F-type represented what one researcher termed a "new anthropological species," one strongly present in evangelicalism, populism, and conservative movements. However, the reality was the F-type personality was not a recent discovery but a fundamental preset for our species. Ironically, the rational researcher was more likely the newly emergent species.

What our trio of authors (Hoffer, Adorno, and Hofstadter) had uncovered was that humans operate within two closed systems. The first system is a biological one. It places a load of unconditional demands on us to survive as primates (for example, air, food, water, sleep, procreation, safety). These demands are uncompromising and categorically must be met. The second system is our dynamic social networks, which are designed to meet our basic biological needs, but beyond that, to also extend our social, intellectual, and emotional needs. While not as closed looped as our biological imperatives, social networks reasonably operate within broader parameters that are generally required to be met, or we become unemployed, imprisoned, hospitalized, or harassed by cancel culture.

Our social networks are comprised of three overlapping processes—parent-child bond, a lengthy process of individual socialization, and the overarching process of social-enculturation of norms, values, and beliefs. Our many network demands are primarily reality-based—brake when the traffic light turns red, be careful with that table saw, pay your bills. But many working hypotheses about reality are also inflated by this process. Reflect for a moment on all the social requirements of the past that now seem so quaint, if not silly and outright harmful by today's standards (feet binding, skull shaping, dueling, penis stretching, horsehair wigs, vaginal suturing, corsets, circumcision, breast enhancement). And yes, we are still making it up as we go along. Watch any BBC Regency period drama on TV or assay the differences for a woman living in Mogadishu versus Malibu Beach.

The fact is, our social reality is comprised of hundreds of thousands of simple routine requirements. For example, complex organizations all have the same hierarchical and management solutions. Financial, medical, energy, and transportation systems all work similarly. A relatively recent grouping called nation-states all have borders; flags; constitutions; judicial, legislative, and executive branches; militaries; currencies; citizenship requirements; and passports. This is our fractal reality—the continuous and self-simulating patterning of micro and macro social networks. It is not only structurally required but also core to our absolute thinking and conformity.

It is probably safe to conjecture that conformity, both practical and symbolic, is the most critical demand placed on any individual operating in these two closed systems. It is our default set point, biologically and socially. In Maslow's hierarchy of needs, after biological needs is our need for safety. And social conformity is primary for sapiens' social order. The question raised here is, What disturbs conformity in these two closed systems? How do the many thousands of pioneering innovations by e-technology impact conformity? How does the endless demand for change and innovation spark the projection of self-loathing, as delineated by Hoffer, Hofstadter, and Adorno? And why does conformity continuously sprout conspiracy theories as if it were a game of whack-a-mole?

We all grow up being socialized to conform. This process is the nexus for both our physical survival and the social network's survival.

The two questions that we should be asking are: What are the limits of adaptive conformity? And at what point does social cohesion begin to break down in the face of over-conformity? The second question really asks, How does an adaptive network co-opt change and non-conformity for its survival? And we should probably ask, What role does absolutism play in making conformity our first adaptation? As Hoffer, Hofstadter, and Adorno have been vigilant to point out, adaptation to change is fraught with inherent dangers. For one, it can challenge conformity and absolutism. But overall, humans have likely been slow to embrace social change for thousands of years. This wanting to slow everything down is what we term today as social conservatism.

With varying refinements, Hoffer, Hofstadter, and Adorno were all identifying elements of the authoritarian personality. Here, we are attempting to step back for a moment and identify what drives this adaptation. Something very elemental to the human condition is taking place. It begins with understanding that conformity is our natural adaptive response to the world around us. These authors have identified a large segment of our population who, for many reasons that will be discussed later, are more narrowly adaptive. In effect, conformity is not just a default adaptation but a rigid parameter. However, it is neither unusual nor pathological in a clinical sense, but it has been a powerful inhibitor to change, which is rapidly upon us.

What has changed over the past several hundred years has been the ascent of a significant modifier to our primary adaptation—*rationalism*, as opposed to the absolutism of conformity. Historians identify the *European Enlightenment* (1685–1815) as the origin of this modern adaptation. This was a celebration of *reason* as our primary source of knowledge about the world. The natural order included radical ideas about liberty, progress, individualism, and human rights. However, one result of this adaptation has been an unabated symbolic war. It is not surprising that Donald Trump identified more with authoritarian leaders than the democratic process or that Republican senators fell in line with his autocratic disposition. They all default to conformity-absolutism, which can be maddening and destructive when change and adaptation are required. The Enlightenment wars have been ongoing now for four hundred years, with no end in sight.

Believing the "Lie"

> The ideal subjects are people for whom the distinction between fact and fiction and between true and false no longer exist.
>
> —H. Arendt, *The Origins of Totalitarianism*

No discussion of the absolute state of mind is complete without exploring the writings of political theorist Hannah Arendt. In the 1930s, she initially fled Nazi Germany as a Jewish refugee. In 1941, she then immigrated to the United States from Israel. After the war, she undertook a big picture analysis of the rise of totalitarianism (fascism and communism) in the twentieth century. Her seminal work is *The Origins of Totalitarianism* (1951).

While it is beyond the scope of this book to summarize Arendt's elaborate theories behind the advent of totalitarianism, she covers all the bases—the evolving nation-state, imperialism, capitalism, modern labor theory, materialism, and the ascent of the bureaucratic state, but also, the despondent aftermath of WWI and the crushing effect of the Great Depression. But her insight into *why* it happened as opposed to *how* it happened is surprisingly psychological. Underlying the advent of totalitarianism was the diaspora of "community" and the detachment of people from the life of the culture and the state. People were isolated, lonely, and alienated from the modern world. She termed it "organized loneliness." And the consequences were worldwide violence and destruction.

Her insights into the use of propaganda to distort reality and the people's need for a false truth offer many clues to our current political circumstances. These insights include the current rise of authoritarian governments and populism, extreme economic stratification, market domination by Big Tech, and the far-ranging impact of social media platforms on social, economic, and political life. One could make the case that today, globalization and the internet have set loose forces around the world similar to those in the 1930s.

Arendt described authoritarian leadership as a criminal element intent on wiping out individual identity and substituting unquestioned loyalty to the state and, if necessary, unleashing mass terror on the populace. The elites were generally co-opted, believing their economic interests were being met behind closed doors. The bourgeoisie's political philosophy was always "totalitarian." It always assumed an identity of politics, economics, and society in which political institutions served only as the facade for private interests. The lower classes generally accepted the propaganda because it was more consistent and coherent than the real world. Arendt observed that the role of propaganda was to "conjure up a lying world of consistency which is more adequate to the needs of the human mind than reality itself." They "offer people what they most crave: an ideologically consistent world aiming at grand narratives that give meaning to their lives."

Perhaps a different lens would help us even better understand Arendt's many insights. It is essential to revisit the concept of the "double bind." Beginning with the parent-child relationship and later, through many tiers of social conditioning and more broadly by enculturation, we learn how to safely reduce cognitive dissonance produced by the problematic exercise of authority in our lives. Core to this programming is accepting a base unreality—the unspoken truth (double bind) that can never be acknowledged for fear of reprisal. Authoritarian leaders are particularly adroit at exploiting the unreality of life created by unacknowledged fear, particularly in times of crisis. Over time, people become conditioned to accepting the lie rather than confronting the truth. And in the case of propaganda, embracing a false narrative and believing in the existence of sinister forces beyond the obviously visible world allow for the infinite projection of our fears and anxieties.

Today, our 24-7 interaction with social media platforms plays an increasingly significant role in propagating fear-based conspiracy theories and distorting reality. The consequence has been to heighten cognitive dissonance in the absolute-minded. We need to seriously consider how contemporary society and e-technology breed loneliness and disconnectedness and empower authoritarian governments to become ever more controlling and repressive. For many, it is more adaptive to believe the *lie*, as opposed to altering their thought processes, changing their beliefs, or altering their behavior to reduce internal conflict or dissonance, particularly in the presence of coercive authority. And in the face of social chaos, defaulting to "tribal identity" has been our historical adaptation, now accounting for a resurgence of authoritarianism and populism. However, the story being told here is the psychology of how we became resigned to believing the *lie* and defaulting to tribal identity.

The Tight Culture / Loose Culture Conundrum

Underlying *Homo sapiens* social life is an all-enveloping cultural construct comprised of *social norms*, literally the rules of acceptable social behavior. These, Michelle Gelfand asserts in *Rule Makers, Rule Breaker*, are the building blocks of culture. And herein lies a critical distinction in our understanding of absolute-mindedness. There is a complex interplay between the parent-child dynamic and social/cultural norms, each supporting and propagating the other.

It turns out that humans are a "super-normative species," with significant behavior devoted to all manner of social rules and conventions, constituting the "deep structure that underlies cultural variation." This is the glue holding our social world together by providing key elements to identity formation and helping organize us politically, socially, and economically. And what we term conservatism is a network of values and behaviors (e.g., child-rearing norms) originating in an evolutionary adaptation to social crisis.

Because social norms are so often evident and conventional, they are largely invisible to us. But hidden beneath the surface, they are highly codified and heavily enforced. The long-term effect, according to Gelfand, has been *tight* and *loose* cultures, reflecting the strength of social norms and the strictness with which they are enforced. One of the earliest known examples of this division is Ancient Greece, with a highly militaristic Sparta continually in conflict with pluralistically oriented Athens. Sounds uncomfortably like Republicans and Democrats in the US today.

An important insight is that the strength of a culture's norms is neither random nor accidental but rather the variation driven by survival needs. Throughout history, social norms have been critical for uniting communities to act in the face of crises, e.g., drought, famine, and pestilence. But also, territorial threats from war, scarce resources, and diseases. Strong social norms minimized internal conflict and allowed for greater responsiveness to threats. However, the tightness-looseness dynamic can and does change over time. As threats appear, groups tighten, and as threats subside, groups loosen. In the twentieth century, we saw this play out dramatically on a global scale during World War II, as nations around the world organized in violent acts of aggression and self-defense. But what happens when this divide persists at a lower level of conflict within nations as it does around the world today?

Gelfand gingerly steps into the topic of conservatism in the US, noting the following tighter characteristics:

- more limitations on acceptable behaviors and what can be expressed
- underlying belief in their superiority
- high demand for social order and resistance to change
- emphasize traditional value
- focus on law and order, with deference to authority
- high percentage of religious believers—generally more intolerant and prejudiced
- reflect a blue-collar world of economic instability and health vulnerabilities
- stricter rules and harsher punishments for children—expect conformity and obedience
- generally, "see the world through a prism of threat"

All cultures exercise high levels of control. But the degree of control varies among and within cultures and nations. Here in the US, the current response to the pandemic poses many questions. The so-called tighter group in the US is resisting social order and adherence to authority, while the looser group has been more conforming and concerned about the overall social impact. In effect, the absolute-minded are operating outside the general societal norms and have insulated themselves in a tighter cultural identity. Now fearful of threats to their status as an attenuating minority, they have come to believe their values and beliefs are under attack (and at some fundamental level, this is true, but primarily because of their rigidity).

Tightness-Looseness Paradigm Big Picture

While tightness is a variable measure of authoritarianism, the degree of variation among cultures and nations is significant. Much of the world today is founded on escaping overcontrol and loosening the boundaries of human cultural life. That is how creative minds invented the modern world. But this tighter/looser dynamic raises an important question: what is the best adaptation for a society going forward? What is unknown in all of this is the rate of change within cultures and why tight cultures can be resistant to change over time, particularly when external threats have subsided. In *Rule Makers, Rule Breakers*, only democratic nations inhabit the sweet spot for governance and people's overall sense of well-being. That's the bottom line.

And lastly, it is important to note there are no historical parallels to the looseness of the twenty-first century world. We are functioning where humanity has never been before, at a new threshold for openness that has never previously existed and is without historical precedent. For the limited nations surveyed by Gelfand, few existing threats require a cohesive and highly organized cultural response. What is driving tightness and looseness appears to be an interplay of primitive social and political norms that no longer comport with the world surrounding these nations.

A reasonable case could be made that 90 percent of all social norms are primarily dedicated routines that make life simpler and more convenient. It is just so much easier if we all just agree to do most things the same way—in effect, we are all on the same page when it comes to the details of life—patiently cueing, walking on certain sides of the sidewalk, which bathroom to use, etc. There are, of course, tens of thousands of these routine details and niceties. And they vary among cultures and nations. These agreed-upon norms allow each person to function smoothly and coherently in a community. Some cultures are more formal in their expectations and the severity of social blowback one can experience for violating these basic norms. Others are less formal and open-ended.

But clearly, there's something more fundamental at play here than preserving routines. Social norms also serve to assure one's safety, rights, and status in a community. All sapiens cultures operate top-down in exercising authority. At various times in our cultural history, it might have been a tribal leader. Today, it is often a dictator and, more broadly, the imposition of status by social caste or class. And throughout history, one's tribe, clan, race, ethnicity, beliefs, and wealth all determined how power was distributed and what norms were enforced. And here is the key—it continues to play out today as it had in our past.

So what is the relevance of tighter versus looser cultures when it comes to exercising authority and the enforcement of social status? Perhaps as we survey nations, it's important to separate social norms that represent daily conformity from those that represent enforcement of social status and authority and not confuse them as being one and the same. Related, yes, but not the same.

One question that needs to be addressed is this: How did the rise of the nation-state, in which all humans are now harbored, impact the role of cultural tightness and looseness as a relevant response to crisis? Clearly, the state has usurped many, if not most, functions of cultural tightness when regarding crisis management. Likely, external crises play a smaller role in the normative reality of most nations, except for leaders and politicians continuously preying on people's fears by heightening a sense of threat.

The unanswered question is, Now that nation-states have taken the tribal-cultural reigns, are conflicts more likely to be internalized to nations that are culturally and religiously diverse? Where are we to go, ask the Palestinians, Rohingya, Uyghurs, and evangelicals? Which partially explains why our cultural war has become so personal and intense. Control of the state and culture dominance are less and less divisible.

The issue we are confronted with is the tension between being normatively conservative (i.e., hostile to change and continually projecting threats that don't exist) and its dysfunction in the modern world. And unless children are raised with a looseness preset, there can be no loose societies or nations. This interplay becomes self-fulfilling, which is why it has taken thousands of years to reach a state of cultural looseness anywhere. When necessary, loose societies can tighten up, but tight societies are slower to loosen up by modern standards. Perhaps the most remarkable transitions have been by South Korea and Japan, which are very tight cultures that have embraced democratic principles. This is something many illiberal nations continue to struggle with.

The cultural norm for thousands of years was simply top-down tightness. It was the barbarians conquering Rome and then leaving without knowing what to do with civilization. Today, it's the Taliban retaking Afghanistan and ruling it as a feudal state. No one really wants it but will settle for peace over the perpetual conflict in the short-term. Much of the world appears to reside in a state of self-fulling authoritarian organization with all manners of justification and rationalization. But always with the brute force of the state enforcing it. What crisis this is serving is unclear, except to enforce privilege and authority.

The division of our world as a measure of absoluteness is obvious. Authoritarian governance versus democratic governance. Within each nation are tighter (conservative) versus looser (liberal) social norms. All other measures become curious but not particularly relevant in the world today. First off are the highly conservative theocratic states. Next in line are the violent tribal warlords and narco-states, followed by the capitalist-authoritarian nations, then the illiberal democracies (dictatorships). And only on the loose side are democracies. Except for democracies, all the other nations qualify as *tighter* (with some variation on specific variables). Only democracies exhibit truly balanced cultures, but still with considerable variation within and among them.

Humanity has spent thousands of years trying to escape repression by insulating itself from crises. The case could be made that so-called tightness is an archaic response that is increasingly irrelevant in our complex and networked world. Its primary effect has been to divide us, claiming "others" are too different, less than we are, or a threat. As apex predators, we wiped out many competing hominid species over the millennia because of this genetic preset. It also enables dictators to thrive by exercising violence, all the while promising nostalgic levels of social order and increased safety and security in a better future.

A state of cultural tightness is a setback when confronted by our modern networked simulation and the coming future. Yes, many will shelter in traditions and customs that make them feel protected and special, not unlike the false security of taking shelter under a tree during an electrical storm. The reality is tight cultural norms around the world can quickly veer from tight to abusive. I, for one, given the long historical record of abuse by tight normed leaders, cultures, and societies, remain skeptical of them in totality. I do not see them as responding to crises but primarily elites fearful for their own safety, prosperity, and status. Whether it is the denial of health care, not allowing women to attend school, tribal violence, or criminal sanctions for criticizing the state or a leader and all the other repressive measures taken against people. Let's be honest, it may be the traditional way, but it is hardly in people's best interest today.

In one of the classic movie lines of all time, a blustering US Army colonel tells a GI in Stanley Kubrick's *Full Metal Jacket*, "We are here to help the Vietnamese, because inside every Gook there's an American trying to get out." But here is the truth: any young person exposed to the future never wants to live in the past. That is our goal. Everyone participates in the future. As we go forward, facing the monumental crises coming our way, tight cultural norms will only lead to conflict, disrupting alliances and ecologically endangering our planet. We have seen this throughout history, the self-fulfilling prophecy of the absolute-minded becoming the very thing they fear—threat, violence, and looming crisis.

Chapter 2

Developmental Origins of Absolutism

The entire man is...to be seen in the cradle of the child.

—Alexis De Tocqueville, *Democracy in America*

The Infant-Mother Relationship

The infant-mother relationship is the single most important relationship in the life of a human being. There is simply no other way to understand it. And any serious review of the literature on this subject overwhelmingly supports this conclusion. What is likely startling about this statement is not that it makes sense or is obvious, but that it is a modern idea that would have been relatively meaningless throughout most of human history.

In our recent past, infant-childhood mortality rates were overwhelmingly high. Resources were often limited and their availability unpredictable. The hold on life was tenuous in the best of times. In a world of hardships, circumstance often dictated emotional detachment, which likely favored older children over younger children. Overfocusing on attachment and nurturing was of secondary concern. In the crudest evolutionary terms, the cost of emotional investment for a marginal return was too high in many circumstances. It made sense to commit resources to a better outcome the next time.

Most earlier cultures routinely practiced infanticide and made harsh decisions about who survived in hard times. And beyond that, primate studies, historical accounts, and field observations document the sacrifice of the young for survival of the mother in highly stressful circumstance (war, famine, drought). Surviving to be a mother again is primary over a particular child's survival. And birthrates naturally fall during difficult times, as it becomes more difficult for women to conceive (a biological defense, it seems). In the US, we continue to see this survival pattern play out in muted form. The infant-mother bond is still largely aspirational for many mothers when one fully considers all the necessary commitments an infant requires.

Voluminous research on infant-mother relationships pretty much supports what most of us have suspected all along. Some mothers seem like naturals. This is not an accident. How a woman was parented by her mother in infancy appears to largely determine later in life how well or poorly she parents her children. And beyond this, having had the experience of caring for children as a sister, babysitter, or nanny more fully attunes new mothers to care for and tend to their children. And developmental psychologists will tell you that this is equally true for rats, rabbits, monkeys, and humans (I do not feel reassured by this).

Positive parenting across the ages has been described by researchers in terms of cyclical patterns (a mother-to-mother transfer of the art of parenting) with demonstrated intergenerational continuity within families. And it should be noted that research demonstrates a mother's early nurturing (both positive and negative) appears to trigger epigenetic changes in the protein structure of her genes, shaping her role as a mother. While it is still not fully understood if one is simply born a competent mother, early life experiences are clearly impactful. Although there are suspicions this may be true, it cannot be demonstrated. The role of genes remains highly suspect. But the ability to be a highly effective parent is strongly formed by how well a woman was mothered herself. It is a learning experience that begins before a child's awareness and shapes a lifelong pattern of parenting. This is not an argument that later life experience cannot reshape this outcome, only that is it not primary. In fact, older mothers are generally more attentive and adaptive.

During the course of a woman's pregnancy and early years of parenthood, the single most important factor impacting the infant-mother relationship are environmental stressors. And the most significant factor mitigating or aggravating the levels of stress are the size and depth of the mother's support network. A highly supportive network reduces stress and positively plays out in more attentive mothering and less child neglect and abuse. And like many of us have known, grandmothers are vital to this process. And just to be clear, chronically stressful environments such as poverty, financial insecurity, drug/alcohol use, or emotional and physical abuse impact a woman's ability to attend to the child during pregnancy and as a developing infant.

Research Limitations

There are significant problems with the research on infant-mother bonding. For one, life seldom breaks along the parameters and distinctions we see in research models, particularly when it is often dependent on laboratory animals for confirmation. And human research subjects seldom represent a random sample of the population, and the scoring by researchers can have subtle biases, and even the variables are frequently subject to confirmation bias. But mostly, too much is extrapolated from laboratory results. And there are never longitudinal studies to validate initial findings. Humans simply don't operate under conditions that facilitate research. Real life is too complex. Subjects' response to researchers and to life can be highly variable depending on the circumstance and the times of their lives. Put more simply, clustering research subjects when it comes to the subtle variation in human response, particularly the infant-mother bond, is nearly impossible. The human condition is so subtle and wide-ranging that we can only speculate in general terms. Which is what is being done here.

If the infant-mother bond is so overwhelmingly significant, does that mean the infant-mother experience is all there is to our destinies? Or is it simply the beginning of how each of us begins to respond to the world as we grow and develop as a person? What is unknown throughout the available research is how subsequent life experiences and relationships shape us and modify our early life experiences. This is literally a "Lost World" in research terms. So we need to proceed with caution. So what about fathers, you ask? They are a potential trust multiplier throughout their lives. Fathers play an important role in identity formation and in the psychological and emotional development of a child. For most children, it is the second most important emotional bond in their lives. But be aware, everything gained at the front end by a nurturing mother can also be lost by a demanding and disciplining father, but not so much the other way around. And this dynamic between child and parents plays out over a lifetime, only beginning to attenuate if all parties can survive adolescence.

But if the infant-mother relationship is primary to the future, it also means that we are not fully captains of our fates because we did not get to choose our parents. And while this relationship is unlikely to preordain a particular outcome, and many factors are influencing who we will become, it reigns as primary. This is true despite all the potential lifelong mitigating factors that support us (fathers, relatives, friends, teachers, and serendipity) or set us back (poverty, neglect-abuse, health problems, and random misfortune). And most important are the hundreds of thousands of unpredictable life experiences and events coming our way that will inevitably impact who we are. While there is clearly a randomness to each of us, it all starts predictably with the infant-mother relationship.

We should also interject into this equation each person's unique genetic makeup, with the realization that not everyone starts out in life with the same baseline. And prenatally, there's a deep hormonal relationship between child and mother, as each influences the other in powerful ways that strongly affect the infant-mother bond. The reality is, there are enormous ranges of differences between each of us right from the start. Far too many for us to predict outcomes early on.

Loss of Trust—the Genesis of Absolutism

Attachment theory, first proposed by British psychoanalyst John Bowlby in the late 1950s, was based on his institutional work with children. He hypothesized that for an adult to grow up mentally healthy, "the infant and young child should experience a warm, intimate, and continuous relationship with his mother [or permanent mother substitute] in which both find satisfaction and enjoyment." He drew his ideas from many sources, including Freud, Piaget, and Konrad Lorenz's ethnographic observations. But the idea that infants and young children need to develop secure dependence on the parents was put forth even earlier by developmental psychologist William Blatz (1940) in what he termed "security theory." The work of Bowlby and Blatz was then followed up by psychologists Mary Ainsworth and B. A. Wittig in their landmark experiment called the "Strange Situation" (1969). For the first time, experimental evidence provided empirical support for attachment theory.

"Strange Situation"

Ainsworth developed an experimental model to observe infant-caregiver attachment styles. One hundred infants between the ages of twelve and eighteen months were observed in a series of eight episodes lasting three minutes each. (Mother, infant, and experimenter; infant with mother; stranger with mother and infant. Mother leaves infant and stranger alone. Mother returns and stranger leaves. Mother leaves infant and infant is alone. Stranger returns. Mother returns and stranger leaves.) In each episode, observers noted the infant's behavior on a scale of 1–7. From these observations, three attachment styles emerged (secure, insecure-avoidant, and insecure-anxious).

Nearly fifty years of attachment theory research broadly supports earlier findings that the dynamics of attachment between an infant and caregiver affect later adult cognitive functioning and interpersonal relationships. Early interactions later help adults organize a social schema of interaction and expectations of how their social world operates and forms the basis for future relationship dynamics. Ainsworth's research revealed that three basic relationship strategies evolved from the infant-caregiver dynamic, which she labeled secure, anxious, and avoidant. Her focus was on what she termed the "caregiver sensitivity hypothesis" as an explanation for each attachment style. That is, sensitive mothers are more responsive to the needs and feelings of an infant. Insecure infants reflected inconsistent primary care. In all cases, anxious and avoidant adaptations were risk factors for future diagnoses of anxiety and depression (Davila et al. 2005; Spadoni et al. 2022). This was true, whether or not there was a history of childhood trauma. A generalized early life instability appeared highly correlated with adult anxiety and depression. Additionally, insecure attachment contributed to dysfunctional attitudes later in life (Beck 1987; Hankins et al. 2005; Gamble and Roberts 2005). Further, negative and dysfunctional attitudes were associated with low self-esteem and vulnerability for depression (Kuiper and Olinger 1986).

Now there are many caveats to these findings. There can be many caretakers in a child's life. A caregiver's behavior can be highly variable over time, and each child may come into the world with presets when it comes to interacting with a caregiver. Research needs to examine cultural differences as well. But overall, this research broadly supports the impact of infant-caregiver interactions on the future attitudes, social interaction, and emotional regulation in adults. And when one sorts through this research, one finding stands out above all others when it comes to the subject of absolute-mindedness. Approximately 60 to 70 percent of the population in the US have secure attachment, and 30 to 40 percent evidence insecure attachments (Shaver and Hazan 1994). One could speculatively make the case that the current Trump base (34 to 37 percent) broadly falls into the insecure attachment cohort in these studies. And the resulting cognitive distortions and negative attitudes form the basis for their susceptibility to rigid adaptation, conspiracy theories, and attachment to authority figures.

Without going too far down the psychological rabbit hole, let's add one more concept to our understanding of *insecure attachment*, and that is *object constancy*. Object constancy underpins whether a child develops a secure or insecure attachment to his or her mother. The origins of this concept are largely from the field of psychoanalysis (Freud, Lecky, Hartmann, and most prominently, the original work of Margaret Mahler). And it likely derives from Piaget's theories of childhood development or what he termed object permanence, a cognitive skill developed by the child between the ages of two and three. The child learns to differentiate itself from its mother as two separate and independent people or what is termed *individuation*. This is the beginning of identity development in the child. It is also the basis for developing emotional trust and managing the uncertainty of the world.

What we observed in Ainsworth's "Strange Attraction" experiment is that at an early age, infants have already developed coping strategies with the world around them, or what Ainsworth described as *secure* and *insecure* responses toward their caregiver. Think of *object constancy* as the process by which these attachment strategies are developed by the infant. An infant with a nurturing and responsive caregiver will quickly develop a sense of trust and feeling safe in its world. Literally, the infant-caregiver interaction encodes the child with a model of the world and forms the basis for the infant's attachment strategies.

When the child has a secure attachment, it learns to manage the caregiver's inconsistencies and maintain trust. When the caregiver is not routinely nurturing or is indifferent or abusive, the infant's world becomes emotionally unpredictable and, in the extreme, chaotic. Here, the child's ability to develop object constancy is disrupted, and trust becomes increasingly difficult to establish. The result is often a deep emotional double bind for the child, particularly having to love and depend on someone who is not emotionally responsive or nurturing. In this latter instance, a duality is formed. People and circumstances are seen through a psychological schema that fixates on people as either trustworthy or not trustworthy.

When object constancy is seriously disrupted, trust does not fully form, and the world is split into a *trust-distrust duality* and becomes a chronic source of dissonance and interpersonal tension in adulthood. How one goes about managing the uncertainty and ambiguity of the world around them, given the chronic possibilities for disappointment, is dependent on their early emotional programming as to whether the world is trustworthy. Without trust, the world fragments and becomes a place without a sense of emotional or cognitive continuity. Managing contradiction and reconciling differences (dualities) becomes a struggle (race, religion, ethnicity, political party, sport teams). This early strategy of splitting typically defaults to a zero-state world, one that is experienced as either good or bad, right or wrong, moral or immoral, with us or against us, patriot-traitor, etc. The same trust-distrust duality that the child learned to cope with in infancy and childhood becomes an adult coping mechanism with underlying fears of abandonment, rejection, or feeling trapped.

From a psychological standpoint, an insecure attachment strategy often forms the genesis of personality disorders (borderline, narcissistic, antisocial). Still, for many, it simply means there is a void in which trust is difficult to establish and maintain. And herein lies the origin of absolute-mindedness, a world in which trust functions as a fixated duality—trustworthy, not trustworthy or "we versus them." Here is the core mechanism of tribal identity. When trust functions in this underlying duality, it becomes nearly impossible to question what one has decided to trust (facts no longer matter and neither does the truth). And in this duality, it becomes possible for paranoia and conspiratorial ideation to form and give explanation to what is being emotionally experienced. Just to be clear, there is a lot to distrust in our world—infidelities, betrayals, advertising, and the human capacity for deception—but also all the travails that befall us and certainly the political process and the power of government.

Individuals who enjoy a secure attachment are better able to differentiate subtle degrees of trust rather than quickly defaulting to an all-or-nothing trust-distrust duality. Put simply, individuals who experience a secure attachment are better able to manage complexity where concerns of trust and distrust are not fully evident, more capable of reconciling inconsistencies in other's behavior and emotionally regulating disappointment without automatically defaulting to a sense of personal betrayal. Trust is managed much like a form of delayed gratification when it comes to addressing complexity and long-term concerns.

Playing the Trust Card

A recent public display of mistrust was Wisconsin Republican Senator Ron Johnson questioning why Americans needed to be vaccinated (2021), stating he was "highly suspicious" of efforts to mass vaccinate the general public and saw "no reason to be pushing vaccines on people." Then defaulting to the right to "decide for themselves." This is what playing the "trust" card looks like politically in times of crisis. Seemingly reasonable on the surface but ruthlessly manipulative underneath. In this instance, it stirred the underlying mistrust issues that affirm people's fears and ambivalence when it comes to being vaccinated. One must wonder what the outcome of this pandemic would have looked like if all leadership from the top had supported public health measures rather than stoking fear and ambivalence. Basically, deploying the same *active measures* Putin is conducting against the West, but only in-house in this case.

The Historical Case for Attachment

The life of man, solitary, poor, brutish, and short.

—Thomas Hobbes, *Leviathan*

The historical picture of child-rearing is truly vague and dismal. In fact, the first book on the subject was written in 1960, *Centuries of Childhood*, by Philippe Ariès. The only record of the infant-mother bond is the European and American historical experience, and it can only be certified with limited authority. The most educated conjecture is what we think of as "childhood" today was mostly conceptualized in the past as little people who became increasingly able to provide labor. Yes, there were apparently eight-year-old adults. It was unlikely that life was seen in stages of development or even quantified by age. For those who read or watch old movies, there was an intense period of rapid industrialization in the eighteenth- and nineteenth-century Europe and America. And child labor was common in textile mills, factories, farms, and coal mines, really many forms of labor we would consider appalling today. The mercantile world was ambitiously trafficking children from orphanages. This was most vividly described and serialized by English Victorian writer Charles Dickens (Oliver Twist, David Copperfield, Nickolas Nickleby). Childhood, for many, was horrendous and exploitive on a vast scale. Similar labor exploitation can be seen today throughout Africa and the third world (e.g., picking cacao and coffee beans, mining gold and diamonds, picking through mounds of garbage, or as child soldiers).

All the literature can really tell us is this. Beginning in the nineteenth century with the arrival of a thriving commercial middle class, remarkable changes began to take place regarding the nature of childhood as it undertook its uniquely modern perspective. Children were children, and the notion of adolescence as a unique stage of life quickly evolved. This was all amplified with the codification of labor laws and the promotion of universal public education as a baseline for functioning in modern society. Unfortunately, cross-cultural and anthropological-ethnological studies of indigenous populations are understood primarily in Western terms and provide limited understanding of infant-mother bonding. But clearly, in all circumstances, past and present, when life is under pressure, what the modern world construes as childhood and adolescence have been sacrificed and continue to be.

In a provocative work titled *The History of Childhood* by psychoanalyst Lloyd DeMause (1974), we are offered a psychological theory of childhood that concludes the maltreatment of children was continuous throughout human history, adding that adult involvement with children mostly occurred at later stages of life. He further notes that the most significant determinate of the adult character were child-rearing practices (nurture shaping nature). The modern conceptualization of childhood is a social construct that likely had no meaning throughout most of human history. What is also evident in the contemporary world is the significant role communities and government play in setting standards of care and maintaining the welfare of children (our little adults).

So what is the digression all about? It is this. If insecure attachment theory holds any validity, it would be reasonable to speculate that throughout most of human history and in most cultures and in most times and places, insecure attachments prevailed with most children and, therefore, with most adults. And the premise put forth here is that this reality pressured society toward authoritarian rule and the unending strife and conflict that has ensued for most of human history. Only with the evolution of Enlightenment values and the rise of a middle class did the ascent of rationalism seriously begin. And most importantly, a nurturing infant-mother bond began to fully evolve, one that extended for many years over the life of a child and was then passed on generationally as that child survived and became an adult. Once this began to occur at scale, it was the likely developmental genesis of the modern world we live in today.

American Children at Risk

So how are American families doing presently? Research psychologists (J. Sung et al. 2015) conducted studies comparing temperamental differences between same age infants from the state of Idaho to Dutch children. The result showed that Dutch children, on average, had brighter dispositions, smiled more, and were more easily soothed. American infants, on the other hand, had "higher overall negative emotionality, fear, frustration, and sadness." Not surprisingly, expectant Dutch mothers were more content compared to American mothers, who were described as worrying and with high levels of unhappiness. Practically speaking, American mothers were running higher levels of stress and felt more isolated and unsupported. And a direct line to this stress could be drawn to mothers having to work full-time and having limited emotional and financial support.

This leads to a very uncomfortable question. What is the infant mortality rate in America? In 2019, America's infant mortality rate was 5.7 deaths per one thousand live births, two-thirds occurring within a month of birth. The states with the highest rates were primarily in the South and upper Midwest, with mothers under the age of twenty suffering with the highest rate of infant mortality (these are also the most absolute-minded regions in the US). The US ranked highest among the industrialized nations of Western Europe, Japan, and Canada for infant mortality, with higher infant mortality rates than Latvia, Slovakia, Hungary, Poland, Cuba, Lithuania, Ireland, Belarus, Estonia, or 176 out of 227 countries.

In international comparisons (2019) of childhood deaths, ages one to five, the US ranked 47 among 193 nations reporting statistics, with a death rate of 6.5 per one thousand births. When we zero in on this mortality rate with the online Health System Tracker (Peterson KFF), it reports that in the 1900s, the primary cause of childhood deaths was infectious diseases. Today, the leading causes of death for children past infancy are "unintentional and intentional injuries," noting that older children and teenagers are even more susceptible to death by "intentional and unintentional injuries." Essentially, children placed at risk is the leading cause of childhood deaths in the US

Let's dig deeper and go darker. The National Child Maltreatment Statistics reported in 2019 that there were 4.4 million child "maltreatment referral reports" filed nationally. Child abuse reports totaled 7.9 million children. There were 491,710 reported victims of neglect; 115,000 of physical abuse; 60,927 of sexual abuse; and 39,824 were psychologically maltreated. The highest rate of abuse was for children under one year of age. Following our earlier line of reasoning, it is reported that 30 percent of abused children will later abuse their own children, and 80 percent of twenty-one-year-old adults who were abused as children met criteria for at least one psychological disorder. And ranging from one-third to two-thirds of "child maltreatment cases" involved parental drug and alcohol use.

And two-thirds of people in treatment for drug abuse report being abused or neglected as children.

The overall picture presented here is that children in America are surprisingly at risk for emotional and physical injury when compared to most developed countries. And it is not difficult to extrapolate from these numbers that neglect and indifference is metastatic in the US. And on top of this are the large number of disciplinarians who demand order and discipline from their children. Herein lies the incubator of the absolute-mindedness.

Perhaps the craziest notion in all this discussion is that we have an environment in which mothers are expected to work full-time to support herself and her family while attempting to raise a newborn. And an even crazier notion would be to provide an at-home nanny for every mother leaving the hospital with her child. Someone to initially help her cope, someone to model infant care and help her find her way in those early months. What about workplace maternity leave for both parents and affordable diapers, baby formula, crib, and home safety devices? Not to mention routine pediatric care with home visits. And if a mother has to work or return to work, why not affordable childcare?

A recent March of Dimes (2022) report found that access to maternity care is decreasing in the South and Midwest in over a thousand counties, demographically described as "maternity care deserts" affecting seven million women of childbearing age and five hundred thousand babies. In these conservative Republican states, which are primarily antiabortion, pregnant women often have limited or no access to obstetric providers and hospital services, resulting in poor health outcomes and higher mortality rates. Dr. Henderson of March of Dimes is quoted saying that the US resides in a "maternal and infant healthcare crisis" and currently is "the least safe to give birth and be born in among industrialized countries" (R. Treisman).

So long as we grudgingly provide the minimum, we will forever be at war with one another. A war that begins in infancy. But no, we will spend grossly more on pet food and video games than investing in the emotional and physical well-being of an infant. Apparently, we are still teaching everyone the unwritten rule of *life* in America at an early age—you are on your own and good luck. "Just like Mom and Dad taught us. Besides, look how they turned out."

Fearing the Spoiled Child

For the past year, all students in the Wisconsin public schools have been receiving free lunches under a federally funded program in response to the pandemic. But in Waukesha, about twenty miles from Milwaukee, the school board had different ideas, wanting to opt out of this program. One board member was fearful families would "become spoiled," and a school administrator was concerned families would gain a "slow addiction" to the program (*USA Today*, 8/28/21).

We need to break the cycle of distrust that rises with each generation in America. To accomplish this, every child needs to be accounted for. We need to accept that every pregnancy is a public concern with long-term consequences for the community. We need to ensure a child's object constancy with their caretakers so that a trust bond is fully formed and maintained throughout childhood. There should be no secret garden where parents get to punish and abuse their children. If that means a financial floor under each parent, so be it. It is an investment in the human infrastructure of the future. The Potemkin Village of many so-called average American households needs to be revealed for what it is. This should be the highest priority of our nation. This is not about state control in some Orwellian dystopia but putting a roof over the head of each child, a floor underneath, food on the table, a chance at education, and stopping the abuse. That is how children will learn to trust and safely find their way to the future.

Undifferentiated and Unending Enlightenment Wars

Our discussion about *object constancy* and *insecure attachment* is essentially a lead-up to the psychological concept of *differentiation.*

That is, how secure emotional bonding leads to an altered and more psychologically complex and discriminating individual. The psychological concept of *differentiation* came into prominence in the 1960s thanks to psychiatrist Murray Bowen's work with institutionalized children. And today, it remains an established cornerstone of family systems theory. But to be candid, it's a somewhat confusing term, having itself differentiated into many meanings over the years. But let's take a stab at it. *Differentiation* is the process of identity formation and defining oneself. Differentiated individuals internalize their values, ideas, and beliefs rather than automatically defaulting to prescribed ideas or succumbing to social pressures around them. They exhibit a positive ability to maintain personal boundaries when pressured to conform, having developed a strong sense of *self* as an autonomous individual. For our purposes, differentiation is the endgame of self-development that begins with a positive infant-mother relationship and the establishment of a trust bond.

But let's take a steep turn down a speculative and theoretical path that also happens to conform with the model of absolute-mindedness presented here. Ruut Veenhoven, in a paper presented at the *International Psycho-Historical Association* (1980), sets forth an all-encompassing perspective on the concept of differentiation (or individuation, to use his term), borrowing heavily from the many insights of psychologist Herman Witkin. While his focus was on the rapidly changing nature of marriages in the Western world, it turns out to have broad implications, today, in the role of individuation as a political dynamic in the United States.

Let's lay out his basic premises. In the Western world, a historical process of psychological differentiation has taken place, resulting in greater interindividual psychological differences and complexity. This process first emerged at the end of the Middle Ages and continues to accelerate to the present. So what does this mean in terms of the distinction made here between the rationally minded and the absolute-minded. For one, the time frames parallel one another. The evolution of Enlightenment rationality and Protestant individualism gave rise, over hundreds of years, to what we now term an individuated person, but really a psychologically oriented individual. And as

Veenhoven makes clear, this resulted not only in an advanced psychological complexity but also "the degree to which individuals in a population differ from each other" following many independent patterns.

Two parallel and interactive processes were taking place in Western history. Our social universe had been growing exponentially more complex than the one that previously existed during the Middle Ages. What I have termed a dynamical social network or *simulation* was evolving alongside a more psychologically complex individual. An individual with a clearly defined sense of *self* that is now more fully differentiated from the world around them. Here, one's values are internalized, and the world is engaged in more rational terms. And importantly, the use of more sophisticated psychological defense mechanisms. Now *intellectualization* and *sublimation* are being substituted for the more primitive mechanisms of *repression* and *denial.* And over the past six hundred years, there has, basically, occurred a reorganization of the personality to adapt to our new world.

Examples abound in how social-cultural factors required a more complex adaptation, one that now fully defines childhood and adolescence as unique developmental stages of life when, in the past, they did not exist because there was no need for them. There was also an increased emphasis on the nuclear family as the key social unit, giving impetus to a greater focus on individuality. This new adaptive family unit placed more emphasis on each child, now increasingly separated from the larger family community that ruled them as small adults. Fronted by changes in child-rearing practices and perceptions of infant vitalization, this process was further pushed along by evolving standards of universal education and literacy. The relationship between parent and child and teacher and student dramatically changed during these times. Parents became more nurturing and reasoning. Teachers became less authoritarian and more sensitized to the learning needs of each student. Children were no longer realized as a form of menial labor and marginal contributors but learners and repositories of the future.

All this took place along with a rapidly evolving and highly stratified economy. Today, job sophistication and organizational complexity are a fleet of starships compared to our recent feudal past with a donkey pulling a cart, further eroding class distinctions and authoritarian models of management, ones that, for thousands of years, rendered workers as indentured servants, tenant laborers, slaves, and industrial chattel. The evolution of the economy from agrarian to mercantile, to industrial, and now knowledge-based requires and demands more complex individuals to invent it, operate it, maintain it, and manage it. The result is a retreat from our previous collective reality to one of greater personal autonomy, one instigated by rising complexity but also by more evolving concepts of individual rights, democratic ideals, and market economy. Society became simultaneously more pluralistic and interdependent.

Complexity became the modern norm, at the same time demanding the same from each individual. Questions about the self and self-esteem and inner emotional life became more defined by greater psychological complexity, as both a means of adaptation and further pushing the boundaries of complexity. As a result, social control of the individual graduated from a shame-based model emphasizing external control to an internalized-based model emphasizing guilt and self-control.

It was further speculated that cultures broadly differ in the degree of psychological uniformity required among their members and that the process of socialization and pressure for conformity vary greatly. The authors of this model suggest the psychological individual is unique to Western culture as the baseline for identity formation, one that stands out as significantly different from its predecessor six hundred years earlier. I don't think these authors are making the case there were no differentiated individuals in the past or elsewhere around the world today, only that in the West, it evolved as an archetype of the *self* that drove rationality, scientific development, democratic ideals, and capitalism. We might call it the "hyper-I" compared to most of the world.

In America, differentiation into a highly independent individual has been a form of radical social philosophy from our beginning and, for many, an outright faith. And failure to fully achieve this state of psychological independence is considered a gross failure of identity formation, which is where the absolute-minded primarily reside. Absolute-mindedness is a failure to fully differentiate and to achieve an independent sense of self from the general societal norms and expectation. Or what has been termed here, the "we." The result is an enduring sense of shame and feeling of less than. And the root cause of this begins with a broken trust bond early in life and later socialization that is structured around *principle and discipline* rather than independent *reasoning and empathy*.

The Dark Side of Principle

A recent CNN broadcast featured a still frame of former Vice President Mike Pence addressing "The Family Leadership Summit 2021" in Iowa. Behind him was a large banner proclaiming, "Principle over Politics." Sounds straightforward enough. But is it? On the surface, it might be proclaiming personal integrity over the corruption of the political process. But with a little jostling, it raises other cynical possibilities. For example, "We stand against the dark forces governing our country." And with the right filter, it's proclaiming, "What we believe is all that matters." Literally, the proclamation for a revolution. And the final reduction is "us against them." This is the experience of being raised with *principle and discipline*, its mindless exposition of the obvious, and its unwillingness to calibrate and deliberate the complex.

The reality is, if trust is severely impaired, it becomes nearly impossible to fully differentiate as a person. If an individual's model of the *self* is one of *principle and discipline*, then they are eternally seeking guidance in life beyond themselves and fail to fully individuate. Currently, that means finding direction on social media, conservative cable news/radio, Republican leadership, evangelical preachers, and conspiracy theories. And in its most radicalized form, the failure to fully differentiate is addressed by attempts to remediate grievance through revenge and ultimately violence. And herein lies the psychological foundation of the populist movement in the US and its fascination with all things Trump. It also informs a long history of violent vigilantism in America and the mass killing sprees we are currently experiencing.

Low-Trust / High-Trust Communities

Identifying who is trustworthy and who is not is not unlike the Supreme Court finding on pornography. You will know it when you see it. And we all can use a healthy dose of skepticism when it comes to surveys of trust, primarily because circumstances can make distrust a reasonable adaptation. So let's try to parse this as best as we can by starting with nation-states. It would be fair to say the government of North Korea is low-trust and the government of Japan is high-trust. And we could go about the world ranking each government on measures of trust. The most obvious is democratic governments are high-trust compared to low-trust authoritarian regimes, etc.

But if we were to look inside each country, we would likely encounter low- and high-trust people and organizations. In the US, it would not be controversial to claim that Girl Scouts function in a higher trust manner than, say, the Insane Clown Posse. Or that some state governments, particularly Republican administrations, function more low-trust than Democratic administrations. One measure of this might be how Republican governors and legislators have gone about enacting voter suppression laws after the 2020 election or curtailed unemployment benefits during the pandemic or have been continuously attempting to gut the Affordable Care Act.

The high/low-trust construct holds across all forms of social organization. It would be reasonable to make the case that people organized around their supernatural beliefs tend to be low-trust. They separate from the community, think of themselves as different and special, and look down on nonbelievers as less than them. They have strict rules and guidelines and continually judge others by their standards and expectations, ostracizing people, condemning people, and imploring supernatural forces to punish those who do not believe or abide by their beliefs. And most concerning, they actively seek to legislate their sense of moral superiority. The reality is, they only trust themselves.

Most of us agree that certain groups tend to fall into the low-trust category—gangs, organized crime, drug cartels, casinos, White supremacists, militia groups, neo-Nazis, and Big Pharma. While others function in a higher trust manner—PTA, Salvation Army, Goodwill, American Cancer Society, kindergarten teachers, and obstetricians. Large corporations tend to reflect both a mixture of low-trust and high-trust values but generally do not trust employees and only relent when competition or government forces them to be more generous than they would like to be. But at the political level, they are all Apple CEO Tim Cook. They are low on trust, seeking legal forms of tax evasion, tax inversion, offshoring profits, lobbying for subsidies and less regulation, price manipulation, hiring foreign visa workers, developing overseas supply chains, and moving manufacturing plants out of the country. When profit is the primary motive, no organization can be fully trusted, but with considerable variation among individual corporations and small businesses.

And all this can be further subdivided along the lines of education and income, urban versus rural, red versus blue regions of the country, faith-based versus atheists, blue-collar versus white-collar, men versus women, and redivide again by ethnicity and race. The regression can be nearly infinite. The Apple mothership in Cupertino is a trust model, but its Foxconn manufacturing facility in China is a model of distrust. And if you work for the Amazon AI research team, high-trust. If you work at an Amazon warehouse, low-trust. America is a blend of all these trust distinctions.

And lastly, we come to conspiracists. They exist at every level of the larger community referenced above. And, by definition, they exist in a state of low-trust. But to restate this, low-trust is not the absence of trust but rather a commitment to other low-trust people, organizations, and ideas. They only trust larger conspiracies that are influencing and manipulating them, often the government. And because they are low-trust, they inevitably place the trust they have in the least trustworthy people and ideas. Why individuals low in trust are prone to primarily trusting those who are deceiving or lying to them is a great conundrum. It appears to be a psychological reenactment of their earliest experiences of failed trust—forming trust bonds with other like-minded people in low-trust circumstances, and continually identifying "others" who cannot be trusted. For example, schoolteachers and doctors. Gangs function this way. Authoritarian regimes function this way, as do political parties and all manner of businesses and private associations.

Individually, we do not exist outside of some form of social organization. There is no "I" without a "we." It is that simple. Individuals who exist in low-trust states often experience an overwhelming need to belong. More so than those in high-trust states. They need to dissipate the internal dissonance that arose from earlier broken trust in their lives. The dissonance then must be externalized as the only safe means of acknowledging it. As adults, they seek out the projected authority figures (faux parents) who will rescue them and identify the immoral or threatening "others" responsible for their internalized dissonance, cast as anxiety, anger, and fear. Dissonance is then resolved variously by identifying the threat and organizing against it, and most simply and efficiently by identifying the conspiracy behind it all.

Worldwide, distrust is the foundation of authoritarian regimes. Regimes that correctly perceive democratic states as threatening to their authority and legitimacy. Why? Because democratic states continually expose elements of broken trust and the lies that obscure this fact. Take, for example, the recent revelation about the deaths of hundreds, if not thousands, of Native American children forced into Catholic boarding schools in Canada; the Tuskegee Syphilis Study (1932) deciding to withhold treatment to African American men to determine the efficacy of treatment; the lead water crisis in Flint, Michigan. These are all lies that have been revealed. But China continues to hide Tiananmen Square, denies the genocidal suppression of Muslim Uyghurs, and Russia pretends it was not at war in Ukraine. Or Belarusian President Lukashenko claiming he won election in 2020 with 80 percent of the vote. In a world so often premised on lies and deception, the two most important questions are, Who can be trusted, and who do you blame? Everything in between is undifferentiated for the absolute-minded. They can only trust those who share their disbelief, and everyone else is to blame.

Nations that govern with a limited ability to trust do so down the barrel of a gun. Apparently, everyone trusts that violence takes care of business. (Here in the US, we let everyone have a gun because this is such an effective solution.) In fact, authoritarian regimes are politically premised on not trusting as core to their identity and survival and respond threateningly to the world around them as a result. And that's why most trust circles are fairly small. The great conundrum for these regimes is they are organized to both govern and suppress the people who are the identified threat to their economic and political power. This is an arrangement that appears to work for many of the absolute-minded, who understand the game and play this lottery daily, all the while gaining herd immunity in return (or at least until the herd requires thinning).

It is reasonable to conjecture that for many people, the hardships and complexities of life and all the mysterious and invisible forces operating throughout the world are bound together by paranoid and conspiratorial conjectures (religion fills this void for many). And equally important, this is normal and has been since the beginning of human cognition. But slowly, through the developing rational mind and science, we have evolved a better understanding of the many mysterious forces in our world, giving us new insights and understanding. However, for many, this process feels evasive and untrustworthy. It also requires a level of knowledge and trust beyond the ability of many, one that subjugates the natural inclination toward conspiracies and quiets the mind and rationally organizes our thoughts and behaviors.

We humans are mental beings, and that has consequences. Once the trust bond is disrupted, the absolute-minded default to simpler associational thinking to explain what they believe, projecting onto others what they are thinking and feeling. This remarkable cognitive trait, the ability to attribute mental states to ourselves and others, is the hallmark of being human. It allows us to both understand and empathize with others, but also to project our fears and anxieties onto others as well. This cognitive trick serves to protect each of us by anticipating the future actions of others, but also to influence and manipulate others if necessary. And in a modern world filled with mysterious and unexplained forces operating below the threshold of awareness or understanding, these forces become the primary drivers of conspiracy formation, continually coalescing around the earlier distortions in their experience of trust.

The historical reality has always been that any disruption in identity formation (broken trust is a precursor to this) portents conflict and violence and is the genesis of today's populism and vigilantism. It is a primitive effort to restore order and, if necessary, challenge existing authority. Today, we are faced with what can only be characterized as the e-tech colonization of the world, a powerful technology disrupting traditional narratives and centers of authority and power, as did European imperialism for five hundred years. It is not going away and is more likely to impact us like a social tsunami. Many are now functioning intellectually and emotionally in a static dissonant state, trapped in rapidly evolving dynamic networks. The world around them is a conspiracy cauldron, much like molten steel flaring into the night air as it's poured into conspiracy molds.

Footnote: Absolutism has never been better portrayed than in the epic television series *Yellowstone*. Here we witness a Montana ranching family's personal delusions of grandiosity and self-righteousness drive their ruthlessly violent response to an expansively changing world, all bound together by their blind loyalty to one another. Unable to see how they have changed the world that came before them or how they are enjoying and manipulating the modern world to their advantage, they pretend to resist the future with massive pickup trucks, murder, political corruption, and shooting from a helicopter, while their grazing cattle herds slowly degrade the environment they fantasize worshiping. What makes it a truly great series is that at some level, we suspect they could be right.

America's Trust Failure

The *Pew Research Center* defines social trust as "a belief in the honesty, integrity and reliability of others." Having surveyed the

American people for the past forty years, Pew reported in 2019 that 71 percent of those surveyed expressed concern that there had been an overall decline in social trust. This finding was consistent with follow-up questions. For example, when asked if most people would be helpful or look out for themselves, 62 percent responded, "Just look out for themselves." When asked if most people would try to be fair or take advantage of you, 58 percent responded, "Would try to take advantage of you if they got the chance." When it comes to trust, we appear to be cautious people, at best. And, I might add, probably always have been.

One simple measure of trust, beyond whether you can trust your neighbor, is how well a community is thriving. The *Bloomberg Global Health Index* ranked the US thirty-fifth globally, between Chile and Bahrain and below Estonia, Croatia, Cuba, and Costa Rica. The *Peterson-KFF Health System Tracker* noted that the disease burden is higher in the US than in any comparable wealthy country, ranking last. The US also ranked last in measures of health care access and quality. Here's the thing. We could track dozens of quality-of-life measures, and the US consistently does middling worldwide and near last among wealthy countries. There is no point in listing them all here. However, we are near the top for violent crime, rates of incarceration, school dropouts, suicide, drug overdoses, and alcoholism. But don't despair. Quality-of-life measures continually rank the US number 1 in defense spending and billionaires (745).

So who is doing well? International surveys of social trust indicate that homogeneous, egalitarian, and well-to-do countries have the highest trust levels (think Scandinavia here) and the *usual suspects* (Japan, Western Europe, South Korea, Canada). Here, the US ranked in the "upper-middle range of trust." Again, we are just so-so. Within the US, minorities and low-income people expressed the least trust. The 2019 Pew survey indicated that trust had fallen over the past twenty years for those over fifty without college degrees, household incomes below $30,000, living in rural areas, and Republicans (what appears to be the home base for the absolute-minded). These findings suggested problems ahead if anyone cared or was paying attention.

But really, the Pew survey and the many similar ones (General Social Survey) don't quite get us fully to the issue of social trust in America. Besides, these surveys are just questions and not actual measures of how we conduct ourselves. If we want to drill down to the core of social trust, it might be better to examine whom we elect to Congress. This is where policies are enacted and money exchanges hands. Here we can clearly differentiate laws and policies that reflect social trust.

So where do Republicans stand on social trust? They are continually attempting to reduce government services and regulations that broadly protect the nation. They are habitually attacking social programs such as Social Security, Medicaid, and the Affordable Care Act. They are nonstop in deregulating financial markets, attacking environmental policies, reducing corporate taxes, grifting tax benefits and shelters to the wealthy, and appointing Supreme Court justices ideologically opposed to social justice issues. They have also been actively suppressing voting rights and have few qualms about dog whistling White supremacists while spouting conspiratorial memes. It does not take a survey to conclude that this is a low-trust environment.

But now, we are confronted by the steaming pile of elephant dung in the tent. Why do so many Republicans vote against their economic interests and support a plutocratic agenda? Well, yes, at some low level, their social values agenda is addressed. But this agenda starts at a low social trust baseline to begin with. Once you are ensconced in an identity tent (Republican, evangelical, White), the theory of cognitive dissonance says internal psychological inconsistencies need to be resolved. In this case, the gaping inconsistencies between self-interest and ideological consistency are resolved by *doubling down* and conforming beliefs and actions to one's ideological narrative. Choosing to be in a tent filled with people who cannot trust those outside the tent is how *conformity* and *absoluteness of thinking* become the primary response for individuals raised in low-trust environments.

When individuals feel threatened by social change and unstable economic times, a tent filled with low-trust people is better than no tent at all (or what has been popularly termed *tribal identity*). But here is the rub. While they trust one another, they struggle to trust beyond the tent, no matter how painful the personal cost. It can become a shame spiral of self-loathing, huddling in their specialness and lashing out at the immorality of the "other." And always with a conspiratorial meme of powerful forces manipulating the world around them (the invisible parent). For them, it's about the personal integrity that comes with having received *principle and discipline* rather than *empathy and reasoning.* So they are needlessly dying from COVID-19 because of a failure to mask up, social distance, and get vaccinated. But taking "horse paste" (ivermectin) for worms and parasites makes perfect sense because the CDC didn't recommend it. Besides, it worked great on their neighbor's livestock (prelogical cause-and-effect reasoning).

There are a few essential things to understand about social trust:

1. Each of us has a personal threshold for trusting (often conditional and not all or nothing).
2. We all greatly vary when it comes to what activates distrust in us.
3. Trust typically must be earned and takes time.
4. Trust is quickly lost when betrayed.
5. We are now at one of those low-trust moments in America.
6. Trust is always a two-way street, beginning with one's capacity for trust, but in close order, the "other's" general trustworthiness. But when it comes to *power*, history tells us power must be the first to demonstrate trustworthiness.
7. If there's limited reliability and honesty at the top, distrust generalizes. In other words, Republican Party leadership doesn't trust anyone in the tent except themselves.
8. In America, trust only exists when everyone is making money, and that is no longer true today.
9. Wall Street and our political parties sold out Americans for wealth creation, falsely claiming we were all in a "rising boat." A conventional and convincing mistruth. As a result,

> trust is low, and the potential for strife and discord is exceptionally high.

If one looks back far enough, it becomes evident that the US has always been a relatively low-trust nation but with a surplus of wealth to buy off civil discord. (Even the Civil War was about an economic model based on slavery. "It's the economy, stupid!") While America's great redeeming qualities have been the rule of law and stable political institutions, it has always been comprised of competing interests and bands of people fighting for their share of the American dream. High on individualism, low on trust outside the parochial tent has forever been our motto (no disrespect to Alexis de Tocqueville). That is the way we have rolled since the beginning. There is one pie, and everyone is trying to get their slice in a zero-sum game. America! As long as we were expanding the size of the pie, things pretty much worked. Why else would so many Americans keep moving West?

From 1585 to 2021, most Americans arrived here impoverished, oppressed, indentured, shanghaied, and many as slaves, outcasts, criminals, or religiously preoccupied on the fringes of insanity, but almost always desperate. And to be clear, the investment overlords owned America from the very beginning. It is a legacy of slavery and the internment of Native Americans on reservations; wars of conquest against France, Spain, and Mexico; and the long and brutal history of impoverished "White trash" Americans forever being forced off their lands. A violent and ruthless low-trust people as experienced by every immigration group who has ever arrived on our shores and, subsequently, the never-ending labor-busting Robber-Baron class. Every social group competes against the other, which is how the rich keep getting richer (today, it includes H-1B visas and immigrants from drug cartel countries).

The only true respite from our exploitive reality began with WWII (1941 to 1964). And by the end, the mindless wars had begun (Vietnam, Afghanistan, Iraq). And finally, an absolutist Republican Party rejuvenated the American plutocracy. But there is a significant difference today. More than ever before, we are all truly economically, socially, politically, and electronically connected. There is no point in going West, young people. California is full, and the handful of expats in Costa Rica aren't going to lead a reformation. There are no more lands to conquer. Denmark is not selling us Greenland. (Suddenly, virtual reality, online gaming, and Second Life are not such bad places to migrate. Mars is looking even better once we terraform it for golf and takeout.)

The true anomaly in American history was the rise of an enormously ambitious and creative middle class following WWII. A product of massive wealth redistribution, a broad social safety net, a highly organized and influential labor sector, available and affordable college education, and significant infrastructure investment (and an economically dominant position in the world following the war). Today, this investment in the future is being strip-mined down to bedrock. Wall Street, large corporations, and the plutocrats are cutting America to the bone to increase their wealth (in much the same way Chinese fishing fleets bottom trawl the ocean floor, creating dead zones), and that is why our social trust is now at an all-time low.

Big financial institutions, declared too big to fail, now have never-ending assets for wealth creation backed by the Federal Reserve. They can never lose, no matter the state of the economy or how reckless their investment strategies. In reality, it's a con game. Any institution too big to fail should be heavily regulated and made risk-averse or broken up. They only give back in token amounts, bottom trawling America. The trust issue is not on the average American but on the plutocrats. It has to start and be earned from the top down. It is in their hands now, as the MAGA wing of the Republican Party continues to stoke division and conflict and Democrats atomize the social landscape. Our current reality simulation is a game of turmoil.

Social trust in a pluralistic and polyglot America is "exclusively" about market dynamics and wealth distribution. That's it in totality! There is nothing more to know or discuss: "Follow the money!" We have succeeded as a democracy primarily because of the promise of high opportunity costs for enough people, but not all, which is less true today than at any time in the past fifty years. In good economic times, trust is higher. When a few have too much in difficult economic times and many too little, trust is lower. Dissonance rises first in the most conforming and absolutist. Here the cognitive bubble begins to fill with fear and anxiety. Then it is projected as anger at the "other" then becomes inflated by paranoid ideation and percolating delusional conspiracies. Yep, that's us today, with too many residing in *resignation syndrome*. But also, because too many are getting screwed. When social trust begins to erode on the left, it's because of broad institutional failures. When it erodes on the right, it's because the lie has been exposed, and there's a refusal to acknowledge it.

And into this primal human drama strides the colossal hubris of Big Tech. A private wealth-creator and tax-dodger, making unending promises of a better future through technology while enabling and amplifying every dysfunction in the American society. All the while claiming no responsibility or even knowledge of what socially ails us. They are only giving people what they want and defaulting to market magic. They have no responsibility to employees, communities, or the welfare of the nation, only to shareholders. On any other planet, they would be part of an organized crime syndicate. In America, they are treated like leprechauns.

Chapter 3

Psychological Origins of Absolutism

> There is only one way to avoid criticism: do nothing, say nothing, and be nothing.
>
> —Aristotle

Reason/Empathy Versus Principle/Discipline

If you watch enough senate subcommittee hearings, you will start to notice a repeating pattern of questioning and interaction with witnesses. Democratic senators typically assert concerns about fairness and social justice regarding the human condition. Why is that, you might ask. Growing up, they were more likely to have been nurtured by parents who emotionally engaged them with reason and empathy. For them, the default for internalized emotional control are feelings of guilt. Republican senators, on the other hand, often project blame and distrust. And you might wonder, Why does their reasoning seem so abstract, distrusting, and self-righteous? The answer is straightforward. They were raised by parents who asserted notions of principle and discipline over reason and empathy. Here, the default emotion for internalized self-control is shame, an emotional state typically projected outward onto the world. They are generally less insightful and more concerned with how they are doing, pleasing others, and making sure they are right and that there will be harsh consequences. And facts and information will be largely distorted to fit this narrative.

Absolute-minded parents tend to be more distant, controlling, demanding, and less forgiving. They are more likely to let children cry themselves to sleep, not wanting to feel manipulated by the child so the child can learn to self-soothe, and, even better, learn to sleep alone and become independent, self-sufficient right out of the womb, not needing anyone. Now any crying or emotional reaction by the child requires discipline, as in "Stop crying now or I will give you something to cry about." Discipline is administered in the belief that sparing the rod spoils the child. The hidden emotional dynamic in this form of discipline is the parents' shamed-based fear they will be perceived as permissive or as bad parents, failing to fully discipline and control their children into well-behaved little adults. The more profound shame is not feeling in control, an eternal struggle for the absolute-minded. For them, the parent-child relationship is primarily about the parent always being in control (which is also an unending source of violence against children).

As the child develops, he or she will be continually disciplined by the withholding of affection, often for reasons the child is unable to discern. "It is my way or the highway!" In reality, the parents' unpredictable moods are controlling the child's emotional life. Physical discipline or the threat of it is rationalized as being in the child's best interest. And inevitably, there is the false narrative that the child needs to learn a lesson. The same parents continually withdraw and ignore the child for no discernable reason. So the child never internalizes a safe emotional schema of its world.

Regardless, discipline, no matter what form it takes, is rarely predictable and almost always an overreaction to circumstances. While there are no perfect parents, an embedded pattern of anger and emotional withdrawal and the use of physical discipline with an obsessive focus on shame-based interactions are the foundation of absolute-mindedness. The sheer unpredictability by which personal boundaries are violated sets in motion the generational passing down of the absolute state of mind. In a sort of "it was good enough for me, it is good enough for you" theory of parenting.

Corporal Punishment

It has been well established in the clinical literature that corporal punishment has no upside for children or adolescents. But a recent study strongly indicates that corporal punishment may actually alter brain activity and neurodevelopment in adolescents, resulting in measurables symptoms of depression and anxiety (Burani et al. 2022). Researchers at Florida State University, studying 149 boys and girls between ages eleven and fourteen, examined their responses to multiple gaming tasks while undergoing continuous electroencephalogram (EEG) monitoring (measuring brain wave activity with electrodes attached to the scalp). From these gaming tasks, they were able to develop a neural response pattern for both error and reward.

During a two-year follow-up, families and participants completed additional assessments for depression/anxiety as well as measures of stress and parenting styles. The results indicated a significant neural response to error (ERN) and reduced response to reward (RewP) in adolescents who experienced "lifetime corporal punishment." This research linked corporal punishment to increased neural sensitivity to making errors and decreased neural activity to receiving rewards, concluding that corporal punishment may alter specific neurodevelopmental pathways that increase the risk for depression and anxiety.

This research on corporal punishment raises an important question. What is the rate of corporal punishment in the US? The answer is we don't know. If we reasonably assume that people might be reluctant to report physically punishing their children to a stranger on the phone, then a nationwide telephone survey of households with children (Finkelhor et al. 2014) sets the lowest possible measure for rates of corporal punishment in America. The rate of surveyed corporal punishment for children zero to nine was an astonishing 49 percent, while the rate for ten to seventeen was 23 percent (both of which had declined from earlier surveys taken in 1975 and 1985).

The World Health Organization (WHO) cites evidence that corporal punishment increases children's behavioral problems over time and is linked to physical and mental ill-health, impaired cognitive and socioemotional development, poor educational outcomes, and increased aggression and violence. Corporal punishment was defined as "any punishment in which physical force is used and intended to cause some degree of pain or discomfort, however light." This includes hitting, smacking, slapping, and spanking, but also kicking, shaking, throwing, scratching, pinching, biting, pulling hair, boxing ears, forcing a child to stay in uncomfortable positions, burning, scalding, or forced ingestion (World Health Organization 2021).

In this environment, the child's reality is unpredictable and emotionally unsafe when a parent's overriding need is to feel in control. The child now resides in a cognitive bubble, struggling to reconcile their need for emotional warmth and object constancy with the unpredictable emotional distortion and physical discipline they receive. Having to depend on and love the disciplinarian places the child in an eternal double bind. What is never resolved is the embedded sense of distrust that arises in this primary relationship. The result is an unending projection of mistrust onto the world. And for many children raised by absolute-minded parents, to conceal their internalized shame, they are driven to succeed, as is often evident in the many absolute-minded Republican legislators thrashing about, projecting blame and fomenting conspiracy.

The distorted emotional reality most absolute-minded were raised with influences the world they now reside in as adults. The world is now distorted to varying degrees depending on the severity of the original double bind. That's why there is skepticism about science (they can't trust experts who become projected authority figures). Paranoia and conspiracy arise in this space to explain the inexplicable mistrust they feel. Their original double bind splits the world into simplistic dualities they cling to (good-bad, right-wrong). The parents who say they love them then harshly discipline them and subject them to unending demands that can never be met create the classic emotional double bind. The child wanting to be loved is now unable to trust or empathize with others. He or she toughed it out and is better off for it, and so should everyone else. And to be clear, this is not a zero-sum game. There can be considerable variability in how each parent disciplines and emotionally interacts with their child or children. As a result, the effect can be highly unpredictable. However, the broader effect is always evident across our communities.

"Don't be a crybaby!" There is, of course, a much subtler edge to the absolute-minded raising children beyond "my way or the highway!" A child is often rewarded with love and affection for complying with their parents' rules and expectations. In effect, affection is given and withheld as a form of emotional manipulation to assure compliance. This is all about control and the use of disapproval to gain compliance, typically, to a set of rigid expectations, values, and beliefs (what God wants or what good people do, but mostly what the parents want and expect). The child is then burdened with a more subtle double bind and carries the dissonance throughout their lifetime. When we see legislators railing about the immorality of illegal immigrants and separating them from their children or voting down stimulus checks during the COVID-19 crisis and filibustering universal health care, it's because the impersonal "other" are undeserving for not having demonstrated the requisite *principle and discipline*. The "other" have failed to comply and earn consideration, typically cast as wanting something for nothing or taking from the more deserving. They have yet to be shamed into conformity and are therefore untrustworthy and unredeemed.

It is all about narcissistic control that derives from shame. Parents are expected to set limits and guidelines for their children and hopefully represent positive role models, but many do it hypocritically and with such unrealistic expectations and demands that no child could possibly meet them. So the child conforms and tries hard and may even exceed expectation, but it is all about the rules for them. They become members of the Federalist Society or the Cato Institute or become respected lawyers and state legislators, always wanting to control the "other" and always subservient to authority. Maybe they become respected journalists and commentators, continually shaming the "other" and discovering hidden agendas (ones that conform to their underlying emotional reality). Their dissonance brims with covert mistrust. Always rigid, narrow-minded, and manipulative, just the way they were raised to be.

Having succeeded on harsh disciplinary terms and unable to see any other possibility, the adult never learns how to care about anyone except those they must please—themselves, those close to them and authority, all wrapped in a bubble of mistrust in the human condition. Often, their childhood experience is closer to Stockholm syndrome than feeling loved. But it is the authoritarian model. The "other" becomes an unconscious projection of their emotional double bind, never trusted and always an existential threat. Yes, they tend to be more concerned about Wall Street, a symbolic parental figure who will reward them for their principles and discipline, than with Main Street, who confronts their double bind, an experience too painful to be examined. As a result, they tend to be outwardly oriented (keeping an eye out) rather than introspective. And this loss of introspection renders them indifferent and unable to empathize outside their trust group.

Just to be clear, we are almost never conscious of the originating emotional processes that formed us. Typically, we engage in simplified dot-connecting, similar to a child's travel book connecting the numbers until a hidden figure is revealed. There is order in the world when our internal emotional states become clarified in the present. That's how one comes to know what they believe must be true and authentic. Projecting blame or uncovering a conspiracy readily dampers internal emotional dissonance. Unfortunately, this clarity is always temporary as the world inevitably reveals repressed distrust. It then becomes emotionally disruptive. Despair arises in the loss of faith, as do anxiety and anger over rising mistrust. Time, once again, to double down on their false beliefs.

For the group, the dissonance is resolved by identifying challenges to its identity and by action that realizes its values. Its benign form is realized by prosocial acts, e.g., charities, voter registration, community service, and religious missions. In its virulent form, it can be intolerant and destructive, as evidenced by violent acts emanating from the word of God, a foreign policy forever identifying threats and more parochially from neo-Nazi, White supremacist, and militia groups. But more personally, by making oneself emotionally invulnerable and by controlling the world around them. Really, any cause or conspiracy to believe in. That is the healing power of the conspiratorial mind, potentially violent and destructive, as we experienced during the January 6 Capitol riot. The truth is, we have been watching this play out for the entirety of our networked social existence.

Betrayal-Resignation

Do the absolute-minded suffer *resignation syndrome*? In the 1990s, there emerged a mysterious illness first diagnosed in Sweden. Young immigrant children began collapsing into coma-like states (mute, immobile, unable to eat or drink) that could last for months. It appeared to be a culturally bound adaptation for responding to loss and trauma. And not coincidently, all these children presented with histories of psychological and physical trauma. The loss of hope when "asylum" was denied appeared to be an unconscious triggering mechanism for this condition.

So what has this got to do with the absolute-minded? Neurological and psychiatric research into *functional neurological disorder* (FND) reveals that trauma histories are predictive of any number of physical and psychological conditions. Early on, patients were mistakenly diagnosed as suffering from *hysteria* and, even later, *conversion disorder* (e.g., sudden onset of seizures, tremors, deafness, pain, blindness, and comas). But subsequent psychological evaluations indicated the presence of repressed trauma, particularly during childhood, with histories of physical injury, sexual abuse, maltreatment, and stressful life events. And a closer examination of these patients with fMRIs revealed a subtle pattern of neurologic anomalies.

Guided by theories that the brain acts as a "predictive processing" organ, continually making and evaluating predictions by comparing past experience with current sensory inputs, neuroimaging supports the hypothesis that predictive processing is altered in FND patients. Risk factors such as trauma appeared to alter brain circuitry. It also turns out that a key to remediating symptoms of FND requires "shifting focus" away from symptoms, which was consistent with the predictive-processing model (Kwon 2020). In other words, focus shifts from the "self" to the negative "other" to resolve internal dissonance.

One could extrapolate from this research that the absolute-minded suffer a subtype of *resignation syndrome*. The predictive outcome of emotional restriction and physical discipline in childhood creates the stressful and traumatic events associated with the loss of trust and a functional neurological disorder (FND). The result is *conformity of behavior* and *absolutism of thinking* in response to early childhood stressors. These responses later become the necessary coping adaptations later in life, e.g., adherence to rigid ideas and beliefs.

Resignation syndrome alters brain structure and functioning, creating a cognitive process whereby paranoid and conspiratorial ideation emerges by "shifting focus" from the symptoms of the underlying trauma. One must ask, How could so many Americans identify with former President Trump, a model of absolutist dysfunction? He is the absolute-minded parent of their childhood trauma and reactive adaptation. Many voters unconsciously identify with him through their childhood traumas and stressors. He had come to symbolize their unconscious resignation in a world that cannot be trusted.

There is also limited research suggesting that individuals with underlying anger deriving from early childhood histories of trauma and trust loss are prone to identifying with authoritarian forms of leadership (Ambroziak et al. 2022). This theory fits well with what we are currently experiencing with Republican leadership mobilizing its base by stirring up anger and fear and *shifting focus* to a wide range of conspiracies and grievances, giving rise to populist discontent across America. This has clearly been identified as a winning political strategy for organizing the absolute-minded.

Intergenerational Trauma Transmission

Research is accumulating that a parent's acute adverse experiences may be genetically passed down to their children in what is termed *intergenerational transmission of trauma*. While it has long been observed that there's a likely trauma pass-through that was behavioral or learned, this new research has chilling implications. Groups who have demonstrated epigenetic changes in their gene expression because of acute and stressful life experiences include Holocaust survivors (Lehrner et al. 2014); genocide survivors (Field et al. 2013; Azarian-Ceccato et al. 2010); war veterans (Yahyavi et al. 2015); victims of interpersonal violence (Cordero et al. 2017); sex abuse victims (King et al. 2001); 9/11 survivors (Yehuda and Bierer 2008); victims of childhood abuse (Brand et al. 2010; Myhre et al. 2014); and of course, many mice in clinical studies. And significantly, these individuals are prone to developing symptoms of posttraumatic stress disorder (PTSD). Let's refresh. Epigenetics is the study of how our behaviors and environment affect the way our genes express themselves by altering the structure of the gene itself. Gene expression refers to how proteins are created from instruction within the genes that can turn genes on and off.

And there's also a paradox at the core of this research. Survivors of trauma tend to exhibit low cortisol levels. The conundrum being cortisol is considered a stress-related hormone. So why is it low in victims and passed on to the next generation? It turns out that low levels of cortisol shut down the release of multiple stress-related hormones, including resetting lower cortisol levels. Psychiatric research (Yehuda 2022) has demonstrated that in instances of childhood abuse, a "freeze" period likely occurs for a child in an abusive circumstance unable to either *fight or flee*. The resulting biological adaptation is lower cortisol levels as a means of reducing harm to the body experiencing chronic levels of stress. The paradox here is that the long-term effect is a proneness to future PTSD symptoms when overly stressed. Cortisol levels are now too low to actively tamp down adrenaline levels. In this circumstance, later trauma events are more readily implanted in memory, increasing susceptibility to PTSD symptoms. What was adaptive to trauma at the front end can now be maladaptive later in life. And this effect can be passed down generationally.

This is crazy, but the big picture is many of us do not come into the world with an emotional *tabula rasa*. Trauma has been passed on to us genetically by our parents. And to deepen this mystery, the evidence suggests men are more prone to this effect. Epigenetic transmission is greater from father to son than from mother to daughter or even mother to son. And the broad impact of events such as war, genocide, famine, and natural disasters may well ripple across generations, making many vulnerable to PTSD symptoms in the future.

Basically, one's gene expression opens the door to future struggles to emotionally cope with trauma or acute experiences. As an example, a high percentage of soldiers in combat who experience PTSD had abusive childhood experiences and low cortisol levels (Costa et al. 2018). And this is consistent with the theme of this book. Families that default to discipline and obedience, where there are high levels of emotional stress because of chaos and disorder (a "freeze" experience for the child), may well be opening the door to increased levels of grievance-revenge and lower levels of emotional adaptability later in life. Further, much of the populist anger and paranoid conspiratorial ideation all about the land today may well be precipitated by both generational trauma but also the freezing experiences of a highly disruptive childhood.

Evidence is now mounting that childhood trauma not only alters brain functioning but also gene expression and our overall adaptability to stress and acute trauma. How we Americans go about raising our children is clearly a significant factor in the violence and irrationality we are experiencing, particularly when it comes to mass shootings and a significant number of our citizens expressing the belief that violence is the solution to our social and political differences. It is also important to note that positive parenting may mitigate gene transmissibility. Diving deeper, this research indicates some children may actually be genetically more adaptive as a result of their parents' stressful experiences. It is not a simple one-way street, it turns out.

Grievance-Revenge Addiction

To fully comprehend absolute-mindedness, we need to step back and survey the bigger picture. And it's not pretty. It turns out that *grievance-revenge* is a default state for humans, a cognitive preset from our earliest evolution. Primed for it from the beginning, research by primatologists and experimental psychologists consistently demonstrates that our primate cousins evidence the same traits of grievance and revenge (chimps, orangutans, gorillas) as do humans, suggesting a long bio-evolutionary demand for fairness among primates. Recently, neuroscientists have begun probing this reality through brain imaging, revealing an underlying neuro-circuitry for these traits. Literally, grievance and revenge are addictions our brain rewards us for. Yeah, that's as bad as it sounds.

Any examination of addiction literature quickly leads back to one key driver—social-environmental confusion. Yes, there can be a genetic predisposition to mental states of grievance-revenge, as well as certain personality types that may be more susceptible to it. And of course, there are the powerful effects of addictive stimuli altering the brain's neurochemistry. But in general, addiction has its roots in social disorder. Addiction literature consistently reveals that addiction starts within the family. Dysfunctional families create high-conflict environments that disrupt emotional bonding. These families are more likely to violate personal boundaries and apply excessive and inconsistent disciplinary measures. The parents typically model negative behaviors, further inducing it in their children and making the family incubators for fearful and angry attitudes, allowing resignation, grievance, and revenge to form.

Pinwheeling Death

Brazilian army ants are rapacious hunters, but they are also blind. In the early morning, they leave their bivouac to explore the surrounding environment. Chemical scents are then laid down, communicating to the ants that follow. However, when they lose the scent, they form what is termed an "ant death spiral." As a group, they then begin frantically spinning like a pinwheel in the wind until they die from exhaustion. This is the plight of the absolute-minded. Losing the scent of reality, they become lost in pinwheeling conspiracies.

Research in the field of addiction offers us several important insights into grievance addiction. In particular, *incentive-sensitization theory (IST)*. This theory postulates that wanting something and liking something operates independently of one another. The brain circuitry that mediates the desire to want something is independent of liking something. Say what? This research initially began with, you guessed it, lab rats in the 1980s. However, a large body of research now supports it and extends it to the human condition (Berridge and Robinson 2016).

The reward system in the brain is driven toward amplifying *wanting* without necessarily amplifying *liking*. And the key hormone in sensitizing this system is the neurotransmitter dopamine. It is so powerful that it sensitizes an individual by altering the brain's structure, rendering it hyperreactive to cues and context that can persist for years. Even if an individual consciously does not want an addictive substance, the sensitized brain creates compulsive levels of wanting, not unlike the absolute-minded obsessive attention to feeling taken advantage of or attraction to extremist ideas online or siloing with people who share their extremist beliefs.

So what is the significance of *wanting* over *liking*? In terms of addiction, it means familiar environmental cues can trigger a powerful desire to want and seek out drugs, independent of whether acting on it is pleasurable or satisfying. A cubicle mate walks by with coffee, and suddenly, you desperately want that second or third cup of coffee but find it increasingly less satisfying. And by the third cup, you are disgusted with yourself. Why do so many Republican senators share the same distorted views on shaming the poor, denial of climate science, or adherence to extremist conspiracy theories about a stolen election? Because they reside in a state of cognitive distortion that is easily cued up by tweets from Trump or right-wing media as if a third cup of coffee.

Environmental cues are primary to *grievance addiction*, triggering one's sense of being a victim and fueling further grievances. Each aggrieved individual is continually encountering social realities that make them feel less than or emphasizing their lower social status as defined by work, income, education, all generating a grievance addiction response. At the same time, powerful secondary reinforcers are further triggering negative responses. The internet has quickly become a hot zone of reinforcers for grievance. It is designed to support and inflate grievances and negative attitudes, spouting dogma, misinformation, conspiratorial memes, and inflammatory rhetoric. We are being continually cued up by a viral contagion of grievances through our connectivity to the deep expanse of online conspiracy theories and paranoid beliefs.

The nature of triggering cues also takes a dramatic shift online, one that fuels grievance. Surfing online quickly moves one past simple personal grievance to a broader and supportive network of generalized grievances (as if the entire world were now triggering grievance). The previously explored underlying neurological process is now subjected to a barrage of unrelenting environmental cues fueling an obsessive preoccupation (or ant death spiral) by those caught up with paranoid beliefs and conspiratorial ideas—the hallmarks of absolute-mindedness.

But wait, there's more. Stress appears to play an independent and active role in addiction, as well as generating grievances. The impact of environmental "stressors" generates a deep cache of negative emotional responses—depression, irritability, anger, anxiety. When these moods are triggered, individuals quickly seek relief through alterations in the brain's neurochemistry (dopamine and serotonin). For most, stress triggers a relapse—drugs, gambling, eating, cleaning, shopping, and online gaming, whatever brings immediate relief and reward. But for many others, it triggers *grievance relapse*—feeling aggrieved and embracing paranoid and conspiratorial explanations for their emotional state.

Stress and chronic emotional states are significant factors in amplifying heightened dopamine reactivity in the brain. That's why it's difficult to quit or stop using drugs or engaging in compulsive activities. The amplified urge created by stress gives urgency to feelings of *wanting*. Equally important, this process operates unconsciously and can be triggered by subliminal stimuli. For the absolute-minded, this state of mind can be triggered by watching Fox News or following online conspiracy links. Equally concerning, the absolute-minded are seldom aware of what is triggering their sense of grievance. They just know it is true, and they feel it passionately. There is a deep state conspiracy, and the COVID-19 pandemic is a hoax, and everything they read and hear supports this, further heightening their awareness of these issues.

It is fairly evident that significant life stressors put all people at risk and potentially open the door for *grievance addiction*, stimulating all forms of compulsive behavior. Conjunctive with creating high levels of *stress wanting* is the subliminal experience of *fear*. And surprisingly, this demanding emotion also appears to trigger chemical rewards in the brain. Recognition of this process has led researchers to theorize that it plays a significant role in instigating "paranoid" ideation in the mentally ill, but just as likely for everyone else as well. Low levels of chronic stress, but especially a fear response, appears to give impetus to the ideological rigidness and conspiratorial insight of the absolute-minded. However, there is one more factor to consider.

Revenge-Violence (Closing the Wound)

Experimental psychologists have conducted human subject experiments demonstrating that when individuals feel unfairly treated, they frequently default to punishing others. This dynamic is on full display in the *ultimatum game*. A player is given money with the option of splitting it with a second player. The second player can accept the money offered or reject it. If they reject it, neither player receives any money. Brain imaging (fMRI) reveals that the act of punishing others engages a part of the brain signaling reward (in this case, player 2 feels rewarded for denying player 1 money for not being generous). It also appears that we would rather sacrifice our own self-interest than feel we are being taken advantage of (Crockett 2017).

But here is the conundrum. *Wanting* revenge may be more rewarding out of a need to emotionally self-regulate, particularly anger (Chester and DeWall 2017), which is not the same as *liking* revenge. Here, the evidence suggests that the post-revenge emotional state is not necessarily satisfying (Carlsmith et al. 2008). But it is all relative to a degree. The more aggrieved a party and the higher on neuroticism and narcissism scales (and if they are men), the more rewarding the act of revenge (Malby 2008).

This has many similarities to the *incentive-sensitization addiction* model (*wanting* versus *liking*) and resides in the same area of the brain stimulated by drug addiction. The significance is there appears to exist a neurological basis for expressing moral outrage and seeing that others are punished for their misdeeds, one that has an addictive quality. It's likely our long history of vigilante violence is triggered by a similar process. It has also become evident that the internet has unleashed this primal drive for millions.

The research findings on *grievance* and *punishing others* are also consistent with *cognitive dissonance theory*, with people assigning a moral lesson to their vengeful behavior. But rather than defining their behavior as vengeful, it is flipped to an altruistic act. "It is for your own good," a refrain many children have heard from their parents as they were about to be punished. Or "This is an important lesson you need to learn." In a harsh world, it is easy for the absolute-minded to feel they are being injured in some capacity and, in the most abstract terms, want to see the "other" punished. Punishment is good. In fact, you will often hear them say later in life, "I deserved to be punished." People getting what they deserve, whether true or not or a fearful projection, is what resignation-grievance demands (and as a child, that is what they received, whether they deserved it or not, and almost always inappropriately harsh and unreasonable). For Republican senators, it may be as simple as filibustering a bill.

Dissonance Contagion

The *Tulsa Race Massacre* is the tragic consequence of mass contagion, with people gathering and acting violently on the basis of irrational fears (and in this case, deeply rooted racism). In 1921, several thousand White males assaulted Greenwood's African American community, a suburb of Tulsa, Oklahoma. It was a community described as one of the most successful Black communities in the United States. After eighteen hours of violence, an estimated three hundred Black citizens were killed, and another eight thousand were left homeless. Over 1,256 homes and businesses were looted and torched. When the National Guard finally arrived, six thousand Black people were under armed guard.

Now, as to the confabulated cause of this violent event. A few days earlier, a newspaper reported a young Black man had raped a young White woman operating an elevator. There is no doubt that the media played a major role in precipitating this violence with its inflammatory and factually unsupported headlines, but also later suppressing reports of this tragic event. (In fact, few Americans have ever heard of this event until the past several years.) It turns out that the accused Black man was in custody at the time of the riot. Later, an investigation determined that he may have accidentally stepped on the woman's foot or had stumbled and touched the woman's shoulder (but there were no indications of violence). It is important to note that no White male who participated in this riot was arrested or charged with a crime. The point being made here is that *revenge contagion* is real, irrational, and deadly, and the absolute-minded are highly prone to it. (The January 6 Capitol riot features all the elements of revenge contagion.)

Grievance affects the brain in much the same way as drugs (based on brain imaging). Harboring a grievance (real or imagined) and acts of revenge activate the same neural reward circuitry as narcotics, triggering cravings in anticipation of pleasure and relief through retaliation, whether imagined or acted out (Rowe and Kimmel et al. 2018). It is no wonder that throughout history, severe punishment was a public spectacle, no less today, as millions reside in chemically induced harmony online over the misfortune of others.

It is well-documented that a primary risk factor for violence is an individual's perceived sense of injustice and wanting to avenge it (Gilligan 2001). Academically termed "retaliatory attitudes," it is a process that fuels cycles of violence in marital conflict, youth assaults, school shootings, gang violence, and acts of terrorism. Feeling aggrieved is also the single most significant variable in deaths because of violent crimes. And victims of violence are at higher risk for engaging in violent conduct as well. Neuroscience points to a link between a neural circuitry of retaliation (amygdala and superior temporal lobe) and the reward processing centers of the brain that activate narcotic addiction. Anticipating reward (wanting) is a significant factor in acts of revenge-aggression (Zimmerman and Schmitz et al. 2011; Chester and DeWall 2015; Akhtar and Barlow 2018).

Consequences of Resignation-Grievance-Revenge

As disappointing as it is to contemplate, acts of revenge chemically light up our brains the same way we experience pleasure and excitement, or what is colloquially termed *schadenfreude*. This process can trigger cycles of revenge violence—the Hatfield versus McCoy, Crips versus Bloods, workplace violence, honor killings, Sinaloa versus the Gulf cartel, WWI. Really, most forms of violence throughout history. If necessary, we can even confabulate grievances where they don't exist to justify acts of revenge and violence.

However, the reality is very different from fantasy. Following the available research, it's unlikely people feel better when they have committed acts of revenge. More likely, the compulsion of *wanting* revenge is what drives the act of revenge and not the outcome. How many times has a family left court after the conviction of someone who harmed them and described the judgment as empty and unsatisfying? A judgment they had pursued for years at great expense, showing up time and again at court hearings.

But really, what does all this research mean? In its simplest form, a grievance model traditionally looked something like this:

a perceived injustice > grievance > revenge > violence

But what we now know is that grievance, for many, is a chronic standalone state of mind, operating independently of any particular injustice. It began with families lacking object constancy and empathy. Then stressors persistently fomented negative emotional states and resignation, and neurotransmitters continually reinforced thoughts of grievance and vengeance. And this state can be instantly cued up by environmental factors triggering a strong sense of grievance. Today, triggering cues exist on cable news, online, and in communities of shared grievances. It is a natural state of mind, one chemically embedded in the human psyche, triggered by enormous economic disparity and endemic social change.

When we look closely at the absolute-minded in America today, they believe that their fears and grievances are not being heard and that they have been getting the short end of the stick for years (primarily disrespected). And their politics suggest that they are motivated by a revenge strategy, even if it is self-defeating and not in their interest (think *ultimatum game*). They can put a moral hat on it, identify revenge as righteous, and feel good about it. Residing in a cognitive bubble, they can project their fear and anger onto the "other" as the cause of their dissatisfaction and sense of hopelessness. And they can feel better for it by triggering a cycle of revenge satisfaction. One could also make the case that the internet is addicting Americans to revenge cycles, chronically looping anger and resentment, not unlike an ant death spiral.

Supposing motivation for revenge is cognitively hardwired, the case could be made that the lengthy social evolution of our legal systems was an effort to break chronic cycles of revenge-violence and facilitate social order. It likely began with tribal and religious councils and eventually followed with a formal codification of law (Ur-Nammu, Hammurabi). Today, this includes a multitude of legal jurisdictional entities most nations employ, but also international treaties and organizations, and more recently, international law. Even the Mafia has a *consigliere* to intervene and keep peace among the families. These systems appease the need for grievance-revenge, assuring that justice occurs and punishments are meted out. It would be reasonable to conjecture that the rise of populism and domestic terrorism in the US today is a direct result of the government's failure to address social inequality (real and perceived), setting in motion cycles of "stolen election" grievances, cued by Donald Trump and the Republican Party.

We are all genetically trapped in a grievance-revenge loop, continuously struggling to extricate ourselves. While we have developed broad and complex systems of jurisprudence and social mores, not so much economic and social justice, which continues to elude us. And *order*, which is notoriously difficult to achieve in democracies, is continually being sacrificed at the altar of a market economy. The reality has been our social, political, and economic systems are largely geared toward perpetuating unending grievance, apparently something we Americans are addicted to and prepared to engage in, forever, if necessary. That is who we are.

Trump's Grievance-Revenge Addiction

Early life stressors alter brain structure and functioning, sensitizing it to fear and paranoid projections, resulting in revenge addiction. And nightly, we watched this model of dysfunction play out on our televisions during the Trump administration. Nearly every night, Trump would obsessively tweet claims of betrayal, election fraud, and fake news, all the while dispersing misinformation, disinformation, and false claims (mostly lies) of ongoing conspiracies against him and his family. He was a model of grievance-addiction, fixated on personal grievances and exacting retribution against anyone he believed betrayed him (and pardoning those who lied for him). This compulsive behavior has all the hallmarks of drug addiction. Only, it's *revenge addiction*.

Trump's family history, anecdotally, makes repeated reference to his having a revenge obsession, one that appeared to have been nurtured early on by his father, who also exhibited the same grievance-addiction compulsion. He continually disciplined Donald not to accept any disappointments or setbacks and punished him when he failed (which appears to have been most of the time). The father-son relationship begins to explain why, in Trump's world, everyone else is to blame except for him.

Trump's public record, it turns out, is a lifetime of angry and fearful striking out at anyone and everything that did not support him in his eyes (and prone to hiring lawyers as his legal hit men). His unrelenting efforts to retaliate against those he believed treated him unjustly appear to be compulsive and uncontrollable, even if harmful to himself or those close to him. His revenge obsession is a model of *incentive-sensitization addiction*, waiting for the next media cue to set him off. He appears to know no limits, as his obsessive-retaliatory behavior has even become a public source of pride and satisfaction for him.

According to Mary Trump, who has a PhD in psychology, her uncle Donald is a "monstrosity [that] is the manifestation of the very weakness within him that he's been running away from his entire life." She further describes him as weak and a bully, meeting the diagnostic criteria for narcissism and sociopathy. These characterizations broadly align with the extreme elements of absoluteness typical of dictators (see chapter 9).

In his unique way, Trump represents the perfect grievance-stimulus for the absolute-minded, helping to focus or shift the object of their fears, giving them the belief that they are right and that the conservative news media and right-wing talk shows are truth-telling. Of course, they are loyal to him. Finally, someone at the top expressing what they knew to be true all along—not to trust anyone in authority. Thus continued the radicalization of a large segment of the American populace. Two excellent references are *Too Much is Never Enough* by Mary Trump (2020) and *Confidence Man* by Maggie Haberman (2022).

Schema for Absolute-Mindedness

How can we begin to understand the conservative orientation of the Republican Party? I would posit that the underpinnings of its *authoritarianism* have been central to human social organization and derives from biological and early life presets, as witnessed throughout history and around the world today. Conformity of behavior and absolute-mindedness are core constructs for the development of both individual and social identity. They are key to attaining herd immunity through tribal identification.

The big picture is the absolute-minded are not fully differentiated psychologically, a fairly recent adaptation that has emerged over the past several hundred years because of our increased social complexity. As a result, they are more externally oriented and looking outward to define whom and what they believe, whether that is a tweet from Trump, QAnon online message, or Bible study. This began with a parental focus on the needs of the parent rather than on the child, for which the child and later adult become forever focused on the external role of authority in their lives and less on internal direction defining their values, beliefs, and ultimately who they are as a person.

The underlying psychological construct at play here is *shame*, an intense emotional state that one has failed the community, that one is less and not good enough. A form of self-ostracizing out of fear of being separated from the community (family, friends, tribe, clan, band).

Note: A *theory* of absolute-mindedness is not all or nothing as often presented here. It comprises a wide range of subtle gradations with each individual and with many varying social cues or triggers. What's presented here is in simplified form, as if it's a zero-sum game. It is not, and exceptions to it abound everywhere. But overall, broken trust is the hidden emotional force behind states of absolute-mindedness.

Phase 1. Negative childhood experiences amplify trust issues for all of us. The origin of absolute-mindedness begins with an *insecure attachment* between parents and child, one in which there is a disruption in *object constancy*. The result is a broken bond of trust and an eternal cognitive *double bind* for the child (having to depend on and love someone who violates their trust). This is the beginning of trust issues in identity formation. The psychological effect is the creation of *cognitive dissonance*. And to resolve this internal emotional state, a number of coping strategies are adapted. For most, it is conformity and adaptation to all the parental figures' unreasonable demands and expectations. For a smaller percentage, it forms as chronic rebellion and acting out (as seen in delinquency and adult antisocial behavior). Generally, the dissonance is repressed and never acknowledged throughout a lifetime. What is being described here is a form of emotional abandonment by the parents. This is then amplified by utilizing corporal punishment to discipline a child, furthering the sense of betrayal and abandonment. But equally significant is that these experiences alter the structure of the brain and subsequent brain functioning, giving rise to depression, anxiety, anger, and aggression later in life. There is also evolving research demonstrating that trauma can be genetically passed down generationally within families in what is termed *intergenerational trauma transmission*.

Phase 2. The second stage of absolute-mindedness evolves developmentally as the child grows to adulthood, now residing emotionally in *betrayal resignation*. Subjected to *principle and discipline* as their primary emotional bond, trust collapses into socially conforming thoughts and behavior, but always with an underlying and unspoken stress and trauma. A cognitive bubble then forms around the suppressed dissonance. Here, reality testing is distorted and forms a portal for paranoia and conspiratorial thinking (where believing the lie is the safest adaptation). This is where *grievance-revenge addiction* forms, whereby one experiences the world as personally unfair, unjust, and without real equity (for many adults, this emotional state can also become a self-fulfilling prophecy that they act out over and over). An individual becomes addicted to grievance through unconscious fear and shame triggered by active environmental cues that are shame-inducing, which are everywhere in the world today. But they become strongly associated with the belief that one's values and traditions are under siege. The demand for justice and fairness is encapsuled by moral outrage seeking revenge and punishment of the projected "other" for toggling long hidden and suppressed emotions of broken trust (as so-called elites and the government are cast as the condemning parental figures of authority).

Phase 3. The absolute-minded *cluster by shared grievances*, united by the unreality of their beliefs. And in the case of the Republican base, any distortion suffices, like deep state conspiracy or Democratic Party pedophile sex rings. From the top of the Republican Party to the base, anything can be believed under duress and with the right triggers (some of which are being exhorted on purpose and with the intent of disrupting our democracy). The most difficult aspect of this entire line of reasoning is understanding that early life experiences of trauma and emotional stress shape the absolute state of mind and alter brain structure and functioning, and assuring the processes of *grievance-revenge* are not only rewarding but also exceedingly difficult to amend, with violence acting as a shared form of emotional resolution.

There is no direct way out of our cultural wars. It is a forever conflict that can hopefully be tamped down. A rapidly changing and complex world triggers a fearful sense of unfairness and grievance. Really, an underlying sense of threat to one's identity and ability to trust that is continually at play. We are going to have to find a path toward trusting the social contract and our democratic experiment. One way is to stop shouting 24-7 that it has all been a massive failure and begin to assert what we can positively agree on. Shifting norms will always be disruptive. And sometimes, the reality is we are simply going too fast for everyone to keep up. But largely, it is the broader issue of social justice that America has been unwilling to fully address.

Psycho-Developmental Model of Absoluteness

Stage 1—Trust Loss The most significant stage of identity development begins with the infant-mother relationship. A significant disruption is primary to the formation of absolute-mindedness.

Disrupted Object Constancy
(unpredictable environment)

Insecure Attachment
(emotionally unsafe)

Trust Double Bind

Stage 2—Resignation-Freeze State Unable to flee/fight can result in adaptive conformity and a struggle to differentiate complexity.

Discipline and Principle
(corporal punishment)

Demand for Conformity of Behavior/Absolutism of Thinking

Incomplete Differentiation

Chronic Underlying Dissonance

Stage 3—Adaptive Responding Acting out grievance-revenge and recapitulating the distrust double bind through group identity and projections onto figures of authority and conspiracies.

Betrayal-Resignation

Grievance, Revenge, Violence Reward

Recapitulating Distrust

Stage 4—Dictators The modern dictator resides in a state of chronic distrust requiring unquestioned loyalty and absolute power and control.

Transactional Social Reality
(developmentally, morally, emotionally)

Dark Personality Triad
(narcissism, psychopathy, Machiavellianism)

Paranoid and Violent Super-Adapters

Chapter 4

Dampening Internal Conflict

Stop the biblical flood of shit that Facebook unleashes on the world.

—*A.* Frank, *The Atlantic*

Over the past sixty years, there has been an intense academic focus on the genesis of what is prosaically termed the conservative mind, variously understood as the authoritarian personality, true-believer, or fascist prototype. Today, the concern in the US is primarily with the radical and populist dynamics of conservativism and a rise in domestic terrorism by White supremacists, militia groups, and neo-Nazi-affiliated organizations. It has also mainstreamed in Europe with the rise of ultra-right parties and a rapid shift toward illiberal governments in Eastern Europe.

The authors reviewed earlier—Hoffer, Adorno, and Hofstadter—were deeply engaged in trying to understand the origins of radical conservatism. And they fully understood there was a psychological component to their theories, one that starts with harsh and restrictive child-parent interactions. How and why this was true remained largely unknown. Presented here is a "theory of mind" that takes a deep dive into the psychology of radical right-wing populism, one closer to Piaget's childhood developmental model than the psychological concepts of personality traits or type.

To understand the absolute-minded, one must begin with a general theory of mind. That is, our ability to attribute mental states to ourselves and others—humans as mental beings able to predict and interpret the thoughts, feelings, and intentions of others. But secondarily, it is important to understand how this projective mental ability is shaped (and potentially distorted) by early childhood interactions with parental authority and the adaptations that follow. These interactions not only serve as powerful reinforcers and negative models of behavior, but recent research in neuropsychology substantiates they alter brain structure and neurochemistry, impacting later functional adaptation. And herein lies the probable origins of absolute-mindedness.

The logic of this paradigm is that there is no reasoning our way out of confronting the absolute-minded but only modifying the environmental conditions and cues triggering their reaction to the world around them. Currently, we are far from undoing this divide. But it begins by dampening reactive social, economic, and political triggers. And blocking any path to resolution is not only a fearful resistance to change but also a Republican party intent on holding power by instigating the latent fear and anger residing in its absolute base.

The Dissonance Effect

The first step in understanding the origins of human discontent begins with an exploration of our default cognitive biases, beginning with a theory of cognitive dissonance. This theory, first put forward by psychologist Leon Festinger in his book *A Theory of Cognitive Dissonance* (1957), has generated decades of validating research. It is also our first step in understanding the many problematic aspects of human cognition. This theory postulates that when a person holds two or more contradictory beliefs, ideas, or values at the same time, they will experience psychological distress. Distress is triggered when individuals act contrary to their beliefs or encounter information that challenges or contradicts their beliefs. An effort is then made to reduce this conflict or dissonance and return to a state of emotional equilibrium. An important factor in striving for equilibrium is a person's self-concept and wanting to retain a consistently positive self-image. This is all premised on the concept that people seek an internal psychological stasis when they experience internal inconsistencies, continually seeking to balance expectations with the realities of the world.

We humans utilize a range of coping strategies when it comes to cognitive dissonance. For example, we may change our behavior to make it consistent with our beliefs, or we may simply avoid any conflicting information or ideas so we don't have to be confronted with our inconsistent practices. Still, others may change or modify their beliefs, values, or ideas to align with their practices. But what most of us do is none of these things. No, we engage primitive mind tricks that allow us to rationalize, minimize, or justify our beliefs, values, ideas, and behaviors, regardless of their inconsistency. It's sort of magical.

No matter how inconsistent and dissonant our experience, we can make it all go away—everything, from mistreating our children to spreading false rumors or committing a murder. No guilt, no shame. Easy-peasy. It's like a get-out-of-mind (jail) card we can play anytime. Just watch your favorite politician deny what he or she said and dispute the facts as smoothly as they can. And truth be told, a large majority simply learns to live with dissonance, sheltering in trust groups and projecting it onto the world around them in the form of anger and fear. While dissonance is not the same as discontent, they are cognitively related. A great deal of online discourse is dedicated to pointing out others' inconsistencies and then shaming them for it. It is one person's discontent trying to shame another for their unresolved dissonance.

Adjusting to the experience of dissonance is forever ongoing. And while most of us can comfortably reconcile the many small discrepancies that confront us daily, unresolved discrepancies of a higher magnitude typically result in increased levels of dissonance. As an example, there are exceptionally high levels of dissonance inherent in the authoritarian or "absolutist" mindset that are typically resolved by *doubling down*; that is, taking confirmatory action, even if the action is inappropriate, harmful, or antisocial. For example, bombing an abortion clinic or storming the Capitol Building.

In our efforts to reconcile dissonance, a favored cognitive strategy is termed *confirmation bias,* whereby an individual seeks out information and people who support their opinions (herd effect). This is a win-win strategy, as one's beliefs and actions gain added support while reducing internal conflict. And coincidently, the internet and conservative talk radio appear to be confirmation bias propaganda machines, configured to silo like-minded opinions and beliefs (Nazi propaganda minister Joseph Goebbels would be overwhelmed with this opportunity.)

The theory of cognitive dissonance has been demonstrated in both neuropsychological research and cross-species experiments with our greater primate cousins. Apparently, resolving dissonance is an adaptive evolutionary strategy supporting group harmony and cohesiveness. The real lesson to be drawn from Festinger's seminal research is that we do not have to do anything to resolve dissonance, and we seldom do. We are pretty much able to reconcile almost any inconsistency without shame or guilt. The only dissonance most of us experience is when our inconsistencies are pointed out to us, which is why we only seek out like-minded opinions on the internet.

Dissonance Prophecy

The classic tale of cognitive dissonance was provided by Festinger in *When Prophecy Fails*. In 1954, a small group gathered on the streets of an Illinois neighborhood on Christmas Eve, ready to depart Earth. Space beings were supposed to appear on December 17 at 4:00 p.m. but were a no-show. This was an apocalyptic religious cult that believed an alien spaceship was about to land and rescue them from the coming destruction of Earth. They had given up all their personal belongings and assembled at a predetermined time and place, only to be disappointed that the ship never appeared and that Earth was not destroyed.

This was the fourth time they had been disappointed. But the real story here is how they handled the disconnect between their beliefs and reality. The resolution of this cognitive conflict was right out of a *Twilight Zone* episode. It turned out that Earth had been given a second chance, and the sect rededicated itself to social and environmental change to help heal the planet. Not ironically, their membership increased. In this instance, their dissonance was resolved by altering their beliefs, which led to a change of behavior.

Research into cognitive dissonance broadly supports a key premise of this book. Reducing predictive error is one of the brain's prime directives. The need for consciousness to anticipate and predict the future is an adaptive strategy. This research demonstrates that the brain is literally an "inference machine," actively engaged in efforts to predict and explain its sensory world by reducing predictive error. The brain has learned to ignore contradictory data as a means of preventing the overprediction of nongeneralized conditions (that is, let's not get crazy over every little inconsistency or contradiction). It is continually screening out background noise to better identify relevant signals. This, of course, opens the door to discussing what is relevant and what is not relevant in our social world and how the brain plays a significant role in identifying and enabling inconsistencies in our beliefs and behaviors.

One unique area of cognitive bias is termed *associative thinking*. Often characterized as prelogical thought, it broadly encompasses the irrational belief that one's thoughts or behavior can influence events that are not causally related. This is frequently termed *magical thinking*. It is also common in religious rituals. For example, believing prayers affect outcomes or sacrificing a virgin will bring a bountiful harvest, or positive thoughts about money will bring wealth. The converse of magical thinking is denial. If one doesn't acknowledge the existence of something, it doesn't exist. Examples of this abound—Republican senators' denial of climate change, that guns are not a cause of violence, and that they never vote the interests of dark money. There is also a subtle variant of this, and that is the confusion of *correlation causality*. Simply because two events occur at similar times or places, they must be related. The notion that vaccines cause autism or health-related problems is so widespread that polio has reemerged in the US.

More deeply concerning is our need to infer an underlying meaning to the perception of causality. This is the genesis of conspiratorial thinking. Because we cognitively reside in a highly deterministic reality, the temptation is to see cause and effect everywhere when it is not. The reality is our ability to reduce predictive error, while residing in complex social networks, has gone haywire. It no longer functions as effectively as it did 1.5 million years ago. And any internet search for conspiracy theories clearly demonstrates this. The point of all this is the human mind is a prediction machine, one that is as likely to be wrong as it is right when the parameters become more abstract. Because our social world has grown exponentially complex, we have evolved neither emotionally nor cognitively at the same rate. As a result, many of us are becoming increasingly irrational, and there is no doubt that internet has become an accelerant for our dysfunction.

Misinformation Contagion

The American Journal of Tropical Medicine and Hygiene (August 20, 2020), in an article titled "Covid-19 Related Infodemic and Its Impact on Public Health," identified 2,311 reports of rumors, stigma, and conspiracy theories in twenty-five languages from eighty-seven countries. Claims were related to illness transmission and mortality (24 percent), control measures (19 percent), causes of disease including origins (15 percent), violence (1 percent) and misc. (20 percent). The same day, Facebook reported that between April and June 2020, it had removed seven million posts pushing COVID-19 misinformation and put warning notes on ninety-eight million COVID-19 misinformation posts.

The conflict between faith and reality is one of our longest ongoing and contentious arenas of cognitive dissonance. For example, today, there is a large group of individuals who believe God created the world in seven days around seven thousand years ago, and that humans and dinosaurs interacted with one another (and there is a theme park to prove it). However, these same individuals are entirely comfortable flying across the country on a 747 commercial jet airliner and using their laptops and smartphones to schedule meetings and watch movies, thanks to the satellites orbiting earth.

These faithful do not appear the least bit uncomfortable or appear to experience any cognitive dissonance over this experience. None! The physics of gravity and theories of electromagnetics and aerodynamics all work just fine for them. But this same science completely refutes every aspect of their faith. And how does that work for them when confronted by the dissonance of faith versus science? It is important we understand how this is resolved to better understand the human condition. It does not appear they have changed either their behaviors or beliefs in this matter but utilize the mind-trick gambits of rationalization and denial of any inconsistencies, essentially doubling down on their trust that God will explain it to them at a later date. It's not unlike a deathbed confession where everything is forgiven, or in this case, all contradictions will be resolved.

There is one other matter that needs to be addressed, and that is the conservative Christian threat of a coming civil war. While the origin of this narrative resides in the nature of faith, it has been bubbling on the surface since the 1960s. It appears to derive from the fact that the world does not conform to everything evangelical ministers preach (in the same way the alien spaceship never arrived for those waiting to depart Earth). It is their oppression narrative. And for the absolute-minded, it is imperative that they have one. Apparently, being a victim keeps them closer to their faith, or what might be termed the *narcissism of small differences.* For example, baking a wedding cake for a gay couple is asking some to openly defy their deepest beliefs. And the great amplifier of these small differences today is the internet, where everyone gets siloed into the status of victim. And if it can't be significant, trivial will work just fine.

Eternal human discontent is now a public relations campaign to gain status as a victim. It is all of us now, whether we want to participate or not. The human requirement for *fairness* features both a genetic and social setpoint. Now that everything inside us is loose in virtual space, it renders all of us victims of someone or something, but mostly of life. We appear to have lost the signal in all the background noise being generated by everyone's discontent. The result is that serious problems are now competing with the trivial ones for our attention. And beyond that, the trivial has been elevated to significance and is drowning all of us in a sea of discontent with the world around us.

Six hundred years ago, you would have been killed for not properly reconciling the dissonance you experienced between your faith and science. I guess that's progress. The primary ways we resolve our scaled-up dissonance, besides our individual experiences of stress, depression, and anxiety, is to find fault and blame others. Projection is a time-honored strategy for raiding and killing people from time immemorial. One possible answer to the sense of threat conservative Christians are experiencing is the profound rejection of their faith by Americans over the past decade. In surveys taken over the past forty years, Americans have moved further from faith in the past ten years than any other nation in the world (R. Inglehart 2020).

Cognitive dissonance is a universally pervasive human condition that is never resolved. All of us struggle with it daily. It has haunted humans emotionally and cognitively for thousands of years. And while faith has imperfectly helped many resolve the many inconsistencies inherent in their mental lives, it has become increasingly less reliable and effective. That's why it has been doubling down for the past one thousand years in confrontation with the rational, secular, humanistic world. Its fantasies were never perfect, but they are even less so today. Daily, this raises the stakes for the absolute-minded and pushes them toward confronting their fantasies in a world increasingly reliant on rationalism to function, explain, and understand itself. Should they be praying or trust the science behind a COVID-19 vaccination? This is a chronic state of dis-ease now being resolved in confrontation and violence.

Because and Effect

Let's briefly visit *cause and effect* thinking. Have you come to believe that the universe is a conspiracy organized against you? I mean, you will die in the end, and before that, you are likely to suffer miserably for a very long time, as will everyone you ever loved or cared about. Does it seem like life is an eternal pissing contest often rigged against you? Why does it seem as if nothing good is ever guaranteed whatsoever? Why can't physicists locate exactly where equality and fairness are in the cosmos? There is never a level playing field, with each of us getting the same advantages and disadvantages. Fate or destiny, luck or serendipity or whatever are always randomly intervening for good or bad. The undeserving often get rewarded, and the deserving often get screwed way too often for this to make any sense. At times, our fates appear to be nothing more than a roll of the dice and, for some, a casual coin flip.

And into all this chaos, we add our individual choices and decisions, and it's not even clear we really are making them. Instead, we keep repeating the same stupid stuff, defaulting to the same assumptions, and acting out the same dysfunctional behaviors as if mindlessly scripted. Really, a lot of it feels like a ritual or habitual carryover from earlier life experiences. In this world, really, what is a decision? Yes, we always get blamed in the end, but how did we get here, and what choices did we really have along the way? Maybe, it turns out, you only had terrible choices to begin with. You didn't get to choose your parents or early life experiences. How do we explain all of this? How do we make sense of this going forward? In the face of this reality, how do you conduct yourself in life, and does it matter? I mean, most of us know how this game ends, and it's not with grace and dignity. You just hope the Buddhists don't have it right, that we keep playing the simulation over and over, in all its many forms, until we get it right.

What Choices Do We Have?

The choices we make all play out confusingly in the criminal justice system. Defendants are accused and convicted based on being held responsible for their actions (with some mitigating considerations). But at the back end, they are harshly punished when it comes to sentencing because there is no belief they can change moving forward. At the front end, they made a choice, but at the back end, they are governed by their past behavior. It appears to be contradictory. If the past is so conclusive, what choice did they have in committing a crime?

At the core of human cognition lies an uncanny ability to connect dots, an unending cause-and-effect process geared to predict the future, and always with the goal of mitigating the randomness and chaos that defines our universe. This process can also become grossly distorted by a lifetime of negative experiences, fears, and anxieties that are projected onto nearly any random event, turning it into a conspiracy. That's what we do. Statistically, cancer clusters are a reality, but searching for an explanation can lead suffering families to seek out someone or something to blame. Everyone wants to understand their pain and grief. As a result, trying to anticipate and prevent a conspiracy of outcomes is a major human preoccupation. And one significant reason for this is humans frequently conspire, if only out of indifference, to screw over others at every level of their social interface.

Almost any two events occurring at the same time and place become predictive in the human mind. That's why casinos light up with a winner. We get that walking into freeway traffic has a predictable outcome, but not so much that mysterious lights in the sky do not portent an alien abduction. But mostly because the future is unpredictable. There is an overwhelming number of random and chance events, as if the earth is being bombarded by subatomic particles of random uncertainty from space. (Why aren't the physicists ever honest about this?)

On the African Savannah, 1.5 million years ago, a simple model of cause-and-effect likely ensured survivability. But today, we live in a world where simple associational assumptions overwhelm all rational thinking (yes, continue to tell your kids not to put their fingers in electrical outlets). We now reside in an environment where we can discern and connect tens of thousands of events daily that have no relationship. Still, we are unable to turn off our reductionistic model.

We appear to lack the cognitive controls for the complex world we have created (maybe Siri is being sarcastic, and your auto mechanic is not overcharging you for unnecessary repairs).

Believing Our Fears

On December 4, 2016, Edgar Welch, armed with a semiautomatic rifle, revolver, and a shotgun, drove from his home in Florida to a pizza parlor in Northwest Washington, DC, convinced that an online QAnon conspiracy theory called Pizzagate was real. He was a father, active church member, and volunteer firefighter who had come to believe that Hillary Clinton was involved in ritualistic child abuse as part of a "corrupt system that kidnaps, tortures and rapes babies and children." Welch received a four-year prison sentence, eventually acknowledging the conspiracy was false. Pizzagate continued to gain online attention by conservative talk shows and cable news channels and on 4chan and Reddit (LaFrance, *The Atlantic*, 6/20).

Update: The *NY Times* reported (Kang and Frenkel) that Pizzagate had reanimated. While on camera, Justin Bieber adjusted the front of his black beanie. This led to an online claim that he was signaling he had been a victim of child trafficking. Activity on social media platforms reached record levels—eight hundred thousand comments on Facebook and six hundred thousand on Instagram. This then morphed into online memes about "powerful elites." TikTok posts with the Pizzagate hashtag zoomed to eighty-two million. The pizzeria owner began receiving another round of death threats. *Out of the Shadows*, a documentary promoting the conspiracy, hit fifteen million views before Facebook shut it down. Later, TikTok took down the Pizzagate hashtag.

This is a frightening demonstration of the internet's power to amplify falsehoods and adjacent fear into mindless conspiratorial memes with real world consequences. But also, our ability to believe them and the underlying mass hysteria generated by unconscious anxieties. This, of course, was all a prelude to the Capitol attack on January 6.

The beauty of a conspiracy is how it nicely ties together all the loose ends and provides an explanation for a tragedy or one feared about to take place. It is also a primary source of our craziness and central to all of us seeing the world in broadly distorted terms. And sometimes we are right. But how do we address what is true, what is false, and what we don't know? More often than not, with lazy thinking, simplistic thinking, magical thinking, cognitive bias, or paranoid ideation. Simplistic cause-and-effect reasoning easily satisfies the mind's need to know, often as the result of our projected fears and anxieties. (Someone defiantly refusing COVID-19 vaccinations but willingly ingesting a bovine parasite medication to stave off the coronavirus because it worked for a neighbor's pet who had worms.) And the arc of human history has been bizarrely destructive because of this cognitive bias. The truth is, we have always been crazy in these terms, which is why it has taken us so long to get here. And if we can't figure this out soon, we may not be here much longer.

Power Dynamic and Cognition

What are the constructs of our modern world, given it is exponentially more complex than at any time in human history? Are the primary constructs more people, more structures, and more things, increased size and complexity, or is it something entirely different? What is holding our world together, and how does it work?

According to Einstein's theory of general relativity, massive objects warp the space-time around them in what we experience as gravity. So when a ball is thrown into the air, it falls back to the ground because Earth distorts the space-time around it. The path of the ball and the ground intersect. Locally, space-time is curved around every object with mass. Mass also has an effect on the overall geometry of the universe. The density of matter and energy in the universe determines whether the universe is open, closed, or flat.

The question arises, what forces are acting upon our dynamical social networks (DSN)? And can the case be made that the effects of "power," in all its many forms, acts to warp the fabric of complex social networks into either centralized or decentralized states, in the same way gravity distorts space-time? While this process assures cultural continuity by suppressing disruption (in the way gravity keeps us from spinning off into space), it does so by inhibiting change. Throw a ball up and it always comes back down. Same with power. It flows from the top down and is a primary attractor for the social organizations of primates. This is as true today as it was 4 million years ago.

Deep inside our human ability to connect dots lies our relationship to "power" and the many forms in which it comes to us. The case could be made that our relationship to authority and its antecedent, power, is the main construct of our distorted human world. As proposed here, power is the social force that inculcates us and, if necessary, imposes conformity to achieve social order, beginning with our parents and residing, today, in absolute terms, with the authority of the state.

Achieving a high level of social conformity in large and complex social networks is fundamental to their efficiency and successful functioning. The requirement for harmony and discord management is central to both our social and economic survival. In our recent past, we often attributed power (and authority) to external forms. We projected it onto animistic spirits and totems or gods. And as a result, our fate could reside in sacrifices, rituals, or religious beliefs and rulers who claimed to be the descendent of gods, anything to make the world more orderly and safer, to placate it and to render it predictable. They sacrificed more animal entrails, more virgins, more youth. Today, most of us sacrifice through military service and taxes, and most importantly, a belief in our political organization (patriotism). The state has become our modern spiritual imperative for comprehending and placating the future.

Our very first contact with power is with our parents and the beginnings of our socialization. Was it arbitrary, mean, cruel, vindictive, and unpredictable? Or was it calm, nurturing, and reasoned? Was it emotionally present and available? Could you safely attach to it and feel secure, or did it abandon and abuse you? The key here is, could it be trusted? When the trust process is disrupted, then trust in authority and how it is exercised becomes central to our relationship with the world. Many become passive in the face of it, some passive-aggressive, others assertive, and many challenging, while still others angry and enraged. And then there are the belligerent, always challenging all forms of authority as untrustworthy and a threat.

Connecting the dots in the face of our initial contact with authority will tell us a lot about how we view the world. It seems throughout history the gods were often angry and vindictive. But when we carefully examine how most people lived and died, this makes a great deal of sense. Life was more violent and unpredictable, and I suspect notions of parenting were not very abstract but more practical and geared toward survival. Today, at one end of the continuum resides physical abuse and emotional abandonment. At the other end of our contemporary parental conundrum is growing up feeling overcontrolled, unfairly criticized, and emotionally manipulated. In other words, you want love, but at what cost? There is no better example of this distortion than the modern dictator, but also all the minor tyrants we encounter in our daily lives as they seek to usurp all the authority and assume the role of gods. Fortunately, angry crowds eventually kill them for their grandiose delusions. But then the crowd may be equally delusional as well.

Where do we begin to intervene in our dot-connecting craziness? How can there be so much randomness in a world comprised of patterns? And how do we coherently identify connected events? But most disconcertingly, connecting dots is pervasive and central to all our private and public discourse. It props up our fears, prejudice, and biases. It empowers us, unites us, and organizes us against each other. It holds us together in the face of doubt and the chaos all around us. However, what is real and what is not real is not easily distinguishable. Nazism was an actual threat, and many didn't see it coming or didn't want to see it coming, no matter how premised it was on paranoid and grandiose fantasies. Climate change is real, and many don't want to see it coming as well, believing it is a scientific conspiracy to take our cars away. We engage in rationalization, denial, and projection. How are we being manipulated and by whom appears to be fundamental to our conspiratorial mindset, and that is determined by our personal relationship to authority. It might be added that it is nearly impossible to modify this trust relationship once it is imprinted early in life. Yeah, we are all in trouble, as this reality is "always" being politically manipulated to considerable effect.

Subreddit Hysteria

Adrienne LaFrance (*The Atlantic*, June 20) offers this insightful take on QAnon:

> The power of the internet was understood early on, but the full nature of that power—its ability to shatter any semblance of shared reality, undermining civil society and democratic governance in the process—was not.
>
> QAnon is emblematic of modern America's susceptibility to conspiracy theories united in mass rejection of reason (and) objectivity.

I would add that the dot-connecting paranoia of this movement should give us all pause as the internet fuels subreddit hysteria. "Q" is an anonymous individual (or individuals) who cryptically message followers about deep state cabals wrapped in evangelistic prophecy. (Dot, dot, dot. Call the California Psychic hotline for more details, $5 per minute.)

In 2020, the Department of Homeland Security commissioned research on the incel culture. Incel is shorthand for "involuntary celibate," an online community of heterosexual men who believe that women deny them sex because they are physically unattractive. What began as an online support group for men struggling to establish relationships with women appears to have morphed to a smaller substrate that has become defined as a hate group. Men turned their frustration and anger into calls for violence against women with expressions of "male supremacy" and even of "violent subjugation of women." While no hard numbers are available, there are documented instances of women being assaulted and killed by individuals expressing incel identification.

The primal threat we face, besides direct threats to our safety, is a status quo in flux. The threat we don't want to see coming, that everything is continuously changing the future and everything we are desperately holding onto. This is the ontological source of our belief in conspiracies or what we broadly think of as conservatism and populism. The rise of women morphed into a conspiracy, for those who identify as incels, now feeling increasingly powerless and needing to blame someone to help resolve dissonance and give explanation and meaning to their anger and frustration. This is also the chronic state of the absolute-minded in the modern world.

Given our propensity to distort reality, how difficult do you think it would be to influence how people think, feel, and believe? History tells us it doesn't take much. Identify their fears and fabricate a conspiracy that ties it to their prejudices and exploit them. They will follow. But when one begins to examine all the potential reasons for an eventual technology intervention, clearly the most logical one (a shout-out to Mr. Spock) is to design an algorithm to straighten out our cognitive biases. I mean, who could care what most people are thinking? Our thinking requires fixing! Mental health professionals have been mostly failing at this heroic endeavor for 150 years, finally giving up and drugging everyone to no one's satisfaction, except "Big Pharma."

The "Hammer"

A sitting US Congressman, Louis Gohmert of Texas, exhorted during a Facebook broadcast of the Global Prayer for US Election Integrity (2020) that a deep state supercomputer, the "Hammer," had switched votes nationwide from Trump to Biden. Okay, routine Republican conspiracy theory stuff. But nope, there's more! US Army Special Forces raided a Spanish server, Scytl, storing US voting data with proof that votes had been altered and that Trump had won California (really CA and not Georgia). At the time, the server was being housed in Germany and being protected by the CIA. A firefight ensued with multiple casualties on both sides that was covered up. But the Special Forces were able to pull off the heist and make off with the server (this distorted reality was reported on by Rachel Maddow on MSNBC, 2021). There are several alternative realities here. Representative Gohmert is delusional and mentally ill, or he is desperately attempting to manipulate the voting base of the Republican Party and doesn't give a damn about the consequences. Of course, both could also be true. For the absolute-minded, it doesn't matter. Reality is whatever they choose it to be. Why is that?

It appears that the primary evolutionary drive behind the development of consciousness 250,000 years ago was to increase our ability to anticipate the future by connecting dots (any dots, apparently). This did not appear to gain serious traction until forty to ninety thousand years ago with a creative explosion of toolmaking, weapon development, and cave drawings. Our big brain is a prediction machine designed to sort the signals and suppress the noise. Day and night, it is weaving together a narrative and continually sequencing moments into a smooth visual and seamless conscious "you" that is easy to identify, while continually searching for patterns and identifying cause and effect. But it's also capable of routinely deflecting data and rendering us vulnerable in a complex environment that is our modern world.

All the cognitive shortcuts outlined here have been amplified by the complexity of our social networks—our modern world. For example, doubling down on a false belief when experiencing cognitive dissonance or defaulting to simple cause-and-effect conclusions in the face of complexity. This is the current plight of the absolute-minded. As a result, paranoia and conspiracy are everywhere in the world, a cognitive bias that connects the most dots with the least amount of effort. And occasionally, getting it right, but not most of the time. And that is exactly what the Bush administration did when it came to Saddam Hussain supposedly having chemical and biological weapons of mass destruction (WMDs), leading to our invasion of Iraq in 2003.

Chapter 5

The Psychology of Conspiracism

Conspiracism: It has no demand for evidence, no dots revealed to form a pattern, no close examination. Dispensing with the burden of explanation, it imposes its own reality through repetition and bare assertion.

—Rosenblum and Muirhead (2019)

Understanding conspiracies as social contagion begins with our model of absolute-mindedness. Here resides the underlying psychological dynamics of mistrust, predisposing individuals toward belief in conspiracy theories. But to trigger a mass belief in a conspiracy, mistrust as an individual and as a social experience have to align. How these two trust factors conjoin is the key. It's also important to distinguish between someone experiencing delusional ideations and individuals with a shared belief in conspiracies. One is a mental health crisis, and the other is a potential political crisis. To better understand how conspiracies propagate and politically converge, we turn to computer science research in the area of network theory, which offers many fresh insights into the spread of misinformation, disinformation, propaganda, and conspiracies.

Delusional Distrust—Demons, Gods, and Ghosts

From the moment sapiens gained consciousness, *reality* was forever rendered indeterminate by a subjective filter that had never previously existed. To better understand this reality filter, it is important to explore a significant cognitive state we are prone to—the delusional state of mind. But also, a state of mind that our e-technology is continuously tapping into with significant consequences, as exampled by the claims of a COVID-19 hoax and fraudulent 2020 presidential election.

The *Diagnostic and Statistical Manual of Mental Disorders* (DSM-5) defines *delusions* as follows: *fixed beliefs that are not amenable to change in light of conflicting evidence.* Common delusions include:

persecutory—one is going to be harmed or harassed.
referential—certain gestures, comments, or environmental cues are directed at oneself.
grandiose—one is exceptional or special beyond common sense or logic, e.g., President Trump's belief that he is an emotionally stable genius.
erotomania—someone is in love with them.
jealousy—one's spouse or lover is unfaithful.
somatic—preoccupation with bodily functions, e.g., alien parasites are eating one's pubic hair.

The reality is, few of us have never been jealous, infatuated, self-inflated, suspicious, or obsessed with health, but we are not all delusional.

Here is the bottom line: Currently, the cause of delusions is unknown, and we are left with mostly unconvincing theories. And to clarify, there are no effective treatments. However, there are several clinical distinctions we should familiarize ourselves with. The DSM-5 makes a distinction between *bizarre* and *non-bizarre* delusions. For example, a bizarre delusion might be someone believing that aliens are talking to them in their dreams, so they have begun avoiding sleep. And a non-bizarre delusion is believing that space lasers started

California wildfires. Obviously, there's a fine line between bizarre and non-bizarre delusions.

A further distinction is made between *primary delusions* and *secondary delusions.* A primary delusion might be a belief that one was abducted by aliens. It occurs without internal logic and exists unto itself, really, without explanation or understanding. A secondary delusion might better be perceived in the realm of a dysfunctional coping strategy. Examples might include "hoarders" or "compulsive gamblers" who are semi-delusional when it comes to denying the dysfunction of their behavior (everyone else sees it, but they can't).

Secondary delusions might be termed "delusional light," veering closer to the notion of "firmly held beliefs." And it appears that we are well adapted to this cognitive mind trick. But herein resides a slippery slope. The DSM-5 opens the door to conjecture that many firmly held beliefs, to varying degrees, are potentially delusional, say, on par with the superstitious, supernatural, paranormal, and conspiratorial. But what about the "firmly held beliefs" of those who pray to God and the celebrities who seek assurance through their E-Meter and Q-Ratings? While others call the California Psychic Hotline. Day traders confidently boot their E*TRADE app every morning, and an unknown number check for QAnon updates. Clearly, we humans have been prone to wanting to believe. And all manner of acceptance is offered when there is a broad social consensus. But this process can become far less discriminating during stressful times. Say, for example, when the internet opens an aperture to an ever-widening distortion in our reality.

The question we are confronted with in times of crisis is this: Are some Americans generally more prone to viewing the world in conspiratorial terms or what might better be termed delusional (secondary type)? When one thinks about the definition of a delusion, the implications are breathtaking. One hundred and forty-seven Republican members of Congress voted to overturn the 2020 election of Joe Biden as the president because they believed that the election results were fraudulent and the election had been stolen. Later, many of them accused the FBI of planting evidence after executing an "illegal" search warrant on the ex-president's Mar-a-Lago estate.

The question has to be asked, Were they just being politically cynical, or were they actively delusional, all spouting delusional ideas as if they were affirmations?

For some time now, it appears that the edges of reality have begun to fray for many congressional Republicans. Let's consult the DSM-5 once again, which adds this remarkably ambivalent qualifier to the definition of a delusion:

> The distinction between a delusion and a strongly held idea is sometimes difficult to make and depends in part on the degree of conviction with which the belief is held despite clear or reasonable contradictory evidence regarding its veracity.

And just to be clear, experiencing and expressing a delusion is a primary symptom for a mental illness, while distorting the facts and confabulating an alternative reality appears to qualify as political discourse today.

Sen. Ron Johnson, R-Wis., testifying before the Select Subcommittee on the Weaponization of the Federal Government (2/9/23), stated that the "left has pretty well infiltrated the major institutions in this country, starting with our university system," and that "corrupt individuals" within federal agencies are acting as "vital partners of the left-wing political movement that includes most members of the mainstream media, big tech, social media giants, global institutions and foundations, Democrat Party operatives, and elected officials" (Fox News.com). This is the face of conspiracism today. No facts, no evidence, no rational case to be made. (The name of the committee says all we need to know. In the end, they will discover that they are really shapeshifting lizards and suppress the committee's findings, as well as their appetite for rodents.)

Conspiracies as Mass Social Contagion

Conspiracy theory: "A theory that explains an event or set of circumstances as the result of a secret plot by usually powerful conspirators" (Merriam-Webster).

All social organisms are prone to spontaneous patterns of movement. This can be seen in the geometry of hundreds of birds spontaneously taking flight or shapeshifting herring evading a pod of dolphins, and all with no discussion. But human patterns of social movement always involve a cognitive process, as seen in the strobing rainbow of car lights as people head home from work on a rainy Friday evening. When conspiracies are not the product of a single individual's mental illness but of individuals numbering in the thousands, tens of thousands, or even millions, they can appear to take a near spontaneous flight as a social contagion. For example, millions suddenly believing that a horse deworming medication can cure COVID-19.

Stated simply, conspiracy theories are a direct expression of an underlying human irrationality in the form of fearful and paranoid projections. From the very beginning, it appears the human mind has been adept at projecting outside forces shaping and controlling the world around us, whether that was our neolithic ancestors at Göbekli Tepe or the rise of monotheistic faiths. Conspiracism is an irrational belief that addresses the perceived threat of the unknown forces acting upon us and manipulating our world. By giving these fears form in the shape of a conspiracy, the hope exists to control these mysterious forces.

Trying to understand how a large number of people can simultaneously come to believe in nonsensical conspiratorial ideas and act upon them is challenging. And for them to fervently believe in a conspiracy and to become emotionally invested in this alternative reality, when it is obviously not true and defies all logic and rationality, requires that we enter murky academic waters.

Americans Believe*

81 percent	God
43 percent	Ghosts and demons
40 percent	UFOs
39 percent	Deep state conspiracy
30 percent	Astrology
25 percent	Covid pandemic planned
15 percent	Government controlled by Satan-worshipping pedophiles
11 percent	Bigfoot
11 percent	9/11 false-flag operation
7 percent	Moon landing faked
4 percent	Lizard people
2 percent	Earth is flat

(*Extrapolated from online surveys and should be treated with skepticism.)

To discuss how conspiracies spread across groups, we will have to conjoin multiple theories. Let's begin with a fact that just about everyone can agree on. We humans are genetically wired to be a social species, just as are all primates. It is who we are and what we do. Being deeply connected with one another is primary to our survival. The second most obvious fact is how our sociability is largely premised on communicating with one another. And herein lies the subjective reality of each individual trying to make sense of the world and coordinate with it as best they can. And looking back over human history, to say this process has been problematic would be a gross understatement. There have been a lot of misunderstandings and miscommunications.

Third, identity, individually, and collectively is the uniquely defining element of what it means to be human. Everything else that is distinctive about us derives from how we come to know and understand ourselves. For our purposes, individual identity has to align with our social identity for a healthy individual to arise and function successfully. When this does not take place and there is a misalignment on the individual level, we have lots of terms—insecure, feeling of inadequacy, low self-esteem, rebellious, and nonconforming behaviors. As this moves from misalignment to an aberrant alignment, we increasingly see personality disorders such as being antisocial or paranoia. Drug and alcohol abuse and homelessness are also evidenced, as are high rates of incarceration.

But what happens when the social side does not align with the individual person? We don't really have a vocabulary for this, even as we watch it play out in front of us. At the misaligned level, there might be layers of bias, prejudice, discrimination, denial of human rights, the routine imposition of authority by violence, and, at the extremely aberrant level, we are subject to acts of genocide and war, and almost always by way of an underlying conspiratorial narrative. (This is Putin explaining to the Russian people why they are at war with Ukraine.) Conspiracies arise when misaligned individual identities encounter a wider social misalignment. This is the discontent of the absolute-minded being signaled a conspiratorial reality by political leadership and thought influencers. For many, a conspiracy reconciles these misalignments.

One more element is required to stir conspiracism and it's mass contagion, and that is a high level of social discontent. Percolating social discontent is the dark lattice holding the conspiratorial reality together. These are moments in which political leaders continually repeat the most outrageous and dangerous lies over and over, sowing distrust in our social and political world. It is Florida governor Ron DeSantis undermining people's confidence in the treatment of COVID-19 and scapegoating Dr. Anthony Fauci. But it is also faith keepers preaching doubt and end of the world gospel, giving the distortion credibility and aligning the individual's experience of disbelief and mistrust with a conspiracy.

Media Actuating Mass Social Contagion

In the twenty-first century, we also have to come to grips with mass media and mass communications. It is key to how we scaled up our social organization and how we stay in the loop and get direction. And it is a recent phenomenon that seriously began ramping up about four hundred years ago with the printing press, the rise of mass education, and universal literacy. Then came the media (telegraph, radio, television, phone, computer, internet), none of which existed throughout most of human history. And simultaneously arose mass transportation, putting more of us in direct physical contact with one another and making tribal migration nearly impossible. Which means, for better or worse, we have lost a 300,000-year-old evolutionary adaptation and are now pretty much stuck with each other in tight quarters.

By the 1920s, the impact of the media on large numbers of people had begun to arouse academic interest. This peaked post-WWII with a recognition of how effectively Nazi propaganda had manipulated radio, print, and film media. Today, we would include televisions, computers, cell phones, and online media as well. All are fully capable of transmitting the mass dissemination of messages "widely, rapidly, and continuously to large and diverse audiences in an attempt to influence them in some way" (Hirst 2018). However, it is not necessarily factually or truthfully.

Understanding how strongly influenced we are by mass media is the first step in trying to make sense of mass social contagion. While mass media is not mind control yet, it powerfully influences how we individually and collectively feel, think, and behave. And it also turns out we enjoy engaging our electronic connection—watching TV, listening to the radio, surfing the internet, texting, emailing, and FaceTiming friends. All of us are now electronically wired. And in the same way a viral pandemic can emerge and spread rapidly across the globe, so now can conspiracies.

What began as a passive consumption of entertainment, commercial advertising, and political messaging and its cognitive, emotional, and behavioral correlates quickly morphed into something very different with the advent of the computer, cell phone, and the internet. What has changed is how interactive users have become with this interface, now free to select and choose what they consume, but also being blindly channeled into an echo chamber of related messaging and content.

Internet surfers are also free to add "comments," and beyond this, they have the ability to repackage and create new content and distribute it out into the metaverse (Instagram, YouTube, Facebook, Twitter). And the audience is now far-reaching, global, and includes 90 percent of everyone on earth. Today, political propaganda is better equipped to exploit mass communications and spread misinformation, as conservative media has grown extremely adaptive at aggressive agenda setting, selectively framing issues, and repeating them over and over, day and night. Beyond this, researchers are documenting the ability of the internet to amplify cognitive biases, spread disinformation, and polarize people. The internet has become the leading component in the rise of "conspiracism"—the embrace of a conspiratorial philosophy. Nothing better exemplifies this than the reach of QAnon across the US.

Social Media Distorting Reality

Amplifying cognitive biases. Social media platforms are designed to amplify preexisting cognitive biases. For example, we are more likely to attend to and share information about perceived risk. We tend to search for and remember those things that more closely fit with what we know and understand. When we encounter contradicting facts and information, we are more likely to double down on preexisting knowledge and beliefs, becoming even more committed to them. And algorithms are designed to exploit these cognitive vulnerabilities and to manipulate us.

Search engine bias. Search engines prioritize information that support our biases and direct us to sites that feed our prejudices and anxieties.

Narrow world effect. Search engines and social media platforms consistently delete content that is inconsistent with our data histories.

Information overload. Social media has saturated the online market with low-quality information, making it difficult to identify high-quality information.

Winner-takes-all effect. Algorithms suppress the quality of information by overfocusing on popularity (wisdom of the crowd effect), confusing popularity with quality in a winner-takes-all scenario.

Spreading disinformation. We are prone to sharing less factual and truthful information. The more extreme content, the more likely we are to share it.

Social contagion. When social media repeatedly exposes us to information or ideas from multiple sources, we become prone to adopting and resharing it.

Virality storms. We tend to pay more attention to information that goes viral. It becomes important by virtue of its ubiquity.

Echo chamber effect. Like-minded people tend to connect with one another. As a result, people are siloed into increasingly large and misinformed communities.

Clickbaiting. Negative content spreads faster than positive content. As a result, people are manipulated by negative narratives that trigger emotional responses, which they are then more likely to share.

Increased negativity. Overall, social media increases negativity by bolstering biases that became resistant to correction.

Extreme effect. Information in a social-diffusion chain is susceptible to distortion and overly influenced by the most extreme content. Efforts to balance the information only served to create even more negative views.

Social herding. The broad effect of online distortions has been to sort us into polarized camps, resulting in an extreme divergence among groups.

(Extrapolated, in part, from *The Attention Economy* by Menczer and Hills, *Scientific American* (12/20).

What Is Social Contagion?

Let's address the elephant wandering around the lab. For the past 125 years, academic researchers have been debating whether crowd behavior and, more generally, the spread of ideas within a community are a form of viral contagion (for example, fashion, popular memes, or conspiracy theories). For our purposes, the term *contagion,* as used here, is an analogy. Upon close examination, the idea of a social contagion does not meet the biological or epidemiological criteria for an actual viral contagion. For example, Mpox or Ebola. And more specifically, the spread of ideas among people do not infect us in the same way as a virus or function in the same epigenetic manner our genes express themselves. The notion of a social contagion is primarily a useful model for communicating its many parallels with a viral epidemic. Until we can better understand human social behavior, that is the best we can do.

Saying the phrase "social contagion theory" is the equivalent of tripping down a rabbit hole that even Lewis Carrol would flinch at going down. But let's take our chances. The first serious discussion of this topic was by Gustave Le Bon in his book *The Crowd,* published in 1895. A hundred years after the French Revolution, many were still horrified and puzzled by the impulse of the crowd to act violently and destructively. To describe this behavior, he adopted a viral contagion model to explain the psychological dynamics of a violent crowd. Broadly, these theories see individual thoughts, emotions, and behaviors becoming irrational and outside societal norms. Crowds are a collective impulse that are suggestible, emotional, and absent reasoned thinking. These are normal people now acting in an abnormal manner because of the "viral" influence of the crowd.

How and why violent riots happen has been the subject of considerable academic theorizing over the past 125 years, with an increased focus on individual interactions and predispositions as key dynamics in crowd behavior. Researchers are now examining how the crowd's emotional impact affects each individual; how similarly predisposed individuals react in unison, reinforcing one another's behavior; or how crowd leaders emerge and influence crowd behavior. Essentially, crowd behavior emerges from the unique dynamic of those composing the crowd. And to put a finer point on this, riots can occur in many social settings, e.g., sporting events, protests, or shopping on Black Friday.

Sociologist Herbert Blumer brings us closer to what we are trying to get at here. (Note: I had the honor of taking his graduate seminar on social interactionism.) Blumer takes a wider angle on the topic of social contagion, one that includes crowds, public opinion, propaganda, copycat behavior, consumer and investment trends, fads, and social movements. And this is important to define our problem. He denotes the concept of "mass" social contagion. Unlike crowd theory, he delineates mass as composed of anonymous individuals who do not directly interact with one another. Here, each person is individually motivated and responds independently. More importantly, after the fact, these individuals can then collectively converge and impact the world around them.

The January 6 Capitol attack is a textbook case for what Blumer was describing. It appeared to have largely begun as a mass media creation anonymously impacting many individuals then evolved into direct electronic messaging among influential individuals, concluding in direct physical assembly and violence. However, once the crowd had assembled, a new set of social dynamics were involved in motivating the crowd toward aggression and violence. There are numerous theories variously describing crowd dynamics as social contagion, group contagion, and behavioral contagion, each emphasizing a specific inter-crowd dynamic arousing it to action.

There is one last element to a theory of mass social contagion, and that is a theory of "what" is being transmitted and how. This is the field of memetics. It is the study of "memes" or what is thought of as a transmittable piece of cultural information, a term coined by ethnologist Richard Dawkins in his book *The Selfish Gene* (1976).

> In human society, almost any cultural entity can be seen as a meme: religions, language, fashions, songs, techniques, scientific theories and concepts, conventions, traditions, etc. The defin-

> ing characteristic of memes as informational patterns is they can be replicated in unlimited amounts by communication between individuals. (Heylishen 2001)

On the internet today, a meme is any popular image, video, or text that spreads rapidly by internet users, as in "going viral."

It is probably safe to say that memetics is a confused academic field of study, but one that still has something to tell us. Basically, it is the study of how social and cultural information and knowledge are passed along (Dennett 1993; Blackmore 1999; Auger 2002). Given that communication is fundamental to human cultural evolution, the meme has often been compared to the function of a gene in biological evolution. At other times, the analogy is to that of a virus that infects and spreads ideas and information. But because there is no physical evidence, memes exist in our minds, and there is only the display of expressed ideas and behavior that can be measured. The consensus is they don't exist except as social constructs helping to explain something we don't yet fully understand.

For our purposes, a conspiracy fits this meme theory as a discrete packet of information that is culturally passed along between individuals or through media. This is important because it has to exist and be transmitted beyond any one individual. When this experience is solely individual, we are typically looking at a serious mental health problem. When it is broader than one person, it is more likely a social-cultural pass-along. Watching the antivaxxer movement grow and evolve over the years fits this model of person-to-person communication or parent-to-parent with a vociferous multimedia and online presence to support it. To expand our thinking on this topic, we need to take a closer look at research in the computer sciences on the subject of how ideas are spread in social networks.

Information Diffusion in Social Networks

Prominent in the field of computer science is social network modeling, particularly of information transfer and how ideas spread throughout a particular subcommunity or network. This research looks across a large expanse of identified social networks to determine how misinformation, disinformation, propaganda, and conspiracy theories are spread. And more particularly, how the speed and ubiquity of the internet, through its search engines and algorithms (weblogs, social networks, online forums, and digital media), is capable of rapidly propagating conspiratorial ideation. And as the study of social networks has surged, researchers have begun to document the ability of the media to exponentially spread disinformation and misinformation.

Individual Factors Propagating Conspiracies

- Individuals in social networks tend to aggregate within homogeneous clusters.
- Conspiracy theories are typically propagated through a homogeneous population of susceptible individuals.
- Conspiracies that easily align with preexisting beliefs are more likely to be adopted.
- Once an individual establishes a false belief from misinformation, changing this belief is extremely difficult.
- Emotional attachment to a conspiracy acts as a cognitive override to logic and rationality, ignoring the extreme complexity and improbability of most conspiracy theories.
- Individuals who believe in one conspiracy theory are more likely to believe others.
- Once a belief is established, confirmation bias influences individuals to actively seek information that confirms their beliefs, but also to discount information that is inconsistent with their beliefs.

(Amblard and Deffuant 2004; Axelrod 1997; Chaudhari and Pawar 2021; Frankel 2016; Franks 2008; Kumar and Geethakumari 2014; Shermer 2010; Stano 2020)

Network Factors Propagating Conspiracies

- Information diffusion in social networks, because of misinformation or disinformation, are increasingly the result of an orchestrated effort.
- The density of a network determines the rate at which an idea is dispersed. The more dense and populated a network, the faster the potential adoption of a conspiracy theory.
- Information is believed to be true when there is a perceived social consensus.
- Idea diffusion, the process by which new ideas are communicated among members of a social system, is optimized by change agents and opinion leaders. These are widely connected individuals within a community who are able to consistently influence the attitudes and decisions of others.
- Familiarity with the sender of a message and the sender's perceived credibility and expertise increases the acceptance of a message.
- Individuals in the most powerful positions of authority are the most successful at influencing others to adapt new ideas or buy into a conspiracy theory.
- A key factor affecting the influence of change agents and opinion leaders within a social network are their shared social similarities with those in the network (this is our tribal identity at work).
- The degree to which individuals in a social network possess and share common attributes (homophily), the faster the rate of idea transmission and diffusion within a community. Factors such as race, ethnicity, faith, and shared cultural values and beliefs predominate in the propagation of a conspiracy theory.
- The interconnectedness of a community and the degree to which members of a social network routinely communicate with one another, particularly opinion leaders within the network, increases the rate of idea adoption.

- The "repetition" of an idea or a conspiracy by change agents and opinion leaders is key to its spread and early adoption.
- The more an idea (conspiracy) is shared by many individuals, the higher rate of transmission and adoption. Typically, because there is very little debate or counterfactual information, a conspiracy is more easily believed and propagated.

(Kauk et al. 2021; Lynch 1996; Sieck and Mueller 2009; Simpkins 2010; Stano 2020; van Prooijen and Douglas 2018)

The Psychological Evaluation of Mass Delusions

Hypothetically, if the court ordered me to submit a *not guilty by reason of insanity* (NGI) evaluation to explain why millions of individuals are experiencing a shared belief in conspiracies, here is what I would report to the court:

These individuals do not qualify for a mental health diagnosis because of their belief in a conspiracy. However, they are highly susceptible to disbelief and distorting reality to fit their fears and anxieties. They have become immune to facts and logic and are more likely to accept disinformation and deceptions that align with their distrust in times of uncertainty. Their misbeliefs are induced by the following key factors:

1. *Triggering conditions.* A high level of generalized social unrest is key to triggering a mass belief in conspiracies. The higher the level of unrest, the greater likelihood conspiracies will arise. Unrest comes in two forms:
    a. Primary is the perception of an attack on one's identity (the group one identifies with and their shared values and beliefs).
    b. Secondary are the emotional and cognitive states generated by feeling trapped in destabilizing personal circumstances. For example, unemployment or health concerns. When both factors align for a large

number of individuals, belief in conspiracies becomes hyperinflated.

2. *Conspiratorial efficacy.* Conspiracies simplify complexity by identifying the powerful and hidden forces manipulating the world.
    a. They act as viral memes that are highly communicable, tightly wound packets of misinformation that co-opt preexisting biases, fears, and anxieties.
    b. They identify the threatening "other" as the focus of one's fear and anxieties.

        Importantly, they distinguish the good "us" from the bad "them."
3. *Collective recognition.*
    a. For a conspiracy to arise, it has to be embraced by thought influencers and be able to reach a mass audience—television, radio, print, and online.
    b. The more frequently voices in the media espouse these ideas, the more likely conspiracies will gain traction.
    c. The single most galvanizing factor in a conspiracy gaining public credibility is its expression and support by political leaders.
    d. Conspiracies that undermine trust in authority and promote distrust in government are a powerful stimulus for inflating conspiratorial belief.
4. *Preexisting dynamics.*
    a. An early life disruption in attachment creates a trust double bind that splits the world into a duality—good and bad, right and wrong, safe and unsafe—which can never be acknowledged.
    b. This distrust is reinforced by parental emphasis on discipline and principle.
    c. The long-term effect is an easily aroused fight-flight response in an effort to identify the source of one's distrust and to give it a projected form or what we term a conspiracy theory.

5. *Online network propagation.*
    a. The spread of a conspiracy can now be conducted individually and anonymously with a significant social impact.
    b. The conspiracy-minded are able to self-select what they hear and see, creating an echo chamber of misinformation and disinformation.
    c. They are able to directly engage and interact with social media and create online memes of misinformation, validating and spreading conspiracy theories.
    d. Online conspiracy theories are able to propagate in a continuous feedback loop of personal associations, social groups, and media interaction that facilitates a confirmation bias.

All the factors discussed here must be understood in their collective context. The key to unlocking the conspiracy conundrum is understanding how all these variables have to align for a large number of normal people to believe in reality-bending conspiracies—claiming lizard people are secretly running a deep state conspiracy, the government introduced microcomputer chips into COVID-19 vaccines, a Jewish space laser started wildfires in California. A conspiracy requires a set of unique triggering events out in the actual world that align with the emotional and cognitive presets of the absolute-minded, forging an often unshakable belief in a conspiracy.

Today, stoking the mass contagion of conspiratorial fear has become political theater given the 24-7 availability of media to spread discontent in the context of a conspiracy, particularly when there is a financial and political agenda. In its most cynical form, thought leaders and influencers stir chaos with the promise of ending it. The modern conspiracy takes calculation, financial resources, the support of many allied people and groups, a means to get the conspiracy out into the world (strong voices and media savvy), the willingness to withstand social and factual blowback, and the insight to strike just the right cord in the public's mind at the right time. Then, for the absolute-minded, all the underlying fear, mistrust, and discontent respond as mass social contagion.

Bad Stuff Fuels Conspiracism

> Half of the American public consistently endorses at least one conspiracy theory.
>
> —Oliver and Wood, *American Journal of Political Science*, 2014

The origins of conspiratorial thinking reside in unresolved irrational fears grounded in a self-protective fight-flight response to the unknown and unseen. An inability to resolve this chronic tension results in the construction of rigid narratives (conspiracies) that give explanation and understanding to one's fears. And by projecting these fears outward, they become identifiable with the fantasy that they are resolvable. This process begins early in life. It's a child wanting to take a security doll or blanket on a car trip or at bedtime, fearing that something is lurking in the closet or under the bed and wanting a light left on and the door ajar after a search of the room. Magically, these fears are resolved. A redefining narration externalizing fear will temporarily resolve inner conflict. Individuals prone to conspiratorial belief similarly externalize their unconscious fears, particularly if there's a significant history of trust violations.

The unresolved anticipation of something catastrophic underlies all fears, even those unlikely to happen and not really catastrophic. This process reflects how our brains are hardwired and how we have been programmed by our experiences. As adults, we tell ourselves paranoid conspiracies to provide explanation to the unseen and threatening forces out in the world. What makes this conspiratorial resolution exceptionally powerful is many people may agree with us, and because real threats exist, it makes distinguishing the real from the imagined impossible for many and difficult for all of us. (There is little doubt that the fears and anxieties let loose by COVID-19 have widened the margins of distrust in government and have given rise to innumerable conspiracies.)

Resolving our underlying fears is the most basic function of conspiratorial ideation, and there are no limits to how insidious, destructive, malleable, and how far-reaching this process can be. This has been true throughout human history and will be true for the foreseeable future. Fear underlies every aspect of human existence. And the great irony here is our rational responding to our fears has made our networked world infinitely safer and more manageable on a day-to-day basis than ever before.

Going to the Cleaners

In a recent TikTok video (2021), an osteopathic doctor, "practicing the truth in Jesus through medicine," is offering "detox baths" for people who regret getting COVID-19 vaccinations. A cup of borax in your bath will provide a "radiation detox" and remove nanoparticles placed there by a "liquified computer system" inside COVID-19 vaccines, which the government is using to track people and make them infertile (NBC News/Yahoo.com).

Any rational appraisal of the human experience would conclude it's highly irrational and not safe. And herein lies the evolutionary origins of conspiracies, anticipating worst-case scenarios. Besides, anticipating a dangerous world has been successfully deployed by primates for millions of years. But today, it is daunting to contemplate "entropy," a universal principle of physics in which stars compress into blackholes, collapsing all light and life before invisibly dissipating into energy after billions of years. (The Earth will be the size of a pebble!) This is the fate of the universe. Everything collapses and dies, and we get to watch it come true during our lifetimes. How random, stupid, and vicious it can be—cancers metastasizing, aortas blowing out, an enlarged prostate painfully squeezing urination, and billions of random, violent accidents raining down on life out of nowhere. And it is disconcerting how all life is either parasitic or eating one another to stay alive. And how we, humans, kill to live, slaughtering animals and annihilating pesky creatures in the process, including the genocide of people we don't like. All the while nature is pretty much guaranteeing you and your loved ones will experience a truly unpleasant death after a life filled with pain and loss, even if you are not killed by a natural disaster, disease, genetic mutation, crazed violent stranger, or a nice person text messaging while driving.

Looking across human history, you may note how most people had been reduced to slave labor or died in meaningless conflicts or by the predatory indifference of someone who doesn't give a shit. Darwinian theory is always chiming in about evolution and survival of the fittest—and some economist telling us it applies to us finding a job, competing for a mate, or having the opportunity to procreate and assure genetic survivability—as millions of sperm with a brief half-life are desperately racing to penetrate an ovum (hopefully in a conscious and consensual act). And every level of society is a survival competition, all of us fighting for basic resources to sustain ourselves and our families.

It's not just taxes but capitalist markets suppressing salaries and maximizing profits by exploiting every resource, including all of us and everything on earth for profit, by monopolizing markets and centralizing command and control in the hands of a few wealthy and powerful individuals. Then there is the disturbing history of centralized authority throughout history, one of the most violent and exploitative forces in all of human existence. All the dictators, emperors, monarchs, theocracies, kleptocracies, autocracies, plutocracies, and their inexorable march to diminish everyone for their benefit. And, of course, there are all the people in opposition trying to co-op this reality and supplant it with their own ambitious designs and murderous intentions. Not to mention the bullies that hounded you in high school.

And war stands out as the most astoundingly destructive behavior ever conceived, with no end in sight, with tens of millions of land mines, machine guns, and bombs spewing destructive hell on people. And apparently, we consider it necessary and normal. And nowhere has this conspiratorial effort been more contaminated than by faith—for thousands of years exploiting people's ability to trust and believe in their everlasting illumination and transformation, and, if necessary, to ostracize or kill everyone who doesn't.

Why, yes, we humans might be prone to confabulating conspiracies from time to time when we live in a world that requires us to be constantly vigilant, scanning the horizons, awake late at night, wondering what the neighbor is up to, what your management team is planning, why your husband/wife is not home, and watching the late-night news pondering all the political machinations and the unending lies and corruption that seeks to manipulate you and the community you live in. There you are tossing and turning in bed with a suspicion that you are getting screwed and that someone wants to kill you. (Not directly, of course. It's just that *they* are unconcerned about whether you live or die.) They really have no idea who you are but are mature enough to realize that "shit happens," and so should you.

However, there is one final kicker to the human adherence to delusional ideation. Once we are fixated on a false belief, it is pretty much unshakeable. A recent study (Mahony et al. 2023) "conducted a systematic review to identify and assess interventions that have sought to counter conspiracy beliefs." (Hint: There is no help coming when it comes to remediating conspiratorial beliefs.) Examining twenty-five studies, utilizing multiple strategies designed to counter conspiratorial ideation (counterfactual argument, informational inoculation, priming intervention, narrative persuasion, and fostering effortful thought), the researchers found that the majority of studies demonstrated no effect, while several had a "backfiring" effect of increasing conspiratorial ideation. They concluded, "Most existing conspiracy interventions are ineffective in terms of changing conspiracy beliefs." However, they would be the first to acknowledge one significant limitation in these studies—no adverse interventions or positive rewards were utilized. But real-world observations suggest neither are particularly effective.

A small subset of interventional strategies demonstrated a limited positive effect but were too impractical to scale up. The most beneficial effect was to take a three-month college "module" to teach students how to differentiate between scientific practices and pseudoscience. (Why are they studying college students to find out about the real world? I guess they couldn't afford laboratory rats.) It was noted that "after taking the module, students endorsed far fewer conspiracy theories." Unfortunately, this finding vaguely suggests that some students continued to endorse bizarre ideas at some unspecified level. And no one knows what the effect was a year or five years later. There are three key takeaways here: (1) debating a conspiracist is likely to do more harm than good; (2) our cognitive biases, hundreds of thousands of years in the making, can be incredibly resilient and destructive; and (3) we reside in an environment that is ripe for spreading conspiracy theories. It is this last fact that offers our only means of direct intervention. Unless, of course, we chose to dampen down the root causes of our underlying anxieties and distrust, which are primarily political and economic in nature.

American Conspiracism

There is no brief history of American conspiracies. Outlined below are highlights of unending craziness. And any examination of the American proclivity for conspiracies can only reach one obvious conclusion. They are primarily the product of the absolute-minded, but not exclusively, cast as religious, social, economic, and political fears and anxieties.

1692—Salem witch trials. Fourteen women and five men were hung to death by the Puritans, believing these individuals were possessed by the devil and practicing witchcraft. More than two hundred people were accused before the trials were shut down by the governor of Massachusetts after his wife was accused of being a witch.

1855—Anti-Catholicism. European monarchs and the pope were plotting the destruction of the United States. Catholicism was perceived as a threat to the American way of life. Samuel Morse, the inventor of the telegraph, warned that the Austrian emperor was orchestrating a conspiracy to undermine the US by flooding the country with Catholics. This was later fueled by Ku Klux Klan propaganda. As late as 1960, there was considerable debate about whether John Kennedy, a Catholic, was qualified to be president.

1820s—Anti-Illuminati. This was an ultraconservative obsession with conspiracy. At its core was a fear by conservative Christian leaders that Enlightenment values would stamp out religion in America. Illuminism was portrayed as an anti-Christian movement. That fear is alive and well today as Illuminati are portrayed as the elites running the world from a military complex in North Dakota, and later, an underground structure at the Denver airport.

1830s—Anti-Masonry. A conservative fear that there was a conspiracy by the elites to deprive the common man and rural Americans of their rights and economic opportunity. In 1931, the Anti-Masonic Party held its first national political convention.

1865–66—Gold cabal. European and American gold traders were attempting to prosper by undermining the financial security of the United States.

1896—Free silver populists. This movement supposedly revealed a gold standard conspiracy by British bankers (code for Jews) as the cause of economic depression, falling values, and the financial plight of rural farmers.

1903—Anti-Semitism. The Protocols of the Elders of Zion, first published in Russia, outlined a conspiracy by Jews to destroy the Christian world and seek world domination. Later, the Rothchild banking family was subject to a similar conspiratorial conjecture of a worldwide Jewish conspiracy. More recently are the Holocaust deniers.

1939–1970s—Anti-Communism. This took two early forms. Roosevelt's New Deal was believed to be a conspiracy to undermine capitalism and bring the economy under the control of a socialist or communist government. In 1951, the Communist conspiracy continued to morph into McCarthyism. Senator McCarthy, during senate hearings, claimed that Communists had infiltrated the federal government at the highest levels. Still later, the John Birch Society and Senator Barry Goldwater portrayed Communism as the force behind Lyndon Johnson's "Great Society" and later, the Equal Rights Amendment, chlorination of public drinking water, and environmental protection laws. The irony is that today, the Republican Party appears to have no concerns about Russia actually hacking our elections if it helped Trump get elected.

1970s—New World Order. Beginning with the John Birch Society and the rise of Barry Goldwater and the Young Republicans, the Republican Party began running against "big government." And in particular, international organizations. This was characterized as a progressive agenda by international global elites and secret societies to suppress conservative political and religious values. Black Ops helicopters and Chevy Suburbans with tinted windows were part of a New World Order (Agenda 21), as were the Federal Reserve, Trilateral Commission, the Council on Foreign Relations, WHO, NAFTA, Davos, World Bank, and United Nations.

1990s—Deep state conspiracy. The CIA was running a drug operation to fund the overthrow of Iran. AIDS was either God's punishment of gay people or government-authorized genocide. This culminated with Trump, Russ Limbaugh, Fox News, and Breitbart News claiming a deep state conspiracy of liberal elites and a stolen election conspiracy denying Trump a second term. In Texas, the governor had come to believe the federal government had been planning a black ops takeover of the state during a FEMA exercise. Violent national tragedies became construed as government false-flag operations—Oklahoma City bombing, 9/11, Sandy Hook mass killing of students, and finally, the January 6 riot at the Capitol Building.

2022—Conspiracy free-for-all. Lizard people are running the government. Jet "chemtrails" are laced with pathogen. Jewish lasers started California wildfires. Alien abductions, shape-shifting reptiles, and "men in black" silencing witnesses. Bar codes are a satanic conspiracy. QAnon claims that Democratic Party leaders are leading a satanic child-abusing, cannibalistic cabal, but also, the "reliable truths" that the Earth is flat, the moon landing was a hoax, and Area 51 in Roswell, New Mexico, is a secret military base experimenting on humans with alien technology. Then there are the germ theory denialists who refuse vaccinations as part of a medical conspiracy because viruses and bacteria don't exist. The National Butterfly Center, near the Mexican border, closed briefly because of online claims that it was involved in human trafficking.

Chapter 6

The Political Dynamics of Conspiracism

I am an American. Fuck America! It's my right!

The Politics of Absolutism

It is time to put all our authors and theories together to better understand absolutism. In complex social networks, absolutism is primarily hyper-conformity to sets of ideas, beliefs, and values, particularly in times of rapid change and turmoil. But for many, it's business as usual, no matter what the circumstance, resolving all manner of cognitive and emotional conflict. In a perfectly rational world, few Americans would vote Republican today, yet 48 percent of our voting citizens make this their ballot choice. So what's up? Sorting through our group of authors and what we can scrape together from bio-evolutionary psychology. At the core of our adaptation to complex social networks resides two key factors: *conformity* as the adaptive base strategy and an *absolutist mindset* to explain the contingent complexities of life. And more often than not, someone or something is to blame. First and foremost, this process suppresses cognitive dissonance and all the attendant fears, anxieties, and troubling inconsistency people experience. In the US, the Republican Party is most closely identified with absolutist thinking, filled with conspiratorial memes that shelter true believers and all their alternatives to the future.

Identity Mistrust

Underlying the development of an individual's identity is the child's relationship to their parents and the enormous amount of decision-making parents exercise over the child. This is a lengthy developmental process that plays out over many years in tens of thousands of micro-interactions that build or chip away at a child's trust. Were one's parents trustworthy? And to what degree is one of the most profound factors in a child's psychosocial development? This process is far subtler than the erosion of mistrust created by physical and sexual abuse. It extends to how consistently parents are available, manage their daily lives, and maintain a positive emotional consistency. How are promises and expectations kept? Did the parents raise their children in an environment that emphasizes reason and empathy or principle and discipline? And most significantly, what were the parameters for physical discipline and punishment? And it is not possible to overemphasize the overwhelming distortions created by drugs and alcohol. And finally, what are the unspoken lessons each child learns from their aunts, uncles, and grandparents? All these experiences are the earliest programming a child receives and set the parameters for all future upgrades and patches (later life experiences). Let's be clear. Each of us comes into the world with a one-off operating system (brain)—no warranty, no return, and no options. It is a remarkable instrument of protean adaptability, but it has its tolerances.

Projected Identification

How do any of us cope with the many levers of authority/power that push and pull us? The two primary strategies are conformity and rebellion, each at opposite ends of a continuum of social adaptation. Conformity typically takes the form of beliefs, values, and norms from our socialization and the larger cultural context that continually defines us. Conformity helps resolve the anxieties and fears of early childhood experiences of mistrust and makes the world a safer environment. For many, the process of successfully conforming is an emotional healing experience. But when a child's relationship with their parents has been disturbed, it is inevitable that an embedded mistrust of authority evolves. This is typically resolved by the child adapting and believing that their parents are all-powerful and the only safe option. In adulthood, this internalized process is later projected onto a charismatic or powerful individual or faith-based belief or conspiracism, which all share many similarities. Here, one comes to feel protected against the contingencies of life in the same way the child does by conforming to the demands and needs of their parents.

Conformity is the first line of defense against the arbitrary exercise of authority in our world. This is how most people resolve their mistrust of authority in the face of emotional betrayal that can't be acknowledged. At the opposite end resides all manner of rebellion. It represents advocacy for social change in its most constructive forms, art revisioning reality through creative endeavors, paradigm shifts across academic fields, and tweaking conformity in all its silly assumptions. At its most explosive, it is crime and violence, acts of self-destruction, and mindless nihilism and anarchy against all forms of authority. Beyond that, it can become violent mass movements. Social conformity broadly allows for everything to work better and more efficiently, personally and collectively, but it is also a rigid barrier to change and too frequently results in the oppression of the "other" and unending violence by those unable to differentiate and negotiate changing social-cultural complexity.

Externalizing Threat

The absolutism of conspiratorial belief lies deep in an emotional construct, one derived from an underlying mistrust of authority. Literally, a conspiracy of powerful hidden forces aligned against the "self." Initially, these forces are hidden in the same way the parent's intentions are unknown to the child, resulting in a double bind for the child that is now completely dependent on the parents and wanting to feel safe yet feeling betrayed at many levels. And it is never safe to acknowledge or act on this double bind, except to conform or rebel, each with different consequences. The cognitive dissonance created by this internal conflict is suppressed by psychological defense mechanisms, typically repression and denial. The child doubles down on conformity to gain emotional relief. But the sense of betrayal and threat never goes away; rather, the fear and mistrust generated by this process are projected onto the "other" to make it safe and acceptable. And in many instances, it becomes neurotransmitter rewarding, as we explored earlier.

The key to understanding paranoia and delusional conspiracies in the absolute-minded is identifying the hidden and mysterious forces organized to harm the faithful, the believers, and the innocent (the child). If a parent could betray a child, what could be more threatening and unredeemable? If this is true, could the world ever be trusted again? In its adult manifestation, this hidden mistrust focuses on outside forces in an unconscious search for the sense of threat they are experiencing (which might come in the form of anxiety, depression, anger, compulsion). Out in the world lies powerful forces beyond any individual's ability to mitigate or control, capable of harming them and attacking their core identity. And this is true for a majority of adults who experienced emotional betrayal by their parents as infants and children.

Understanding the conspiratorial mind is to confront its eternal search for the sources of its distrust and subsequent fears. Typically, this involves searching for an all-knowing individual and acolytes with secret knowledge of hidden forces or, in times of crisis, a conspiracy. Here, one is oriented toward projecting their hidden fears and giving them form. And without form, they do not have meaning, and without meaning, identity remains diffuse and unformed and conflicted. And now, at last, being able to identify the hidden forces that threaten to shatter one's sense of self, mitigating the underlying fears and anxieties and giving one's sense of threat form provides a powerful healing experience. The healing effect of finding form to one's internal dissonance is powerful and effective. It resides in identifying with like-minded individuals, groups, or charismatic leaders, which provides validity to their struggle for identity. Primarily, absolutism is a response to feeling under siege by powerful outside forces (parental analogs) in a world changing around them, including shifts in status, values, and sense of security. Now the world is reduced to a zero-sum state, "we" versus "them." The threat no longer resides with one's internalized parents, which can never be acknowledged, but now physically and symbolically out in the world.

Being Unique and Special

There is a base narcissism to being *Homo sapiens*. Being able to quickly identify threats renders each of us unique and, hopefully, safe. And a belief in a conspiracy achieves this for many. And given our social nature, our uniqueness often needs affirmation because authority is experienced as innately harmful and not to be trusted outside the safety of the trust group. Here, identity is surrendered to the group, and trust in the group is elevated above reason.

Those who generally subscribe to reason (for example, scientists, academics, intellectuals, and technical elites) are seldom involved in spouting conspiratorial memes and, more often than not, are the subject of them. They are quickly identified by the absolute-minded as the internalized parent, acting in charge, patronizing experts claiming to know everything, perceived as controlling and telling everyone what to do, signaling they are superior know-it-alls, talking down to everyone and treating them as "deplorables." This is why during Senate subcommittee hearings, Republican senators continually attack the character of expert witnesses, typically distorting the record or dismissing the facts and presenting their alternative facts and theories. Senator Rand Paul of Kentucky stands out in his contrarian ability to distort facts and challenge experts. It is a House subcommittee hearing on Russian influence on the presidential election and Republicans denying it and making the case that it's a deep state conspiracy fueled by FBI malfeasance and spying by the Obama administration.

Underlying the conspiratorial mind is a foreboding sense of shame or feeling less than that is projected onto the conspiratorial "other." Identifying those who cannot be trusted is key to feeling safe. Identifying the forces out in the world working against them or wanting to harm them is essential to quieting their internal dissonance. As a result, there is forever a deep state conspiracy. In fact, searching for it is necessary for emotional regulation. This process almost always takes the form of paranoia and conspiratorial beliefs contrived from prelogical reasoning, embedded with superstitious theories and cockamamie doctrines (Ayn Rand, Milton Friedman, Friedrich Hayek, Laffer Curve, and trickle-down economics) to protect against the arbitrariness of life. This process helps identify one's tribe against both real and imagined threats (John Bircher, Young Republican, Christian Right, Neocons, Paleocon, NatCons, Tea Partier, Libertarian, Rhino, Freedom Caucus, MAGA). This is the breadth of the Republican tent. And the key to its success is that group identity makes each individual feel safe and significant in all their shared absoluteness.

Healing Absolutism

If someone believes in the paranormal and supernatural, they will more easily subscribe to conspiracies. One of our earliest experiences to inhabit distrust were faith systems. Those who experience an early loss of trust are forever seeking an explanation as to why. Systems of belief were keen to jump on this with notions of original sin and the eternal need for ritual, confession, atonement, and salvation. There was a hole in the human psyche it sought to heal by making the problem universal rather than personal (the latter of which is the role of psychology). And the solution was a rigid devotion to the irrational as a means of healing. And as faith splinters, it turns out, there is an infinite number of new irrationalities to fill the void, which we are experiencing today.

Systems of belief seek to heal the distrust that initially forms in the child. This is also a binding feature of conspiracism and its adherence to the absoluteness of belief, that the child can never acknowledge the parent's betrayal but are now forgiven, having found a healing path forward. And part of what makes this group identity cohesive are "causes" that offer active direction as an expression of their faith and its ability to protect everyone who believes. This also requires identifying and projecting sinister intentions onto others, which creates a unifying tension overriding the individual's mistrust in all authority and makes trusting the group possible. But once an individual subscribes to the mystical and irrational as governing his or her existence, any deception, lie, or manipulation can potentially appear to be true, often with a need to double down on one's belief when dissonance arises.

Action is also a critical factor in forming group solidarity. In times of perceived crisis, anxiety and fear (and hidden self-loathing) are projected onto those seen as attacking the group's identity. The world is then cast as a simplified duality—good versus evil, weak versus strong, or patriots versus traitors. The negative "other" is cast as dangerous to them and their system of belief. In reality, it's a projection of their inner state of being (child versus parent). The world is divided between "us" versus "them," resolving into a binary zero state. Conspiracies always simplify the contingent and unpredictable world. Often, there's a strong personality or leader organizing and formulating the identity, beliefs, and actions required for inclusion in the "cause" (QAnon and Pizzagate, Senate Republican's unending hearings on Hillary Clinton's emails, and currently, Hunter Biden's laptop). Hence, for thousands of years, there was human sacrifice, torture, burning at the stake, and hanging those accused of disbelieving or violating belief norms.

Base Paranoia

Deep within human consciousness lies the neuro-substrates of distrust, where fear is biochemically induced in the brain and, more specifically, in the amygdala and hypothalamus. A sense of threat is capable of initiating a chemical flight-fight response that can trigger as many as 1,400 physiological and biochemical changes in the human body. And residing in a chronic state of "symbolic threat" is fully capable of triggering paranoia in response to a fight-fight state, the bedrock of all conspiracies. Here, deep-seated fears toggle off the internal regulation of emotions and cognition. In the child, it is the "freeze" state of emotional resignation, and in the adult, it is the projected conspiratorial other. The power of an organized narrative or a conspiracy helps to dampen the internalized conflict. In its most disorganized form, an individual's paranoia is deeply personal and subsumed in interpersonal dysfunction. In its social form, it exists as a projected identification with individuals, groups, beliefs, and conspiracies that validate the individual and outwardly identify the threatening other, whether real or imagined.

A key factor underlying absolutism is the formation of crystallized or rigid narratives, or what most of us think of as conspiratorial thinking, a common delusional state we humans appear to routinely resonate in. It turns out that consciousness only exists in narrative form (awake or dreaming, as far as we can tell). One in which all our emotions and perceptions require understanding. For a significant number of people, rigid narration exists as a default state, lacking an overriding rational toolkit. In times of personal stress or social and economic disturbance, hidden anxieties arise and are an antecedent to rigid narrative-thinking, at the front end defaulting to simple cause-and-effect schemas and, at the backend, the formation of complex conspiratorial ideation.

But what truly gives the absolutist conspiracy model powerful legitimacy is that the world is filled with powerful hidden forces continually undermining and attacking an individual's beliefs, security, and identity. And unfortunately, capitalism, our predominant economic model, is more often than not aligned with social instability. Inevitably, it potentiates profit-seeking, monopoly power, and induces economic fluctuation. This is often applauded in entrepreneurial circles as "creative destruction." The result is a classic double bind, a destabilizing marketplace that rewards a few, conjoined to a democratic process with a core expectation of fairness and justice. But capitalism is just one of many unpredictable factors churning havoc in the larger world, continually impacting individuals, families, and communities in often unforeseen and harmful ways and opening the door to conspiratorial mindedness.

As a source of political strategy, a conspiracy is protean in its ability to organize fears and mistrust in the face of confabulated threats, the secret sauce of the absolutist mindset that all autocratic leaders intuitively grasp. As the one-percenters rise and Wall Street and corporate America dominate the political and economic landscape, it gives credence to the belief that the world is out to harm people. And in some basic sense, this is true. And the cognitive dissonance (anxiety and fear) is real, and the response will likely be chaotic and anarchical. But for the absolute, the internalized narrative is seldom able to identify the source of the dissonance, except as it becomes organized as a conspiracy of hidden forces. Look across America. Whom can you trust, and what are your legitimate options in the face of this distrust? For the past fifty years, the reality has been that both political parties have failed the American people, opening the doors to even crazier conspiratorial narratives.

To clarify, absolute-mindedness is not what we conceptualize as psychopathology (though an alien might disagree). Rather, it has been the ordinary course of the human experience for many thousands of years. But aren't we just bashing parents and blaming them for everything? I would make the case that this argument is overly reductionistic. The answer is more complicated. But no, parents are not fully to blame. What choices did they have? Did they get to choose their parents or early life experiences? And so, it perpetuates generationally. Our evolutionary adaptation is designed to induce random and chaotic elements into our lives. Parents, it turns out, are simply another mechanism for this process. Besides, no one gets to choose the unpredictable contingencies of life that shape who they will become. But one partial way out is for more stable social networks supporting the influential role families play in the long game of our social adaptation. The reality is, it's still far too chaotic out there in the daily lives of way too many people for any other option to make a difference.

Acute Republican Delusional Disorder

Many of us tell ourselves that Republican lawmakers privately know that Biden won the election with 306 electoral votes but refuse to acknowledge it publicly. This held true even after the courts rejected sixty plus postelection lawsuits challenging the election outcome. But what about when they go public and embrace all manner of bizarre conspiracy theories to explain how the election was stolen? Do they still really know that Trump lost? When they incite violence to overturn the election, do they know the real truth? Okay, they are incredibly desperate to hold on to political power. We get it! But do they know that it was a fair election and that Trump lost and Biden won? National surveys eighteen months after the election reported that 66 percent of Republicans believed the election was stolen, or roughly fifty-one million voters.

At what point does it become concerning that Republicans might not really know the truth and reside in a distorted reality? That the truth, for them, appears to be flexible and subject to "alternative facts." Even as you desperately hold on to the faint hope that they must really know the truth, you now understand they will never acknowledge it, regardless of the consequences. Increasingly, it is hard to distinguish who is more delusional, Republicans for claiming the election was stolen or those believing that deep down, they know it wasn't.

Here is our dilemma: How long will the rationally minded hold on to their fantasy that Republicans are not crazy and are not trying to overthrow our democracy? For example, if Republican lawmakers were imprisoned in Guantanamo Bay and tortured (under Bush administration guidelines), surely, they would admit they knew the truth all along. Or would they falsely claim they did when, in fact, they just want to stop watching 2020 election returns twenty-four hours a day? All we can do is default to the DSM-5. A delusion is a *fixed belief that is not amenable to change in light of conflicting evidence.*

It also appears that Republicans are willing to suffer any consequence from asserting the election was stolen, which is a real problem because there appear to be no adverse consequences. And we are in deep trouble if this is true. But what about those of us who watched the January 6 mob attack on the Capitol Building and pondered, *What would have happened if Vice President Mike Pence had been strung up for his supposedly traitorous conduct?* We might be left pondering how many Republican lawmakers would dismiss it as "legitimate political discourse," per the RNC's later characterization of the riot. Only later to strongly assert that if Democrats are serious about healing the country, they should quickly move beyond this "troublesome" event. Nostalgically noting, we used to hang people all the time; that's why we want to "Make America Great Again." (What really happened—the White House gift shop ran out of Trump bobblehead dolls, and a few tourists became upset.)

We are required to look deeper than this one election to understand what is transpiring here. The larger existential question we are confronted with is this: Are the conservatively minded prone to delusional thinking? And how and why is that? The DSM-5 attempts to parse the difference between a delusion and normality. First, it asserts that delusional ideation results in some impairment in work, relationships, or overall adaptive functioning. But then it adds this caveat: "A common characteristic of individuals with delusional disorder is the apparent normality of their behavior and appearance when their delusional ideas are not being discussed or acted on." Our broader concern might be what opens the door to delusional ideation in people who are prone to it? And what triggers it?

Batshit, Crazy Calculating?

Let's debrief the case of Marjorie Taylor Greene, Republican Congresswoman from Georgia, elected in 2020. She has publicly endorsed the following: 9/11 was a hoax, Barack Obama is Muslim, the Clintons were involved in the death of John Kennedy Jr., a Jewish-sponsored space laser started CA wildfires, there exists a cabal of Democratic pedophiles, President Biden's infrastructure agenda is a Communist takeover of America, the mass shooting at a Parkland High School was a false flag operation to suppress gun ownership (she also publicly harassed a student from this same school where seventeen students were killed and seventeen wounded), expressed support for the mass execution of Democrats and moderate Republicans in Congress; and has asserted that Democrats are hunting down and killing Republicans.

In mental health terms, a homeless individual on the streets expressing these ideas would likely be diagnosed with delusional disorder or schizophrenia and treated with anxiolytic or neuroleptic medications in a state-designated mental health facility on seventy-two-hour hold. The diagnostic outcome is typically poor in these cases. When it comes to our congressional person, the general reasoning is she can't be crazy because too many people agree with her (a benefit of doubt conferred on religions but not cults). When one resides in a filter bubble, as in this case, the more outrageous her pronouncements, the more others agree with her. In their trust circle, there are no counterfactual challenges to this giant heap of false beliefs. As a result, people begin to lose their ability to distinguish between fact and fiction and, in time, between reality and nonreality. Their *reality testing* is impaired and in some fundamental sense but normal or what Trump likes to call "nice people." What's particularly disturbing is a so-called state of normalcy can apparently be functionally delusional. I think we have always understood this but reside in a state of denial because it implicates too many people we know, particularly leadership within the Republican Party.

We know this much. When subject to stress, trauma, or threat, the brain organizes itself to highlight grievance and seek revenge. This was as true in Nazi Germany in the 1930s as it is in the US today. To be clear, under real and urgent threats, nearly everyone defaults to simplistic truths as a means of survival. But the absolute-minded appear prone to generating a heightened sense of threat and confabulating cognitive distortions, or what mental health professionals term delusional ideation, unconsciously deconstructing the world in a looping, distorted and rigid narrative.

Conspiratorial delusions are primarily simplified dot-connecting, great for coloring books but not so much for real life. Conspiracies connect unrelated dots to reveal a sinister plot about a world intent on harming those who can discern the message (there is almost always an underlying narcissism to this). While this is not uncommon among drug users, it also appears to be a preexisting condition for many Americans. It's a narrative mindset that provides an explanation of one's *resignation* and *grievances*, to which one feels helpless to do anything.

Delusional conspiracies provide narrative relief and are comforting by focusing one's fears and anxieties onto their imagined problematic source. And a shared delusion is exponentially more powerful and effective. In general, conspiratorial delusions in normal functioning people are a maladaptive response to high-stress levels when there is an underlying *resignation-grievance syndrome*. The case being put forward here is that early life stressors have rewired the brain, leaving individuals prone to secondary delusions as a coping mechanism. And that this is a default state for many absolute-minded.

COVID-19 Prelude to Capitol Riot

The red button on Trump's oval office desk was to order diet Coke.
Looks like we dodged a nuclear strike on the Capitol Building.

The COVID-19 pandemic of 2020 to 2022 shines the brightest light on absolute-mindedness in the US. After three hundred thousand virus-related deaths by late 2020, sixteen red-state governors signaled to the incoming Biden administration they would not issue statewide mandates for wearing masks as a public safety measure (*Politico*, 2020). Even more inflammatory, Scott Atlas, a Trump White House adviser, called for the citizens of Michigan to "rise up" against any COVID-19 restrictions (CNN, 2020). Mystically, a Catholic priest conducted an exorcism to rid voting machines of demon Democrats (*The Hill*, 2021). And more directly, an online headline read, "South Dakota emergency room nurse says some patients insist Covid-19 isn't real, even as they're dying from it" (MarketWatch, 2020). And two years after the advent of the pandemic and nine hundred thousand deaths (one in five hundred Americans), Republican governors in Florida, Arizona, and Texas passed laws banning local mask mandates.

The entire absolutist conspiracy playbook is on display with COVID-19. At the very top, Republican leadership strongly implied that the coronavirus was a hoax not to be taken seriously. The so-called elites, doctors, and public health professionals were portrayed as misleading the American public and profiting from it. An external agent, the Chinese, were blamed for purposely releasing it, thereby assuring everyone that it was, in fact, a conspiracy. This latter fact is important because it supported all the other conspiratorial lies supposedly being told. Trump and his sycophants went about endorsing multiple fake cures (bleach, disinfectants, UV lights, hydroxychloroquine, ivermectin) while continually minimizing the risk. In a bizarre claim, Trump repeatedly asserted that testing for the virus should be curtailed because it continually reported higher COVID-19 rates. In a complete denial of reality, it was implied that the virus would go away if we stopped testing for it. The leader of the free world was down a rabbit hole.

Republican elites across the country coalesced in large public gatherings without masks, making them viral super-spreader events. People were continuously advised by Republican leadership to oppose the most basic public health measures, e.g., wearing masks and social distancing. The Trump administration then falsely inflated its efforts to control the virus while limiting federal oversight and defaulting to states, even threatening to withhold assistance if governors were politically critical of the administration. Made-up time lines for the virus's remission were distributed, continually emphasizing it was in remission, no matter how many people were dying or its transmission rate. Efforts by the CDC to issue public safety guidelines were muzzled and contradicted. And CDC health professionals were openly criticized for relying on facts that contradicted the administration's false claims. When all else failed, vaccines were promoted as the solution, but not surprisingly, resistance to vaccinations increased. When nothing can be believed, why trust anything?

With direction from Trump and his administration, congressional Republicans, governors, and the conservative media, along with the most conforming and absolute-minded, all immediately self-identified by publicly gathering and refusing to wear masks as a public safety measure in the face of the COVID-19 pandemic. But why? Because underlying trust issues are the true super-spreaders of this pandemic. Yes, people don't like being told what to do. Really, who does? Equally important, there's an intense distrust of the federal government by the absolute-minded, along with the perception that their right to exercise choice in this matter was being violated (something that Republican leaders repeatedly emphasized in the media). The cognitive dissonance that arose between individual rights and public safety was no longer suppressed, as fear and anger gained traction from a conspiratorial campaign of disinformation on the right and affirmation from leadership at the top.

Where the Meerkats Don't Plan on Enrolling!

A private school in Miami, the Centner Academy, with two campuses and three hundred students paying $30,000 per school year, informed staff and parents by email that any teachers who have been inoculated against COVID-19 would no longer be employed. The concern was these teachers may be transmitting something from their bodies that could be harmful to the "reproductive systems, fertility, and normal growth development in women and children" who have not been vaccinated (*Miami Herald*, 4/26/21).

It is no wonder that fraudulent 2020 election claims gained so much traction in such a brief time. If one can believe that the coronavirus is a hoax, then stealing an election makes perfect sense. The viral hoax campaign opened the door for a militant response to claims of a stolen election. And stacking conspiracies appears to make each one more valid, especially the secret knowledge being spread by Republican lawmakers that an "elite" Venezuelan strike force had hacked US voting machines (even Marvel Comics couldn't have made this up). The same people who believed the virus was a hoax were now encouraged to invade the US Capitol by Trump and his *fellow traveler* congressmen. All to thwart the confirmation of Biden as president. And it all made perfect sense if you are absolute-minded.

Subduction of Democracy

Over the past twenty-five years, the absolute-minded have become safely sheltered in a cognitive bubble inflated by the

Republican leadership over the four years of the Trump administration. Each false claim made the next one easier to believe, as dissonance further formed around people's high personal cost of having their economic and social lives disrupted. But rather than adapt to this reality, they preferred to believe the virus was a hoax and the election a fraud, all the while resenting "elites" telling them what to do.

Early in the lives of the absolute-minded, grievance was shaped by their parents in roles similar to those now played by politicians. As a result, they fail to fully discern their own social reality, especially in the face of real economic loss and struggle. It is safer to believe the "lie," as Arendt asserted, and take their chances. If one is unable to trust, then double down on the *lie*. Residing in a double bind of broken trust is the most familiar and safest place for a significant percentage of Americans. Perhaps the most challenging thing to understand is that once a lack of trust is unconsciously embedded, individuals will provoke it to assert its reality. It becomes a self-fulfilling prophecy and a chain of disbelief that comes to permeate the world around them. That is why there is no reasoning with it.

But what about those at the very top of the Republican Party spreading false information, sowing doubt, and attacking authority? Were they raised similarly? Most likely, they were raised in high discipline, emotionally remote but intact families with minimal physical punishment. The result is, they are conventionally better able to conform and succeed. Yes, they are echoing the distrustful child but also mimicking the detached parents. They do not perceive their inconsistencies, manipulations, and distortions as lies or deceptions but rather doing what needs to be done to protect their interests and hide their disrupted emotional lives. Shame-driven distrust is suppressed and intellectually rationalized.

So a Supreme Court justice defines him or herself as a constitutional *originalist*. No surprise here. So were their parents. Only their parents were *parentes originalists* when raising their children. And in the world of parental originalism, personal insight rarely exists, raised in environments hostile to introspection where one might encounter their emotional lives. Everything emotionally intolerable is projected onto the "other." They do not experience themselves as exaggerating their concerns or acting deceptively but rather acting on principle and doctrine. They become sheltered in the so-called "institutionalist" reality, offering up harsh punishments, rigid policies, shadow rulings, and dated legal theories two hundred years after the fact. Better to intellectually project their distrust than face their emotional lives. We should pause for a moment and ask ourselves, What is the antonym for institutionalist? It would be peoplists or peoplism. That is all we need to know about the rigid intellectual shortcuts taken by the conservatively minded.

The harsh reality is, there are no moral or ethical boundaries with the logic of the absolute-minded that suppression and projection can't resolve (they are better for having been raised in principle and discipline, and so will everyone else). This is how totalitarian and fascist regimes have reigned throughout history. At some primitive level, the "lie" is a rigid and crystallized narrative or what we now understand as a conspiratorial false belief. And at some fundamental level, all autocratic rulers understand that *fear* is how one governs in this distorted reality. Their transformation from a distrusting child to an untrustworthy parent is natural.

Shame-bound absolutism is a core construct for nearly all members of the Trump administration, Republican congressional members and governors, as it is for someone living homeless in a cardboard shelter on Wilshire Blvd. in Los Angeles. It is a model of how White evangelical ministers insist that God will protect their congregations from COVID-19 and that any efforts to restrict services is a suppression of religious freedom. And, at the same time, overlook how Trump's actions and statements entirely disavow their beliefs. They have all been residing in and adapting to high levels of distrust from early on in their lives. Unable to envision a different world, they reside in disbelief that anyone doesn't feel and see the world the same as they do.

But for the non-absolute minded, the most astounding aspect of all of this is how so many people trust the Republican political and economic agenda, telling people there are no limits to their sacrifice and at the same time affirming the inability of the government to help them (for their own good, of course). And the way through their fear and economic pain is by denying the reality of COVID-19 and attacking election results as fraudulent. True believers are put at risk by being fed disinformation and sowing their distrust then abandoning them. Individuals with the highest levels of distrust are routinely manipulated and taken advantage of in this manner. But how is that possible? Why are they not able to see this? Why do the most distrusting continually believe only those who are deceiving them and lying to them?

For one, they have already paid emotional admission to the Republican identity tent in the form of a distrust circle, one supported by a broad network of people and conspiracy theorists supporting their underlying distrust of authority and elites in particular. This is all amplified as never before by ubiquitous online forums and the conservative broadcast media. The grift is they only trust those who covertly reenact the damaged trust double bind configured early in their lives. It is that simple. Believing the lie only hurts if it's revealed. This manipulation and adaptation have gone on generationally for thousands of years. However, it has become increasingly self-defeating and destabilizing in a modern networked world where the past is rapidly receding.

Republican "Lost Cause"

Perhaps the most confounding absolutist adaptation has taken place in the US Supreme Court. Why do so many conservative Supreme Court justices, having graduated Ivy League law schools and clerked for former justices, adhere so rigidly to conservative legal doctrine as faithfully as any evangelical Christian minister does to the Old Testament? Voting for all the world to see, they share a reasoned belief they are acting with unquestioned intellectual integrity consistent with legal principle, as evidenced by quoting the Declaration of Independence, Constitution, Bill of Rights, English Common Law, and deep diving into the Federalist Papers. All the while claiming they are channeling "original intent" and faithfully upholding the ideals upon which our nation was founded.

Here is a sampler of the court consistently voting against the future (without citation): upholding slavery, authorizing forced sterilization, the internment of Japanese citizens, supporting segregation and racial discrimination, criminalizing homosexuality, authorizing child labor, anti-labor rulings on workplace safety, blocking the democratic process by handing Bush the presidency (2000), proclaiming that money equals free speech in *Citizens United*, overturning fifty years of precedence to end abortion rights for women. The broad framework of this voting pattern has been to champion elitist economic interests and limit individual and civil rights.

Conservative Supreme Court justices are literally the last vestige of the Republican's "Lost Cause" movement in America. They would put King George III (or his contemporary progeny) back on the throne if the donor class insisted, citing a majority of Americans in 1775 did not support the revolution (which was true). There was no legal basis for revolution under British law (also true). It was unlawful domestic violence extremism (DVE) or White militia groups fomenting seditious rebellion (true from the British perspective). Besides, the British were only upholding "law and order" and tax rights (true enough).

What we see on the court is what typically takes place on the intellectual Right—ideological principles being mistaken for reasoned thinking. Over time, one quickly realizes that it's not possible to reason with the conservative mind. It inevitably defaults to a simple-minded set of principles to explain complexity. They will claim their findings are principled and reasoned, but the truth is they always start from a shaky premise, rendering their conclusions intellectually empty. And beneath the surface, it's easy to detect the open hostility to their emotional lives. In the legal system, they appear to have found a secret garden from having to reason or feel—bending reality, twisting words, nuancing phrases and ideas to conform to a broad distortion of reality. They are hailed as legal scholars when, in truth, they are only upholders of the past in the face of an ever-changing world. If there's any irony in this, it's that the Founding Fathers were rationalist children of the Enlightenment.

Are Conservative Supreme Court Justices "Partisan Hacks?"

On September 12, 2021, standing before an audience at the University of Louisville's McConnell Center, Supreme Court Justice Amy Coney Barrett offered that "judicial philosophies are not the same as political parties," adding "this court is not comprised of a bunch of partisan hacks." The first question to be addressed here is why is a US Supreme Court justice publicly addressing this concern? But then the answer becomes obvious. Seated right next to her was Republican Senate Minority Leader Mitch McConnell (who the center was named after). Perhaps we can all agree the optics for impartiality were not good here. On the surface, it appears Barrett was pandering to a conservative audience by letting them know that their shared agenda (wink, wink) was nonpartisan. And the fact that Mitch McConnell had previously manipulated the political process in an egregious act of partisanship to get Barrett confirmed, and now claiming she does not "legislate from the bench," was stated without irony. This is the same Mitch McConnell who defines the term "partisan hack," now trying to cleanse the charge of partisan hack Barrett carries. (They are waist-deep in muck pretending these conferences are golden showers.)

Justices Barrett, Kavanaugh, and Gorsuch were nominated by Trump after being vetted by the highly conservative Federalist Society to ensure their ideological purity. An extremely partisan Republican Senate confirmed them without bipartisan support because of their conservative credentials. McConnell worked tirelessly to manipulate the confirmation process to ensure their confirmation. Was this because these justices were independent-minded or because they were as close to a sure bet the nation's conservative legal community could produce from the hundreds of more qualified attorneys and judges? If these justices were not partisan hacks, they would never have been nominated. That was the primary criteria. But they could not see this. All they could see was every day in judicial paradise. Why is that? Had none of them wondered who or what was influencing Trump to nominate them or considered the highly partisan context in which they were confirmed?

In 2016, after the death of Justice Antonin Scalia (the most ideologically weaponized justice to have served on the court but well-liked by his peers at lunch), President Obama nominated Merrick Garland. Then Senate Majority Leader Mitch McConnell, without historical precedent, blocked Garland's nomination, stating, "One of my proudest moments was when I looked Barack Obama in the eye and I said, 'Mr. President, you will not fill the Supreme Court vacancy.'" This was done to later let Trump nominate a justice who just happened to be Barrett. (Consider, for a moment, being nominated by Trump to the highest court in one of the most politically partisan acts in the history of the Senate and not wonder what your role is in this.)

We can only conclude that Barrett was indifferent and willing to play the partisanship game. Then near the end of the Trump presidency, McConnell reversed course and confirmed one of the most fragile judicial nominees since Clarence Thomas. Refusing to wait for the next president to be elected, Trump nominated Ivy League frat boy and partygoer Brett Kavanagh, who understands judicial restraint but not so much personal restraint. (On this latter matter, he and Justice Thomas share a history.) Here was politics and not integrity at work, usually a sign you are a partisan hack.

What a coincidence that the voting history of these justices on issues before the court clearly square with Republican psychopathology. It was not a coincidence in 2022 that the court's conservative majority overturned *Roe v. Wade*, basically allowing states to severely restrict and even ban abortion. A draconian ruling that had *The Handmaid's Tale* written all over it. (Basically, the court was taking on the role of Gilead's "Commanders of the Faithful.") Barrett was unable to see how her biases influenced her judgment. She doubled down on her faith (a conservative strain of Catholicism) rather than manage the complexity (dissonance) of the case before her.

Confronted with the eternal dilemma of being absolute-minded, conservative justices like to refer to themselves as "originalists" regarding judicial philosophy. Lacking insight and operating in a narrow moral vacuum, they are the opposite of court "pragmatists." Originalism is simply judicial moonshine for doubling down on *prin-*

ciple and *discipline* over *reason* and *empathy*. That saves them from having to think outside the box. So what about the so-called liberal or *pragmatic* justices? Aren't they just as biased? The short answer is no. When the logic of the law is guided by reason and empathy and the broader objective is for the law to be "fair" and "just" and not an ideological test of purity or the consistency of rigid principles, it is the opposite of being a partisan hack.

After an adult lifetime of marinating in conservative propaganda, the past tells these conservative justices how to deliberate and vote, which is almost always against individual rights, social justice, and the future. It is simple. If they were independently minded, there would be greater variability in their voting records on important cases before the court. Their votes consistently skew toward partisanship that support Republican policy positions.

Trump appointed all three justices to assure that his corrupt administration could legally violate democratic norms and that, if necessary, they were the backup plan for a political coup in 2020. Barrett's invitation to speak at the McConnell Center was further confirmation that she is what she fears. In 2022, Justice Barrett addressed the Federalist Society's National Lawyers Convention. One can reasonably ask, How is it that Justice Barrett keeps insisting that she is independently minded but continually attends the most conservative-minded legal forums in America, typically to standing applause (as do Alito, Thomas, Kavanagh, and Gorsuch)? Does she ever wonder why she is being applauded by the audience?

Supreme Court Justices

Just politicians in black robes.

—W. Shaub, former director US
Office of Government Ethics

The question has to be asked, Why do so many conservative Supreme Court justices, confirmed to the court for their rigid ideological principles, struggle to avoid the appearance of impropriety?

Just saying, without attribution of wrongdoing. Let's hit the highlights of our conservative justices, beginning with Clarence Thomas. At his confirmation hearing, he was accused of sexually harassing Attorney Anita Hill, and no one cared. He is also politically yoked to a White supremacist wife who was actively involved in an attempted overthrow of the US government, and no one cared. Now comes the revelation from *ProPublica* (2023) that the extraordinary power and prestige that comes with being a justice are not enough for Thomas. He has been on a dark money grift with a powerful Republican megadonor for twenty-five of this thirty years on the court, claiming an anonymous individual told him that the lavish personal gifts, chartered jet flights, and superyacht stays at exotic vacation locales did not have to be reported on his taxes. And no one cares. But also slipping Thomas's wife a yearly $170,000 in pocket change salary to run her advocacy group while buying and remodeling his mother's home. (Really, what are friends for?) This is what sexual grooming looks like above the C-PAC level. (Although, a part of me empathizes with Thomas's desire to have all these wealthy plantation owners kiss his Black ass.)

Real estate speculator and Supreme Court Justice Neil Gorsuch potentially made as much as $500,000 on the sale of a property he jointly owned through an LLC. This property had been on the market for two years until it sold for $1.825 million nine days after he was confirmed to the court in 2017. Two factors stand out here. The court's annual financial disclosure statement indicated that he reported this income as the sale of an interest in an LLC and not real estate. The property was actually sold to the chief executive of a law firm that did extensive business before the court (a fact omitted from his disclosure forms). In fact, this firm has appeared before the court in as many as twenty-two cases since Gorsuch's confirmation (*Politico*). The chief executive of the law firm has stated that he had no prior knowledge that Gorsuch owned the property. (My response is "Yo-ho-ho, and a bottle of rum!)

Now comes the revelation that the wife of John Roberts, Chief Justice of the US Supreme Court Jane Roberts, made a casual $10.3 million in commissions from 2007 to 2014. Now you might be curious how she did this and why you can't. Simple. She went to elite law firms and solicited their business as the wife of the chief justice (wink, wink) and suggested it was in their best interest to hire the attorneys she represents and pay her an exorbitant commission of a few hundred thousand dollars. And they did this over and over because it seemed like a good business or what most of us think of as a *quid pro quo* they couldn't refuse. I mean, it can't hurt to be on the good side of the chief justice if you are before the Supreme Court. Coincidently, most of the law firms Mrs. Roberts solicited routinely appeared before the Supreme Court. (In it most cynical form, this looks similar to a mob protection racket. You pay for protection even if you don't need it.)

Amy Barrett is a "handmaiden" in People of Praise, a Christian charismatic sect that teaches women to be submissive to men. Brett Kavanaugh was accused by three women of sexual misconduct, including attempted rape. And lastly, that leaves us with Samuel "Immutable" Alito, who strongly believes women should not have any rights that were not specifically granted to them under English common law, when they had few or no rights unless they were virgins, which was an exception that required considerable legal protection.

The currents of the immutable one's misogyny run deep. In overturning *Roe v. Wade* and a woman's right to an abortion, he displayed the type of cajones you find hanging from the back of pickup trucks in small Southern towns. He cited seventeenth-century English jurist and devout Puritan Matthew Hale on how aborting a fetus was the equivalent of murder. While coincidentally, Hale advocated it was the contractual right of a husband to rape his wife. In 1662, he sentenced two women to death for witchcraft, arguing that the existence of the law against witches is proof that witches exist. Hale's ruling on this matter were later influential in the Salem witch trials.

But do not fear. Alito's logic will start to make sense if we are patient, when the court will eventually rule that husbands can rape their wives and women can be tried and burned at the stake as witches. Really, how does Alito go back four hundred years and separate Hale's logic on abortion from his Puritan attitudes toward woman? Here women were considered instruments of Satan, inferior and subservient to men, unable to possess property, sign contracts, or engage in business or politics. Why did Alito only focus on abortion when there is so much more the court could be doing for and to woman?

ProPublica (2023) revealed that "Sammy the Immutable" was also engaged in a racketeering influence-peddling scheme (with plausible deniability) with billionaire hedge fund manager and GOP megadonor Paul Singer. In 2008, Alito accepted a private jet flight that would have cost most of us a $100,000 one way (or $200,000 round trip) to a $1,000-a-night Alaskan fishing lodge. His lodging expenses were a tax write-off for another conservative billionaire who owned the lodge. Coincidently, Alito failed to report any of this on the court's financial disclosure forms or to recuse himself from the ten cases that Singer almost or maybe had an interest in before the court.

On the editorial page of the *Wall Street Journal*, Alito penned a rebuttal to his critics that made ChatGPT4 laugh out loud for the very first time and describe it as a deepfake for its simplistic reasoning and lack of ethical nuance. (No need to inquire as to why so many billionaires seek out friendships with lonely Supreme Court justices. It is a courtesy of the Federalist Society's Leonard Leo, a Jeffrey Epstein wannabe who has the degrading task of passing out money instead of sexual favors.) One is left asking, Is this the best that legal conservatism has to offer America in the twenty-first century? It's something that Senator Sheldon Whitehouse, D-RI, characterizes as "a noxious cocktail of creepy rightwing billionaires, phony front groups, amenable justices, large sums of money, and secrecy (that) has been brewing at the Supreme Court for years now."

Are Conservative Justices Stupider? Maybe!

In the *Journal of Personality and Social Psychology (*1983), researchers examined *cognitive style* as a predictor of ideological voting consistency among US Supreme Court justices. Before this, they had examined US senatorial speeches (1975–76) across three Congresses and determined that moderate and liberal senators "showed significantly more integrative cognitive complexity than did politicians with conservative voting records." Perhaps more disturbing, these results were replicated in a study of Supreme Court justices. The general finding was there is a significant relationship between lower cognitive complexity and political conservatism. The authors concluded their findings "lend indirect support to the rigidity-of-the-right hypothesis" and that a "general trait interpretation of integrative complexity appears to apply more readily to conservatives than to liberals and moderates." In laymen's terms, conservative justices aren't dumb. They're just not as smart and open-minded as moderate and liberal justices.

Chapter 7

Does Authoritarianism Exist on the Left?

A study at Northwestern University indicated that conservatives are more receptive to disinformation:

> Republican users are more likely to mistake bots promoting conservative ideas for humans, whereas Democrats are more likely to mistake conservative human users for bots.

Over the past twenty years, a handful of academic researchers have attempted to establish the existence of left-wing authoritarianism, chaffing at prior comparisons to finding "hens' teeth" or the "Loch Ness monster." This included an effort to demonstrate that two of the primary constructs underlying authoritarianism, paranoia, and conspiracism coexist equally among Democrats and Republicans (Uscinski and Parent 2014). The first serious effort was by Altemeyer, a psychologist, with the creation of the Left-Wing Index (2004). He noted that several variables overlapped his earlier and well-respected Right-Wing Scale (RWS). Later came an even more ambitious follow-up study by Costello et al. (2021), who also presented qualified findings regarding the existence of left-wing authoritarianism (LWA). What follows is a brief review of this research. But the most charitable assessment is that the "needle" has moved on LWA and can now be found in a haystack.

Academic Debate 1—Left-Wing Authoritarianism

A few researchers are convinced that authoritarianism exists on the political left if they could only prove it. To clarify, there is no doubt authoritarianism substantially exists on the political right, and now there is a limited consensus to continue probing the left for its presence. And just to be clear, current research on LWA concludes with many qualifying caveats, rending the results more a ghost in the machine than a locomotive. However, the case presented here is there may exist something on the left, but it's not authoritarianism but a subset of absolutism. And, unfortunately, as with all academic research, we will have to go into the weeds to make sense of it.

It is important to explore a few of the many research caveats on LWA to better understand this shaky hypothesis. The first question that pops up is, What populations did these researchers sample to produce measures of left-wing authoritarianism? And beyond that, how big were the sample sizes, and how was it stratified (subdivided)? Did they have deep samples of individuals who were clearly identified as authoritarian to validate their findings and create a measurable baseline? The answer is no. Not illogically, they defaulted to safe assumptions about survey and voter data to reveal self-identified patterns of voting and party identification. In other words, it was secondhand. But who were the people they measured for authoritarianism, and who do they truly represent? Beyond the fact that many of the sampled populations were primarily students, these concerns are never satisfactorily addressed. But also, what happens to these students fifteen or twenty years later regarding their so-called authoritarian traits?

A major concern is trusting what researchers identify as authoritarianism. Even the definitions of it can widely vary among them, making comparisons inconsistent and unreliable. Findings are primarily based on secondary and tertiary measures, meaning it's nearly impossible to establish what was measured versus the real world or what researchers call *concurrent validity.* In the end, we are forced to ask, How do they know what they know? Yes, they administered a multitude of tests, assessment instruments, and surveys, but do these results in any way represent their limited claims? This research raises as many questions as it answers, not about their competence or ethics but about what their findings actually mean. Significantly, this research never conveys to us how their findings result in real-world expressions of authoritarianism. There is no follow-up research to determine how accurately these measures predict future behavior (and that is a giant problem when it comes to extrapolating research findings to the real world). Limited sampling size and overinterpreting independent measures often clump findings together that do not reflect the real world at all. But might suggest RWA and LWA are similar in some respects.

Still, many questions remain as noted by researchers. For example, what does the general population look like on these measures, but also cross-culturally or among nations? An important question never addressed is, What percentage of the population exhibits authoritarian traits? And importantly, how do a few overlapping variables reflect the real world, beyond academic conjecture? And perhaps most unknown is how prone are measured variables of authoritarianism to cultural triggers, and to what degree? And to be clear, authoritarianism has a direct relationship to environmental triggers, and its presence is relatively indifferent to the world without them. Which raises the eternal research conundrum of *sensitivity* versus *specificity* of test measurements (*sensitivity*, the true positive rate of authoritarianism, versus *specificity*, the true negative rate authoritarianism is not present). When a *trigger* is required to assert authoritarianism, this can all become muddled, if not incomprehensible.

Costello and his team of researchers (2021) assert a most remarkable finding, claiming their measures of LWA "powerfully predicts behavioral aggression and is strongly correlated with participation in political violence." This assertion should raise serious doubts about the validity of this work since it would represent the Holy Grail of research, if true. But when one examines the political landscape, correlating political violence to measures of LWA is impossible to determine from tests and surveys. Let's look closer at one of the findings supporting their assertion that those high on LWA "expressed stronger support for a political system with substantial centralized state control." On the surface, this appears to support a model of authoritarianism. But really, what does this mean in real life? Is this as true in Hungary or Belarus as it is in the US? In the US, this could reflect the left's greater confidence in our democratic institutions than the right's high level of distrust for authority and the federal government. It may not be the left pining for dictatorship, but rather for a social safety net, immigration reform, and voting security, as Republicans go about undermining democratic norms. Likely, it reflects the left's higher level of trust in government rather than the specter of authoritarianism (or advocating "substantial state control" typical in authoritarian and autocratic countries). So when these researchers claim variables on RWA and LWA overlap, it has to be conjectured, only in their imaginations.

This all began with Adorno in the 1950s and has brachiated over the past seventy years into many instruments and measures that basically mean whatever the researchers say they mean. Rigorously, of course. But clearly, authoritarianism has come to mean many different things as a result. Let's focus on another small example. From the beginning, a core definition of authoritarianism included "submission to authority." But what does that mean exactly? To Adorno, it meant a passive submission to the authority of the state, as exampled in Nazi Germany and Fascist Italy.

So let's forward to 2021 and look at right-wing populism in the US. The far right is paranoid about the "deep state" and the reach of the federal government. It has formed any number of armed militia groups opposed to the state and a Republican Party that is actively undermining the authority of the state. So where is the supposed submissiveness? Well, the submissiveness is to Trumpism and authoritarian Republican leaders and evangelical ministers preaching anti-state vitriol. In the face of this, Costello noted that political violence can be directed either against the system or to support the system, adding that the LWA uniquely emphasizes anti-state violence, whereas RWA emphasizes pro-state violence. Really! After the recent Capitol riot, one would likely question this assertion. In fact, it is not an accurate statement of fact at all.

Costello goes on to emphasize that:

> LWA (Index) uniquely predicted participation in use of force for a political cause within the last five years as well as support for, and participation in, anti-state violence during the summer of 2020.

They speculate the fact that anti-state political violence has, heretofore, been largely excluded from the authoritarianism construct exemplifies the shortcomings of an exclusively right-wing account of authoritarianism. (While the conclusions about the limitations of this research are accurate, it totally fails reality testing. For example, exactly how do they assess how Black Lives Matter protests compared to violent White militia activity?)

The idea that research instruments are predictive of future violence, whether individual or mass behavior, should immediately raise red flags. I would offer, after a career of studying violence prediction, this research is reaching for a bar too high. But are these researchers accurate about where violence is emanating from? In the eighteen-month period from January 2020 to June 2011, more than thirty thousand demonstrations took place in the US, and 94 percent were without violence. They were, in fact, remarkably peaceful. And here is an important caveat: when violence did occur, it was with the presence of armed right-wing counterprotesters (where authoritarianism is clearly identified).

The notion of *submission to authority* may be accurate but not necessarily to the state. That's just how it had played out in the 1930s in Europe. So is current violence by the right pro-state or anti-state, when it entails the overwhelming submission of millions to deception, lies, paranoia, conspiracy, and a violent attempted coup against the US government? The fact is right-wing militia groups, for decades, have been founded on subverting and overthrowing the federal government. No such drive or impetus exists on the left beyond radical reform. The Antifa, considered by many on the right to be the violent tip of the spear for LWA, is mostly in reaction to aggression and violence on the right and confronting authoritarianism, and are not opposing the state or government but rather those disrupting the exercising of protesters' rights.

The deeper one explores this research, the less convincing are its findings. And the more complex their research, the less likelihood anyone will understand it or offer critique. On the surface, one could cynically conclude they are publishing to confirm research biases, as the range of subtle overlapping constructs can no longer be sorted or even understood. And it all begins with this: Do the instruments they use measure what they say? And most importantly, who did they sample? These studies are never repeated, and the populations sampled appear to be only vaguely relevant. The entire process appears to be a house of cards, identifying one more card (variable) to be placed on top. And if the house of cards doesn't collapse, the measure must be valid.

Academic Debate 2—Left Wing Paranoia and Conspiracy

In their book *American Conspiracy Theories* (2014), political scientists Uscinski and Parent advance the argument that political conspiracy theories are not limited to one particular ideology or political party but are equally present on the right and left. This was offered as a counterpoint to Richard Hofstadter's influential article "Paranoid Style in American Politics" (1964). Hofstadter made the case that underlying the conspiratorial mind was a base paranoia that could be triggered by high levels of social and political conflict. More to the point, it primarily existed on the political right, and more specifically within the Republican Party.

Our two researchers posit that believing in a conspiracy is not a mental disorder and relatively normal, and that everyone is potentially subject to conspiratorial beliefs to varying degrees. They appear to be on solid ground here. But then they assert that there is an underlying predisposition toward believing in conspiracies that exists equally among "Republicans" and "Democrats." But is this true? Consider their description of those prone to conspiracies: "poor in terms of formal education and money, less likely to participate politically, more accepting of violence." Then later adding for emphasis, "more positively inclined towards guns and violence than the average American." It would not be a biased generalization to conclude from their description that it more accurately describes the authoritarian mindset and the political right than it does the left.

The authors then add this bit of mystery, noting, "Conspiratorial predispositions are ingrained early in life and persist much like other orientations." And here the discussion comes to a dead end. How is this "predisposition" created and fostered is not addressed (which is the subject of this book). The fact that it is "ingrained early in life" tells us it may not be the same for everyone and that there may be considerable variation depending on one's early life experiences. The answer to this conundrum might also tell us a great deal about how and why political conspiracies exist at all and whether they equally transit the political right and left.

The key issue is how the authors go about identifying and measuring conspiratorial belief on the left. They offer limited empirical evidence and considerable conjecture from anecdotal sources. And this has been a continuing problem for researchers seeking a one-size-fits-all theory of conspiracies. I would proffer that voting patterns are the single most reliable measure of underlying conspiracies that can be meaningfully scaled up.

In the past two presidential elections, who was more likely to believe, support, and vote for politicians espousing conspiratorial and paranoid ideation? Who has been most likely to publicly act on their conspiratorial beliefs? Which party consistently dog-whistled its base with false information and conspiracies? The answer is clearly the political right and the Republican Party. And this has been historically true for the past one hundred years. When one examines the many examples of the conspiracy-minded put forward in their book, they mostly reflect the political right, whether it's on Fox News, social media, podcasts, or radio. There are no voices or organizations on the left mimicking Alex Jones, Glen Beck, Tucker Carlson, QAnon, Proud Boys, or proselytizing Christian nationalism. And when conspiracies exist on the left, they are more immediately subject to being influenced by facts and information. They correctly conclude that conspiracies that prevail "have to appeal to the right people, at the right time, in the right way, and adapt to survive." The fact is, we have known this for some time now, as well as those most susceptible to them.

To bolster their case, the authors added a dubious historical footnote: America's Revolutionary War against England was based on the conspiratorial beliefs of the Founding Fathers. Historically, it has been well-documented that George III, the English monarch at the time, suffered bouts of "insanity" because of a lifelong mental illness. He has been variously described as "agitated and talking incessantly and incoherently" and becoming so unmanageable that he had to be placed in restraints. I somehow doubt our founders were overly conspiratorial, as opposed to being deeply concerned about the arbitrariness with which they were being governed by an unstable king, in a repressive manner, residing some four thousand miles away. They didn't require a conspiracy to advocate for independence, even if they expressed their deepest concerns and fears about the future with a measure of hyperbole.

Outside Academia

Sometimes it is important to step out of academia and examine the surrounding world, which researchers can be reluctant to do. Let's revisit the political impulses in the US over the past 170 years. This refresher might help us better align with what takes place on the political left and right. Please note, this is not intended to be a complete compilation but rather a cursory review.

Right. Southern succession from the Union to maintain the institution of slavery, vigilantism, Ku Klux Klan, Jim Crow laws, hanging of African Americans and violent destruction of Black communities, labor suppression, Charles Coughlin, J. Edgar Hoover, Joseph McCarthy, George Wallace, Donald Trump, Oklahoma City bombing, White hate groups, violent resistance to the civil rights movement and school integration, Christian nationalism, White supremacists, neo-Nazis, Sovereign Nation, Proud Boys, Three Percenters, QAnon, Aryan Nation, bombing abortion clinics, subverting election laws, attempted coup of the US government, threats to kill and kidnap Democratic governors, armed militant border patrols, mass shootings, fixation on school shootings as red flag operations, stolen election claims, Capitol riot, coronavirus as a hoax, hate speech toward LBGQT, vaccines as a threat to individual rights, deep state conspiracy, attacks on the US power grid, and dozens of paranoid conspiratorial theories. And let's not ignore the wave of mass shooting across the US over the past twenty years because of a failure to regulate firearms.

Left. Abolition of slavery, women's right to vote, Prohibition, civil rights movement (Thirteenth, Fifteenth, Nineteenth, Twenty-Fourth, and Twenty-Sixth Amendments to the Constitution), union and labor rights, Prohibition era, anti-war movement, Weather Underground, Black Panther Party, feminism, LBGQT rights, abortion rights, environmentalism, Black Lives Matter protests, critical race theory, advocacy for a social safety net, social security, Affordable Care Act, immigrant rights, Antifa, *woke* culture, Wall Street protest, Women's March on Washington, DC, exchanging Columbus Day for Indigenous People's Day. There are no outstanding conspiracy theories, but there is a belief that the wealthy have too much money and need to share, and that the marketplace needs more regulation and safeguards. Okay, climate change also needs to be addressed. (The broad theme here has been to establish and protect civil rights.)

It is no wonder the academic world took as long as it did to examine authoritarianism on the left. When it confuses expressions of hate and intolerance with nonviolent civil rights protests but also a willingness at the highest levels of the Republican Party to subvert the political process to achieve aims that are largely paranoid and conspiratorial, generally missing the mark for reality testing. The extreme right is premised on distortion, deception, and lies to achieve a narrow political and social agenda that is antidemocratic and authoritarian. While on the far-left, Bernie Sanders and Elizabeth Warren are struggling to get national health insurance and affordable education for every American. (And here is the point—absolutism, as defined here, exists on the left, but not in the same form as authoritarianism does on the right.)

Violence on the Left (1960s–1970s)

The *Weather Underground* was a left-wing radical group active in the 1960s and 1970s that advocated Marxist ideology and carried out bombings of government buildings. The only deaths from the bombings were three of its members when their bomb accidentally exploded. In addition, two members of the Weather Underground, along with four members of the Black Liberation Army, were responsible for the deaths of a security guard and two police officers during an attempted robbery in 1981. The Weather Underground had an active membership peaking around twenty individuals.

The *Symbionese Liberation Army* (SLA) was a small group of left-wing terrorists active in the 1970s. The group aimed to politically radicalize people but ended up killing an Oakland school superintendent and later a bank customer during a robbery. The group gained notoriety for the kidnapping of Patty Hearst, a student at UC Berkeley and the heir to the Hearst family fortune.

The *Black Liberation Army* was a far-left Black nationalist movement active from 1970 to 1981. Its goal was to initiate a war against the United States and liberate Black people. The group was responsible for the deaths of an estimated thirteen police officers, multiple robberies, a prison break, and the hijacking of a jet passenger plane on its way from Detroit to Miami, which ultimately landed in Algeria and resulted in the arrest of the hijackers in Europe.

The *Black Panther Party*, founded in 1966 in Oakland, California, was inspired by the shooting death of civil rights leader Malcolm X. It expressed belief in Black nationalism, Marxism, and armed self-defense. The goal was to create social programs to benefit the Black community. But within a few years, the BPP became involved in numerous violent confrontations with the law enforcement and faced internal personal and political conflicts that turned violent. By 1980, it had collapsed. (It is important to note there was clearly a violent effort to address racism in America by a small number of people.)

Antiwar Movement was a direct consequence of the Vietnam War (1964 to 1973). The war resulted in the deaths of 58,220

American soldiers and the wounding of 153,303. At its the height, five hundred thousand American soldiers were stationed in South Vietnam. Estimated Vietnamese war deaths range from 950,000 to 3 million. The war sparked largely peaceful nationwide protests and widespread defiance of governmental authority among college-age adults. (In 2019, 132,798, American tourist visited Vietnam.)

Political Right versus Political Left

One further distinction is required here. Many social scientists confuse the political left and right as reflecting authoritarianism on the left and right. For instance, politically, fascism is on the right and Communism is on the left. But is that true? Hannah Arendt correctly surmised that both were authoritarian reactions and that fascism and totalitarianism derive from the same social, economic, and political factors. While there is an absolutism on the left, there have been few violent expressions of it. It can be intolerant, demanding, and confrontive. A primary one was the American Revolution. At some point, repression unites left and right. But the left does not stand alone as aggressive and violent as does the authoritarian right.

Now you might ask yourself, "Why is academia concerned with validating the presence of left-wing authoritarianism?" The answer appears to be, at least on the surface, one of academic objectivity. Because there is RWA, a fair measure of this phenomenon would examine the entire political spectrum. But objectivity does not make it true. Let's examine. A glance about the world today would suggest that the expression of absolutism on the left is relatively limited compared to its overwhelming expression on the right. It would also be fair to conjecture that any expression by the left is primarily in reaction to resistance to social change by the right, one often violently enforcing existing social biases and inequalities. That is, the more prominent and aggressive the right attempts to impose order and control (repression), the more likely it will encounter an absolutist response on the left.

There is a temptation to believe that the political expression of ideologies derives solely from their underlying philosophies. But nothing could be further from the truth. They also derive from a power dynamic and only secondarily from philosophy. While the French Revolution was, in part, inspired by the earlier American Revolution and the ideals of "liberty, equality, and fraternity," it did not give rise to a democratic France or Europe until after the Second World War. Instead, Napoleon arose and basically imposed dictatorships as the antithesis of monarchy throughout Europe. Yet it was the beginning of the end of a feudal Europe and the rule of monarchy and the rise of nation-states and a constitutionalism based on "natural" rights.

The two most virulent ideological movements that followed 150 years later were communism and fascism, both authoritarian models of government, each representing different philosophical elements of the French Revolution but equally focused on the top-down rule of the state. What did not fully arise was democratic norms and capitalism, except in Great Britain. The point being the true political left has always been democracy, and the true right has always been authoritarian rule.

The only political movement to the left of democracy is democratic socialism. In fact, when one looks closely at communist states today, such as Russia and China, they are highly authoritarian models that primarily mirror Nazi Germany and all the other theocratic, plutocratic, and autocratic regimes around the world, whatever their underlying ideologies. The primary dynamic is always about the concentration and distribution of power and wealth as influenced by ideology. And today, the focus is on the shift to the right by increasingly illiberal democracies. If you really want to know what the right fears from the left, watch how dictatorships around the world are deadly afraid of democracies exposing their lies and hypocrisy to their citizens. The point being, Marxism, as an ideology, lies to the left of democracy, but communism as a political expression of it lies to the far right of democracy. That is just a pragmatic fact that researchers struggle with when trying to identify authoritarianism on the political left.

A question that appears to flummox many social science researchers is whether authoritarianism is similarly expressed on the political left as it is on the political right. I would conjecture that authoritarianism is primarily a response to circumstances. But it is also the product of a specific mindset derived from a unique developmental history and a specific set of social triggers. But that does not mean there is no "absolutism" on the left. There is a rigid and ideological focus on the left that has an underlying irrationality. In fact, we see it all about us today in *woke* culture. But is it the same? If one were to take all the adults in America and sort them along a continuum of right to left, we would discover the majority of those who express authoritarian values would reside on the right. As one approached the moderate middle, the proportion would begin to quickly diminish, and at some point, it might overlap the conservative side of the left. But by the time one got to the middle of the left, it would completely disappear.

However, an *absolutist* response on the left is more latent and fluid. It entails a more idealistic response to circumstances. It does not arise out of paranoia and conspiracy as on the right, but rather out of a reality assessment of circumstances. And if need be, it can organize top down, impose discipline, and use force if necessary. When one looks at partisan resistance against Nazi occupation throughout Europe in World War II, the left was highly organized against a real threat, not an illusion or conspiracy. And here in the US, as a large number on the right refuse COVID-19 vaccination, it is easy to detect the left wanting to impose mandatory public health measures as their assessment of the problem accurately reflects the reality-bending fear and distrust of the right. And as the public health consequences rise, so did an absolute response on the left. It simply is not triggered as easily and operates in a more reciprocal relationship to reality. And yes, all types of fanciful and nonsensical ideas arise on the left, but seldom social violence or mass repression.

The Absolute Continuum

The model of absolutism offered here is a more coherent model of what researchers are searching for on both the left and the right. Absolutism is a universal construct underlying the human condition.

We all operate along a continuum of absolute responding. Those on the right are the most easily triggered and overresponsive to their fears and anxieties. While those on the left are better able to navigate their social reality emotionally and cognitively. But there is a threshold when the two are not overtly distinguishable as circumstances grow more threatening. The response by the US public during the Second World War to German and Japanese aggression didn't require a debate among Americans, regardless of their degree of authoritarianism. It was immediately responsive, highly organized, and uncompromising across the entire spectrum. The point being it is a spectrum we are looking at, with everyone residing along it with varying degrees of absolutism. Each one is triggered by their own unique social cues.

Developmentally, there is no perfect trust. Object constancy and a secure emotional attachment are always disrupted to varying degrees. No one differentiates as an individual without developmental setbacks. And we are all genetically geared to respond with *grievance-revenge* to personal insult, and more generally, to perceived injustices and unfairness socially and culturally. This is the homeostatic reality of our social universe. The primary difference between an absolute response on the right, as opposed to the left, is the right is more easily cued and quickly triggered. Here resides a large segment of the populace who struggle to repress high levels of dissonance and cognitively double down on issues of trust. They struggle to manage complexity emotionally and cognitively. As a default, they respond in a more rigid and fixed manner, frequently subject to reality-bending distortions and conspiracies. And they are more likely to shelter with other like-minded individuals.

Perhaps the best way to understand this distinction is that violence on the right aims to support the status quo and is resistant to change (which is inevitable and unavoidable). Violence on the left is an attempt to overturn the status quo as repressive, unjust, and discriminatory. The right (monarchy, aristocratic elites, plutocratic and theocratic rule, dictators) all fear the left seeking to change the foundations of governance as potential democratic reform. Today, all Communist governments are authoritarian and governed as dictatorships. Regardless of their political origins to overturn monarchy and colonialism.

Many times, membership in left-wing movements against social injustices can be quite diverse and even absolute—rigid, demanding, and aggressive. These movements have all the required elements to attract the absolute-minded—strong leadership, group identity and conformity, narrow ideological focus and purpose that reflects their own grievances and revenge motives, provides direction and focus for their fears and anxieties, etc. They take on a "we" against the world attitude, as exampled by the environmental movement. Absolutism is a mindset before it is a political expression. It simply requires a great deal more to organize the left to violence than it does the right. In fact, the thresholds are remarkably divergent despite efforts to suggest they are the same. The bandwidth of absolute-mindedness is neither as broad nor as deep on the left as it is on the right. On the left, a fear can arise they are being denied the future, while on the right resides a fear the past is being taken from them.

Authoritarianism versus Conservatism

There is an ongoing academic debate, of no consequence as far as I can discern, as to whether or not *authoritarianism* and *conservatism* are two separate states of mind. For the record, the theory of *absolute-mindedness* does not offer a significant distinction between them, except as a matter of degrees along a continuum. But there is one, and it should be noted. If there is a distinction to be made, it is this. The conservative mind likely came from family circumstances that emphasized order and discipline but with greater emotional connectedness. Life proceeded in a more orderly fashion with less neglect and abuse. While the more authoritarian experienced greater disruption in emotional bonding that was negatively reinforced throughout infancy, childhood, adolescence, and adulthood.

An example of the distinction between authoritarianism and conservatism took place in Nazi Germany as Hitler rose to power in the 1920s. The Nazis deployed the SA (Sturmabteilung) or "brownshirts," a paramilitary organization primarily derived from the lower classes, utilizing thuggery, intimidation, and violence against political opposition. The architects of this violence, however, were conservatives (and many just went along). By the 1930s, a more middle-class SS (or Schutzstaffel) took command. They were more socially connected, better educated, becoming the administrators and theorists of Nazism and better able to administrate the "Final Solution."

Perhaps an analogy closer to home would be the 2021 Capitol riot, and before that, militia groups, neo-Nazis, and White supremacists marching in the streets—more absolute-minded. But Trump and the Republican leadership were instrumental in fomenting this violence and dog-whistling their base for a show of violence—the conservative mind. Now can you be conservative and not support an authoritarian agenda? Absolutely! Can you be authoritarian and not support a conservative agenda? By all means. Because the key is always the press of personal circumstances and the degree of disorder and disruption experienced. Depending on the circumstances, these two groups exist on an overlapping continuum that no one knows how to measure. Only time and circumstance reveal the extent to which these two states of mind are interconnected.

But whether conservative or authoritarian, both generally operate with varying degrees of distorted reality testing, bending it to fit their distrust. And this all plays out in many confusing ways. Conservative Supreme Court justices sit back and implement a conservative agenda based on "originalist" interpretations of the Constitutional framers. They are, of course, confabulating a reenactment fantasy by believing they are channeling the Founding Fathers 250 years later, as if the world has not changed. This is like Civil War reenactment battles, except they have the good sense not to use live ammunition. President Ronald Reagan and Republicans instituted economic policies based on a completely made-up economic theory called the "Laffer Curve" and "trickle down economics," all fabricated from nonsense. Federal Reserve Chair Alan Greenspan believed that the market was self-correcting in absolute terms. Yet another confabulated notion he later acknowledged in his autobiography was partially based on the writings of novelist Ayn Rand (where all sound economic theory derives from).

Republican Congressmen are perfectly comfortable denying health care benefits to millions of people, especially those who are poor because they don't want or need them. Evangelical ministers preach that religion is under assault because they have been frustrated legislating Christian sharia-style laws in the US and dictating morality to the country at large. So much for the separation of church and state that the Founding Fathers enshrined in the Constitution. The conservative mind resides within an intellectual invisibility cloak of false premises and reasoning, continually grappling with distortions in their reality testing by contriving concepts to fit their beliefs. And to be clear, this is different from simply having a conservative orientation. The conservative mind functions around bending reality to fit its distrust, while a conservative person can venerate the past and embrace change in gradual terms without self-deception or distorting reality, but with a rational calculation that all change is not necessarily for the general good and that costs need to be calculated and accounted for. Going forward slowly may be a wise alternative in many, if not most, circumstances. So let's keep this distinction in mind here.

In a true crisis, the conservative-minded and the authoritarian enable one another, and that is what needs to be understood. One is implementing violence in the streets; the other is assaulting democratic norms in the halls of government in the name of principle. And it is important to understand that exceptions abound to all these generalizations and may even be the rule in many instances. But not to see the current Republican Party, from the top down, as a violent threat to our democratic institutions, as it abandons conservative doctrine, would be naïve and self-harming, not all Republicans and not all conservatives. And all those who quietly stand by in resignation are as responsible as those who take to the streets or filibuster legislation. (We should not let the academic distinction between conservatism and authoritarianism trouble us.)

Perhaps the best way to understand the distinction between the conservative-minded and the authoritarian is the authoritarian are prone to conspiracies that are, for practical purposes, delusional (e.g., Democratic Party leaders are part of a satanic child pedophile ring). The conservative-minded are more prone to confabulating a narrative reality that better fits their distrust (claiming a "deep state" conspiracy or COVID-19 hoax). The reality testing of the authoritarian and conservative-minded are triggered under the right circumstances by their underlying distrust. And at times, it is not possible to distinguish the difference between them. When Republican members of Congress assert that a rogue Italian general commandeered a satellite and used it to switch votes in electronic voting machines, one is now down the same rabbit hole, whether conservative-minded or authoritarian.

Letter to Editor of *Foreign Affairs* (March 4, 2021)

A New Conservatism by Oren Cass advocates for a new "conservative coalition" that would appeal to a wider range of voters. I also have watched journalist David Brooks struggle with this for years. In the Republican lexicon, they are generally labeled RINOs. As he puts forward his big "C" vision, one must worry for Cass's safety at a CPAC or RNC convention. Besides, what he advocates already entirely exists. First, if Edmund Burke were alive today, he likely would have voted for Biden, a "gradualist" who supports community over fractured identity politics of the left. Biden is the voice of the Conservatism advocated by Cass. And the authentic voice of modern conservatism is democratic socialism in Northern Europe. Here the community is deeply supported as a basis for healthy identity formation. The individual is celebrated in a meritocratic fashion and the market respected, but its excesses are blunted for the general good.

The reality is, conservatism is no longer relevant to the future of America. It is mostly hawkish foreign policy and a plutocratic economic and political agenda, with "bread and circuses" for the masses (infrastructure investment). It has nothing to define itself except for holding onto political power by exploiting racial and class divisions to assure the sanctity of wealth creation while forever distorting democratic norms to assure it. The conservative mind is fully revealed for what it is with Trumpism—rambling, broken, and self-destructive, drunken on conspiracy theories and empty rhetoric, always bending the knee to its authoritarian origins. We may not be at the end of history, but we are certainly at the end of an aging and irrelevant Republican conservatism.

Is There an Authoritarian Personality?

Given we have taken this turn toward academic distinctions, one other area of academic pursuit should be addressed. And that is the continuing efforts to create a psychological measure that would identify the authoritarian personality. The earliest effort was by Theodor Adorno and his development of the F-Scale in the 1950s (F stood for fascist). Subsequently, there have been more recent efforts to improve this research (e.g., Altemeyer's *Right-Wing Authoritarianism Scale*). Still, nothing substantial has come of this through Altemeyer's extensive use of surveys, questionnaires, and polling/voting data. There have also been efforts to examine personality traits underlying political behavior, including a prominent psychological measure of personality called the "Five-Factor Model" (openness, conscientiousness, extraversion, agreeableness, and emotional stability). Attempts have been made at utilizing standardized psychological testing (MMPI/MCMI) with limited success. And more narrowly are measures of specific social dynamics (dominance, political intolerance, belief in certain knowledge, confirmatory thinking, need for closure, conspiracy minded, etc.). And if you are wondering, there are no diagnostic categories or clustering of symptoms identifiable within the *Diagnostic and Statistical Manual of Mental Disorder* (DSM-5) that substantiate the concept of an authoritarian personality.

So what's the problem? Here it is in a nutshell. Absolute-mindedness is not a psychological abnormality or condition. It is not a personality type but a state of being around which identity is formed. When trust is disturbed, the individual and their social reality are altered, and in the face of stressors, the loss of trust is reconstituted through belief in a stable and predictable environment (making resistance to change endemic). It is not pathogenic but the result of human evolution. It is, in fact, normal. The second major problem is that most research indicates absolutism derives from early life experiences, which means it is rarely available to be studied on a relevant scale. But also, the only way to confirm its early origins would be longitudinal studies, which seldom happen given the academic need to publish and the inordinate amount of time and cost involved. But none of these matters because inevitably, the sample sizes are always limited in size and of marginal predictive value. (It should be noted that developmental and longitudinal studies on the impact of attachment disruption have been ongoing and are a basis for the theory of absolute-mindedness put forward here.)

Perhaps the biggest hurdle in assessing for a personality type is that the key factor at play here is what's termed "conditions of normative threat," triggering a uniquely authoritarian response. This means, for example, sampling the Capitol rioters and the White supremacists marching in Charlottesville both before and after these events. And if there are no triggering events, this entire process lies fallow. It takes two to dance here. It is not just the underlying personality factors but environmental cues and triggers. To conduct this research on a scale that would be reliable and valid is challenging. You eventually ask yourself, "What's the point?" Desperate people act desperately. What constitutes desperation and what triggers it has wide latitude, it turns out. And this is true for all of us.

A review of the past seventy years of academic research on the topics of conservatism and authoritarianism is condensed below. And in all candidness, it does not fully detail the range and complexity of this research. It primarily outlines the basics. And what makes this research particularly confusing, beyond the depth of jargon, is the overlapping use of terms and theories of origin and causation, offering mostly vague distinctions that are challenging to parse. Perhaps the best summary is by Jost et al. (2003): "People adopt ideological belief systems to satisfy their psychological needs and motives for order, structure and closure" and the avoidance of *uncertainty* and *threat*.

As one surveys the chart below, it's important to understand how unlikely it is any one individual encompasses all these characteristics. This is a collective picture, and each factor resides along a continuum of expression. And the mix and match are exponential and beyond measurement in a large population of citizens, except as generalities.

The Social Psychology of the Conservative Mind

Early Childhood Development
Harsh, demanding, and punitive
Focus on discipline over empathy
Avoidance of negative outcomes
Absent emotional warmth
Expression of authoritarian values and ideas

Prediction and Control
Lack integrative cognitive complexity/flexibility
Seek cognitive closure to avoid confusion and uncertainty
Prevention-oriented for security and stability
Decreased openness to experience
Avoidant of change, disruption, and ambiguity
Closed-minded, rigid dogmatic thinking, and moral rigidity

Response to Change
World as threatening and dangerous
Respond with fear and aggression
Intolerant of ambiguity and uncertainty
Overly responsive to negative messaging
Express high levels of pessimism and contempt
Seek to reduce negative emotional states
Beliefs mitigate feelings of fear and threat

Adaptive Resistance
Security seeking as opposed to change seeking
Seek order and structure to avoid uncertainty
Prioritize conformity, tradition, and security
Adhere to social convention to satisfy needs and values
Preserve existing hierarchies of status, power, and wealth
Engage in group-based social dominance
Submissive idealization of authority figures

Chapter 8

Virtue-Thought on the Left

There is no swifter route to the corruption of thought
than through the corruption of language.

—George Orwell, *1984*

On the political left, there exists a powerful expression of absoluteness dedicated to improving the flawed human character. Here, guilt is the primary driver of their virtue-seeking absolutism rather than shame. Unable to countenance or dispute their striving for virtue, they act as thought police to absolve themselves from past errors in their thinking. This is a powerful impulse to right all wrongs, both individually and collectively, confusing righteousness with being right. The desire is to be on the right side of history and reform the disputers, doubters, and less virtuous and to find absolution for their guilt. In Freudian terms, they are being squeezed by the superego, still hoping to become a more perfect child. With virtue as the goal, this faction on the left is pretty much intolerant of anyone disputing their premises.

In recent years, researchers have begun to explore whether authoritarianism transits the political right-left continuum. But by focusing on similarities and the legacy of fascism and totalitarianism, they may have missed the differences. And while the right is more prone to paranoid and conspiratorial authoritarian memes, the left is no stranger to absolutism. On the left, there is a substrate of belief that is driven by an idealism that envisions a more perfect world, one that is more pristine with visions of Gaia. Here, everyone gets along. The world is a safer and more equitable place, and no one ever has to see how pit vipers are fed. And while absolutism on the left is often sheltered in its naivete, it is not always right in the face of reality.

The arrival of virtue-thought or what many call *wokeness* was the inevitable consequence of the European Enlightenment and our liberated contemporary mindset. In the turbulence of daily life, many formally sheltered individuals are now seeking temporal emotional relief in self-righteous indignation. At last, freed from the psychologically suppressive and the politically repressive, arose the triumphant "me." Consequently, the internet and social media have lit many Gen Z and millennials into a smoldering dumpster fire. In academic terms, we are living in the postmodern zombie world of *critical theory*. And yes, that's as bad as it sounds. Think of it this way. Each of us resides in a snow globe, and no two globes are exactly alike. Each globe has its own inner reality. This is a private snow world, and whoever or whatever shakes our globe is responsible for how the snow settles. Here there is only personal truth—my hurt, my pain, my discomfort. What I say and feel is the only truth in the world. And anyone who disturbs my globe is oppressive, unthoughtful, and indifferent to how I feel. Each time someone offends or ignores you, they are shaking your snow globe and obliterating you again and again in an assertion of political power.

Underlying this state of mind is a modern relativism, one that attempts to see past our social pretenses and to discover the oppressive power dynamic that lies behind our social facades. We are now confronted with the individual's subjective experience as defining of reality, or I feel therefore I am. This is quite the opposite of a thousand years ago when people were all suppressed/repressed and how one felt was mostly irrelevant to social life. Now, however, how one feels overrides the rational and objective and has become the eternal source of one's personal truth, as opposed to a universally shared one. The truth is what each of us says it is and derives from how each of us experiences it. In this reality, all relationships are brokered by the exercise of hidden power, the genesis of oppression. This mindset is intolerant of debate, discussion, or disagreement, which is a power differential between people that serves to deny the other's experience by shaking their snow globe.

One unanswered question in all of this is: Are all feelings real and true, or are there false feelings and emotions in the same way that we confabulate false beliefs, misbeliefs, and conspiracies? Are we capable of emotionally overreacting, emotionally misunderstanding in ways that disrupt our inner and social worlds? Do we default to our emotions because we are unable to modulate and understand them better? Have our emotions been distorted by a subjective filter through which we interact and understand the world, the detritus of past experiences that have little or nothing to do with the present? This is life as posttraumatic stress disorder. In the same way we have all experienced or seen someone raging out of control, some people are ragingly oversensitive and inevitably feel dismissed and ignored? Now residing in a social media contagion of entitlement (cancel culture), they have become enthralled with outing the indifferent and the supposedly oppressive while internet anonymity empowers their hysteria to new heights.

Thoughtcrime

Eric Blair, born in India in 1903 to English parents, would later take on the pseudonym George Orwell and write two of the most famous novels in English literature (which is a considerable achievement when you think about it), *Animal Farm* and *1984*. Novelist, journalist, and teacher, Orwell was a penetrating observer of totalitarianism in the twentieth century. In his novel *1984*, he envisioned the totalitarian state of Oceania, ruled by a political party that sought to control people's actions by controlling their thinking with an ideologically cleansed language. Everyone was required to speak Newspeak and could not hold any thoughts that conflicted with Ingsoc (English socialism). In the official language of Newspeak, *crimethink*, *thoughtcrime*, and *wrongthink* referred to anyone who held any unacceptable political thoughts. The party sought to control the speech, actions, and thoughts of its citizens through the Thought Police, responsible for the detection, arrest, and elimination of all thoughtcrime that challenged the party's ideology. Because it was impossible to directly police every citizen, there was also Thinkpol, a two-way television technology that monitored a person's speech and behavior.

"In the end, we shall make thoughtcrime literally impossible, because there will be no words in which to express it." "We do not destroy the heretic. We convert him, we capture his inner mind, we reshape him." The ultimate goal was *crimestop*, the ability for each individual to immediately rid themselves of unwanted and incorrect political and personal thoughts, a process that would become unconscious and normal. We would each become self-censoring and unable to perceive the contradictions or illogic in any idea or decree we are required to accept. (Watch the brilliant dystopian film *Brazil* deconstruct *thoughtcrime*.)

This brings us to a recent Stanford University IT project titled "The Elimination of Harmful Language Initiative" (2023). It sought to eliminate "harmful language," deemed "racist, violent, and biased," including "disability bias, ethnic bias, ethnic slurs, gender bias, implicit bias and sexual bias" in the Stanford website and codes. The guide provided ten harmful language sections: "ableist, ageism, colonialism, culturally appropriative, gender-based, imprecise language, institutionalized racism, person-first, violent and additional considerations."

Included among the words considered harmful are *American* and *brave*. Of course, there is no point in addressing any of the reasoning behind this act of Newspeak. It is clearly an attempt to control people's thoughts by editing their language. While this is also prevalent on the right wanting to control what our children read and learn in the classroom, the left is all out on wanting to protect us against *wrongthink*. What might be most concerning here is not this list, per se, but what happens once we are all on the slippery slope of everyone wanting to eliminate language they personally consider unacceptable. *Fuck*, for example. This is modern-day book burning. There is simply no end to this until we are all silent (which may have some advantages).

"Newspeak" Now at Stanford University

Here is an annotated list of words deleted by the Stanford IT project: American, addicted, blind review or study, committed suicide, crazy, handicapped parking, mentally ill, walk-in, wheelchair bound, brave, tribe, freshman, he, she, ladies, you guys, Hispanic, Indian summer, peanut gallery, straight, survivor, thug, victim, black mark, black box, blacklisted, brown bag, gangbusters, grandfather, master, red team, white paper, convict, disabled person, prisoner, prostitute, abusive relationship, rule of thumb, war room, African American, long time no see, normal person, and process. (I am not sure why they didn't decolonize *white* as a term of abuse—Snow White, white Christmas, White power. But I lament that the staff at Stanford will never be able to quote Snoop Dogg in an email: "Fo shizzle, my nizzle.")

Virtue Seeking

The mass hysteria infecting the internet is now on full display when it comes to virtue seeking. It has become the arbiter of who you are, and in many instances, you become defined by your online proclamations and endorsements as evidence of incorrect thought. It amplifies the strongest emotions and organizes the weakest thinking. Everything you have ever written or uttered online can become a damning measure of your character. Today, having your online brand is being supplanted by being branded for not being woke sensitive. Ask the Google software engineer who was let go after expressing his concerns about affirmative actions and hiring quota practices. He also expressed his belief that women, in general, are not as adept (at least today) at programming as men, mistakenly believing he was starring in an episode of *Silicon Valley*. Wrong! Or comedian Dave Chappelle offering humorous commentary about the demands and expectations of the transgender community. Whether they were right or wrong or somewhere in between, there was no room for a public hearing. It turns out that this is settled virtue. And just to be clear, there's an overwhelming amount of settled virtue these days as we approach *crimestop*.

Shaken, Not Stirred

James Bond spy novels are undergoing a "sensitivity review" to remove offensive language (*Time*, 3/13/23). Does this mean goodbye to the wonderous femme fatales—Pussy Galore, Xenia Onatopp, Honey Rider, Mary Goodnight, Strawberry Fields, Holly Goodhead, and all the double entendres that made these films endlessly fun for earlier generations?

It appears the internet has hardwired us to a new level of sensitivity to the world around us. We are going down an anthill that is a sensitivity gauntlet of 7.5 billion people. Somewhere, someone will be unhappy and blame someone for whatever, which is likely to happen a few hundred million times a day. Some of us will be able to walk this tightrope better than others. But just remember, there is no herd immunity here. Just because you finished the *American Ninja* obstacle course in record time, there is no guarantee you won't fall the next day. Very few will succeed. What could any person possibly say or do that wouldn't offend the sensitivity of someone? And if you are working hard at this, you might want to ask, "Who have I become?"

The two primary sins of the *unwoke* are being insensitive to other's feelings and making someone feel uncomfortable. Several problems arise here. It's not really possible to know what everyone feels or what might make them uncomfortable. We already have complex social guidelines for personal and private conduct bursting with reams of fine print most of us have never read. Until we get a social contract reader, similar to software that reads legal documents that upgrades daily, we will forever be ignorant of our social world. That about sums it up. We are forever operating at low temperatures in a Crock-Pot. The safer conjecture here is that we are all guilty. It is just a matter of time until we are outed then having to prove to the entire world's satisfaction that we are repentant, or until there are no more online comments. The darker subtext, of course, is the underlying reality of racial, gender, ablest prejudices and biases (and the modern-day *Scarlet Letter* of being accused of them, whether true or not).

How do we ever accept that our private self overlaps with our public self and that these two states of mind can never be fully reconciled? And that this is exponentially true with the advent of the internet. Today, the left is increasingly refusing to make this distinction, seeking to reconcile the personal with the public and "out" anyone who fails to reconcile. The so-called "failed" are labeled racist, misogynist, xenophobic, fascist, and fragile. And worst of all, unwoke and insensitive to the power they wield and the feelings of those they are harming. If college professors commit a virtue offense, they will be hounded from their job first by students and parents. Then faculty fall in line, and finally administrators pile on in fear for their jobs, all satisfied in the virtue of their correct thought and belief. There appears to be very little forgiveness or redemption here. No, every thought offender is consigned to hell, no matter how trivial the transgression. But then there are no trivial virtue offenses.

In 2022, Hamline University, a "small liberal arts college" in St. Paul, Minnesota, decided not to renew the contract of an adjunct art professor. This occurred after a number of Muslim students claimed that their faith had been offended because the professor had displayed medieval and Renaissance art depicting the Prophet Muhammad in their online art class. In the Muslim faith, depiction of Muhammad is considered, by many but not all, as blasphemous and forbidden. But here is the caveat. The professor alerted students to this in the course syllabus and offered a workaround for any student who might be offended. Further, she offered a warning that students could turn off their video feeds before she displayed the images.

But in virtue dogmatism, this was not enough. In not renewing the professor's contract, the university asserted the professor's actions were "undeniably inconsiderate, disrespectful and Islamophobic." Much to the chagrin of this university, the Council on American-Islamic Relations subsequently asserted the actions of the professor were not, in fact, Islamophobic. And in its own online attempts to address this controversy, the school's president, in administrative speak, equivocated and carefully parsed language framing the issue as academic freedom v. student rights, but never addressed why the professor's contract was not renewed. PEN America, an organization dedicated to artists' and writers' freedom of expression, offered that this was one of the "most egregious violations of academic freedom" it had ever witnessed. No doubt this professor will get her bag of money, after her reputation had been completely trashed in the name of virtue.

Halloween Zombies

On Halloween, your son wears a ghost costume and a neighbor, in disbelief, sees a Klan outfit. Definitely no Indian headdress or witch costume (offends Wiccans) or demons or Dracula (neighbors are conservative Christians). No fake guns anymore or being a soldier (could be reported to the police). Cowboy costumes are definitely out. And definitely no more "little princesses" with their sexualized gowns and plastic tiaras fetishizing royalty (and no, the boys are not invited). Forget anything reflecting ethnicity, race, or nationality. It's cultural appropriation. Does anyone dare dress up as a police officer?

A neighbor dressed his daughter as a construction worker and his son as batgirl until it was explained that this was reverse gender stereotyping. Another neighbor intervened and made the case for these costumes as non-cisgendered. Your daughter and son could both be nonbinary and identify with these costumes later in life and appreciate your openness. You quietly suggest everyone should go as zombies.

But as the police approach and casually inquire if you are here with your children, you point to the ghost outfit and immediately get a high five. Subsequently, you are let go at work after multiple online posts show you giving the okay sign to another parent in a MAGA hat, who playfully gives you the finger. There were also a number of anonymous online comments expressing offense at your going around as a White male, indifferent to the oppressive attitude you confidently exuded. You have declined all media interviews. Your wife is filing for a divorce, claiming she had no idea who you really are. But your kids are excited about going out with you next Halloween.

Crisis with Obvious Authority 1—School Violence

You can easily find the hidden crisis facing American public schools online, a darker tranche of what colleges and universities are submerged in. Without being able to verify any of these numbers, I am just going to assume they put us in the ballpark. It is currently estimated that there is a shortage of approximately three hundred thousand schoolteachers across the United States. And the two most common factors cited for this are low salaries and teacher burnout. But let's burrow a little deeper. Currently, 163,500 positions are being filled by teachers who are not fully certified, which means the shortage is really closer to 450,000 (or one out of every seven teachers).

Teacher surveys also indicate as many as 25 percent may leave their jobs in the future, while the norm in recent years has been 16 percent (which is remarkably high in itself). Recent national surveys also indicate that as many as 55 percent of teachers would like to leave teaching as soon as possible, and stress appears to be the key issue, with public schoolteachers reporting stress-related issues at nearly twice the rate as the general adult population, while they are three times as likely to experience symptoms of depression.

It is important to juxtapose this retention crisis with another reality facing public schools—violence. An American Psychological Association survey (2020–2021) of fifteen thousand teachers, administrators, school psychologists, and school staff reported that 43 percent of teachers said they wanted to quit, 6 percent reported being physically attacked by a student, and 10 percent said they were threatened with injury. In addition, 15 percent of administrators reported instances of physical violence, as did 18 percent of school psychologists, and 22 percent of school staff. Teachers also reported that a lack of administrative support was a secondary trauma for them (a form of administrative-induced helplessness to either address or change their circumstances).

These numbers don't begin to scratch the surface of the discipline and behavioral problems in classrooms today. In this same survey, 33 percent of teachers reported enduring verbal harassment from students. It is pretty clear that classroom order and discipline are out of control, and very little is being done about it. And there are many reasons for this. The first one is obvious, and I experienced it many years ago after discharging from the Air Force and substitute teaching for six months. At one predominantly Black high school, I was politely informed by several students that there was no point in reporting individuals misbehaving or disrupting the class. The administration was not going to do anything that would jeopardize attendance and cost them federal funding. These were young adults informing me to stop wasting my time and theirs. Eventually, to my relief, one very assertive teen girl stood up and instructed the class to "quiet down so we can learn." Which actually worked for a while.

There is a second factor affecting the lack of classroom discipline, and it is also about money. And this is the decision to mainstream kids with developmental and behavioral problems into public schools, no matter how impractical and disruptive. This problem was recently captured on video footage taken at a Florida high school (February 21, 2023), when a six-foot-six-inch, 270 pound, seventeen-year-old male student with special needs knocked down and punched a female teacher's aide fifteen times until she was unconscious. On his arrest, he threatened to "kill her." The sheriff later noted "this could have been a homicide." It turns out this adolescent was allowed to attend this school despite a history of serious behavioral problems, including three prior "misdemeanor battery charges."

On January 6, 2023, a Virginia elementary schoolteacher was shot in the chest by a six-year-old student in her class. She subsequently underwent four surgeries and later filed a $40 million lawsuit against school officials for gross negligence. Here is the kicker. Two days earlier, the same student had grabbed the teacher's cell phone and smashed it to the ground, for which he received a one-day suspension. However, a year earlier, he had "strangled and choked" his kindergarten teacher. Plus, there were numerous instances of aggression toward other students and school staff, often requiring a parent or guardian to be present in the classroom.

While the mother was not present on the day of the shooting, her gun was. And yes, the school board subsequently installed metal detectors throughout the district and fired the school superintendent. Currently, there appears to be only two options for teachers and school staff, and that is to "pat or pack," as in pat down students or self-carry firearms (maybe children should wear Kevlar vests and helmets with popular anime logos and Winnie the Pooh characters). School security is a politically broken process that is always late to the catastrophe. But let's look on the bright side. After every school district in the country (13,452) suffers a violent incident, many of them will become more secure.

Incidents of school violence are not only tragedies without real foresight by the left or right but are also a grievous message of how our one-size-fits-all school experience is demoralizing students and teachers. These incidents appear to be exceptional for their violence, and most of us grew up never experiencing or encountering anything like them. The time has come to reenvision K–12 as something different from educational bootcamps for everyone. Here is an important question: What are the practical alternatives to today's educational model?

The driving force behind rising school violence has two parts. One is what is taking place in homes, and the other is the feckless exercise of authority by school administrators. In this latter instance, we have a shame parade of middle management decision-makers. They are afraid of angry parents, school board politics, lawsuits, and a reduced revenue stream, but all under the guise of a woke consciousness mindful of the terrible abuses inherent in the exercise of authority. And for this, they sacrifice teachers and students.

Case in point: two high school administrators in Denver were shot and wounded by a seventeen-year-old student on March 22, 2023. The student committed suicide a few hours later. Here is the "rest of the story." Before this, the student had been placed in a school "safety plan" after being arrested two years earlier for possession of a "ghost gun" (one without a serial number) and placed on probation for a weapons charge. As a result, he was required to be "patted down" for weapons each day he attended school. But there is more to this backstory. Armed security had been banned from Denver's high schools after the death of George Floyd in 2020. The school board reasoned that the death of Floyd was because of systemic racism and that school security officers were disproportionately "criminalizing students of color."

After this tragic event, the school board voted to "temporarily" suspend the ban on armed security in its school. So what is it? If security is a rational requirement, why is it only being temporarily implemented? What is the rational basis for a temporary school policy that is racist by their definition? Either security is a necessity or it's not. Let's be honest, the school board is not capable of predicting the next violent incident in its schools. It looks like they are engaging in a media campaign to demonstrate they are concerned until most people forget what happened. And then they can lean back in their upgraded desk chairs and reinstitute the security ban until the next incident. This is not dissimilar to a local branch of a national bank near my home. I always know when it has been robbed because a security guard suddenly appears and paces about for six months. Then for some unknown reason, just as I have learned his name and he recognizes me, he disappears, as if the threat no longer exists. Thank goodness, it was just a six-month threat. This disappearing bank security is the same logic being used by the Denver school board.

This is what authority looks like in educational settings that are in continuing crisis, a confused tangle of half measures in the desperate hope they reconcile with reality. But here again, denial gnawed away inside their snow globes. During this same school year, ten guns had been seized from Denver school students, while eight hundred students had undergone threat assessment. Perhaps most egregiously, a middle school principal, despite his many pleas to expel a student, was required by the district to pat down a student charged with first-degree murder and the illegal discharge of a weapon. The board reasoned that the student couldn't be expelled because his offenses didn't take place on school grounds! By this logic, they would hire a teacher because their sexual relationship with a student took place off campus. (Having had a son who attended an academically exceptional high school, I could never fully express my gratitude and relief that an armed police officer was present on campus every day. Of course, this was all years ago, before school districts decided they didn't like the way the numbers were trending).

In the end, administrators are afraid to act with authority because of the blowback that comes their way. Authority is power, and power is biased, hurtful, and arbitrary when there are so many more practical alternatives, like sending teachers into retirement, watching them quit in fear and disgust, or capping college teacher education programs because no one in their right mind wants to be a teacher today. Inevitably, there are student protests and the humiliation that comes with an online post becoming newsworthy, one portraying the school administrator as a biased power monster living in another decade, particularly when it comes to dress codes.

The Pious Weight of Doing Good

The administrative weight of the US Department of Education is carried on the shoulders of every school administrator in the United States, as if bias and bigotry toward the student with disabilities is rampant in school districts across the nation. Nothing better captures this pious mandate than the department's latest guidelines (2022) titled "New Guidance Helps Schools Support Students with Disabilities and Avoid Discriminatory Uses of Discipline." To quote:

> Helps public elementary and secondary schools fulfill their responsibilities to meet the needs of students with disabilities and avoid the discriminatory use of student discipline. These newly released resources are the most comprehensive guidance on the civil rights of students with disabilities concerning student discipline.

Let's get to the core of this document: "Too often students with disabilities face harsh and exclusionary action at schools." In developing today's guidance and resources, the department drew from experience with enforcing and administering federal laws relating to students with disabilities, including section 504 and the IDEA. (It is important to note that no statistics were offered or any data outside the department. In other words, they mostly made it up based on individual cases that came to federal attention.) This is the tip of the iceberg when it comes to understanding why schools are failing to discipline students. It has slowly become an administrative minefield fraught with legal ramifications, beginning at the front end with issue of civil rights. Yes, school administrators are walking a minefield, and so are teachers and, unbeknownst to them, students.

This is not meant to be a diatribe against the need to address discrimination in schools when it comes to students with disabilities. But the elephant in the room that is not being addressed by the Department of Education is that these students appear to represent a serious disciplinary problem in the classroom. One so clearly out of control that it is being addressed at the federal level. And addressing it as a civil rights issue is irrelevant to solving it. No matter how many Individual Educational Plans are written mainstreaming students with disabilities, it is politically correct thinking running into a reality wall.

That teacher salaries are ridiculously low is not the primary issue driving teachers from the classroom. It is the lack of control and consequences in the classroom that prioritizes the disruptive individual over the class and the teacher. It is important to note that no-tolerance policies, when it comes to enforcing school disciplinary codes, often result in statistical trends that will later be characterized as biased. This interpretation of the data makes it easier for school administrators to default to a systemic problem they can't do anything about. For example, racism, than having to be confronted by parents coming at them like a pack of rabid wolverines for trying to discipline their child. These same parents are also one of the reasons bullying is out of control in many schools. The quiet child who is being bullied can be easily ignored while the bully is misunderstood. Better for one child to commit suicide than for the school to acknowledge it has a problem exercising authority. This, of course, is not the school policy but how it often turns out to be. In this scenario, it's always a tragic individual circumstance and not a system-wide failure by the school district.

It is crazy, but the one area of discussion no one wants to address is that disorder in public schools begins with the disorder at home. While schools can't solve this problem, they can do a better job of containing it by acknowledging it and responding to it as a serious problem rather than treating it as if it's a foreboding career blocker. Schools are being tasked with solving societal problems they are ill-equipped for. And schoolteachers are speaking up by leaving the profession. This all starts with the left's naïve and fanciful assumption that "it's a beautiful day in the neighborhood," no matter how much disorder and violence permeates our schools. Schools have evolved into an environment where discipline is considered corrupting and where "equitable" and "inclusive learning spaces" are the answers to every problem. Sometimes a "positive relationship" and "redirection" require setting clear limits with real consequences, or one just becomes an enabler of the underlying problem.

Any student that requires a personal aide or guardian in the classroom, a safety plan, or has to be patted down belongs in a specialized program and not in a public school classroom. And no, not everyone is going to be happy that many individual problems require specialized attention. But this is better for the child and the school in the long run. Given the rising level of school violence across the nation, the use of metal detectors, restricted campus egress and ingress, no-tolerance policies, and the presence of security officers are no longer outrageous but represent a rational response to our violent culture. That is how the proper exercise of authority works—order and discipline are the foundation of all functioning communities.

Crisis with Obvious Authority 2—School Suspensions

A report by *Child Trends* (2021) analyzing the use of out-of-school suspensions from 2011 to 2012 and 2017 to 2018 for grades K–12 offered this finding: While schools' reliance on out-of-school suspensions continues to decrease, Black students and students with disabilities were twice as likely to be suspended as their White and Hispanic peers. And here is the key caveat:

> Previous research has found that nearly half of Black-White disparities in exclusionary discipline can be explained by the differential treatment of Black and White students within the same school.

This research finding is frequently cited to demonstrate overt racism in our educational system. The US Department of Education also references it in its guidelines for supporting students with disabilities and avoiding discriminatory use of discipline in schools. But is it true? The research supporting this idea leads back to "one" study, "Unpacking the Drivers of Racial Disparities in School Suspension and Expulsion" by Owns and McLanahan (2020).

Let's start at the beginning. This study leads off with an objective finding: Research shows that Black students are 3.2 times more likely to be suspended/expelled from school than White students, while Native American students are 2.0 times, and Hispanic students 1.3 times. So what accounts for this disparity? Two sociologists, Owens and McLanahan, report that there is a 21 percentage-point racial gap in the suspension of Black students (28 percent versus White students, 7 percent), ages five to nine, in inner-city schools. In effect, four Black students are suspended for each White student. Further, half the difference (46 percent) between Black and White students being suspended could be accounted for by what they term "differential treatment." They make the case that bias by school principals accounts for half the variance. In other words, without this bias, the ratio of suspensions would be closer to 2:1 rather than 4:1.

However, these findings are highly qualified by their research review:

1. There was no difference between "well-behaved" Black and White students.
2. Black students' behavior worsens more than White students' behavior between ages five and nine.
3. Differences in school's racial and socioeconomic composition account for a large share of the racial gap in suspension.
4. Black students may have less access to resources like supportive parents, social-emotional learning opportunities, and rigorous and engaging instruction.

But the key detail from this research is their qualifying statement:

> Omitted variables from our inability to link suspension to a particular infraction and thus to determine whether Black and White children are differentially suspended for the same infraction.

In effect, this means they found nothing to support their assertion that there was a differential effect between Black and White students when it came to suspension/expulsion. They were unable to directly demonstrate that Black and White students were treated differently in the same school for the same infraction. In my opinion, they used considerable statistical sleight of hand to demonstrate bias on the part of school principals.

The researchers are candid in acknowledging the limitations of this study, noting they could not distinguish between "in-school suspensions" and "out-of-school" suspensions. Let's be candid, there is a gaping difference between these two disciplinary measures, rendering this research irrelevant in distinguishing the significance of discipline given Black versus White students. Adding to a limited chain of evidence was their inability to account for each student's history of suspension or discipline, which could help explain why students were expelled/suspended. They also offered this statistic: nationally, only

0.1 percent of students are expelled/suspended, which means that in their total sample population of 856 students across 352 schools, none may have been suspended. And if two students were suspended, it's unlikely they attended the same school, were in the same grade, or had similar infractions. In fact, only 35 percent of their sample included Black and White children in the same "inner-city" school. Essentially, they were comparing apples to oranges.

In addition, they noted that their research results were not generalizable to suburban and rural schools. And perhaps most remarkably, they relied on the self-report of students as to whether or not they had ever been suspended (children between the ages of five and nine) and not the available record. Given all these limitations, it is difficult to place a great deal of confidence in their findings, let alone use this research to guide federal educational policy.

They also expend considerable effort in questioning research that did not support their findings. In one instance, they appear to downplay research indicating that racial variations in rates of suspension are because of difference in student behavior, such as "rule-breaking and aggression, inability to pay attention, and inability to get along with peers and teachers." In response, they offer a vague refutation premised on how suspensions are preconditioned by a pattern of disciplinary referrals to the principal's office.

Looking deeper into the "office referral" problem, one finds an entire academic industry advising educators that the problem is the teacher and not the student. For example, "if an African American student 'talks back' or 'mouths off' to a teacher, the teacher may interpret this behavior as completely disrespectful and intolerable. The student may be behaving this way because of peer pressure, not wanting friends to see him or her as weak." This same logic goes on to add, "Teachers and students do not ascribe the same meaning and intentions for the student's behavior" (no shit). The above quotes are from "Why Are Students of Color [Still] Punished More Severely and Frequently Than White Students?" (*Urban Education* by Sage Publishing).

Students disrupting a class and rudely and disrespectfully talking back to the teacher are being cast as the new normal. Teachers are being advised to get used to it and stop referring these students to the principal's office, which is harmful to the student (this latter fact is true in that mounting office referrals may lead to suspension). What is not evidenced in this logic is how challenging this behavior can be if a teacher is sworn at, angrily challenged, or subtly threatened, not to mention how much class time is taken attending to these disruptions. And does tolerating this behavior encourage more of it or cause it to escalate? (Let's get real. Children and teenagers who cannot exhibit self-control and respectfully interact with their teacher don't belong in a classroom. Now what? Let their internal chaos rule the school day?)

Learning is a disciplined activity. If a student feels threatened (inadequate or insecure) by the learning process, the best way out for them is to disrupt it (proving to his or her peers they have no fear) and get referred to the office or suspended (a badge of honor). If he or she is bored or indifferent, then disrupting the process often becomes the goal. Problem solved. Stay tuned. (What we require is an option to our current one-size-fits-all educational model. Education is too passive and abstract for far too many young men who require more direct and active hands-on learning experiences. One might go so far as to describe grades K–12 as anti-male.)

In an effort to add validity to their research, our trepid researchers indicate that "laboratory experiments" present the strongest evidence for their findings. In other words, not use real-world data or even their own study. I would characterize their findings as unproven. In my humble opinion, they were unable to account for too many variables to offer a conclusive result regarding the differential suspension of Black students. Yet this research is guiding federal and state educational policies across the country because it fits a preconceived notion for the left as to the underlying problem (racism).

The cascading failure of social and economic policy in the United States is now being blamed on principals and teachers. Let's be blunt. What no one wants to acknowledge is the possibility that Black students are less adaptive to school for a variety of already acknowledged reasons and that this is reflected in more severe disciplinary problems and not prejudice. In effect, there may be different structural and behavioral factors accounting for the difference between Black and White students when it comes to school disciplinary rates of suspension.

I am not trying to make the case that there is no bias operating in our educational system, as many parents and students can attest to. Only that research has not demonstrated it in the matter of suspensions. And future research may support this idea, but if I had to gather my educational resources, I would focus on supporting Black families and communities and spend less time investigating school principals.

Zero-tolerance policies in low-income school districts are an empty, highly punitive solution with potentially serious long-term consequences. But searching for an alternative to this by trying to uncover covert racism is an equally empty solution. More likely, the answer lies in finding alternatives to our conventional educational model that does not work for many of these students. While some of them are beyond the reach of education, most would benefit from positive alternatives. But asking teachers to bear the brunt of this is beyond absurd and well above their pay grade.

There is a prominent discussion on the academic left about *decolonizing* education in America. But when one wades into this research on racism in education, there is only one logical conclusion that can be reached. In a perfect educational world, schoolchildren would be separated by race, ethnicity, and gender and only taught by teachers who reflect their heritage. For instance, a Black female student would only be in a school with other Black female students, with a Black female principal and Black female teachers. And similar segregation for boys by race, gender, and ethnicity. Let's be clear, this research does not advocate this, but their skewed findings and often fragile logic seem to support this unstated conclusion. Given the left's clear pessimism for deracializing White America, per critical race theory, what options really remain except for a segregated model of education? In this model, every student is better understood and appreciated and not subjected to the harmful racism of White teachers and principals. More to the point, education could finally escape its White, racist, and Eurocentric origins. The dilemma here, of course, is there is no clear alternative, given the Western origins of public education as a tried-and-true model that has been adopted worldwide.

A Young Man's Anecdotal Experiences

Getting out of the Air Force with a master's degree in educational psychology and just before starting a PhD program in clinical psychology, I briefly substituted as a teacher at three high schools in Shreveport, Louisiana—one upper-income, one middle-income, and one that was primarily in the Black community. The challenges around simple order in the classroom and casual challenges to authority were exponentially more blatant in the high school in the Black community. After one day, it was clear to me that I had no intention of returning. The classroom felt less about education and more about getting through the day without incident. The saddest part was seeing how many students were there to learn and the underlying classroom tension they experienced every day. There was no evidence of this challenge in any serious form in the other two high schools.

I generally support a no-tolerance policy in schools that benefit students who are there to learn. But we also require an alternative beyond suspending/expelling the many students who are struggling to conform. Really, there are lots of ways to learn that are not evident in our schools. (I highly recommend the critical work on education by Postman and Weingartner, *Teaching as a Subversive Activity*.)

The Promise to Undue History "Forty Acres and a Mule"

In 2020, the San Francisco Board of Supervisors appointed the African American Reparations Advisory Committee to help redress the legacy of racism and slavery in the United States and, in particular, "institutional, city-sanctioned harm to African American communities." The committee initially proposed that each eligible Black resident be awarded $5 million, a guaranteed annual income of $97,000 for 250 years, personal debt elimination, and converted public housing turned into condos and sold to each eligible family for $1. It is estimated that about fifty thousand Black people currently reside in San Francisco. And by some estimates, these proposed reparations would cost each San Francisco household $600,000 (Hoover Institute). The total cost could be as much as $800 billion. As of this date, no one knows who qualifies, what form the reparations would take, what the total cost would be, or how they would be financed. The committee's final report is due out in June 2023.

The Left's Reparations IOU Note

We can assume it wasn't a coincidence that California Governor Gavin Newsom also decided it would be politically savvy to appoint a state reparations task force in 2020: To consider the compensatory case for the historical injustices experienced by California's Black community. Three years later, in 2023, the task force recommended $1.2 million for each slave descendant, with an estimated total cost of $800 billion. To put this in perspective, the annual California budget is $296.9 billion.

And in a complete shock to everyone in the Democratic establishment, the governor rejected this proposal as well as all other recommendations for financial compensation (no mention of mules, however). When asked about this, cynical political insiders speculated his bid to run for the presidency in 2024 was disrupted when Biden decided to run for a second term. Yet another political miscalculation by the left to pay off their constituent base with a fairy tale. (Wisely, Newsom didn't offer to fly Black Californians to NYC, Chicago, or Boston with one-way tickets.)

On the federal side, in 1989, House Resolution 40 proposed that Congress make reparations to descendants of slaves. To ensure this resolution died in committee and never made it to the floor, it took the time to calculate the value of cotton harvested by Black people as slaves. By some estimates, this resolution could cost as much as $14 trillion. Enough said! Thirty-five years after the fact, we can all feel confident that this money thing is never going to happen. It is a leftist virtue trope to make themselves feel better.

Here is what I don't understand. Why not offer reparations in a form that matters right now and on which a consensus can be built? How about free health care, college tuition reimbursement, low mortgage loan rates, or early qualification for Social Security? Why is the left always pretending to calculate the ginormous historical cost of injustice when many low-income Black families could probably use some tangible assistance right now?

The idea of reparations for the African American community has been floating about the country since the end of the Civil War when the federal government promised newly freed slaves forty acres and a mule (which did not happen). More recently, the cities of Boston, Chicago, New York, Detroit, and Washington, DC, have reviewed how to atone for the historical injustices against African Americans. But a survey by the Pew Research Center (2021) reports that 68 percent of Americans oppose reparations, and that pretty much assures reparations will not occur on a significant scale in the United States.

Now the pushback to reparations has many counterarguments. The primary one is that the cost is exorbitant and unaffordable, given all the social issues we need to address. But who exactly is going to pay for them will have to be kept mysterious because no one wants to, not even those who support the idea. Many point out the absurdity of California paying reparations when it has no history of slavery, so the scale of the proposed reparations makes no sense. Others make the case that their immigration history postdates slavery, and that they do not carry any historical burden of slavery or racism and do not owe Black Americans anything except respect.

Pundits on the right are already arguing that the idea of reparations furthers the indoctrination of Black people as inferior and dependent. Adding that reparations are a cynical political manipulation that is never going to happen, or what has been termed virtue signaling, whereby pretending to care is apparently better than not caring at all, even if they pose serious consequences going forward. Some speculate violence rippling across the country by those who support reparations and didn't receive them, but also by those who oppose them. A Black person in Chicago, Detroit, or DC might not understand how a few people in San Francisco could get so much while they got nothing.

But beyond this chatter, it is also evident that many Black people have thrived despite this legacy, so offering a simple and broad categorical solution is more foolish than restorative. Having to decide who receives reparations poses many unknown questions about fairness. For example, who is Black or how Black could set off contested debates not unlike determining tribal affiliation. There might be two tiers of reparations, one for the legacy of racism and one for the legacy of slavery. Does a family of five each get separate reparations? It will get crazy. And many would argue that the juice is not worth the squeeze for the country as a whole.

Besides, any effort to distribute reparations would likely send the right and the militia movement into hyperdrive and further raise the potential for violence across the country. Some have made the case that reparations were already paid by the nation 370,000 Union casualties during the Civil War. While others note that the Southern slave states never paid Civil War reparations. (I think we can forget this one.)

But where does the arc of historical justice end on the question of reparations? The history of the world has been largely written in the violent and oppressive subjugation of peoples. Shouldn't the nations that traded in slavery and brought slaves to the New World also chip in? And what about the African tribes that enslaved other tribes and bartered them into the slave trade? Where this all leads to is not only a very uncomfortable metric of measuring every identifiable group's historical suffering and pain and prioritizing who is to be recognized and compensated but also each group's degree of culpability. I wouldn't want to be the one making up these lists. Better to leave it to an algorithm. (Now we are starting to play God.) When one looks at all the immigrant families at our southern border, how will their pain and sacrifice be measured? And how will our accountability be taken into consideration in the future? This raises an even more uncomfortable question. What are the limits of justice?

Clearly, it is not infinite, and we have to pick and choose what is to be addressed. There is no doubt about the grievances of slavery in America, but what about the indigenous people who were here when the Europeans arrived? Shouldn't they be first in line?

A nation's primary responsibilities when it comes to being a just society have never been adequately addressed at any political level by any nation and probably never will be. The universe is too random and humans too intransigent for justice to fully prevail, whatever that is, given our struggle to agree on the abstract principles of justice. But it is satisfying when it occurs. Whether any nation, democratic or not, is required to or is even capable of addressing historical injustices is up for debate, given the unending instances of injustice and nonexistent efforts to recompense (but we appear to be beyond the eye-for-an-eye doctrine). When one looks closely, it is pretty evident that past tragedies can never be undone, and all efforts at amending their future reality have been unsatisfactory (for example, the internment of Japanese Americans or the history of Indian reservations in America). Just try to do better the next time appears to be the upper limit of most reasonable expectations. And at some point, wanting justice and the world to be "fair" becomes an infinite regression, until there is only each one of us unhappy in our unique way in an imperfect world. Now what?

Most of us would likely agree that suffering the injustices of today is generally not as grievous as suffering them two, four, or six hundred years ago. And looking about the world today, suffering injustice in the United States is not nearly as severe as in many parts of the world. What we are attempting to measure has a degree of historical, cultural, and moral relativism. And clearly, some groups in the United States suffered a historical legacy of injustice, while many others are free of this burden. But what is the factual measure of this is not as clear. While we can't change history, whether we can alter the projection of this legacy is also unknown. The real question is, what are our social justice options? Here, we run up against a moral philosophy that concerns itself with how much responsibility each individual or social group bears for their circumstances. The truth is, we lack both the will and resources to make everyone good in some apparition of a perfect society. There are too many real-time grievances out there right now to start picking and choosing winners and losers on the scale of these proposed reparations.

We are far from perfect as a political union, but something beyond further fracturing our identity and emboldening exception seeking has to hold us together. In a heterogeneous democracy, reparations are probably not a good idea, but rather one that will incite those who feel unseen and diminished by these efforts, further rupturing the body politic. Addressing injustice has to be a communal effort, or it will fail. And creating just circumstances might be a good place to start. Guaranteed health care, food equity, minimum income, affordable education, equality before the law, child support, and an assured retirement plan could be a basis for a more just America. Any justice metric beyond this opens a Pandora's box of self-interest.

There is no place on earth where life is fair and never has been. But some places are fairer than others, at least for now. A wave of pandemic or global warming could upset all notions of social justice going forward. Maybe the real outer limit is trying to do better next time rather than trying to undo the past. Sorting out who exactly is to blame and who shares in it is a potentially treacherous path forward. While tracking down and trying Nazi war criminals was satisfying, the bar has been raised. Morally, all of us have too much blood on our hands today. We better hope we are never called to testify at an International Tribunal for World Justice and Compensation.

Institutional Racism

One vision of the left's absolutism is that racism is institutionalized in American culture and that all White people are racist. This type of dogmatism almost always defies reality and typically fails to address the reality of those paying the price. Let's be honest, racism and its comorbid analogue, prejudice, exist everywhere on earth, and there is no respite from it. None. But it is good when the law and social conscience attempt to correct it. But if we are equally honest with ourselves, these efforts have limits. "White fragility" is a projection that fails to account for a two-term US president, vice president, three Supreme Court justices, chairman of the Joint Chiefs of Staff, national security adviser, two secretaries of state, attorney general, congressional representatives, senators, generals, governors, elected state representatives, mayors, and police chiefs in America who are Black. Clearly, we have to search deeper.

Absolutism on the left often fails to see how the hidden power of capitalism and money exploits everyone time and again, regardless of race or ethnicity. Yes, White privilege is real, but not every White person actually benefits from it. More often than not, the ones who would benefit most from it are privileged to begin with and do not require this added bonus and derive very little from it, which is also why they can't see it. And they exercise this privilege over everyone, regardless of race or ethnicity. And many at the bottom never rise to gain much from it. I, for one, would not want to explain to a struggling blue-collar family that they should be grateful for their White privilege when their twenty-three-year-old son, who was the first in their family to graduate college and became a second lieutenant in the Marine Corps, was killed in Iraq. White privilege is neither as deep nor all-pervasive as it is being made out to be. That doesn't mean it's not real. But we should seek a higher level of clarity and less absolutism.

Lecturing people who are struggling that they are privileged and should continue sacrificing is not going to be fruitful in any form, even if there is some vague generalized truth to it. We all have to get better at this. The effort to invoke a shame state in privileged White America will be short-lived but hopefully long enough to roll out some realistic reforms—reforms that the majority of Americans understand, believe in, and support.

The Persistence of Wildflowers

The recent commencement address (2023) at City University of New York's law school by Fatima Mousa Mohammed, a Queensborough resident by way of Yemen, appears to have confused repression (the necessary exercise of authority for social order) with oppression (the imposition of excessive order by violence and terrorism). She then proceeded to name the NYPD, the US military, Immigration and Customs Enforcement, and the prison system as "fascist." Then she asserted that the CUNY School of Law had "failed students by supporting...the city's Police Department and the country's armed forces." More broadly, she characterized the "law" as "a manifestation of White supremacy that continues to oppress and suppress people in this nation and around the world." And in a final plea, she asked for support in the "fight against capitalism" and a US government that is an "empire with a ravenous appetite for destruction and violence." (I. Keane, *New York Post*, May 29, 2023). It might be fair to say that she called out everyone except for Dr. Seuss and gravity.

Ms. Mohammed is not completely wrong, and most of us can empathize with her anger at the scale of indifference and violence committed by the modern bureaucratic state, or what Nietzsche called the "coldest of all cold monsters." However, being unable to distinguish between the violence taking place throughout the Middle East and the excessive use of force by the NYC Police Department suggests she might be idealistically impaired. Curiously, she resides in a time and place that is among the least repressive that has ever existed yet sees hidden and abusive power everywhere. Why is that? This phenomenon is a demon illusion peculiar to the left and is the heavy burden carried by the idealized child confronted by an imperfect and amoral world, or what has become clinically termed late-stage Greta Thunberg syndrome.

Unfortunately for Ms. Muhammed, she believes she lives in a nation in which the police are not suppressing crime, the military isn't preventing violent aggression against our nation, the law is not subjugating vigilante justice, prisons are not incarcerating violent criminals, and not everyone is getting to be a US citizen (which is true). Hopefully, Bernie Sanders will take her under his wing and teach her to fight the unwinnable battles with less hyperbole, more like Representative Alexandria Ocasio-Cortez.

Tomahawk Chop

The American Psychological Association, in 2005, recommended that the use of American Indian mascots and symbols, typically featured by sports teams and schools, be discontinued. The available research suggested that this practice was racist in nature and detrimental to Native peoples. And in protest of this practice, the Not in Our Honor Coalition has been seeking to bring attention to the systemic racism inherent in the use of Native images and mascots, such as wearing Native headdresses, painting faces red, and the tomahawk chop at sporting events.

It is in this context that we should consider the decision by the New York State Department of Education in 2023, ordering all public schools to stop using any Native American references, including names, mascots, logos, and imagery, without tribal approval. This is being done to create a school environment free from discrimination, harassment, bullying, and reinforcing negative stereotypes. What makes this particularly asymmetrical is that none of the Native American tribes in the state of New York (Cayuga, Oneida, Onondaga, Seneca, Shinnecock, Mohawk, Tuscarora, and Unkechaug) have come forward complaining of discrimination or harm in this matter. For the record, Lake Erie is named after the Erie Nation, and the city of Buffalo derives its name from the Seneca Nation. Shouldn't they be asked about these names as well?

In America, this protest seems inevitable but also raises a broader question about the use of mascots in sports and by educational institutions. To varying degrees, all mascots are "reductionistic" of the real world. By definition, they simplify and objectify images in some stereotypical form. So why isn't People for the Ethical Treatment of Animals (PETA) out protesting the use of animals as mascots that are unable to speak up or defend themselves? Typically, with an overemphasis on their predatory violence (hawks, eagles, wolves, wolverines, bears, tigers, lions, grizzlies). And why are we allowed to diminish yellow banana slugs or anteaters as humorous team mascots but celebrate beavers and horned frogs?

Perhaps unions should protest how reducing blue-collar labor to sports memorabilia is demeaning to a lifetime of sacrifice and historic achievement—49ees, Steelers, Oilers, Cowboys, Lakers, or Tar Heels. And when will descendants finally rise and protest the distorted images of "Vikings" or "Spartans" or "Knicks." Really, the "Fighting Irish" and "Ragin' Cajuns." In a sense, this use of mascots trivializes the world around us, and we should probably stop using them. I went to a high school whose mascot is the "Farmers," featuring a one-dimensional figure in a straw hat, blue overalls, and pitchfork (really, a hick). How absurd is this? Come on, most of the kids in my graduating class didn't know what a farmer was. And this mascot did nothing but marginalize the idea of farming and its traditional role in our society. We can all do better than this. Maybe Stanford University gets it right for once. It has no official mascot.

But let's examine the current example of the Atlanta Braves baseball team. The liberal media have, for decades, been attempting to shame the Braves organization into dropping its name, claiming it is demeaning to Native Americans. And even more scandalous is the fan favorite tomahawk chop, where a foam hand makes a chopping motion as if using a tomahawk. This name and conduct have been variously characterized as racist and belittling of indigenous people, yet when local tribes are asked to offer comments and express their concerns, they have none whatsoever. In fact, they take some pride in it. But this has been changing over time. (It is seldom mentioned that French and English colonialists introduced bounty incentives for the scalps of tribes at war with the settlers. So this may be way more racist than has been assumed—White people celebrating violence against Native tribes—but I somehow doubt it.)

Racist or not, we should at least understand the intent of pro sports mascots. And none, to my knowledge, was an effort to demean or make fun of anyone. All sports team names are meant to be a source of pride. Yet these battles over the sport's representation of Native Americans have been raging for years among privileged White Americans because the woke are convinced of their virtuousness. It may take them a little longer to convince Native Americans, but in time, they hope to show them the error of their thinking on this matter. With a little more effort, they may be able to wipe out the civic memory of Native Americans altogether. It seems we should be encouraging sports franchises to find better ways to honor our Indigenous tribes.

In the United States, the names of twenty-six states are derived from Native American words/names (Alabama, Alaska, Arizona, Connecticut, Hawaii, Idaho, Illinois, Iowa, Kansas, Kentucky, Massachusetts, Michigan, Minnesota, Mississippi, Missouri, Nebraska, New Mexico, Ohio, Oklahoma, South and North Dakota, Tennessee, Texas, Utah, Wisconsin, and Wyoming). Let's not go deep into the hundreds of towns, cities, and counties that share this legacy as well. For example, Chicago, Miami, Detroit, and Seattle. And we haven't even scratched the surface of rivers and geographical landmarks. Maybe we should be querying tribes about how they feel.

The larger question raised by deleting Native American references from any civic context is, Why not erase all references to everyone's heritage in the United States? Why bother with voter approval if these names are deemed discriminatory and harmful in some imaginable way, say, to Native Americans who originally inhabited these lands? (This is the slippery slope of revisionist history.) And to be clear, all the schools, parks, buildings, and statues bearing Confederate names were a revisionist attempt, long after the war, not only to alter the historical reality of having lost the war but also to assert the righteousness of their cause and to maintain the Jim Crow suppression of Black Americans.

Maybe it's time to poll Native tribes about the European names they find offensive and would prefer changed to their original tribal names. Wait! On November 2, 2022, the National Park Service agreed to rename Indian Garden as Havasupai Gardens, after the tribe that originally inhabited this land before it was designated as part of the Grand Canyon National Park. (But here is the point of all this. The great thing about being on the left is never having to say you are wrong.)

Identity Politics

The question that has to be asked is, How much is a community willing to disrupt itself to validate the transgender community (i.e., gender identity incongruent with their sex assignment at birth)? Current estimates vary from 0.21 to 0.39 percent of the population or a third of 1 percent are transgender. This process of redefining gender identity extends far beyond civil rights and protections under the law, to redefining 99.95 percent of the entire population's own sense of identity, which will certainly sow confusion, disbelief, and a backlash. And beyond this, it may create a social agenda for nearly every other identifiable subgroup that demands validation. Given the fluid nature of identity, this may be an act of perpetual motion.

Somewhere in this debate lies chaos for our networked communities. When people we have traditionally referred to as "woman" for thousands of years have been reduced to impersonal phrases that objectify them, such as cisgendered (assigned female at birth) or "people who menstruate," "menstruators," "people with vulvas," "people with cervixes who can become pregnant," or "chromosomal female," we are truly lost in the virtue-absolutism of the left.

Currently, Facebook offers fifty different gender identity options, e.g., agender (a person without an identifying gender), bigender (a person who identifies as having two distinct genders), and gender-fluid (a shifting gender identity). This does raise additional questions, such as, how many types of males and females can be identified? Are all males assigned at birth, who identify as male as adults, really represented by one group, or are there dozens of sub-identities that need to be respectfully acknowledged? Certainly, gay males represent one major subgroup, but how many beyond that? And are they being discriminated against? It appears that anything less than accepting these redefinitions has now been virtue-formed as discrimination, denying an individual's equality and "grammatical dignity."

The attempt to define equality as the correct use of gender-neutral pronouns is certainly unique from a historical perspective, as is defining it the equivalent to denying an individual's "social inclusion" (a right I am not sure is in the Constitution). There is also considerable debate over whether the use of the term *preferred pronoun* is even acceptable, as if its use is potentially discriminatory. But also, that one should not directly inquire as to one's sexual identity, which may be a private and not a public matter, with the admonition that one should only use a unique pronoun as an individual refers to themselves, but also with an awareness that they may use it at different times and places, so try to stay congruent and don't make any assumptions. One underlying difficulty here is there have arisen many pronoun variations, each asserting individual identity. In other words, chaos. And the big caveat in this is anyone who questions or challenges any of this is, you guessed it, "transphobic" toward gender nonconforming people.

The question we are all faced with is, How does the social world make the distinction between personal preference and social bias? Let's face the pregnant woman in the room. (You are probably asking yourself, Why did this author automatically default to a menstruating vulva? Because in the end, it is her body, and she represents 99 percent of those who give birth.) Parents want their twenty-two-year-old daughter to marry someone who they prefer—same race and economic and educational background. Someone who wears the same ties Dad does, supports the same sports teams, enjoys the laid-back family fish fry, goes to the same church, and gets the family jokes. They also want him to be tall (a bias against shorter men) and handsome, smart and ambitious (shout-out to the truth only the incel movement understands). Here is the question: How many biases and prejudices have they committed, and can they ever be rehabilitated? They probably want him to be heterosexual and preferably not a non-cis woman. Who haven't they offended?

I hate being the one to say this, but simpler is generally better on a large social scale (Occam's razor). It doesn't have to be binary, but fifty plus alternatives is too many. And having to be sensitive to each person's personal pronoun depending on the circumstances is exponentially mind-boggling. In one's limited social life, it may entail thousands of nuanced distinction. Everyone's rights need to be assured (we), but we are descending into chaos around the notion that each of us has our own individual rights (I).

Failed Expungement of a Federal Judge

In 2023, a conservative federal judge was invited to speak at Stanford University by the school's Federalist Society chapter. Even before he had an opportunity to address the audience, student protestors were heckling and verbally harassing him until he was escorted off the stage.

Perhaps most astonishing was the conduct of the school's associate dean of diversity, equity, and inclusion (DEI). She commandeered the podium by interrupting the judge as he prepared to speak then verbally excoriated him in a self-righteous outburst, asserting all the "harm" he has done to the LGBTQ community while serving on the Federal Appeals Court. She also expressed her belief in free speech while proceeding to describe the judge's past speech as "abhorrent" and "harmful," further inciting protesting students to deny the judge an opportunity to speak. Stanford University later issued a formal apology.

While this appears to have been an absurdist drama from the start, one of the judge's legal opinions appears to have incited the most anger from the students. In an opinion rendered in 2020, he failed to use a transgender sex offender's preferred pronoun. Think of this as virtue-thought's passionate loss of perspective. Apparently, no one was protesting that more needed to be done to prevent sexual abuse or to help victims of sexual abuse or to treat and incarcerate offenders. No one was challenging the judge's legal opinion, claiming the defendant was innocent and there had been a miscarriage of justice, or that the sentence was not long enough. Nope. Pronouns were the drama. This is not unlike protesting the order of the letters in LGBTQ as discriminatory and marginalizing the TQ community. Better yet, Stanford University should be required to hold a forum to decide the proper order of 2SLGBQIA+. (Everyone, please go to YouTube and type in the name of former professional basketball player Allen Iverson and the word *practice*. Then as you watch this video, substitute the word *pronoun* for *practice*.)

Injustice Outrage

We are all the heroes of our own personal tragedies.

It isn't just Fox News that knows how to orchestrate public hysteria. The liberal media has been in the muckraking, doing yellow journalism business for hundreds of years, every day searching for just the right incident to stir public outrage and sell newspapers and now online clicks and comments. So while tens of thousands are dying in the fight for Ukraine and thousands of migrants are suffering at our southern border, the New York media has turned the unfortunate death of a homeless individual into a Kurosawa-style *Rashomon* urban tragedy. Here is the unadorned back-page version:

> On May 1st, 2023, a homeless man died after being restrained by three Manhattan subway riders when he began behaving erratically and in a threatening manner.

The tabloid version of this event is how a former Marine preyed on a "beloved street performer." The victim was a hapless and guileless Michael Jackson subway "busker" who merely wanted a bottle of water (a modern-day Oliver Twist surviving on the mean streets of NYC). The subplot deeply reflects what the media believes is the cynical failure of the body politic to not only protect this helpless subway denizen but everyone who is down and out. (Note: If you are not familiar with the term *busker*, you might conceptualize it as entertainment entrapment, which is popular in NYC and Las Vegas.)

And, of course, we were exposed day and night to the unremitting pain this family has had to endure in front of the media. And the streets were filled with outrage protesters demanding justice (street performance agitprop). But the parade did not stop here. The political left joined in with a self-righteous crescendo about the evils of racism and the murder of a young Black man. New York Democratic State senator Julia Salazar, fully in on the hyperbole grift, compared this death to "lynching" and "the public extermination of a Black, marginalized person in the name of restoring public order."

Everyday Tragedies

None of this is intended to make light of or diminish the unfortunate death of this individual. In fact, it is this media exclamation that is disrespectful in this matter: Turning this man's death into a carnival-barking circus of faux outrage. An event that was no more a tragedy than all the other unpublicized deaths that occur every day in the United States. This death, unfortunately, seemed inevitable more than not when one looks more closely at the factual details (which is not an argument for justifying it).

In an average day, 7,974 people die in the United States. There are sixty homicides; 1,906 deaths from heart disease; 1,658 from cancer; and 616 by accident, per the Center for Disease Control. The CDC also predicted 294 deaths per day from a drug overdose in 2023. There were a lot of tragedies on this particular May 1, and every other day.

But what exactly is a tragedy? Is it the eight killed and seven wounded in a mass shooting at a mall in Allen, Texas? Or the seven killed when a drunk driver ran into a group of migrants waiting at a bus stop in Brownsville, Texas? Or the twenty-nine-year-old female sheriff's deputy, with a young son, who was shot and killed when she pulled over to assist a drunken driver who had crashed off to the side of the road? This was all in the same week that our subway rider, Mr. Neely, died.

The reality is subways are a part of New York City and all the crime and social dysfunction that goes along with that. Perhaps the 2022 headline below was on the minds of more than a few people on that Manhattan subway on this day in May.

The *New York Post* headline read, *"Killings in NYC subway system skyrocket to highest level in 25 years—even as ridership plummeted."* The details were pretty disheartening, maybe even tragic—"Three people stabbed to death in NYC transit system in 10 days." Maybe the subway riders recently read that "overall felony crimes on the subways is up a whopping 42% compared to the same period in 2021—and this year's death toll is on pace to eclipse the eight murders clocked last year." More recently, "Two Big Apple dads...were separately knifed to death on their commute home from work in random attacks that have left experts scratching their heads" (*New York Post*, Oct. 11, 2022). These details might possibly influence you when someone is behaving in an erratic and threatening manner on the subway you are riding.

And the Creek Don't Rise

The NeighborhoodScout "Crime Risk Report" assesses property and violent risks and rates for every US address and neighborhood, using algorithms and crime statistics from more than eighteen thousand law enforcement agencies. The total crime index for New York City neighborhoods ranked fifteen out of a hundred. In other words, in 2021, the total crime index was worse than 85 percent of neighborhoods across the United States. The chances of becoming a victim of a violent crime in Manhattan was one in 192, and a victim of a property crime was one in fifty-one.

For absolutists on the right, life is often reduced to a moral drama. Their story is about the eternal conflict between the forces of good and evil and how temptation leads one down the wrong path. But for the left, life is a narrative illusion of redemption in the face of an unjust world. In the case of Mr. Neely, the liberal press badly wanted to redeem him, given all the injustices he had suffered, wanting to make his death even more tragic than the other 7,794 that occurred in the United States that day. And they succeeded, which is why the media became saturated with injustice outrage, but also unhinged when it came to the facts and circumstances of this one death.

A second victim of this unfortunate death was twenty-four-year-old Daniel Penny, a former Marine whose intervention resulted in the death of Mr. Neely. The political theater that ensued was over whether or not he was a good Samaritan or a violent vigilante. To redeem Mr. Neely, this ex-Marine's actions had to be characterized as those of a violent vigilante taking the life of a harmless, mentally ill homeless person. With this projection, the left's internal dissonance was resolved. How good it must feel to be all outraged and self-righteous, now residing in the contrition of demanding restorative justice. But not actually having to do anything.

As a forensic psychologist, I was never allowed these restorative moments, whether writing a psychological evaluation or testifying in court. The reality was always much more complex and much less satisfying. In every case, injustices always prevailed on all sides if one wanted to examine the truth closely. And I often had the opportunity to explore it all to understand how we arrived at the tragic present.

During the course of my work, I have encountered hundreds of cases of violence by individuals living homeless on the streets. They are often suffering from mental illness, drug and alcohol addictions, and severe personality disorders. And all too often, their behavior is highly unpredictable, aggressive, and threatening. And, in too many instances, violent. (And for the record, individuals on the streets are considerably more violent and subject to more violence than any other population in our society. I have encountered many who actively sought out prison as a respite from the violence and hopelessness of the streets.)

Victims of Urban Intervention

Let's examine what we know about the case of Jordon Neely, who was on a Manhattan subway train when he was placed in a chokehold and held down by two other men and died by suffocation. Neely had been described in the news media as a homeless person with a documented history of mental illness and substance abuse. He had also been arrested forty-three times from 2013 to 2021, including four prior assaults plus an outstanding warrant for a fifth assault that took place in 2021. (Importantly, the earlier assaults have yet to be detailed in the press.)

Before devolving into what happened on the subway train, let's look more closely at Mr. Neely's history of interaction with public health and law enforcement officials:

- His interactions with his family had been fraught with discord for many years, including frequent arguments, chronic drug abuse, and numerous death threats to his family. In 2010, he was reported as threatening to kill his grandfather. His behavior had become so threatening that his family would not let him in the house at night because they were afraid of him.
- In 2013, police escorted him to a hospital after he complained of hearing voices and that his body had gone numb.
- In 2016, he was escorted by officers to the hospital after several complaints of "an irate, intoxicated man threatening other around West 168th Street."
- In 2018, he came to the attention of the police on six occasions but refused hospitalization or public shelter.
- In July 2018, he was hospitalized after threatening a conductor and scaring passengers on a subway train.
- From 2019 to 2022, he had frequent contact with law enforcement, psychiatric services, and city outreach services, often many times a month. There had been at least forty-three calls during this time for an "aided case" (someone sick, injured, or mentally ill) in reference to this individual.
- At the time of his death, there was an outstanding arrest warrant for him having assaulted a sixty-seven-year-old woman. This was a serious assault, and we should not let the press reduce this to a passing reference. He punched a helpless and aging woman in the face, knocking her to the ground, fracturing her orbital bone, and breaking her nose, with her suffering considerable bruising, swelling, and substantial head pain, according to the charging documents.

For this latter assault, Mr. Neely was in jail for a year before being released. It is unclear why he was released and what was legally pending from the available reporting. I am guessing that he failed to appear in court, and a bench warrant was issued. This assault should have our utmost attention in the escalating pattern of instability and violence on the part of Mr. Neely. (The personal history outlined above was reported by the *New York Post*, which appears to have been the only media outlet for investigative journalism regarding this event.)

What seems abundantly clear from this limited history is that Mr. Neely consistently refused considerable efforts to provide him social services. It also suggests that he was personally devolving on the streets, as seen by his high level of contact with law enforcement and the repeated incidents that involved threats and violence. The big picture that emerges here is that homeless and patient's rights advocates had come to treat aggressive and threatening behavior as the new normal and unrelated to future acts of violence. I also suspect this is because there is so much of it that they feel helpless to intervene.

The number of contacts with law enforcement by Mr. Neely is quite astonishing and portrays the limits of helping people who do not want to be helped or are unable to accept help because of their mental illnesses. And herein resides one of the most stunning insights into this whole affair. NYC has a "top 50" list of homeless people most in need of outreach, which Mr. Neely was on. (Guaranteed all fifty refused social services that would have taken them off the streets for more than a day.) Here is a lesson on how to handle a serious social problem—make a list of everyone you are not going to help. For crying out loud, crowdfund it! (Clearly, homelessness does not have the same priority as say the "Top 50 Socialites Calling 911" on opening night of the Met Gala pleading for dog care or ticket requests for the "Top 50 Off-Broadway Plays That Aren't Musicals" or the "Top 50 Aging Street Rappers" who know what funk is.)

The question unanswered here and in communities across the nation is, What happens when an individual is unable to survive on the streets and continually comes in contact with law enforcement but refuses all assistance? The answer from the left appears to be you are free to die, but under no circumstances will your civil rights be infringed upon, not even when it comes to your own safety or that of the community. Unless you seriously hurt someone, you are good to go (okay, you may be briefly detained, but then you are free to go). This is as true in California and Arizona as in New York City.

Here was an individual who should have been committed long-term to a psychiatric hospital. (Do they even exist any longer?) Instead, he was left on the streets until he could find a way to die or go to jail. And we should be clear about this. Jails have become the primary mental health treatment facilities and substance abuse treatment programs throughout many communities. I have encountered many families thankful that their son or daughter was in jail and off the streets, where they might finally get some help.

The First Day in May

As for what took place on the subway train that day, one passenger on the subway was quoted as saying Mr. Neely did not appear to be seeking to assault or harm anyone (however, this observation appears to be the exception). Another passenger was quoted as stating, "He erupted in the train and then started yelling violent language, 'I don't care if I die. I don't care if I go to jail. I don't have any food. I don't have any beverage. I'm done.'" Another described him as "came onto the subway, threw his jacket on the floor, and began screaming and yelling aggressively, pacing up and down the train car." Yet another passenger described him as "increasingly hostile and began throwing trash." One noted that Mr. Neely stated his willingness to "hurt anyone and was unbothered about the prospects of returning to jail or being killed."

A Mr. Vazquez, who was on the train and captured some of the altercation on his cell phone, told NBC News that Mr. Neely got on the train and "began to say a somewhat aggressive speech, saying he was hungry, he was thirsty, that he didn't care about anything, he didn't care about going to jail, he didn't care that he gets a big life sentence." NBC News also noted, "Some witnesses reported that Neely allegedly acted very aggressively toward other riders and threatened to harm them."

Kawasaki Railcars

An online search for the subway cars in NYC tells us that they are 151' long and 8.5' wide or 434 SF and can carry up to 188 passengers. That works out to 2.31 SF of standing space, per person, at full capacity. That is a tight space in which to determine if you are about to be attacked by someone acting out verbally and physically near you.

I would like to interject a note here. The type of anger and hopelessness expressed by Mr. Neely is a predictable overture to violence. A desperate, incoherent individual, one abusing drugs and mentally deteriorating, should always be treated as a threat to act aggressively. And suicidal ideation is often a precursor to a violent act. Just look at all the mass shootings across the United States by individuals prepared to die. This type of violence is all around us if we care to look. My work did not allow me to look away very often.

And perhaps most significantly, the available videos of this incident failed to capture the events leading to this confrontation. Mr. Penny, through his attorney, described Mr. Neely as engaging him in a "verbal dispute" and that Mr. Neely "began aggressively threatening" him, which then "escalated into a physical altercation" and his subduing him. His attorney, Thomas Keniff, interviewed on CNN by Cooper Anderson, noted that Mr. Penny "put Mr. Neely in a 'recovery position' and rendered direct aid when police and EMTs arrived."

This is a part of the story the media does not want you to read or watch because it undermines their unjust premise. Attorneys for Mr. Penny have repeatedly stated that their client "never intended to harm Mr. Neely and that he could not have foreseen his untimely death." After the medical examiner ruled Mr. Neely's death as homicide, the district attorney, caving to public pressure, charged Mr.

Penny with one count of second-degree manslaughter (and not the lower offense of negligent homicide, implying some degree of intentionality). However, it will be up to a grand jury to formally indict him. To date, his legal team has raised over $2.6 million from public donations. (However, for those who were impatient, this case was immediately tried in the more relevant court of public opinion.)

You've Been Bustered!

The reaction on the political left was predictable: all cueing up as if this were a casting call for a guerilla performance of *New York, New York*, with community leaders and activists hyperventilating over justice for the victim, Mr. Neely. And, of course, the mandatory antagonist. In this case, a young man recently out of the service, who stepped up to intervene in a moment that was out of control and threatening. One that, unfortunately, resulted in the accidental death of Mr. Neely. How much Mr. Neely's deteriorating physical state and drug use played in his death will probably remain a mystery.

Just maybe, the political class should stop routinely reaching for hot words such as *exterminate*, *racism*, and *lynching* as a bland form of political tithing. A formally good person was now being characterized in the media as a "murderer" by newspaper writers pretending to be journalists. The governor of New York stated Mr. Neely was "killed for being a passenger." (Wow is all I can say. Never let the facts or details get in the way of political strategizing.) The New York Council Speaker immediately jumped on the racial angle: "This killing puts on display for the world the double standard that Black people and other people of color continue to face." (From this statement, I can only guess it would have been better if a White person had been killed.)

The New York lieutenant governor jumped in: "The consequence of mental health problems in New York should not be death." (But not a comment about how the mentally ill have been put in harm's way for decades.) And Rep. Alexandria Ocasio Cortez (D-NY), who seems to have an opinion about everything, tweeted, "Jordan Neely was murdered." Then she perseverated on the word *killing* to make her point, self-righteously believing she is the final word on this matter.

But the nadir of hypocrisy was not reached until the White House decided to weigh in with a statement ten days before President Biden was heading to New York City for two campaign fundraisers. "Our hearts go out to his family and loved ones." Then adding, "Events surrounding his death demand a thorough investigation." Talk about jumping the empathy shark to keep the money rolling in.

If the administration really cared (and in America, that is measured in money, not words), how much were they offering the Neely family or NYC? Apparently, no comments were offered about the other 7,794 deaths that day or the 77,940 who died in the ten days before commenting. This tells us all we need to know. Really, what's the point of the legal process when our elected officials are a *de facto* judge and jury? And not one mention of the broader social failures here. The comments above reflect the deepfake reality of the left's outrage theater in America today. (And to clarify, as this was being written, the right actively entered the political fray as well. But I am writing about the left because the sensationalizing and politicalizing of this unfortunate death originated there.)

Murder, of course, presumes a motive or intention as if this event was all somehow premeditated. And make no mistake, adrenaline was high on the part of individuals choosing to intervene, and an unfortunate consequence occurred. This Marine was also assisted by two other individuals during this confrontation whose actions clearly supported his version of events. At times, the left appears to have no altimeter when it comes to perceived injustices. They are like a helium balloon being battered in a polar vortex of outrage that, once again, the world has been unfair, and someone has to be held accountable. (When many times it's bad weather.)

Was our antagonist a vigilante or a good Samaritan? The left's narrative illusion is always cast as outrage for healing the wounded. This is really simple. Yes, law enforcement is not available when it is needed, and security on subways is inadequate. The rise in violence on city streets and throughout the land is significant and making us ever fearful for our safety. Social services are a failing stopgap to the task of helping manage the plight of the mentally ill on the streets.

We seldom have the required resources and services to help those with drug and alcohol problems. Homelessness is an ever-aggravating social problem for which we have no answers at this moment. Besides, patient's rights advocates and state financial considerations emptied out the mentally ill from state hospitals onto the streets of our communities, where they are desperately living homeless but free of the abusive power of authority. And perhaps most disturbingly, the left, which claims to care, is clearly making matters worse on the streets of many cities.

The question not addressed here is, What are the limits of community social services? What if this wasn't so much a failure of the system but rather the case of an individual who stress tested the limits of what could be done? The media and the left's need to cast blame and find fault shines a light on the unreality of their expectations and their fear of how civil authority is exercised. Mr. Neely was a beneficiary of a system that prizes personal autonomy and freedom over authority and control. He was sacrificed for his own good, and for ours as well. This is what the left tells itself once the injustice-outrage subsides.

All the failures noted above are likely true and contributed to the death of Mr. Neely, which also led to the response of the three men who subdued him. But none of this mattered in those final moments. All of it is completely irrelevant if you were sitting on the subway train with your family—husband, wife, and two young children—and had no idea of Mr. Neely's history of threats and violence. What you are witnessing is an out-of-control individual, likely high from drugs a few feet from you and acting in a threatening manner, while you and your family are all crammed in the claustrophobic confines of a subway car traveling at seventeen miles per hour. (Fortunately, this was not someone heading to the exit door of a commercial airliner at thirty-five thousand feet. You know, with everyone curious if these doors open from the inside, even pondering if you should say or do something.)

You, me, and probably most people on this subway would have been enormously grateful that someone was willing to step up and diffuse a volatile situation. Just ask all those who have been assaulted, robbed, raped, kidnapped, and murdered on the streets of our cities because people just watched and didn't want to get involved. Too much risk of injury or legal blowback when they would rather finish their shopping and get back home without the inconvenience of violence entering their lives.

Better yet, sit back and read and listen to all the politicians and journalists bloviating for months on MSNBC and CNN before forgetting how grateful you are for not being involved. Then move on to the next tragedy and struggle to figure out who is to blame. On the left, outrage is synonymous with virtue. By the time you are reading this, it will all have been forgotten, except by the victim's family and the ex-Marine who chose to act when confronted by a threatening circumstance. For the absolute-minded on the left, the Manhattan F train was not a community of subway riders but a collection of unaddressed grievances.

Sidebar: One intrepid reporter (E. Snodgrass, Yahoo News, May 5, 2023) interviewed a psychologist who presented himself as someone "who conducts bystander intervention training." (Only in NYC could this job description be true.) He also shared a number of simple ideas about the causes of violence and how it is provoked. But then he offered there are "effective ways to intervening as a bystander." (Contemplating the liability of these recommendations left me wishing I had gone to law school.) But here is his most interesting observation: "Passengers on that subway train could have intervened to help Neely before he was ever put in a chokehold," suggesting that someone could have "offered to give him a granola bar or water bottle."

Now my reading of events suggests this is a questionable tactic. I would advise anyone in close contact with an erratic, hostile, and verbally aggressive individual to get as far away as possible, then immediately call the police. Given one is stuck in this circumstance, one has to be very careful about any direct interactions, particularly if you are hypnotized by the belief that you are "intervening."

Here is the problem. I have spent many years interviewing thousands of individuals in jails, prisons, and state hospitals throughout California and Arizona, and it is one thing to approach an inmate or patient from a position of authority in which offering them something can be seen as respectful and minimizing the power differential. But a stranger risks directing anger and aggression toward themselves if they are perceived as acting superior or implying this person shouldn't think, feel, or act the way they are in that moment. In this instance, they may feel judged by you, which was never your intention.

Always be respectful. That is the coin of the realm. But a helpful act can be interpreted as condescending or even controlling and provoke an even angrier and more aggressive response. In emotionally elevated circumstances, a supposed act of considerateness can be a trigger. You are now pointing out to everyone on the subway car that you are in control and they are out of control or needy. They may feel humiliated by this. Just saying that there are no simple bystander interventions with an angry individual. Best to avoid them whenever possible.

Altruism's Event Horizon—Immigration

By any historical measure, immigration has been an overwhelmingly net positive for the United States (but not so much for the preexisting indigenous peoples) and will continue to be well into the future, but not as currently structured. Our current immigration policy requires the left to come on board for serious discussions and to change their attitude. There are limits to believing you can do nothing but good. Their open-ended immigration policies are a significant factor in driving immigration and creating the humanitarian crisis at our border. The fact is, if it wasn't so easy for people to cross our border, fewer would come. While this is blatantly obvious, the left does not want to see its role in this. It has now gotten to the point that immigrants are demanding they be allowed to cross and that it is their right.

First off, we are a nation of immigrants who suppressed and nearly exterminated the entire indigenous peoples of the so-called New World. We should hesitate for a moment when we self-congratulate ourselves as a great melting pot and a moral beacon to the world. Forget it. We are not. Let's move on from this delusional sentimentality about who we are. Time for everyone to reread *White Trash* by Isenberg. No one was ever welcomed here, and everyone fought for what they got. Many never succeeded, and even fewer are today.

In my lifetime, the US population has grown from 150 million to 328 million (a 125 percent growth rate in a relatively few years). A significant factor in this rate of growth has been immigration. In 2010, forty million US citizens were foreign-born. We have been generous, but there are practical limits.

Just because we did something in the past (for example, high rates of immigration) is not a reason to keep doing it over and over (which is its own kind of craziness). It feels mostly like a specious argument for immigration that many, if not most Americans, have grown weary of. Laissez-faire immigration policies are an overly simplistic solution to a complex problem. Wake up! It's time to recognize that sweeping global migration is occurring and that everyone can see on their smartphones that they live in what Trump colloquially called "shitholes."

And it is tiring to hear the continually buffering Democratic side of this equation. That individuals and families who show up at our borders should get special consideration (some form of "due process" out of humanitarian consideration) because they come from countries filled with violence. The reality is, nearly two-thirds of the world's population meet this irrelevant criteria. Besides, every citizen of Guatemala, Honduras, and El Salvador qualifies, including Detroit and Chicago. Let's stop the bullshit and develop a rational criterion for citizenship.

Yes, nearly unlimited immigration has significantly cut labor costs, resulting in the suppression of wages for sixty years. While profits were high for the upper class, this process hurt the previously existing American underclass in the job market (particularly Black

Americans). Immigration has also been a primary tool of the plutocracy to suppress organized labor in America, one that millions of illegal immigrants can easily testify to.

Current rates of human population growth are projected to result in large-scale global population migration. This is in the face of dramatic climate change, water scarcity, loss of arable lands, species eradication, proliferating intranational conflicts, and terrorism. Heck! There is now open discussion of guaranteed incomes in the United States because of the loss of real jobs from technology, and we want to import millions of people who don't speak English and are undereducated. The world is facing a coming humanitarian crisis on a scale never before experienced, with a projected four hundred million people on the move over the next thirty years. This doesn't add up, people. Maybe it's time for an immigration moratorium until we sort this out?

The truth is, immigration has been an unresolved political conflict in America throughout its entire history. Few people have ever been welcomed here, and all struggled after they arrived. It's only going to get worse. What the left can't bring itself to accede to is the use of authority in this matter. And this authority requires complete control over our borders and deciding who enters and who becomes a citizen, and that this is completely nonnegotiable. This is not an act of a totalitarian state or the absence of humanitarian character, but one of common sense that the right intuitively grasps.

The current US immigration rate is at its highest since 1910, with forty-four million immigrants currently in the United States or 13.5 percent of the population.

Our immigration policy is broken because it serves the interest of both Democrats and Republicans not to fix it. The disturbing reality we are all confronted with is every legislative, administrative, judicial, and law enforcement immigration policy/decision has a real human consequence, which is why immigration issues are always ethically and legally challenging and why there are no simple solutions. In the end, it pits the best overall interests of the United States against the best interests of migrants worldwide. And the whole world gets to watch this very modern ethical conundrum.

There are cynical aspects to the current immigration crisis that broadly fit well-worn stereotypes (and unfortunately, all of them are true). Business prefers the confusion because it provides cheap labor and suppresses wages. Republican because it plays on the xenophobic and nativist fears of its base. And Democrats champion the moral high ground regardless of the potential long-term negative consequences, all the while waiting for a demographic voter shift.

Let's get real! There really is an "immigration-advocacy complex" actively working to obstruct the current system, stymie reform, and keep the immigration doors wide open, and it needs to be quieted or at least tempered. It is comprised of attorneys, religious organizations, ethnic interest groups and self-righteous people who have created an immigration network, all topped off by false legal claims of "sanctuary" by churches and cities. While the fact is, immigration is an ongoing moral, economic, and political crisis no one wants to resolve, and it is only going to worsen in the coming decades.

Here is the important question: Is there a practical middle ground between all the involved self-interested parties? No, not really, because someone is going to be disappointed at every attempted solution to this problem. The solution requires that all parties to this troubling reality be able to point to positive outcomes and accept considerable disappointment. (Currently, this is not the American way.)

First, a few facts. If one goes to the US Customs and Immigration Services' online website, they will quickly discover numerous legal means to come to the United States. One can apply directly for *citizenship*, seek a *green card* for lawful permanent resident status, or a *visa* for temporary work, business, tourism, or study. So what do we do? An individual comes here to study and work at the highest levels and contributes to our intellectual and scientific advances and we deport them. While millions illegally or semi-legally cross the border in Texas and are welcomed by attorneys, addressing them in Spanish, handing them business cards, and connecting them to networks to help them avoid apprehension and deportation. This is nuts.

There is also what is called a *humanitarian visa* that allows individuals to enter the United States on "humanitarian parole" on a temporary basis for a compelling emergency, usually for up to twelve months (then everyone disappears into the United States and is never accounted for again). But by far, the most popular and successful means of admission is to illegally cross the border between the United States and Mexico.

Birthright citizenship was a rational eighteenth- and nineteenth-century policy that doesn't make any sense in the modern world, as easy as it is to travel and move about the world today, whereby today, families come to the United States to give birth to their children to gain US citizenship. Corollary to this is that "chain migration" is one of the largest sources of legal and illegal immigration to the United States.

Legal "due process" for so-called "catch and release" immigrants who have entered the United States for humanitarian reasons has, in reality, become a cynical legal tool for claiming both the moral high ground and to obstruct the government's administration of immigration. It's a judicial end round that proceeds from the shaky legal premise that individuals who enter the country illegally are entitled to all the same legal rights as US citizens. This process, of course, has proven to be a complete farce.

There are currently 332 immigration judges with a backlog of seven hundred thousand cases, taking up to six years to hear. This does not even begin to address attempts at communication between the court and involved parties scattered across the United States. Issues of legal representation, language barriers, financial barriers, or anyone's ability to provide evidence of humanitarian abuse in their country of origin. (In 2015, these courts held hearings for 2,753 children under the age of five. Exactly how does this proceed legally, ethically, and morally? How about even practically?)

The underlying result of the "due process" agenda has been to incentivize immigration into the United States. The more immigrants enter, the more who seek to enter in a never-ending loop of immigration hope. But no doubt, the three largest immigration magnets are security, opportunities for work, and chain-migration connectivity. To ultimately control immigration, these avenues have to be controlled. One obvious place to begin is with the workplace, an unending magnet for illegal immigration. Until employers are required to clean up their act, there is very little hope for reform.

A chronic element of illegal immigration into the United States is violence and extortion. On the southern side of the border, we have the cartels, and on the northern side, we have gangs. In between, we have an immigration underground composed of thousands of people extorting the immigrants seeking to gain access to the US. This process is coercive, violent, and extremely dangerous for immigrants. Essentially, a criminal syndicate exploiting immigrants entering the United States because of our broken policies.

On the back end of arriving here illegally is the chronic anxiety of deportation and the struggle to gain legal identification and to participate in communities. This has resulted in an immigrant shadow world that is subject to exploitation by the labor market, subject to lawlessness for fear of reporting crimes, and reducing an individual's or family's ability to learn English, attend schools, work, and receive health care. There needs to be a process by which immigrants are welcomed and assisted without fear.

Based on current projections, the US population is expected to increase from its current size of 325 million to 438 million by 2050. Sixty percent of this growth is projected to be due to immigration or the equivalent of adding forty-eight cities the size of Chicago.

One question never publicly addressed is, How much is the United States going to allow Mexico to determine its future? Mexico is the single largest source of illegal immigration into the United States and will continue to be in the future, currently with ten to twelve million Mexican citizens residing here illegally. The single most important factor in immigration reform is to incentivize Mexico to control its side of the border.

We require a more candid and plausible public discussion of humanitarian immigration into the United States based on the so-called claims of "violence" and political asylum. The reality is, millions throughout the world would qualify, as would 100 percent of the citizens of most Latin and South American countries. This is simply not a satisfactory or politically realistic criterion. And if we are being candid, most of the claims are not provable. Everyone who wants to enter will likely make this claim, whether true or not.

All the issues outlined here are not a justification for separating children from their families when they arrive at the border of the United States. But the trauma of children being kept in detention centers does not compare to the serious risk-to-life and health risks these children are subjected to by their parents bringing them to our border. Yes, the "immigration-advocacy complex" is overplaying this issue, but it is a serious concern that needs to be addressed by rewriting lax admission policies. There will probably never be a satisfactory government option to this problem until families and oftentimes children stop arriving at our borders. The government is simply not prepared or adaptive enough to solve this risk riddle posed by immigrant families. The outcome will always be unsatisfactory, no matter what the efforts or concerns. But we can do much better.

Illegal immigration is the beginning of a new permanent underclass of poor in the United States. This process also undermines economic gains for those who have already arrived. And with the advent of new technologies and a reduced need for unskilled labor, lacking the language skills and education required, newly arriving immigrants are being forced to survive on the margins generationally. This process is extraordinarily costly at both the front end (security and border control) and the back end (long-term assimilation into our communities). While we are now just beginning to explore the concept of a "guaranteed minimum income" for citizens because of diminished labor demands, permitting unlimited immigration of the poorest into the United States has the makings of a future social and economic crisis.

Some intellectuals (on the left) have proposed an "open-border" policy in the belief that the immigration process will self-regulate itself and that allowing a free flow of immigrants across the border will, in the long run, decrease overall immigration pressures. And yes, those on the sentimental bandwagon will cry their damaged hearts out about the injustice and unfairness of it all. (But they probably believe their dogs are really unicorns and should have the same rights as children.)

There was never a "golden era" of immigration into the United States. Focusing on the '60s and '70s is not a reliable optic for this problem and ignores the real labor unrest and social problems leading to the unionization of farm laborers by activists like Cesar Chavez. This "happy" version of reality was unraveling before it existed. The times have changed, and going back to the future is sheer naiveté, no matter how altruistically intended. The immigration process into the United States is no longer about seasonal migrant workers and hasn't been for sixty years.

The open-border argument suffers from the same self-regulating marketplace delusion as those who promoted "globalization." It only exasperated economic problems in the United States in the long run, and so does undeterred immigration. Look, no one is leaving to return home; rather, they will seek to bring their families and relatives here. They all have cell phones and internet connectivity and can easily judge their best options and what they want for their children's future.

Given the coming global humanitarian crisis, there is no opt out. We have many difficult choices before us, but they are ours to make. If we don't, they will be dictated to us by a fear-driven agenda. We need to approach this with cautious humanitarianism, which will require many difficult choices.

Not to address immigration will further divide the American body politic, particularly on the right, which could give rise to even greater extremism in our country, as is playing out in Europe. It's a tribal world after all and the left needs to wake up. While we cannot cave to fear, these fears need to be addressed legitimately, even if they cross ethical and moral boundaries on the left. If it takes a useless wall to reassure the right, so be it. Build a wall.

The reality is the world is overfilled, and the only question is: How are we going to rationally cope with it? Think of Germany's Angela Merkel and do the opposite. (Between 2015 and 2016, Germany allowed for 1.25 million immigrants. Five years later, half were unemployed, violent crime rates were up, and Germany's politics had become radicalized.) The rise of Trumpism in America and illiberalism worldwide, Brexit, and the political division of the

European Union should be a wake-up call to America. Liberals need to realign themselves and stop being the "usual suspect" in party politics and fake immigration reform. The reality for the left is when one acts from an altruistic impulse, it is difficult to see the harm being done. This is not forgetting about who we are as a nation or people but paying attention to what is coming our way.

Paradigm Lost

We can all be candid in this safe space. There is no such thing as cultural appropriation. It is a wokist fantasy that they are able to evoke special powers that magically identify the hidden power differential ("structural discrimination") they have encountered in the video game of life. Here, they are asserting the irrelevance of the past as a spell they can cast over the present. While the right tends to be preoccupied with conspiracies, the left suffers the illusion of having revealed yet another hidden dimension of power (not unlike descending Dante's nine rings of hell). The formal definition of cultural appropriation goes something like this: "the unacknowledged or inappropriate adoption of the customs, practices, ideas, etc. of one people or society by members of another or more dominant people or society." This is commonly evoked when the "imagery, fashion, practices, music, or artifacts of a culture are removed from their original context" (Oxford Online Dictionary).

As an aside, it needs to be emphasized that no one owns any of the imagery, fashion, practices, music, or artifacts of a particular culture. Cultural appropriation is solely about someone's sensitivity to their use or depiction. More to the point, no individual can authorize the use of the imagery, fashion, practices, music, or artifacts of a culture but can apparently protest it. It should be noted that no nation owns any of their cultural expression either by deed, title, copyright, patent, or contract. In fact, to my knowledge, there are no Bureaus of Cultural Sensitivity anywhere in the world exercising this particular kind of authority. And there is the strong likelihood that the existing imagery, fashion, practices, music, or artifacts of a culture were appropriated from a preexisting culture and is not unique to them at all. As a result, in Las Vegas, we have a fake pyramid, Roman forum, and a replica of the Eiffel Tower in the tackiest form possible.

Appropriation Blues

What are we to make of the unique form of blues music that emerged from the Mississippi Delta region in the early 1900s that later migrated north and became the "Chicago" style of blues in the 1920s? The synthesis of blues, jazz, country, rock, and soul all drew on this early blues music, including the Rolling Stones, the Beatles, and Bob Dylan.

> The diverse efforts of these musicians have attested to the vitality of the Mississippi sound within the broader stream of American popular music. ("Mississippi Delta blues," *Britannica.com*)

While it is important to honor the legacy. The gift of this unique sound does not belong to anyone.

Can I say, let's get real? In a completely subjective sense, how many people have to be offended, and to what degree before cultural appropriation rises to a broader concern? Is anyone complaining online apparently enough? In totality and without exception, all of human social-cultural evolution has been about the confluence of cultures, both in polite exchanges and in violent subjugation. This confluence is as true for us biologically as it is culturally. Genetic assimilation is a process by which a phenotype or trait produced in response to an environmental condition becomes genetically encoded by natural selection in a population. This same adaptive dynamic also applies social-culturally. It is you going down to Panda Express or Chipotle for lunch and enjoying what you think of as Chinese and Mexican cuisine without any sense of guilt or remorse. And no one is verbally assaulting you in the restaurant and accusing you of cultural appropriation.

This is also the story of the clash of cultures, whether subtle or oppressive, and where everything is exploited. That has been the human legacy for three hundred thousand years and the dominating precondition for modernity. Let's not pretend that tea and gunpowder from China or chocolate and plantains from the New World were friendly exchanges. The answer is always to move on. Look across the human condition—Kuala Lumpur, Singapore, Beijing, Tokyo, London, Abu Dhabi, New York, Paris, and Sau Paulo. We humans are all the same, and everything else is irrelevant or will soon be. This is similar to arguing that speaking English to better function in the world is oppressive colonization. And you could point to the rapid loss of language diversity worldwide. But if it is in your interest to learn English and succeed, better to learn English and stop complaining.

Trying to undo our evolutionary reality is not only frustrating but ultimately not possible. The exchange of social realities between cultures is continuous and inevitable and has never stopped for even one fraction of a moment in time, and especially not by those complaining about it today. In fact, that is what I thought it meant to be an American—to make everything that works our own. Fortunately, the complainers are mostly being ignored as trapped in a nostalgia matrix. (Having served in the military during the Vietnam War, I cannot begin to express to you the shock I experienced reading about how welcome American tourists are in Vietnam. My esteem for these courageous people cannot be fully expressed here.)

When my grandfather arrived in the US from Portugal in 1896, he Anglicized his name, changed his faith from Catholic to Protestant, and never spoke Portuguese again or taught his children the language of the old country. He never went down to the Portuguese cultural center or read the local Portuguese newspapers. He had no Portuguese-speaking friends. It was mostly by accident that I even knew of my heritage.

All the cultural artifacts of his past had been discarded. No nostalgic stories about his youth. He began as a ranch hand in

Montana as a young man, became a chicken farmer in the California Central Valley, and I knew him as an insurance agent in San Lorenzo, California (in the San Francisco East Bay Area), who drove a Studebaker Golden Hawk and whose lawn I mowed for a dollar every weekend. He was a model of what an American is, without a hyphenated name or holding on to the relics of the past. He lived in the future. The past was a ghost that never haunted him.

In America, it is not where are from but who you are now. That is what makes America different from any place in the world, ever. We should be rejoicing in it. *America was the first and only time in human history that an individual could be defined by the future and not the past.* Clearly, this process has not been perfected but is the beginning of this new reality. And this will not necessarily be easy or accepted by everyone. You have an American passport, and it is the most desirable one. You are a citizen of the most powerful nation in human history. You can be a proud US citizen wherever you go in the world. It is the most important identity there is, and there is an aircraft carrier out there to prove it and millions of people rushing to become Americans.

Of course, the pushback will be that I am White, and my family never directly experienced the violence and prejudice experienced by many others. True enough. But my response is still the same. Your path will be more difficult, same as it is for everyone not born perfectly into this world: Why did my child have cancer? Why are we starving to death in a world rich in resources? Why do we live in a town carpet bombed by jet planes? But calling others out for cultural appropriation by shouting profanities in a college student center seems profoundly irrelevant to the problems that exist. And there is much that is wrong. People just scurry away and are not going to contemplate the existential nature of their lives and how they intersect with yours because of someone's grievances about cultural appropriation. Not in the face of their everyday struggles.

You can go all Amish if you want. You can cling tightly to your cultural past. Nothing inherently wrong with that. But asking the world around you to retreat with you into your nostalgia is a waste of time that does not address the so-called hidden power differential. In fact, it covertly expands the differential bandwidth and continues to diminish those holding on to the past. Acculturation, enculturation, and assimilation are factual distinctions after the fact and not portals to the future, similar to believing in the special powers of Harry Potter rather than marveling in the storytelling.

Bonfires of the Vanities

If we really want to address grievous and outrageous acts of bias and prejudice, we will have to get over much of our sensitivity and have clearer public markers and guidelines. Media platforms feed the bonfires of our virtues. In 1497, a social movement known as the "bonfires of the vanities" erupted. Supporters of Dominican friar Girolamo Savonarola organized against the excesses of power and luxury during the Italian Renaissance. They gathered and burned personal belongings that might tempt people to sin, such as mirrors, cosmetics, fine clothing, paintings, books, and musical instruments. That is pretty much the absolutist mindset of the left in America—gathering and burning all the cultural biases of the unvirtuous past that offend them and then lighting their defenders on fire. Who among us today is so virtuous that they can withstand the judgment of the future? Of course, we should try and do better, but Thomas Jefferson and Woodrow Wilson? A hundred years from now, if you ate meat, got your bills in paper form, shipped overnight from Amazon, and drove a car, you will be a virtue criminal with an asterisk next to your name (the same as steroid users in Major League Baseball's Hall of Fame).

This sudden infection of virtue has many venues. It appears to have begun on college campuses around the country, as students filed complaints and protested about professors who wouldn't let them retake a test because it had been scheduled on their birthday, used words that made them feel unsafe, and worst of all, assigned texts on topics that made them uncomfortable. They also protested conservative speakers who had been invited to speak on campus. This woke state of mind then began to spread throughout the academic environment and infect faculty and the administrations, particularly sensitive to the university's finances. This then appeared to spread throughout online platforms, comorbid with protests over fat-shaming, the rise of the #MeToo movement, transphobia, and Black Lives Matter. In the end, virtue testing does not stand the test of history. It just makes those practicing it feel better by briefly settling their snow globes. Did witch burning and the Inquisition make people more faithful or quicker to point out a witch?

Woke absolutism is wide-ranging on the left, believing that some people are not woke enough and insensitive to others and fail to adhere to politically correct orthodoxy out of bias and a careless exercise of power. And the proof is they don't accept the accusations made against them. They continually violate safe spaces, use offending words, and fail to listen to or accept what they are being lectured about, claiming that others are talking down to them. The unwoke are dismissive of those who accuse them of cultural appropriation and insensitivity, while the woke assert they are being revictimized, having to explain all this to all their unwoke critics. Here, one's identity struggle is resolved through virtue-seeking in others (projection), in which their critics don't understand them because they lack correct thinking. On the superficial surface, this looks a lot like Chairman Mao's *Little Red Book* and the Communist Chinese Cultural Manifesto, where forgiveness was reeducation and farm labor camps. Today, you get an internet ankle monitor until the day you die, but that will not be good enough, because it will electronically track you until the end of affordable energy.

Large Confused Tent

The left's absolutist mindset is like a "box of chocolates," a large tent with something for everyone. In response to journalist Wesley Lowery's call for "moral clarity" in journalism and "ending its attempt to see all sides of a story, when there is only one" and to give up the pretense of objectivity, Andrew Sullivan responds, in *Interesting Times*:

> Question any significant part of this, and your moral integrity as a human being is called into question. There is an increasingly ferocious campaign to quell dissent, to chill debate, to purge those who ask questions. The orthodoxy goes further than suppressing contrary arguments. It insists that anything counter to this view is itself a form of violence against the oppressed.

Undoubtedly, the process of virtue-seeking is not well organized. It is generally less conspiratorial than the right but absolutist, nonetheless. It's about projecting guilt and shaming the world around them to help resolve their internal emotional conflicts (dissonance). While the causes are often justified, and there is a need for a course correction in America, the impetus appears personal and fails to address the broader "Reformation" America requires. An example of needed reform is with policing in America. But making this about virtue will not guarantee that too many Black Americans will continue to be shot to death throughout inner cities. The morbidity for the obese will continue to rise, and women will suffer under the workload of multitasking and becoming sex workers. Students will continue to be shocked by reality. Virtue reform is not reform and is more about making the virtuous feel better about themselves than changing the world. When the solution all along was to actively participate in the political process of consensus building.

As we bog down in micro-debates, we are failing to attend to difficult reforms. This situation is a classic sapiens default state—struggling to accurately distinguish the signal from the noise because it's easier to connect the obvious dots and overfocus on small differences. Not dissimilar to conspiracy theories, whereby the left finds a rational lens by which to view the world and then explains everything through it. This failure inevitably drifts into unknown consequences. And we are left wondering, "How did we get here?" Worse than that, the "noise" is amplified to a deafening level by the internet, so much so that the signal may never be fully discerned. And for that, we will pay a high price. We appear to be far too distracted by the unreality of daily life, unable to separate the genuine grief and tragedy of our times from our unending seeking of identity and validation, again steering the ship toward the shoals (Plato's *Ship of Fools*).

In the future, it's important to understand how unlikely a second America revolution will take place, no matter how imperfect we are or how violent we were in the past. There will be revolutionary change, and there will be violence, but not a genuinely violent transformation. So what remains is how we make structural reform in the American society. We will have to wait for the sclerotic death of the Republican Party, and it could be a violent implosion rather than not waking from sleep. It is near the end, still waiting for the *rapture* when the past catches up to the future. But hidden in all this debate about the nature of our discontent is a simple reality. Only until financial markets are rendered less speculatively volatile and wealth meaningfully redistributed more fairly, broadly, and deeply will there be trust. This is the real hidden power in America. To be clear, what comes next could be violent, but it will not be revolutionary. The world is too invested in complexity and dynamical networks for that to happen.

Virtue-Denial

The most difficult videos to countenance are those of unprovoked police violence. What is even more difficult to comprehend are the risks police officers undertake every day and humanity of their actions we seldom see. No television footage of how much they put their sanity and lives on the line for us and how the actions of a few are distorting the overall picture. Reform is necessary when it comes to the use of force of any type, but the challenges of their work are overwhelming, and we need to better understand this. At times, they are literally operating in a war zone, and for everyone's safety, their decisions must be instantaneous (and unfortunately, the outcome can sometimes be catastrophic).

As a forensic psychologist having worked for many years in the criminal justice system, I can personally attest that knowing when to slow down and give up being in control of every interaction is a virtue that must be learned (and not everyone is capable of it). What we have discovered from our smartphone videos and police body cams is the police are not perfect and many times unnecessarily aggressive and violent. And some are unqualified to be officers of the law. But all this talk of defunding the police department is a bizarre denial of reality and a complete capitulation to absolutist virtue-think.

One of our greatest failures to law enforcement has been to put them on an island in a sea of craziness and violence, where none of us want to be. I mean no one in Flint, Michigan, wanted to give up drinking water because theirs had been poisoned with lead. No, they wanted clean water, not less water. Same with police departments.

We should reflect on the Roman Empire, conquered many times from 387 BC to AD 476 by "barbarians" (Ostrogoth, Vandal, Gaul, Hun, and Visigoth). And after they entered and sacked Rome, they all left, having no idea what to do with the architectural marvels, running water, public sanitation, paved roads, the wealth of technology, landmarks of literature, and the administrative, legal, and philosophical advances. They retreated to their villages and towns while civilization waited another one thousand years to reemerge. We can't do that today and survive.

Chapter 9

American Warlords Vigilantism

Vigilante. A member of a self-appointed group of citizens who undertake law enforcement in their community without legal authority, typically because the legal agencies are thought to be inadequate (Oxford Dictionary).

Unsanctioned Hierarchy, Order, and Identity

From time immemorial, the exercise of authority (power) has been to suppress the individual impulse and ensure social conformity by a ruling elite or clique. The goal has always been to reduce conflict and organize an interactive community against the contingencies of life. Our survival has been wholly dependent on it. It is also how all higher primates construct their social worlds. The result, throughout most of human history, has been authoritarian rule and unending conflict challenging the privileges inherent in exercising authority, e.g., assassination, overthrow, putsch, takeover, coup, revolt, purge, mutiny, revolution, rebellion, civil war (we got terms for it). And always the never-ending conflict to assure hereditary succession and the maintenance of order and, of course, privilege.

However, the powerful dysfunction in all this has only recently been highlighted by Enlightenment rationalism, the rise of human rights, and the modern liberal state. Here, leadership is elected, and the transfer of power is more orderly. And broadly, people are directly involved in the affairs of the state through elected representatives. In other words, a relatively decentralized social network in the US and Western Europe as opposed to the more traditionally centralized networks in Russia and China. Although a recent attempted coup by Trump Republicans and conservative media has tested this in the US.

Many who immigrated to America were revolting against repression and an orderly world that had ground them down. A window opened in America that allowed for a less orderly world, partly because a continent was being exploited, but also because of limited government. But trailing along were Protestant and Enlightenment values. And into this more individualistic and disorderly space evolved what de Tocqueville was the first to observe and comment on—the enormous energy in America to self-organize. And in this self-organizing bubble, one that rarely existed on this scale anywhere in the world, arose vigilantism, a challenging form of self-organization that is seldom tolerated in authoritarian nation-states, except as a proxy for state action, organized criminal activity, or a failure of centralized government. But in America, the impulse to vigilantism has been nearly impossible to irradicate, as if embedded in America's social contract.

This is all predicate to better understanding the driving elements of vigilantism in the US today, or what the Department of Homeland Security prefers to term "domestic violence extremism" or DVEs. The roots of this form of usurping authority are primeval. It is the assertion of dominance to maintain social order through an established hierarchy. It comes in two primary forms: the suppression of "others" to enforce order or hierarchy and a direct challenge to the exercise of authority by the state. And in America, they are often combined with an all-encompassing extremist ideology to justify acts of violence.

America's founding "vigilantism" has been a recessive but enduring trait. It is founded in multiple primitive impulses—an armed response to maintain social order, challenges to the misuse or illegitimate use of authority, and to assure a base identity in the face of an existential threat. Throughout our history, vigilantism has had many faces. For our purposes, we will refer to it as nonstate-sanctioned violence in the service of order.

While all the forces creating the impulse to vigilantism latently languish in our national character, underlying it is a profound distrust of centralized authority. There is also the assertion of a White Christian identity, which requires the continuous projection of an identified "other" as a threat to the social, economic, and political order (Native Americans, African Americans, Jews, Catholics, Hispanics, Muslims). And let's never forget that any sense of threat to identity (real or imagined) is always dangerous and capable of triggering a violent response. This is as true for an individual as it is for threats to collective identity.

When in Doubt, Resort to Violence

A survey undertaken by the nonprofit *Public Religion Research Institute* (PRRI) reported that 30 percent of Republicans agreed with the following statement: "Because things have gotten too far off track, true American patriots may have to resort to violence to save the country." This number jumped to 39 percent for those who believed the 2020 election had been stolen. Overall, only 18 percent of Americans agreed and 11 percent of Democrats. A similar survey taken by the conservative *American Enterprise Institute* found 39 percent of Republicans agreed with this statement: "If elected leaders will not protect America, the people must do it themselves, even if it requires violence." If there is a caution here, it would be the polling samples appear small and unstratified, and the wording of questions lead to an either-or response that makes violence seem like a reasonable option. But troubling nonetheless, given America's proneness to vigilante violence.

Native Americans

When Europeans arrived on the North American continent in 1492, historians estimate fifteen million Native Americans resided here. By 1592, 90 percent of the population had died from disease brought by European settlers. Today, there are 574 recognized tribes and a population of approximately five million. But by the close of the nineteenth century, there were only an estimated 238,000 Native Americans according to the *Equal Justice Initiative*.

Militia vigilantism among European settlers initially began as organized self-defense in circumstances where formal government rarely or barely existed. In November 1775, the Province of Massachusetts issued a declaration giving "His Majesty's Subjects" a license to kill members of the Penobscots for the "entire month," including men, women, and children. In today's currency, their financial reward could be up to $12,000 per scalp. A documentary on this subject, titled *Bounty*, reported more than seventy bounty proclamations were issued in the New England area encouraging colonists to kill members of the Penobscots tribe. It turns out this was common practice in colonial America.

> Colonial governments paid out bounties for scalps of at least 375 indigenous peoples across New England between 1675 to 1760.

In many instances, settlers could also be rewarded with tribal lands, with the aim of displacing Native tribes (D. Sharp 2021).

Following the *Pequot War* (1636–1637), the New England colonies formed a military alliance (New England Confederation) and later fought the Wampanoag, Pocumtuck, Nipmuck, and Narragansett in the *King Philip's War* (1675–1676). This was fifty years after the Pilgrims had landed at Plymouth (1620) and survived their first winter thanks to the Wampanoag, who later showed up that year uninvited to a harvest festival. Subsequently, most were killed by disease or war. Many were enslaved.

The American expansion westward gave rise to what historians call the Indian Wars and endless conflict with Native tribes over the next 350 years. Historians document many dozens of vigilante attacks and massacres of villages as a primary means of taking native lands or as reprisals. In what has been termed the *California Genocide*, from 1846 to 1871, settlers enslaved twenty-four to twenty-seven thousand Native Americans as forced laborers, including four to seven thousand children. An estimated nine to sixteen thousand died as a result. *Legends of America* records 159 "wars" between Native tribes and settlers, militias, and American soldiers between 1540–1898, with the last armed conflict taking place in 1924.

African Americans

Nothing evidences the ethos of American vigilantism, by its modern definition, than violence against African Americans. This second wave of American vigilantism engaged the violent suppression of African Americans, first as slaves (under legal pretense) and later as supposedly free citizens. For our purposes, let's begin post-Civil War with the Jim Crow South and the rise of the Ku Klux Klan. Here is the authentic face of vigilantism that speaks of the depth to which suppressing the rights of others can go in America. This includes a lengthy history of lynching Black Americans, culminating in the massacre of African Americans in Greenwood, Oklahoma, in 1921. Prominent were acts of violence committed against Black individuals and communities by the Klan from 1865 until the 1960s. *The Equal Justice Initiative* documents 6,500 "racial terror killings" in the US. The NAACP has documented 3,446 lynchings.

The Vigilante Killing of Ahmaud Arbery

On February 23, 2020, Ahmaud Arbery, a twenty-five-year-old Black man jogging in a primarily White suburban neighborhood of Satilla Shores in the southeast Georgia, was shot and killed by three White males, two armed with guns. They chased him down in two trucks and videoed it on a smartphone. One was a former police officer. When the victim reached toward the shotgun pointed at him, he was shot three times at point-blank range and killed. Later, when police arrived, one of the defendants was quoted as stating the victim "was trapped like a rat." The vigilante logic in this case was they suspected, without knowledge, that the victim had trespassed a construction site and possibly burglarized it, warranting a citizen's arrest. The individual who shot Mr. Arbery later claimed he felt threatened and acted in self-defense and therefore justified in the use of lethal force.

Clearly, if anyone had a right to feel threatened in this instance, it was the victim and not the individual pointing a shotgun with another armed individual next to him. At trial, it was acknowledged the victim made no verbal threats and was unarmed. What started as a hate crime ended in a murder of an innocent individual. Let's add another perspective to this act of violence. Laws supporting citizen's arrest date to 1863 for the sole purpose of recapturing escaped slaves. This irony is tragic, to say the least. This was really a lynching. From the time the first African slaves arrived in the Virginia colony in 1619, about five hundred miles from Satilla Shores, this form of violence has existed in America against African Americans.

What truly underpins vigilantism in America today is the Second Amendment right to keep and bear arms. Whether it's the death of Mr. Arbery or White militia groups showing up armed at peaceful demonstrations. Without guns, this form of violence would be virtually nonexistent today. Guns themselves empower people to lethal violence in acts of anger and omnipotence, a primeval form of violence from the dawn of human history. And to be clear, guns exist only as instruments of violence. The individuals who most need guns to exercise control are mostly men who feel empowered by the use of force, Which turns out to be a lot of Americans.

Let's go deeper and examine this homicide through the theory of absolute-mindedness. The absolute-minded reside in a perpetual state of emotional resignation, a fear-bound state easily triggered by threatening social cues. On the surface, the victim had violated de facto territorial boundaries in the minds of the defendants and was perceived a threat. This was then amplified by preexisting racial biases. The presence of a threat triggered a sense of shame over their feelings of helplessness, one immediately resolved by anger and retaliatory acts against the projected threat. And acting in concert gave increased viability to their aggressive actions, each prodding the other to act (a form of masculinity challenge inherent in primate males). This act of violence was emboldened by the preexisting social order (racism) and the defendants' belief that they were acting under color of authority, one being a former police officer. But also being asked by a sheriff to keep an eye out for a trespasser. Clearly, their need to genuflect to authority and the fantasy of acting with authority played a role in empowering this senseless act of violence. (A White jury convicted all three defendants of felony murder.)

The confounding aspect of this crime was these men did not have criminal records or histories of violence or antisocial behavior. In fact, they were conforming members of the community. Nor were drugs or alcohol involved. Why! If you were to ask me, having interviewed many thousands of criminal defendants and violent offenders, I would offer the simplest explanation is they set out to teach the victim a lesson—that he didn't belong there and needed to know his place. But also with the righteous belief they were protecting the community. And as is often the case in the use of guns to enforce vigilante justice, it escalated to violence. But the real reason is they were emotionally triggered by external events they will never understand. The chronic plight of the most absolute-minded.

Post–Civil War Vigilantism

Mobile County Alabama Massacre (1865)—White mob killed 138 Black people over several months.

Opelousas Massacre (1868)—two hundred plus African Americans were killed attempting to join the Democratic party.

Millican Massacre (1868)—armed White mob killed 150 Black people.

Colfax Massacre (1873)—153 African Americans were killed by Ku Klux Klan at a Louisiana courthouse and later as prisoners.

Vicksburg Massacre (1874)—White mob killed fifty Black people who were protesting the removal of an elected Black sheriff.

Polk County Massacre (1886)—a mob of White workers attacked Black workers, killing three and wounding eight in what has been termed "labor-related racial terrorism."

Thibodaux Massacre (1887)—three hundred striking Black sugarcane workers were killed.

Wilmington Massacre (1898)—White supremacists killed sixty-four African Americans while driving thousands from their homes.

Slocum Massacre (1910)—in East Texas, twenty-two African Americans were killed by a White mob (with some estimates ten times higher).

Elaine Massacre (1919)—estimates of a hundred to eight hundred African American farmers seeking better pay and cotton prices were shot and killed by a White mob.

Red Summer Chicago (1919)—three African Americans were killed and thousands of homes destroyed.

Ocoee Massacre (1920)—fifty-six African Americans were killed near Orlando, Florida, and their town destroyed.

Tulsa Race Massacre (1921)—an estimated forty plus African Americans were killed and eight hundred wounded and their town destroyed.

Rosewood Massacre (1923)—eight African Americans were killed and 350 driven from their homes.

(Please note this annotated list is primarily derived from the Equal Justice Initiative.)

Territorial Expansion

If you were President Santa Anna of Mexico in 1835, you directed the Mexican army to finally suppress ten years of domestic unrest, or what the Mexican government thought of as "pirates" attempting to declare an independent state of Texas. On the Texas side were privately organized militias (or what the Department of Homeland Security today terms *domestic violence extremists*). These wars of independence raged throughout the West. In 1846, a small band of thirty plus American settlers initiated a battle for California's independence from Mexico that eventually succeeded. Federal troops later fought armed engagements with Mormon militiamen in what became known as the Utah Wars (1857–1858). And in a rarely discussed massacre, the Mountain Meadows Massacre of 1857, Mormon Utah Territorial Militia killed 140 immigrants traveling through Utah by covered wagon.

America's "militia" days, however, are long gone, no matter how much nostalgia they generate. The only legitimate militias under the Constitution and federal law are those appointed by the states. No exceptions. And beyond that are what are termed "unorganized" militias, which are also state-authorized reserves backing up to the National Guard. But there remains a militia vigilantism legacy that many absolute-minded cling to, continually trying to undo their resignation by striking out in revenge at the projected "other."

Sidenote: Twenty-five states have a State Defense Force (SDF), and all states have the authority to authorize them. These are state militias that report directly to the governor and are not subject to federal control. A relic of the First World War, Congress legislated them into permanent status in 1956.

Range Wars

From the nineteenth century until the early twentieth century, there was nonstop violent conflict across the western United States. Most Americans today are only aware of this from old Western movies. This was violent vigilantism through and through as law enforcement barely existed. These wars had names such as Pleasant Valley War, Lincoln County War, Central Oregon Range War, Johnson County War, etc. And the conflict was over land rights, particularly "open range" for cattle grazing, but also over water rights, land ownership, and property borders. The conflicts were between large cattle barons and smaller cattle operations, but also with homesteaders, sheepherders overgrazing lands, and ranchers fencing lands. Most of these disputes were not resolved until the Taylor-Grazing Act of

1934. Here's the point. These conflicts ostensibly involved ranch hands, hired security agents, and bounty hunters attacking, shooting, and hanging anyone in their way.

In 1892, in Johnson County, Wyoming (Johnson County War), fifty-two armed men, first riding a train and then on horseback, were on a mission to shoot or hang seventy men identified as small cattle operators. This was the result of a long-running dispute with the goal of driving these operations off open rangelands. The cattle barons were also fearful the smaller operations would gain legal claim to the lands. Cattle and sheep wars engulfed Central Oregon from 1885 until the early 1900s from the overgrazing of open range lands by sheep. This conflict escalated as vigilante cattlemen burned sheep camps, poisoned, and shot sheep until the government intervened in 1906 and began regulating public lands. In New Mexico (1878), in what has been called the Lincoln County Wars, twenty-five plus cowhands and local citizenry formed a vigilante group called the Regulators to avenge the murder of a cattle rancher by a sheriff's posse. They were subsequently deputized by a local justice of the peace, whose actions were later declared illegal by the governor. The sheriff and many of his deputies were captured and killed, while a second sheriff's posse was formed to arrest the Regulators. This ended in several violent confrontations until federal troops finally intervened.

Labor Suppression

In the late nineteenth century, waves of labor-related violence ranged across America as industrialization ramped up and immigrants poured into the nation to meet labor demands (27.5 million between 1865 and 1918). And conflict ensued as a result of low wages and long hours of grueling work, often under dangerous conditions. And America's industrial monopolies during this Gilded Age were run by a Robber Baron class whose wealth far exceeded that of our tech titans today. They were also intent on breaking up all forms of organized labor. Typically, this meant hiring "private security" (and paid thugs) to threaten and, if necessary, attack striking workers (this was vigilantism corporate style).

In 1892, there had been 1,298 strikes across the country involving 164,000 workers. And more often than not, local police, state militias, and federal troops sided with the industrial class to break up these strikes. In 1897, nineteen striking miners were killed by local police in the Lattimer Massacre. During the Homestead Strike in 1892, the Carnegie Steel Company, determined to break the steelworkers' union, had upped production quotas violating an earlier contract agreement. A strike ensued, and Carnegie Steel hired three hundred private security forces to attack the strikers. After a day of gun battles, the state militia restored order, but only after nine strikers and seven security agents were killed.

Among the most notorious acts of vigilante violence against striking labor was the Ludlow Massacre in 1914. An unprovoked attack by National Guardsmen and private security, using machine guns, resulted in the death of twenty-five people, including two women and eleven children. But immigrant racism was also at the heart of labor violence. During the Rock Springs Massacre, twenty-eight Chinese workers were killed and fifteen wounded by 150 White coal miners. In the Los Angeles Chinatown Massacre, five hundred White and Latino men rioted and killed eighteen Chinese residents. The Ford Massacre took place on March 7, 1932. Five thousand employees of Ford Motor Company, who had been recently laid off, marched from downtown Detroit, Michigan, to the gates of the Ford Dearborn plant, where they were attacked by armed police and private security who openly fired into the crowd, killing five people and wounding and injuring sixty others. The injured admitted to a hospital for treatment were handcuffed to their hospital beds. No police officers or security agents were arrested (Wikipedia).

Where the Buffalo Used to Roam (High Roaming Fees It Turns Out)

I would assert that the legal, illegal, and immoral need to impose order on nature through violence originates from the same place in the human psyche as does the vigilante need to use violence against other human beings. They are both an effort to impose order on their world, typically with economic justification or from some sense of threat. The vigilante organization of killing animals appears to have few limits in our history and continues today. But perhaps the most egregious acts were against bison. In the sixteenth century, there was an estimated twenty-five to thirty million bison in North America. By the 1880s, they were near extinction, with less than one hundred remaining in the wild.

The ongoing predation by hunters of wolves, bears, otters, beavers, mountain lions, bison, bighorn sheep, and raptors brought them all near to extinction. This killing has been unending and is still promoted today as sound ecological practice. It is sport killing for the good of the herd. But there is also an underlying assertion of the "right" to do this. Or as Molly Carter stated in Wideopenspaces, "These are the ones every hunter deserves, no game animals are off-limits." On horseback, from a train or helicopter, we have slaughtered the mammal wildlife of North America without prejudice.

We can sense the fury of a Montana rancher who has lost a calf to a mountain lion and the need to hunt it down and kill it. And, of course, American big-game hunters travel to Africa to kill lions, elephants, rhinoceroses, leopards, and water buffalo as a fictitious means of supporting local economies, but really as a means by which to dominate the natural world. We can probably give our prehistoric ancestors a pass here. Still, they were efficient in killing off most of North America's *megafauna mammals* (over a hundred pounds), including mammoths, mastodons, giant beavers, saber-toothed tigers, ground sloths, and dire wolves. This "overkill hypothesis" is debated by researchers, but it's clear that beginning eleven thousand years ago, when humans first arrived, thirty-six mammal species became extinct.

Kill Every Buffalo You Can! Every Buffalo Dead Is an Indian Gone

The author writes that in 1873, depression struck the country and that "thousands of buffalo runners came, sometimes averaging 50 kills a day. They sliced their humps, skinned off the hides, tore out their tongues, and left the rest on the prairies to rot." Throughout much of the prairie, buffalo had completely vanished. Quoting correspondence from a Colonel Dodge:

> Where there were myriads of buffalo the year before, there were now myriads of carcasses. The air was foul with a sickening stench, and the vast plain which only a short twelve months before teemed with animal life, was a dead, solitary desert. The wasteland was so scattered with the bones of dead animals and buffalo that all the prairie felt like a graveyard risen. (J. W. Phippen, *The Atlantic*, 2016)

Today there are an estimated twenty to twenty-five thousand buffalo on public lands (for each one, there used to be a million). On May 9, 2016, President Obama signed the National Bison Legacy Act, making the American buffalo our national mammal.

Today, it is still legal to shoot and kill bison, with a permit.

> Do people hunt buffalo today for sport and/or meat? One large buffalo typically provides some 600 pounds of meat, which feeds a lot of people. People like eating buffalo meat because it's considered leaner and healthier than beef. (TiogaBoarHunting.com)

In May 2021, the National Park Service authorized killing two hundred buffalo (from a herd of five hundred) near the north rim of the Grand Canyon. Once again, they were trampling vegetation. I am sure we are all relieved the Park Service is on top of this problem. The real problem was the herd was thriving and posed a nuisance to tourism, all those people wanting to experience the awe of nature.

Anti-government

An enduring element of American vigilantism has been the long arc of anti-government sentiment challenging the federal government's legitimacy. Distrust in government came to America with its earliest European settlers. And yes, many were grifters and exploiters and religiously preoccupied Protestants, each now a private author of their own delusional reality and a founding source of unending conspiracies. We were founded on a basic distrust in government, and our Constitution was a shining legal document assuring protection from government. And as soon as the federal government was established, there was vigilantism to challenge its authority.

Let's first look back at the beginnings of the American Revolution and the Boston Tea Party. Yes, it was an act of "vigilantism" by merchants fed up with tariffs and taxes. Sixty colonists, disguised as Mohawk Indians, dumped 342 chests of tea into the harbor to protest against taxation policies and the monopoly on tea the British government gifted to the East India Company. And as highly repressive measures by the British government followed, it escalated America's drift toward revolution. From the British standpoint, these taxes were a means of paying for the huge debt incurred by the French Indian Wars twelve years earlier.

The first significant vigilante challenge to the newly established American government was Shays' Rebellion in 1786. Following the Revolutionary War, a debt crisis ensued, one that created enormous economic hardships throughout the country. Veterans of the Continental Army and state militias had received very little in the way of compensation for their service. Shays' Rebellion was a violent uprising in Massachusetts (but also a wider one throughout the states) against debt collection, particularly by rural farmers losing their lands as debts were called in. Twelve hundred militiamen attempted to storm the federal armory at Springfield, Massachusetts, but were defeated by the nation's new army. Eight years later, in 1794, settlers in western Pennsylvania revolted against a liquor tax to help pay the cost of the war in the Whiskey Rebellion. Washington led an army to suppress it, fearing challenges to the legitimacy of the federal government.

We need to be candid here about the threat of vigilantism to the government. The only true threat to the federal government was the Civil War. This conflict has been the only true act of vigilantism in American history that was a threat to the Union, when eleven Southern states succeeded in 1861. Some would make the case that this was state sanctioned in a loose federation of states called the United States. But others would argue, from a federalist perspective, that it was unauthorized vigilantism by states acting in defiance of federal authority.

Today, a core group of Americans has come to question the legal and political legitimacy of the federal government and see it as a direct threat to their rights and identity. These movements go so far as to challenge the federal government's authority to exercise the rule of law, determine citizenship, collect taxes, exercise monetary policy, and manage federal lands. And always the mistrust that the government is in the business of suppressing their rights to control and subjugate them. Examples abound. The government wants to take away their Second Amendment right to bear arms, deny mineral rights to western landowners, or use FEMA to set up concentration camps. And as the government grows in authority and power, the more threatening it becomes. As a result, we are in a spin cycle that is nearly impossible to interrupt.

What is not included here is the action taken by gangs, criminal syndicates, and drug cartels operating in the US. By academic standards, they do not qualify as vigilantes or violent domestic terrorists. But given the level of violence, their reach into our economy and the destruction wrought by them, is that really true? Their actions largely mimic many earlier vigilante groups—nonstate-sanctioned violence, highly territorial, revenge-minded, and enforcing hierarchy. While they do not directly challenge the legitimacy of the government or seek to enforce the broader social order, within their limited scope of operations, they act vigilante-like, with enforcers and hitmen and sporadic episodes of mass violence that defies the rule of law and challenges the authority of the state.

Political Assassination

It's great to be the king, but it is also very dangerous. But it seems someone always wants to be the king. Why is that? The answer is again, it's great to be the king. Let's take a deep breath for a moment because America is forgetful. Four US presidents have been assassinated in office: Abraham Lincoln (1865), James Garfield (1881), William McKinley (1901), and John F. Kennedy (1966).

But let's also contemplate the seventeen or so plotted and attempted assassinations of American presidents and how close many presidents came to being assassinated. It is chilling. And yes, this is an incredibly long list, including Andrew Jackson (1835), Theodore Roosevelt (1912), Herbert Hoover (1928), Franklin Roosevelt (1933), Harry S. Truman (1947 and 1950), Richard Nixon (1974), Gerald Ford (1975), Jimmy Carter (a vague threat was made in 1979 by a mentally ill individual), Ronald Reagan (shot and wounded 1981), Bill Clinton (1994 and 1996), George W. Bush (2001), and Barack Obama (two uncovered plots and two attempts). But there also have been other notable political assassinations, including Huey Long (senator), Robert Kennedy, George Wallace (wounded), Martin Luther King, Malcolm X, and civil rights leader Jordan Vernon.

Interestingly, the vice presidents of the United States have not been important enough to bother assassinating. Maybe former vice president John Nance's (1933–41) description of the office as "not worth a bucket of warm piss" is fairly accurate. Really, who remembers him? Out of forty-five presidents, there have been assassination attempts against nearly half of them. And in some instances, multiple attempts were made. It is not difficult to imagine the potential chaos that would have ensued if many of these attempts had succeeded. In every known instance, these assassination plots and attempts were largely by dysfunctional individuals and not by organized vigilante groups. (It is also important to note that in 1914, Bosnian terrorists assassinated Archduke Franz Ferdinand of Austria. The result was World War I.) In the US, no political assassination has ever led to a conflict. No, the vice president becomes president (except for Secretary of State Al Haig, who claimed in 1981, "I'm in control here," after President Reagan was shot).

American "Anomie" or Solo-Vigilantism

Today, when we drill down, we quickly come to understand that our violent history of vigilantism has been largely suppressed by the overwhelming police and military powers of the state, particularly when compared to our long history of violence. There are still occasional breakthrough acts of violence, such as the Oklahoma City bombing. And while we continue to experience it in the guise of the militia movement, QAnon and Sovereign citizens, and dozens of other populous vigilante groups, the real mechanisms of expression are individualistic acts of violence and narcissistic rage—randomly attacking people at worship, work, shopping, partying, and attending school, often out of a personal sense of anger, despair, and revenge. This is classic *grievance-revenge-violence*, with limited planning and forethought, but always in a desperate and despairing mode: "I am going out and taking someone with me." And there's a lot of this rage in America, as are the ubiquitous and affordable means by which to carry it out—guns.

From 1982 to 2002, there were a reported thirty mass shootings in the United States (defined as four or more people killed or wounded). But from 2003 to 2022, there have been 101 mass shootings, over a 300 percent rise (Statista). The FBI reports there were sixty-one mass shootings in 2021 alone. Since 2013, there have been forty-five mass school shootings, all by students (or former students) using semiautomatic weapons, including Virginia Tech, Sandy Hook Elementary School, Marjory Stoneman Douglas High School, Umpqua Community College, Red Lakes Senior High School, Oikos University, West Nickel Mines School, Northern Illinois University, Santa Monica College, Marysville Pilchuck High School,

Columbine HS, Santa Fe High School, and the Robb Elementary School in Uvalde.

Violent Catharsis

We shouldn't ignore that we live in society saturated 24-7 in simulated violence (TV, movies, and video games). To a certain degree, it has normalized violence for generations of youth, and not just as graphic images but as an immersive experience. While it's difficult to demonstrate this connection, the rapid rise in mass shootings should give us pause. For most people, video games are vicarious experiences that are nothing more than private fantasy of no particular importance beyond their entertainment value. But a few may be pushed across a threshold, particularly the sense of omnipotence and indifference to reality they impart. Watching eighteen-year-old Kyle Rittenhouse testifying at trial for shooting three people and killing two of them during protests in Kenosha, Wisconsin, in 2020 respond to the prosecutor's question as to why he owned a semiautomatic military-style weapon, he responded, "It looked cool."

In America, the most powerful psychological driver in an act of mass violence is feeling one has been redeemed by imposing their personal sense of justice on the world in an act of retribution. These individuals marinate in grievance, and mass shootings are the definitive statement of the inflated rage they anonymously suffer. Now the entire world knows who they are and the power of their feeling disrespected, unvalued, and unseen. And people's fear and anger provide them the significance they have never experienced. Many are then content to take their own lives as a final "fuck you" to emphasize they meant it. For them, it undoes all the past rejections, slights, mistreatment, insecurity, and invisibility. Really, their sense of insignificance. Still, others are content to live their lives out in prison, satisfied they have made the world pay attention to them. "Look at me. Look at how powerful I am. I have to be locked up for everyone's safety." They are telling the world, "Hey, payback is a bitch." And they are content as never before. They were here, capable of great tragedy and injustices in a world that is obsessed with it. Finally, everyone is paying respect (we especially see this with mass and serial killers and their Charles Manson moments in the media).

The gun ethos embedded in the American psyche has many hidden elements, and one of them is the belief that an entertainment media saturated in violence has no blowback. The secret sauce in gun violence is the sense of empowerment and fear generated by carrying and wielding a gun. Creating fear empowers those who feel powerless, and that may be enough for some. As many list toward anonymity or suffer the indifference of those around them, they sense they are "failing," which is the greatest sin of all in America. The rise in mass shooting was inevitable. A man and his gun on the frontier doing "what a man's got to do," this is their WWII *Wake Island* movie, going out in machine gun bravado. It is our *Rambo* act of retribution and payback. It is a *Scarface* moment: "Say hello to my little friend." And Dirty Harry's 44 magnum: "Go ahead and make my day." Or actor Liam Neeson proclaiming in *Taken*, "But what I do have are a very particular set of skills. I will look for you, I will find you, and I will kill you." (And the tens of thousands of choreographed scenes of gun violence we are all routinely exposed to.)

Being immersed in thousands of hours of entertaining violence renders violence-omnipotence even more heroic and empowering, emphasizing a dark honor in killing (as one neighbor shoots another for violating their property boundary and calmly waits for the police to arrive or a jealous or rejected boyfriend killing his girlfriend and dialing 911). At some point for the absolute-minded, a rigid personal boundary that is defining and inviolate has been crossed, literally reducing one's sense of self to an undifferentiated caricature, not unlike removing a block from a game of Jenga and toppling the entire edifice. It is always this moment for violent action, the personal sense that one has been decimated and that shooting someone momentarily makes one whole again.

But really, it is all of us saturated in violence and residing in chronic subliminal fear. In a not unsubtle way, mass shooters are acting out our shared fears, hurting people where they hurt the most in random acts of violence against the most innocent—our children. And this points us to where many of these offenders believe they suffered the most—as children in school. They want to wipe it out because they live with it forever, the humiliation, embarrassment, discontent, rejection, the lost sense of self, and not being good enough that follows them forever. These early formative experiences are that powerful when trust has been dissolved.

We should stop kidding ourselves. Guns are the instrument that kill people because of what rages inside us. The availability of guns and the depth of gun ownership in a dysfunctional America is the major cause of our mass violence. Selling guns to Americans is, in part, arming a paranoid and delusional subset of Americans who are at war with the world around them. The governor of Texas, Gregg Abbott, recently advocated making Texas a "gun sanctuary state." He doesn't understand America is already a "violence sanctuary" nation. His grandstanding is a cynical manipulation of people's fear for his own political ends.

In absolutist America, mass shootings and all other acts of gun violence are a right, one fully permitted under the Second Amendment. The key for most of us is suspending disbelief until after someone exercises their constitutional right. The result is mass gun violence is pretty much the new normal for those who want to be America-free. A right repeatedly affirmed by the US Supreme Court. Gun violence is the cathartic arbitrator of one's underlying outrage and general sense of grievance (while NRA is content requesting a clean-up on aisle 3 and offering 10 percent off your next ammo purchase).

Republican leadership does not publicly make the case that gun violence is good, only that it is a small price we pay for the right to own and carry a firearm (and polls suggest a high percentage of Republicans agree). Apparently, no amount of gun violence is too high a price to pay for gun ownership, especially if one is expected to be prepared for war and oorah-ready to bring down the government at a moment's notice. There is no violence threshold if war is the ultimate concern. But with more gun violence, the greater the need for everyone to be armed in an escalating arms race with ourselves or what is seen as a win-win on the political right. Currently, there are an estimated 393 to 434 million firearms in the US, give or take a few. But when you are battling conspiracies, occasional collateral damage is to be expected (same if Vice President Mike Pence had been hanged during the January 6 riot). And let's not forget all the government false flag operations confusing righteous killing with false prophecy.

Gun politics is one reason the United States is among the most violent nations on earth. What gun advocates don't understand is the "militia game" has been over for 150 years. It's time for us to publicly lay down our weapons. The war in our heads, in reality, is over, and we won. We are like the two Japanese soldiers hiding out in the Philippine jungle and surrendering sixty years after the war (2005), at ages eighty-seven and eighty-five, asking if they could go home. It is time for so many Americans to come home. We are only murdering each other now (mostly forming "I don't trust you" circles and shooting one another). In reality, no one is seeking to suppress White America. And when the right can't blame a racial or ethnic group or immigrants or the amorality of others, that only leaves the government for many. And that appears good enough. Anything is better than nothing. Otherwise, what would be the cause of all their anger, fear, and distrust?

Boys to Men

There has been a great deal of research over these past few years (Peterson and Densley 2021; Schweit 2021; Follman 2022) to help stem the rising tide of mass shootings, beginning with trying to understand the state of mind of the mass shooters and the circumstances giving rise to their horrendous acts. And an identifiable pattern has emerged. The problem is, for everyone who fits this profile, there are many thousands of individuals who will never commit a mass shooting, which means identifying dangerous individuals is beyond our capability. (And having spent an entire professional career largely devoted to the prediction of violent behavior, I am confident of this assertion.)

Perhaps the more relevant question we should be asking is, Why are there so many more violent acts in the US than in any other developed country? Now we are getting somewhere. And yes, the ubiquitous availability of semiautomatic weapons is the number one reason. But there are many other reasons as well. The underlying American ethos of hyper-independence and violent retribution play a role. And we have already covered the media saturation effect. But if we really wanted to honestly drill down, we would look more closely at the fracturing of American family life and the general instability of families. This would require us to look at the rising tide of feminism and its insatiable focus on an #MeToo-ism that is oblivious to the realities of young men today.

In the US, more women graduate high school than men (and boys are far more likely to be physically bullied in school). More women graduate college than men. More men fall into substance abuse than women. More men get arrested and go to jail and serve prison sentences than women. There are more men in state mental hospitals and more men admitted daily to emergency mental health care facilities. More men are homeless and live on the streets than women. More men engage in work that puts them at greater physical risk for their health than women. On average, women outlive men by five to seven years (and men are more likely to die doing stupid things and taking greater risks). And male suicide rates are greater as well. Men are subject to greater levels of physical abuse and assault throughout their lives than women (regardless of what you watched on Dateline or ID Discovery channels). We as a society have been more than willing to sacrifice men when it comes to war and all physical risks (our genetics and primate genealogy probably accounts for much of this). And making the case that men are doing this to themselves does not absolve men or women from how so many men have become increasingly violent and destructive in America.

Gender Cage Match

From its inception, the field of psychology was dominated by men, from academic researchers to clinicians, but by the time I graduated and entered practice, this reality had begun to flip-flop, and today, women dominate this field of mental health. So why am I mentioning this? Only because the American Psychological Association (APA) could never explain to me why it had a Women's Directorate and not a Men's Directorate. A few years ago, I pointed out how this field had primarily become a career for women, one still being actively promoted by the APA. Asking what they were doing to bring men into the field was met with complete silence. This is only noted as an example of how we have become so singularly focused on blaming and shaming men that we are failing to take notice of their plight as well. The momentum of women's rise in America will never be perfect or complete. But we are going to have to do more than one thing at a time to bring down rates of violence in America. Of the 163 documented mass shootings in America since 1966, only three were by women. And notably, 83 percent of gun death victims were men.

Just to be clear, this is not, in any way, meant to be a diatribe against women or their rise in the world today, but only to shake out a few basic realities men face that are not being addressed. And this is not an either-or problem. The solution is not sacrificing the gains of women to help men but just honestly addressing what we are obviously missing. It is typical to point to the male dominance in upper management, on corporate boards of governance, pay differentials and the rates at which women experience discrimination and suffer all forms of abuse at the hands of men (particularly in Hollywood), which are true and need to be addressed. But we don't want to address how men are being failed because we are more willing to sacrifice them. What America is failing to address is, Why are so many boys and girls and men and women being subjected to abuse and violence? And because of this failure, violence is one of the consequences we are suffering from. What we need to do is garner greater support for families in general, from neonatal care through early adulthood, and finally out into the world. It is all too haphazard, and we are now paying the price. The solution is long-term and has no immediate resolution, except to support families in a way we have terribly neglected and to limit access to guns.

Government Overreach

While government overreach is not formally vigilantism as defined here, it is government broadly operating outside norms and violating social trust. Let's call it governmental vigilantism. And there is little doubt that incidences of government violence against citizens is a powerful antecedent to the rise of the modern militia movement in the US.

While many of us today struggle to understand people's distrust of government, one needs to only look back at government overreach to understand how distrust has been sowed. This includes a long history of supporting a White majority over minorities, business over labor, and the economic well-off over the impoverished. The fact is, America has always been a punitive community that deals harshly with people who fall down and are struggling, offering little in the way of hope except for the promise of more grief to come for their failures.

Reservations

Clearly, the unofficial goal of the Indian reservation system had been to confiscate Native American lands and culturally assimilate indigenous peoples. The first reservation was established in New Jersey in 1758. Only in 1824 did the government establish the Office of Indian Affairs. It would be fair to say that the entire history of treaties until 1934 has been one of violation by settlers and the federal government. Between 1778 and 1871, over five hundred treaties were violated. After the Louisiana Purchase (1803) and the military defeat of the Creek at the Battle of Horseshoe Bend, the Creek ceded twenty million acres of land to the federal government. In 1830, the *Indian Removal Act* was signed into law, permitting the government to apportion lands west of the Mississippi to compensate tribes. This led to the forced resettlement of the Choctaw, Creek, Chickasaw, Shawnee, Huron, Ottawa, Miami, and Delaware to the Oklahoma territories. In 1838, federal troops marched Cherokee in Alabama, Tennessee, and North Carolina 1,200 miles to Oklahoma reservations, resulting in deaths of thousands, in what came to be called the Trail of Tears.

In 1851, the government passed the *Indian Appropriations Act*, creating the Indian reservation system. Native people were not allowed to leave the reservations and were forced into farming. Disease and starvation were common. In 1887, the *Dawes Act* allowed the government to partition reservation lands into farming plots. This resulted in a further loss of tribal lands, opening it up to settlers and railroads. In 1934, the *Indian Reorganization Act* was passed with the goal of aiding tribes to self-govern with the assistance of federal financial aid, now under the supervision of the Bureau of Indian Affairs (and operating independent of federal law). Today, there are currently 326 Indian reservations in the US. Total reservation lands are approximately the size of Idaho. Currently, two-fifths of Native American (one million) reside on reservations. (They can now leave when they want.)

DC Massacre

In 1932, during the height of the Great Depression, forty-three thousand demonstrators, primarily seventeen thousand WWI veterans and family members, demonstrated in Washington, DC. They were demanding cash redemption of their war "service bonus certificates" (issued in 1924 and due in 1945). President Hoover first ordered police to break up the demonstration and clear the campsites. (There were fears this was a communist-inspired demonstration. For the record, it wasn't.) In the course of rioting, police shot two demonstrators dead. General Douglas MacArthur was then ordered to break up the demonstration. Using infantry with fixed bayonets and tear gas, calvary led by Major George Patton and six tanks charged the demonstrators, injuring fifty-five veterans. When Roosevelt later won election that same year, he set up field kitchens for demonstrators, and First Lady Eleanor Roosevelt visited the site to meet with veterans during a second demonstration, leading to the creation of the Civilian Conservation Corps.

Internment

Two months after Japan bombed Pearl Harbor, President Roosevelt signed Executive Order 9066 establishing the "War Relocation Authority." The stated goal was the prevention of espionage by evacuating all people deemed a national security threat. (Initially, German and Italian Americans were also considered.) This order applied only to those of Japanese descent living in Hawaii and on the West Coast. In total, 120,000 people, including eighty thousand American citizens, underwent forced relocation to ten prison camps in restricted military zones (California, Arizona, Utah, Colorado, Wyoming, and Arkansas). They were given six days to report to Assembly Centers, including seventeen thousand children under the age of ten. Most lost their land, personal belongings, and businesses as a result. In 1945, the Supreme Court ruled in *Ex parte Mitsuye Endo* that the executive order was unconstitutional. The last camp was closed in 1946. (In 1943 or 1944, the military formed a unit of Japanese Americans, the 442nd Regimental Combat Team, that became the most decorated combat unit serving in Europe.)

Kent State Shooting

On May 4, 1970, student protests formed with the announcement that President Nixon had secretly expanded the Vietnam War into Cambodia after an election promise to end the war. After several nights of violent clashes between police and protestors in Kent, Ohio, near Kent State University, a thousand members of the Ohio National Guard were called in to restore order. Confronted by three thousand protestors and spectators, twenty-eight members of the Guard fired seventy shots into a crowd that had refused to disperse. Four students were killed and nine injured. In a later court settlement, the Guard acknowledged it was not in danger and "the tragedy should not have occurred."

Ruby Ridge and Waco

These two violent events formed the origin myths of the modern militia movement in the United States. In both events, overwhelming violence on the part of the government against citizens fomented anti-government conspiracy theories. Ruby Ridge, Idaho (1992), an attempt to enforce an arrest warrant on a fugitive for the illegal sale of guns, who had evaded appearing in court, led to a shootout. Randy Weaver's fourteen-year-old son shot a marshal after the marshal had shot his dog. Both died. The FBI intervened in the standoff, killing Weaver's wife and wounding him and a friend of his son. Nine days later, the friend, Weaver, and his three daughters surrendered. A year later, in 1993, the *Waco Siege* took place just outside Waco, Texas. There had been a fifty-one-day standoff between federal agents and the Branch Davidians (a millennial Christian sect). The siege ended when fire consumed their compound, resulting in seventy-five deaths, including twenty-five children. This all began when eighty ATF agents raided the compound on reports the Davidians were violating federal firearms regulations. Four agents and six Davidians were killed in a gun battle. Soon, nine hundred law enforcement officials and the FBI laid siege to the compound. To end the siege, tanks were used to deposit four hundred tear gas containers. Fires soon broke out, leading to the deaths. There was no evidence the fires were the result of the tanks or gas canisters.

Incarceration

In the US, there are currently 2.3 million people serving prison time in 1,833 state prisons; 110 federal prisons; 1,772 juvenile correctional facilities; 3,134 local jails; 218 immigration detention facilities; eighty Indian Country jails, as well as military prisons, civil commitment centers, state psychiatric hospitals, and in US territories. With a per capita rate of 698 per 100,000, the US has both the highest number of people and the highest rate of incarceration worldwide. Each year, six hundred thousand enter prison and 10.6 million enter jail. And there is little doubt that our failed "war on drugs" is at the heart of what is taking place, as one in five incarcerations are for drug-related offenses. There are approximately 840,00 people on parole and 3.6 million on probation. And if you believe the poor and people of color are overrepresented in this population, you would be correct. And for those without financial means or support, jails have become modern debtor prisons, with bail and all the fines/restitution levied by the courts (Sawyer and Wagner 2020).

Guantanamo Bay Detention Camp

This forty-five-square-mile site was originally leased in 1903 from the Cuban government to support US naval operations. Since the US military detention facility opened in 2002, 780 men have been detained at this extra-legal prison (nine have died in custody). Currently, thirty-nine detainees remain incarcerated. To date, eight have been convicted by military courts. Total cost for its operation is $6 billion. The camp was established outside the US to ensure that US courts did not have jurisdiction. The Bush administration (2001–2009) also made the legal argument that because the prisoners were nonstate actors, they were not party to the Geneva Convention or qualify as POWs. As a consequence, CIA was then brought in to interrogate detainees. However, a subsequent Senate hearing determined there was no evidence that "enhanced interrogation" has been effective in obtaining vital national security intelligence or preventing terrorist attacks. It also turned out that the majority of prisoners had no ties to al-Qaeda or the Taliban. (Bottom line, human rights violations are not a good look for the beacon of democracy. Perhaps more to the point, here was a Republican administration undertaking subterfuge to work around the law, something we saw on full display with the Trump administration's attempt to overturn the 2020 election. This is a dangerous playbook.)

Constitutional Sheriff's Movement

This is a coalition of conservative, far-right-minded sheriffs asserting that their law enforcement authority legally supersedes that of state and federal officials within their counties (which sounds grandiose, if not outright delusional). The Southern Poverty Law Center has labeled them an extremist group. The upshot of this has been an active effort by these sheriffs to pick and choose which laws are unconstitutional and refuse to enforce them, whether federal gun laws, issues of border security, federal land management, or federal public health guidelines. In a recent survey by the Marshall Project (Farris and Holman 2022), 40 percent of the sheriffs sampled broadly supported the idea that their authority overrides state and federal authority.

And here is perhaps the most concerning aspect of this movement. These sheriffs also believe they have the authority to investigate and, if necessary, intervene in the administration of elections, independent of all other legal authority. This facet of the movement quickly emerged as it began to align with conservative vote-monitoring groups pushing election fraud conspiracies. Of course, there is a prologue to this assertion of legal omnipotence. It is preceded by the "county supremacy movement" (which most of us never heard of), but all derive from the same anti-government sentiments of the "Posse Comitatus" and "Sovereign Citizens Movement."

This is a dangerous alignment of law enforcement and extremism at a precarious moment in US history. The key takeaway should be that all law enforcement in the US, including sheriff and police departments, Homeland Security, FBI, and Secret Service, are staffed by many like-minded individuals who are opening a doorway to an authoritarian America. Our "thin blue line" is wavering in many agencies and departments across the country. And we have to consider the likelihood that highly organized public attacks on law enforcement across the county, over the past ten years, have pushed many in law enforcement further to the right and toward the delusional and conspiratorial edges of our social reality.

Rogue Department of Homeland Security

While it is vital to follow the money, it is equally important to closely investigate the chain of command (as the House Select

Committee to Investigate the January 6 attack on the US Capitol is so aptly proving). The higher up, the greater the authoritarian threat to America. And this was fully previewed for us by the Trump administration. It is now being reported that an internal Department of Homeland Security (DHS) investigative report, released by Oregon Senator Ron Wyden (Gizmodo) in November 2022, revealed that the DHS, operating across multiple federal law enforcement agencies, local law enforcement, and private security contractors, implemented an administration plot to detain, arrest, and create secret intelligence dossiers on anti-racism protestors, all in an effort to give legitimacy to Trump's claim that these protests were being fomented by radical leftwing groups.

Intelligence officials were attempting to connect protestors to a completely fabricated left-wing terrorist plot in an effort to boost Trump's poll numbers in the upcoming presidential election. But the most troubling aspects of this are in the details. Anyone on the streets the night of the Portland protest in 2021, whether arrested or not, could be the subject to federal investigation and labeled an "anarchist extremist," even if only charged with misdemeanor trespassing. To further this plot, Justice Department lawyers attained a court motion allowing law enforcement to force reporters off the streets, with later reports of protesters being abducted off the streets without provocation by federal agents and private security contractors (Triple Canopy, formally Blackwater).

This brings us uncomfortably close to Nazi's brown shirts being directed to attack political opponents in 1933, after Hitler was appointed German chancellor. It is one problem if local law enforcement overreacted with water cannons and mace, but creating federal dossiers out of whole cloth takes this to a new and troubling level that we can observe in nations like Turkey, Russia, and China. What has been unveiled in the actions of DHS is how easily internal norms and legal boundaries can be violated time and again without consequence while distorting the law for political gain. In fact, there may be no protection against this reality in the coming future. This is the might and weight of federal law enforcement organized to commit criminal acts on the pretext of state security.

Anonymous, Endless Proxy Wars

For the past twenty years, American Armed Forces have been engaged in dozens of clandestine intelligence and counterintelligence operations around the world—secret wars—as recently reported by the Brennan Center of Justice (2022) and online by the *Intercept* (Turse and Speri). And here is the key takeaway. This activity has gone largely unknown to House and Senate armed service and intelligence committees, who have constitutional oversight. In fact, it appears that these covert operations were designed to evade oversight. There is vague legal authorization—Authorization for Use of Military Force (2001) and National Defense Authorization Act (2018) Sections 127e and 120 that allow for "support to foreign forces, irregular forces, groups, or individuals." And the even more vague authority of US Code § 333. US military personnel have been active in Afghanistan, Cameroon, Egypt, Iraq, Kenya, Lebanon, Libya, Mali, Mauritania, Niger, Nigeria, Somalia, Syria, Tunisia, and Yemen, as well as an unknown number of unidentified countries in the Asia-Pacific region. How these programs are even funded is obscure and largely unknown within the government. While they may yield considerable foreign policy value, we still have to operate as a democracy. Perhaps more to the point, none of these operations are blunting a direct threat to US security. It is the US picking sides worldwide and meddling with the potential for serious blowback in the future.

The Vigilante Game—American Style

It just so happens that the absolute-minded are hyper-triggered by social cues to organize and respond violently. And today, they are being played by dark money, Republican governors, and conservative media in what is politely termed the "cultural war." There are really three simultaneous political challenges to the authority of the federal rule of law in the US. One is by the Republican Party to hold on to political power. Second is by its base to defend what it perceives as threats to its rights and identity. And third, dark money thrashing America to hold on to its financial clout. And the base is cued by the

Republican leadership, who are being funded by conservative money in an absolutist death spiral of delusional conspiracies. The real danger is more from the top than from the base. The top is more desperate and has the financial and political power to disrupt the American experiment. The base's need is for conformity. As long as their basic needs are being met—employment, health care, education, etc.—the current trend of populism and militancy will remain largely fallow for the majority.

Vigilantism is a violent response by the most absolute-minded to perceived social disorder. To a varying degree, it has always been present in the US and always potentially violent and destructive. But today, it is as ubiquitous as UFO sightings, and it would not be crazy to believe that the two are related to one another. To say that paranoid conspiracies are a modern contagion is a gross understatement of reality. Yes, there were fears about the Illuminati in the eighteenth century and about Papists and Freemasonry in the nineteenth century. By the early 1900s, it was Bolshevism and Zionism. But by the time Communist conspiracies consumed the United States in the early 1950s, so did UFO sightings. Today, conspiracies have metastasized—black ops takeover, New World Order, jet chemtrails laced with pathogens, anti-vaccine theories, space lasers starting wildfires, Satanic cults, deep state takeover, shape-shifting lizard people running government, false election results, alien abductions. The list is endless and mindless in an evolving system of belief or conspiracism for many. And not coincidently, the media is saturated with craziness—television, social media, print, online forums—all orchestrating craziness for profit (none more so than the History Channel. How ironic).

And now the craziness is on our doorstep once again—an armed standoff in Oregon (2016) disputing federal land rights, a White supremacist torch parade in Virginia (2017), a threat by domestic terrorists to kidnap and hang the governor of Michigan, armed "Judgment Day" protest at the Michigan state capital over COVID-19 safety restriction (2020), and invasion of the US Capitol Building (January 6, 2021) in an attempt to overthrow the election and potentially hang the vice president. What makes this latter event interesting from a historical standpoint was the government's complete failure to use lethal force to disrupt the rioters and force them to stand down, which they should have. Not at all like Kent State, the 1968 Chicago Democratic Convention, Waco, or Ruby Ridge. Here, law enforcement's complete laxness and ineffectualness actually caused violence to escalate. Currently, there are an estimated two hundred militia groups throughout the US, including Oath Keepers, Proud Boys, Boogaloo Boys, American Firsters, and Three Percenters. Various estimated are for over 1,020 hate groups in the US (Southern Poverty Law Center). Numbers for both groups have increased substantially (30 percent) since the beginning of the Trump administration.

Today, vigilantism is primarily manifested in right-wing, anti-government, and White supremacist organizations, including the Posse Comitatus in the 1960s, Sovereign Movement in the 1990s, Minutemen (2000), and of course, the grandfather of all of them all, the Ku Klux Klan, beginning post-Civil War and reconstruction. And currently, all this fear and violence is being stoked by social media and conservative news, with the Republican Party providing oxygen (legal legitimacy) to setting America on fire. Our new reality is that the current Republican Party hides a consortium of fascist agendas with a willingness to subvert the democratic process to hold on to political power.

But the absolute-minded are always in eternal rebellion without a cause, and with plenty of delusions. Get a COVID-19 vaccination? Hell no! But show up to riot at the Capitol Building or rally at Sturgis? What time? The difference is that the first one shames them, and the second one validates their anger over feelings of shame. In the first instance, they are responding to the parental expectations, and in the second instance, rejecting these expectations. They are continuously oppositional to externalized forms of authority they feel controlled, judged, or threatened by.

Why attack the government? It is experienced as omnipotent, distant, and inattentive to them and always potentially harmful. This is why the Second Amendment issue is core to their identity and why they self-organize in violent groups like the Militia Movement, the only means to protect themselves from their fantasized fears. For many, enlisting in the military or joining law enforcement creates a projective and protective identification with powerful figures of authority. But once out, the government once again becomes threatening, no longer providing tribal identity and protection.

I would like to add one contemporary footnote to the reality of militia violence in America today. As a nation, we have been continuously at war for the past sixty years. It would be foolish not to understand how this has radicalized millions of young men (and women) now lost in America, as if there would be no communal blowback coming our way for waging war. The price is now being paid across America, medically, psychologically, financially, and in organized militias forming communities of people desensitized to violence, and who have also come to believe that violence is how problems are resolved.

We should not ignore the numbers of men and women who serve in law enforcement (police, sheriff, rangers, highway patrol, corrections, border security, DEA, Secret Service, Treasury, FBI, US Marshals, private security). Altogether, military and law enforcement, active and retired, constitute nearly 16 percent of adult voting age males in the US. They are largely noncollege-educated individuals who are adaptive to the use of force and skew socially conservative.

In the eighteen months from January 2020 to June 2021, there were 560 demonstrations in the US in which armed right-wing militia groups were present, including at more than a hundred government facilities across twenty-five states (state houses, vote counting centers, etc.). The findings of the *ACLED US Crisis Monitor* are that armed demonstrations are being driven by far-right mobilization and reaction to left-wing activism, opposition to BLM (48 percent), pro-Trump organizing (18 percent), pro-Second Amendment organizing (10 percent), and opposition to COVID-19 restrictions (10 percent), accounting for the 77 percent of armed right-wing demonstrations. In 84 percent of BLM demonstrations, there was an armed presence opposed to the BLM movement (Proud Boys, Three Percenters, Patriot Prayer, Boogaloo Boys, Oath Keepers). The key finding was that "armed demonstrations are nearly six times as likely to turn violent or destructive compared to unarmed demonstrations."

Throughout the US is a loose network of domestic violence extremists (DVE) in various states of rebellion and disorganization, and it has been that way from our beginning. And this is unlikely to go away anytime soon. Rebellion is foundational to the American character. And today, while the threats and resentments they represent need to be addressed as a primary law enforcement concern, they are not currently a direct threat to the federal government, the rule of law, or an orderly society. For all their violence and posturing—Timothy McVeigh's bombing of a federal building in Oklahoma City in 1995, a militia plans to kidnap the governor of Michigan, and the Capitol riots in 2021—none were a direct threat to unseat the legitimate government. But their continued encroachment on the First Amendment right to assemble and express oneself without fear and intimidation needs to be legislatively addressed.

Our recent history of domestic terrorism speaks to our need for an American Reformation. And this is not to minimize their potential violence and destruction. If DVEs represent any serious threat, it's the tip of the spear for the fascist-authoritarian elements of the Republican Party. Any cursory review of violence in America would lead us to understand we are as peaceful today as we have ever been and are becoming more so.

Without trying to justify it, America has always been a violent community. It was largely founded on violence, and it continues to express itself violently, including violent crime, gang violence, organized crime, drug-related violence, gun violence, mass killings, serial killers, domestic violence, political assassinations, automobile deaths, police violence, and violence against police officers. And into this primordial soup resides vigilante violence and domestic terrorism.

Violent domestic extremism is primarily an individual affair in America. Everything else is mostly delusional conspiracy, not unlike online gaming or battlefield reenactments. While there have been a small handful of organized acts of violence against the state and hundreds of armed confrontations, the state was not in any way impaired or threatened. If China or Russia wouldn't dare attempt it, we can rest assured that a few hundred men armed with AR15s are not about to wrest rule of this nation from the federal government.

But violent assaults on schools, strip malls, night clubs, churches, and all manner of neighborhood killings, for reasons that are never fully understood or comprehensible to most of us, are a daily occurrence in America. America is not only a gun sanctuary country but a sanctuary for those who want to commit extreme domestic violence. In fact, we are better at it than anyone. No, the real violent domestic extremists are Republican legislators and governors. They threaten the legitimacy of the federal government as an institution devoted to serving the nation. They want to lock it up, tie it down, and break it if necessary. And the pawns in this endeavor are the absolute-minded, those most easily aroused by their fears, the ones most susceptible to conspiracy theories and reactive to authority.

Vigilantism is an arcane vestige of our past that remains very much alive today, but primarily in individual acts of mass violence and secondarily in armed confrontation by small ineffectual groups of citizens confronting the state. Events, I suspect, most of us have grown weary of but also surprisingly tolerant. And the vestigial organs of vigilantism are very much with us today—the authority to carry out a citizen's arrest, bounty hunters, "self-carry," "concealed carry," and "stand your ground" statutes. Then there is the right to high-capacity magazines and military-style AR-15, which a federal judge in California recently likened to "a Swiss Army knife," adding, "good for both home and battle."

And, of course, there is our unending fantasy that a "well-regulated militia" is a bunch of guys down the street getting together after work to blunt an imaginary invasion force (or take over the Michigan State Capitol). Each of us armed and holed up in our compounds, much like the White couple in St. Louis who stepped out onto their front yard with weapons pointed at Black Lives Matter protesters. (They were later found guilty of a misdemeanor charge of "harassment" and having to surrender their weapons. Both happened to be attorneys.) America, always waiting for someone to break in—robber, brother-in-law, black ops—and always angry and fearful someone or something is after us. Our unending search for problems to solve with violence saves us from having to look at what is hiding in each of us.

If it weren't for *we the people*, America would be the safest nation that has ever existed in human history. There is great irony in the fact that no one would dare attack us right now, yet we are continually shooting ourselves at an astounding rate from the inside out. And we have been invading a lot of nations recently. For their own good, of course. For those of us who are serendipitously inclined, we can only hope for the coming alien invasion from space. Here, the absolute-minded get to be heavily armed, encamped in compounds with a surfeit of survivalist skills and technologies, and can make jerky from roadkill. And to be clear, they are not sharing with all the techies and woke liberals panicking over what to do next because Amazon no longer delivers food the same day. But deep in our subterranean unconscious, every American, no matter when they arrived here, still believes they are surviving on the frontier somewhere, someday, sometime. It is who we are.

Chapter 10
Cultural War

Peculiar parasitic fungi discovered growing out of
the rectum of a fifty-million-year-old fossilized
ant nicknamed Mitch *fungi* McConnell.

A.
White America

At the top end of our cultural war is a struggle for wealth and power. At the bottom, there's unending conflict in an ever-churning world. To turn Clausewitz's aphorism on its head, *politics is the continuation of war by other means*. This is the state of our democracy in the twenty-first century—two cultures, two parties in open conflict with everything on the line, including democracy itself. And most predictably, this conflict is primarily internal to White America.

Since the end of WWII, White Americans have been slowly realigning left and right politically and becoming increasingly entrenched in their differences. What is unique about this moment is the right feels existentially threatened and under attack, unable to find room for compromise. They have begun to believe that the future is against them and have hunkered down, unwilling to politically recalibrate, giving rise to an autocratic presidency and continuous attacks on our democratic institutions.

White Demographic Tribalism

Democrats	Republicans
Liberal	Conservative
metropolitan	rural
college	high school
white-collar	blue-collar
open values	traditional values
secular	evangelical
MSNBC/CNN	Fox News/Newsmax
86 percent vaccinated	45 percent vaccinated
$309 million*	$371 million*

*2016 billionaire campaign donations

The US population in 2019 was 328.2 million. Approximately 197.3 million identified as White (58 percent). In 1980, it was 80 percent. In 2000, 69 percent. And 2010, 64 percent. Over the past forty years, there has been a clear demographic shift in the percentage of White Americans in the US, one that is projected to continue, if somewhat slower, for the next several decades. Multiple factors account for this, including lower birth rates, mixed marriages, and an aging population combined with increased immigration.

Currently, among registered White voters, 34 percent identified as independent, 33 percent Democrats, and 29 percent Republicans. However, a 2020 Gallup Exit Poll indicated this was closer to 50 percent Democrats and 39 percent Republicans based on how they leaned or voted. Demographically, Republicans are concentrated in the South, Midwest, and throughout rural areas. Today, America is less blue-collar, less religious, more suburban, better educated, and white-collar. In a trend, this is ascending.

America dividing between Democrats and Republicans is not unlike the doctrinal divide between Shia and Sunni Muslims 1,400 years ago. The parallel is how deep and uncompromising the divide can be based on core values and beliefs. This process might better be described as cultural mitosis (cellular division). What was once primarily a divide between conservative faith and secularization has significantly widened over the past sixty years in the face of economic instability and an attenuating White majority.

First came a rapid shift in the role of education in creating a highly educated technical-professional elite that is driving economic growth. This also coincided with globalization and outsourcing a previously industrialized labor force that supported a thriving lower-middle America. And simultaneously, rapid technological automation began supplanting factory work. As a result, a large swath of America economically shrunk, reflecting a radical shift in identity for many. For one of the few times in American history status, faith, race, identity, and values all align in a starkly divided America in terms that appear increasingly nonnegotiable.

A part of this story and the crisis we now face is how obsessed America has always been with the scramble to the top, making us relatively indifferent to everyone around us. Our unique brand of Puritanism still insists the struggling pull themselves up by their bootstraps and not become dependent on the largess of the community or government for income, food, housing, health care, security, and safety. No, that is not our brand of individualism and can-do spirit. Better to suffer in silence than to need, the way it has always been, now supporting an increasingly bipolar America.

And at some fundamental level, this is a familiar conflict between many of the same feuding parties since the Civil War, with Republicans having successfully played the race card over the past sixty years. And here is an important insight we all need to understand:

> The South didn't so much lose the Civil War as outsource it, spreading new theories and techniques of segregation beyond the region itself. (King 2021).

The Civil War is currently America's longest ongoing conflict and remains unabated today as cultural war, both its racism, underlying class politics, and antigovernment vigilantism.

Theory of Social Division

There is an academic give and take when it comes to understanding social unrest in America. It's best framed by Hofstadter's dichotomy of "interest" versus "status" politics. The abridged version goes something like this: Are communities in which people experience high rates of joblessness, poverty, and violence more likely to drive populous unrest? Or is it primarily a product of larger scale social change, e.g., school integration, immigration, and LBGQT rights? That is, do personal events drive unrest, or does wholesale cultural change drive social unrest? While the former can directly impact one's economic status, the latter may feel threatening to one's social status (a threat to the herd or one's group identity). But this simplicity begins to unravel when there is broad social-economic loss by an identified social group (say lower-middle class White Americans). Then both can be catalysts for social unrest. Which is where we are today—"interest" and "status" politics aligning at a deep level in America. It is important to understand that for most Americans, social stability (and tradition) functions as an important proxy for trust.

B.

Education: Ground Zero

If one factor best accounts for the values conflict we are experiencing in America, it is education. Today, education drives income, social status, and demographics—who you marry, where you live, the news you watch on TV at night, the music you listen to, who you vote for, and what you believe. It reflects the informal demarcation between the *differentiated* and *undifferentiated*, one mediating complexity and the other embracing tradition. Currently, 39 percent of Americans have a bachelor's degree, and 9 percent have a graduate degree (Educationadata.org). Among White Americans, the number of college-educated individuals is about 32 percent.

If education is the primary battleground that divides White America, then the classroom has been ground zero for nearly a hundred years. Republicans have continually challenged public school curriculum on conservative religious grounds over the teachings of evolution and sex education. And there has been endless debate over the acceptable content of textbooks. And in the 1970s, there was conflict over establishing Common Core State Standards across the nation. Today, it's about the rights of transgender students and critical race theory. But the earnest challenges began in 1954, when the Supreme Court ruled, in *Brown v. the Board of Education*, that school segregation was unconstitutional and violated the Fourteenth Amendment's "equal protection" clause. The war was on.

It was not until the 1960s and the civil rights movement that segregation was enforced by the courts and the federal government. In 1962, the Supreme Court also declared mandatory school prayers unconstitutional, as communities across the nation opposed school integration and student busing. Simultaneously, violent protests over integration were confronted by the presence of law enforcement and federal troops. And soon thereafter, Republican state legislatures began passing bills promoting vouchers programs to support private charter and religious school as alternatives to public schools. And let's not look away. The real goal was to gut funding for public education and at the same time give tax breaks for those who could afford private schools.

Nearly forty years after the Scopes "Monkey Trial" in 1925, which challenged and overturned a Tennessee state law prohibiting the teaching of evolution in public schools, began unending curriculum challenges and the frantic promotion of *creationism.* In 1987, the Supreme Court ruled, in *Edwards v. Aguillard*, that teaching creationism as science in public schools was unconstitutional. This subsequently led to legislative advocacy for teaching *intelligent design* as an alternative fact-based theory in the classroom. For the past five years, numerous state legislatures have introduced hundreds of bills to teach "creation science." To date, none have been passed into law.

The passage of *Title IX* in 1972 set off a new wave of legal challenges over issues of sexual discrimination and harassment in public schools. And today, school boards across the country are being shouted down by angry parents over COVID-19 mask mandates, school policies for transgender students, and most vehemently, over the teaching of American history. And yes, that does seem odd. The key to understanding this sudden concern is to know it's being largely financed by conservative think tanks and institutes trying to gin up outrage that leftist propaganda is intent on tearing America down. Although the reason is not exactly clear.

On one side of this debate is the "1776ers" and its celebration of American exceptionalism and patriotic virtue (a Trump-backed team). On the opposing side are the "1619ers" (underwritten by the *New York Times*) and its advocacy of critical race theory (CRT). In this latter instance, White students are confronted with America's history of racism and how their White privilege continues perpetuating institutional racism. This appears to have evolved into a contest over rewriting America's founding narrative. (Gosh, all of a sudden, it seems like we've forgotten that we teach the "other" unmentionable in school—sex education. And part of the reason is it has proven effective in reducing unwanted pregnancies.)

The ironic question we are confronted with is this: Is the American "New World" myth just a variant of the Southern "Lost Cause" myth about the noble cause of the Civil War? And as we tear down the statues of Robert E. Lee and Stonewall Jackson, should we be tearing down those of Washington and Jefferson as well? The reality is that America has arisen to become the greatest and most powerful nation in history, but not a perfect nation. But then there have been no perfect empires, kingdoms, or nations. And any accounting of our history has to account for all the stories, the heroic and the inglorious, which neither team appear to appreciate.

In 1513, Spanish explorer Juan Ponce DeLeón, then Spanish governor of Hispaniola, led an expedition to Puerto Rico and La Florida. He was rumored to be in search of the "fountain of youth," or at least waters that rejuvenated, depending on who was telling the story. But herein lies the absolutist parable for the New World, the dream of eternal sameness. While classrooms today are literally fountains of eternal transformation of the self and the world around us. No wonder education is continually under attack by the right in America. And apparently, never more so than in La Florida.

Framing Assault on Free Speech as Promoting Free Speech

The *Tampa Bay Times* reported that the wily Republican governor of Florida, Ron DeSantis, signed legislation (6/21) requiring public universities and colleges to survey students, faculty, and staff on their beliefs and viewpoints as a means of ensuring "intellectual diversity." The fear on the part of Republicans appears to be that higher education is "indoctrinating" students and has been reduced to "socialism factories," as prosaically framed by Florida Senate President Wilton Simpson (there's that frightening word, *socialism*, again). The House speaker characterized universities as devoid of "diversity of thought." (What he really means is right-wing ideology, conspiracism, and religious doctrine are not treated seriously except as propaganda.) It was emphasized that students would be allowed to record lectures to "shed light" on classroom wrongdoing. The governor then extolled the bill as ensuring "robust First Amendment speech on our colleges and university campuses." This is practically verbatim from Mao's *Little Red Book*, turning students into snitches for the thought police to shut down incorrect thinking not approved by the state. The fact of the matter is, education (analytical thinking) liberalizes the mind and differentiates the individual. And that's a problem for many.

Burning the Past to Halt the Future

Book burning is on the rise again. And for the absolute-minded, this appears to be an imperative, whether they read or not. Since

1529, the Catholic Church routinely published lists of books (and later movies) that were considered heretical (*Index Librorum Prohibitorum*). However, in 1966, this venture into mind control became treated as a private matter and not one associated with ecclesiastical law or censure. The first banned book in the American colonies was *New Canaan* by Thomas Morton. And if you guessed this was done by the Puritans, you are correct. Published in the Netherlands in 1637, this three-volume set later led to his arrest for savagely satirizing the Puritans for their religious hypocrisy and mistreatment of Native Americans. Skip forward to today, and we have a Texas lawmaker, running for state's attorney general in 2021, submitting a list of 850 books for "review" (focused on topics of gender and race). In Spotsylvania County, Virginia, two school board members advocated banned books be "burned." In September 2021, seven states removed books that were of concern to local citizenry, and twenty-eight states are in various stages of restricting curriculums on topics of gender, sexuality, and race.

Of course, two factors currently stand in the way of banning books. First, in 1982, the Supreme Court ruled (*Island Trees School District v. Pico*) school boards cannot preemptively remove books because people don't like the subject matter. Libraries are considered spaces of "voluntary inquiry." Second, any student can go online and read about any topic or subject no matter how distasteful to others, without limits. In this sense, the library books and school reading lists are antiquated technology. But we should all take notice that closing avenues of inquiry and curiosity is a primary preoccupation of the absolute-minded, but always claiming for the good of the community. In what alternative reality do they reside where library books are a primary source of information for kids about the world around them? Apparently, one in which parents and politicians never watch TV and movies, listen to music, visit the internet, use a smartphone, engage social media, or read e-books. Aside from the obvious efforts at censorship in the hope of turning back the future, the underlying irony is that every concerning topic is likely being watched by their children on a Netflix movie tonight.

Going forward, the educational divide is only going to increase as college degrees have become the gateway to economic advancement. The US now stands at approximately 4,627 colleges and universities, and worldwide, there are twenty-five thousand colleges and universities. (In Florida, forty public colleges and universities currently enroll 793,372 students.) And make no mistake about it, US universities attract the most intellectually talented students from around the world. In 2019, there were 19.6 million students enrolled in US colleges and universities. This is the spigot driving our cultural divide, and it cannot be turned off. It is also the foundation of modernity and the future.

C.

Wealth Inequality

The American oligarch class is driving
authoritarian capitalism in the US.

The top 20 percent of Americans now own 77 percent of household wealth in the US (2016), triple that of the middle class. As recently as twenty-five years ago, this was reversed (Brookings online). In 2020, the top 1 percent of households (about 1.6 million) accounted for 38.5 percent of privately held wealth in the US (Federal Reserve), with an average annual income of 4.4 million, while half of the American households reported incomes below $50,000 (Statista online). Today, 37 percent of Americans cannot afford to pay an unexpected medical bill of more than $100 (MarketWatch). As of 2016, there was only a 50 percent chance that children born in the 1980s would earn more than their parents. And the largest decline in social mobility over the past eighty years has been within the middle class (Brookings).

Sidebar: The current student loan debt in the US is $1.6 trillion, increasing 150 percent between 2006 to 2018. This is what happens when millions of low interest loans backed by the government hit the educational market. It created an inflationary spiral in the cost of education, but also saddling families with long-term debt. And as these generous loans came onto the market, Republican-controlled state legislatures began defunding education and passing on an even greater financial burden to families. Getting ahead in America was never easy and still isn't. And for a large segment of America, it is increasingly out of reach. Score one for fleecing America's aspiring students and families by colleges, loan agencies, and states.

Note: The average salary of a Division 1 college football coach is $1.75 million (*Newsday* 2021). The annual salary of college professors ranges from $44,000 to $141,000 (Martin Center 2021). The highest paid public employee in every state is likely the football coach.

American Oligarchy

Between 2010 and 2018, the number of American billionaires increased from 401 to 586 (32 percent). They possessed an estimated combined wealth of $4.6 trillion. In 2018, twenty-five "ultra-high net worth" individuals or couples contributed a total of $573,892,284 to political campaigns. The majority were White males between ages sixty to eighty. The top 100 all had wealth above $4.5 billion, typically made in finance, technology, and retail, in that order. And according to research into their politics, the "vast majority" were "right-wing" and largely engaged in "stealth" political activity at the federal, state, and local levels (Jacobin 2021).

There should be no doubt that spending on local elections is by far the most effective way to go with your voter influence dollars, which is why Republicans control the majority of state legislatures. It has also been highlighted that most billionaires seldom, if ever, publicly speak about having a political agenda (going all possum on us and pretending they don't have one. How clever). But the truth is more concerning. Their primary political agenda is to not pay taxes. *ProPublica* gained access to fifteen years of IRS tax returns for the twenty-five wealthiest billionaires in America and discovered they essentially pay no taxes. Between 2014 and 2018, they earned $401 billion and paid around 3.4 percent in taxes. And the federal government's response? Neither party had the guts to revise the tax law. It was easier to go after the people who leaked this uncomfortable tax data. But the solution is simple—tax capital gains. That's it. Pay as you go, like most Americans have to. Better yet, just tax wealth in all its hidden financial instruments.

The consensus by those studying billionaires is that they are economically and politically conservative and support cutting the social safety net, and, of course, eliminating taxes and scrapping the minimum wage. But to reduce their agenda to these naïve wants would be foolish. They want to block efforts at reducing climate change, deny health care to low-income families, bust unions, promote carbon-spewing and polluting industries, roll back consumer safety and environmental protection laws, and generally buy political favor, but really, gut tax law. At the top of any list of conservative campaign donors are Sheldon Adelson, Charles Koch, Robert Mercer, Rupert Murdock, Paul Singer, Ronald Cameron. And yes, there are Democratic-leaning billionaires—George Soros, Warren Buffet, Bill Gates, and Tom Steyers. They are all financial vigilantes here in the wild, wild West.

What's important to know about having this amount of money is that money, by definition, is conservative, whether it's leaning right or left. It packs enormous influence on the democratic process in an undemocratic manner. Much of its outsized influence is never directly accounted for or even known about—writing the fine print in bills up for a vote, backroom lobbying, free private jet trips, invisibly influencing voters, and financially propping up hack politicians. What is not obvious is the amount of unaccounted for money pouring into hundreds of conservative foundations and institutes. For example, the *American Legislative Exchange Council* or *Americans for Prosperity*. In its most predatory terms, wealth is about supporting the face of Republican fascism from behind the anonymity of offshore accounts, shell corporations, and untaxable wealth.

The wealthy industrialists who supported Hitler during his rise to the chancellorship of the Weimar Republic in the 1930s were not ideologically Nazis. No, they were simply following money logic, politics be damned. Same here in the USA today. This should make all of us cautious about not wanting to make money more accountable. Contrary to the Supreme Court, money should not be the equivalent of free speech and should not have a right to vote. Otherwise, billionaires would have all the votes. You make $50,000 a year, you get fifty thousand votes. Charles Koch gets a hundred billion votes. Besides, most families living on $50,000 might only have discretionary spending of $500 for political influence peddling. But this is all speculation about the invisible. The myth used to be "one person, one vote." But this has never been true and is even less so today.

Note: There are eleven thousand well-paid registered lobbyists in the US. The top 100 earned between $500,000 and $1.2 million per year (CEOupdate.com), all the while enjoying the lifestyle perks of influence peddling and buying off democracy one vote at a time behind closed doors (seven lobbyists served in the Trump cabinet). Then there is Senator Manchin of West Virginia torching President Biden's agenda as the coal industry pays him off or Senator Sinema of Arizona gutting efforts to control drug prices as she is paid off by the pharmaceutical industry. The quid pro quo is so obvious in these two instances, we forget Hunter Biden's career as both a wealthy and successful artist and adviser to Ukraine on gas and oil development.

D.

Republican Authoritarianism

There are simply too many elements to the Republican authoritarian orientation to cover them all here. Here are the highlights. Beginning in the 1930s, the Republican Party became steeped in government conspiracy (Freemasonry and Illuminati) and opposed all efforts to provide a social safety net to Americans following the "Depression." In particular, Social Security. In the 1950s, it morphed to "McCarthyism" and the paranoid fear Communists had infiltrated the federal government. But the final implementation of their distorted reality began with the libertarian bent of Robert Welch's John Birch Society and Barry Goldwater's Young Republicans in the 1960s, raging against Communist conspiracies and how chlorinating the public water supply was poisoning people.

The subsequent election of Richard Nixon (1968) and of mediocre actor but charismatic politician Ronald Reagan (1981–1989) was the beginning of the end. Here, the Republican Party aligned with racist elements in the South and with evangelical cultural conservatism. The party platform featured the federal government as the "the problem" and not the solution to whatever ailed Americans, giving rise to Newt Gingrich and the Tea Party faction. The aim was no longer to govern from the right but to break government so it could no longer function properly. This came out of a desperate concern about their ability to hold on to power, as moderates were driven from the party with glee, still naively obsessed with hawkish foreign policy, deficit spending, and principled conservatism when the object was to lockdown government. And we can now add obstructing voting rights. That's it in a nutshell—paranoid deep state conspiracies, attacks on government as the problem, playing the race and cultural conflict cards, obstructing the government's ability to function, and propping up Wall Street (and a hawkish, if not militant, foreign policy). And always eager to take dark money—"the Grand Old Party." Just saying, if we are a two-party democracy and one of the parties is the Republican Party, we are no longer a democracy.

Note: In President Reagan's first inaugural address (1981), he concocted one of the most effective pieces of conspiratorial propaganda in American history: "Government is not the solution to our problem, government is the problem." Here, he not only reflected the sentiment of Wall Street but also tied it to the underlying fear and distrust of the absolute-minded in the Republican base.

Voter Suppression—Flying Monkeys

The Founding Fathers set out to deny the voting right to a majority of Americans. You might wonder, how is that possible? America, the beacon of liberty to the world and founder of modern constitutional democracy? Let's review. After signing the US Constitution in 1787, only White male landowners were permitted to vote. Okay, most of us knew that one. Besides, that was a long time ago. However, in some states, you also had to prove you were a Christian. Didn't know that one. And they purposely left it to the states to determine the voting procedures. That's odd. Why would they do that? Because it essentially gave states a veto over the election process and made it nearly impossible to standardize voting rights across the nation.

Being very prescient and wanting to protect their economic and political interests, the Founding Fathers then inserted the Electoral College into the Constitution. Today, we would call it malware. It was designed to activate after the election and switch the vote count as a means of mitigating the anarchy of the popular vote. It seemed innocuous for a long period and only truly activated as the nation grew larger, prioritizing smaller states over larger states. But the real purpose of the Electoral College was to make sure that someone like Donald Trump was never elected president. The underlying fear was a populist rabble (think absolute-minded type) would seek to crown someone king. Which proved to be prescient, it turns out. The Electoral College was a hedge against tyranny, or so they thought. They failed to imagine a large well-educated population of differentiated people representing a majority of the populace.

During the early nineteenth century, some states began eliminating the property requirement to vote. And after the Civil War, the *Fifteenth Amendment* was passed in 1869, adding that race could not be used to deny a person the right to vote. This, of course, led many states to enact poll taxes (have to pay to vote) and literacy tests (given few African American men were able to read or write because of slavery). Whoops, then came the ratification of the *Nineteenth Amendment* in 1920. Holy moly, women were allowed to vote 140 years after we became a nation. Okay, we knew this one too. As late as the 1960s, states were actively restricting voting access for immigrants by adding English language requirements.

In 1962, Congress approved the *Twenty-Fourth Amendment*, making poll taxes unconstitutional. Then in 1965, Congress passed the *Voting Rights Act*, which essentially prohibited practices used to limit voting among African Americans. States and local jurisdictions, with a historical pattern of suppressing voting rights, had to submit changes to their election laws to the US Justice Department for approval. Then in 1971, the *Twenty-Sixth Amendment* lowered the voting age from twenty-one to eighteen. This came about when young men who had fought in the Vietnam War had not been eligible to vote (mature enough to die for our country but not to vote).

In 1993, Congress passed the *National Voter Registration Act*, allowing citizens to register to vote when applying for driver's licenses and for mail-in registration. *The American Vote Act* was passed by Congress in 2002 to help streamline election procedures across the nation. Mandates were placed on states to replace outdated voting equipment, create statewide voter registration lists, and provide provisional ballots to ensure eligible voters are not turned away. The law also made it easier for people with disabilities to cast independent ballots.

Okay, now comes the pushback from the right, both legislatively and through the courts. In 2013, the Supreme Court ruled, in *Shelby County v. Holder*, that key elements of the *Voting Rights Act* were unconstitutional. In a 5–4 decision, the court gutted provisions requiring states with a history of voter suppression from having to report and justify changes to state voting laws. We can guess what happened next. Almost immediately, states began restricting voting by tightening voter identification laws and gerrymandering aimed at diminishing the vote of low-income and minority voters. And after the 2020 election, many states began closing thousands of polling sites, limiting voting days and times to further suppress targeted voting populations.

Which brings us to 2021 and *Brnovich v. Democratic National Committee*. Here, a conservative Supreme Court, in a 6–3 vote along ideological lines, pretty much finished off the *Voting Rights Act*, permitting states to manipulate voting access and shifting the burden of proof for equal access from the states. It also prohibited ballot harvesting (people collecting ballots and then depositing them at polling sites). The basic ruling is only a relative or caregiver can collect absentee ballots. States were also permitted to throw out ballots cast in the wrong precinct. (I guess this means we can look forward to a lawsuit against the US Postal Services as a ballot harvesting conspiracy. All those people mailing their ballots in and then the post office collecting and delivering them hardly seems safe and secure.)

What makes the *Brnovich* ruling remarkable is the court found that just because there was no evidence of voter fraud, it does not mean states cannot act to protect against it, even if it restricts voters' access. Essentially, protecting the vote from a nonexistent threat justified limiting voter access. For example, voting sites could potentially be struck by a meteorite, so why not restrict voter access out of concern for voter safety and election integrity? With this logic, anything can be used to chip away at voting rights. There you have it. In fact, research by the *Washington Post* into the 2016 presidential election found only four fraudulent ballots cast out of 135 million. Clearly a problem that needs to be urgently addressed by the Supreme Court.

The Court's direction is clear here—limit voter access to prevent something that's unlikely to occur. This is similar to what Conservatives were doing in their early challenges to *Roe v. Wade*, the constitutionally protected right to abortion. Conservative states slowly chipped away at the edges of the law's basic premise—that voting rights or an abortion are being restricted, giving a conservative court just enough room to overturn precedent. But what is truly remarkable about all of this is the number of Constitutional amendments and laws that have been required to assure our right to vote.

In the 2020 federal election, 73 percent of all voting age citizens were registered to vote. Sixty-seven percent reported voting. Among White voters, 71 percent voted, Black 63 percent, Asian 59 percent, and Hispanic 54 percent (US Census). This means eighty million people failed to vote in 2020, 29 percent because they failed to register (NPR). The effects of voter suppression is primarily an effort by Republicans to win elections by whatever means necessary. But there is no doubt that today, the election "kraken" has been released. But the real effect and impact of their efforts are largely unknown. On the basis of voter turnout, one could conjecture that the biggest impact was on minority groups. The conundrum Republicans face is that despite their many and varied attempts at election manipulation, they lost the popular vote in 2020 by seven million votes. That is the primary reason they have moved from disrupting the election process to subverting it, delegitimizing it in the eyes of voters and, if necessary, corrupting the election process itself. Elections have become a dark cloud on the American horizon.

Election Suppression in America

Disrupt

English language requirement
Restricted voter ID
Ban student ID cards
Limit voter registration access
Prohibit out-of-state student voting
Prohibit mail-in ballots
Prohibit ballot collecting
Discard miscast ballots
Reduce polling sites
Reduce ballot drop boxes
Restrict ballot drop-off hours
Restrict days polls are open
Reduce hours polls are open
Eliminate weekend voting
Close polls early
Frequent voting location changes
Poll watchers to intimidate voters

Subvert

Poll tax
Literacy test
Gerrymander
Purge voting rolls
No mail-in ballot renewal notice
Politicize local election district / board officials
Act as faithless elector

Delegitimize

Unsupported demands for election audits/vote recounts
Baseless lawsuits to overturn election results
Baseless legislative challenges to electoral slates

Foreign influence/interference in election
Declare election fraudulent/stolen/manipulated
Claim election results product of bizarre conspiracy

Corrupt
Dark money campaign influence
Attack state capitols
State legislature appointing alternate slate of electors
Legislators seeking to overturn vote count
Overturning election results by insurrection

Examples abound of voter suppression. For example, not accepting a student ID to register to vote, move polling sites between elections so it is difficult to find the correct site, or reducing the number of ballot drop-offs in minority or student communities. For individuals who work or have limited transportation, limiting available days and hours is effective. Showing up to vote and finding out you are no longer on the active voting roll or that your mail-in ballot never arrived in time to vote is frustratingly effective. But for most of America's political life, the real game changer has always been gerrymandering, something Republicans have made a stealth art form for the past sixty years, redrawing district boundaries to diminish the voting impact of minorities communities.

In desperation, Republicans have gone all audacious on us in 2021. Fearful of losing the vote count, even in supposedly conservative states, Republican state legislatures are now enacting laws giving partisan appointed election officials greater control over election oversight. Essentially, they are attempting to usurp the voting process to overturn election results, if necessary. After the failed effort to overturn the 2020 presidential election, Republicans have seen the light—control and restrict state election officials, the turnkey to the future.

These movements on the right are the absolute-mindedness forever at work, ever fearful, distrusting, paranoid, and self-righteous in the conspiratorial belief that change and the loss of status is apocalyptic. Their underlying sense of danger justifies all efforts to subvert what they perceive as hidden and destructive forces at work against them. We have seen this playout for centuries now, and it was what our Founding Fathers were most fearful of and tried to cap early on. Good try, but after 250 years, a "king," or at least someone who desperately wants to be king arose in America.

E.

Conservative Media

There have been many emergent paths for selling conspiracy theories or *conspiracism* to America. The majority of which have only entered the public consciousness in the past thirty years, and they have proven to be highly profitable, starting with conservative cable news (Fox News, Breitbart, Newsmax), print media (the *Federalist*, *National Review*, the *Wall Street Journal*), right-wing propaganda radio (Glen Beck, Alex Jones, Sean Hannity), social media platforms (Drudge Report, White supremacists links, and QAnon), podcasts (Dan Bongino and Joe Rogan), and conservative think tanks (Claremont Institute, Heritage Foundation, Bookings Institute, Cato Institute, Hoover Institute; there are too many to list). And the most hidden but significant Trojan horse has been dark money supporting university foundations and grants to propagandize conservative ideas, all giving voice to anti-government conspiracy theories.

Conservative media is where conspiracies become immersed in rage outreach 24-7 by an audience enraptured by an alternative universe, all sheltered in a "self-sealing" bubble in which the lack of factual evidence becomes proof of how well the truth is being hidden from them. Every bizarre notion that has ever existed has found safe haven in what is now being termed the *inforwars*—attack news, shock radio, and filtered online platforms. For every subtle nod at a deep state conspiracy or "okay" sign affirming the massacre of schoolchildren is a false-flag operation are millions of enraged online voices shouting outside the bounds of reason at each other. A universe of lost people teetering on a shared disbelief of reality, all drinking the same conspiracy Kool-Aid to make sense of the world they live in.

This is where the conservative mind safely wanders in crisis or just idly passing the day.

We have a long way to go in making America media-sane again. But we can begin by shutting down media *conspiracism*. First off, we should not permit foreign ownership of media outlets that broadcast in the US. For example, Fox News. It appears to function primarily to legitimize disinformation and promote conspiracy, e.g., actively promoting Russian *kompromat* to destabilize the electoral process in Trump's run-up to the 2020 election. And on matters of foreign policy, Fox News has been expansive in promoting Russian foreign policy propaganda, with host Tucker Carlson routinely featured on Russian state media, questioning if Ukraine is a sovereign nation. Even suggesting that the Biden administration orchestrated the war in Ukraine to avenge Donald Trump's election in 2016.

It's time to limit ownership of cross media platforms as well. For example, a corporation owning a print media and cable news media outlet. Media corporations buying up local newspaper and television outlets across dozens of geographic markets needs to be restricted or prohibited. The FCC needs to reassert the "fairness doctrine" requiring broadcast licensees to cover controversial issues in a fair and balanced manner and to really put some oversight and teeth into it and make it inclusive of the internet. And there needs to be an acknowledgment that conservative news channels are not newsworthy and should not be licensed to broadcast as news or entertainment.

The FCC should be regulating the media and internet and providing oversight for what have become propaganda machines and engines of mass hysteria disrupting the American commons. There is too much hate speech, disinformation, and delusional conspiratorial ideation masking as free speech without boundaries, and we are crazier and in more danger as a result. For a Fox News broadcaster to go on the air and advise Americans to not wear protective masks against CDC public health safety recommendations during a pandemic, in which hundreds of thousands have died, should end this person's broadcast career and suspend Fox News' broadcast license, with a financial hit that would make Rupert Murdock contort in agony. Donald Trump was shut down under voluntary guidelines by Twitter and Facebook for much less.

We need go beyond the niceties of corporate policies and market jitters and shut down shouting "fire" in a crowded theater under the false journalistic piety of balanced news. If the standard legal analogy for a hundred years (thanks to Justice Oliver Wendell Holmes Jr.) has been that an individual cannot falsely shout fire in a crowded theater—that here resides the limits on free speech—how many have to die believing Fox News' disinformation about COVID-19, which is closer to nuking the Super Bowl and claiming it is protected speech?

Watching Fox News is not unlike watching a documentary of Hitler addressing a huge "Nuremberg Rally" in 1934. The broadcaster commenting how articulate Hitler is, how he projects being in command, how wonderfully forceful he gestures, the power of his message, and how he has moved his audience to cheer in adulation (and to salute respectfully). Then casually noting that Hitler wants to help Jews as humanely as possible if it is technically and logistically feasible but wishing him well in making Germany "great" again. Then blaming the liberal media for the bad press he's getting, the broadcaster lashes out at Hitler's critics for distorting his message of *principle and discipline* as "fake news." Besides, the commentator adds, "Jews can always wear gasmasks," winking at the camera. This is pretty much conservative cable news.

Footnote: As of January 2022, Donald Trump had raised $1.3 billion to finance Trump Media, primarily from hedge fund investors. (This is how discontent is being sowed in America, making it a great investment opportunity.)

F.

Religious Fundamentalism
The Faith Grift

(Joseph) Smith obeyed an angel's long-standing order to become polygamous or die, he married thirty women in two years, eight of them during one three-month period, six of those teenagers.

—K. Anderson, *Fantasyland*

From the beginning, the practice of religion in America has been a carnival sideshow running a fantastical gamut. But always a money-making lollapalooza for talented grifters and the suspiciously delusional. Or what Alexis de Tocqueville described, after witnessing a Shaker service in 1831, as "religious insanity." But we are not required to revisit history to fully understand what is taking place today.

Under the "Big Tent" of charismatic televangelism, the grifting never stops, selling "sincerity" to the distrusting and a chance to participate in the largest conspiracy pyramid scheme in human history—Christianity. It's Americans making a down payment on a homestead in heaven.

Televangelism MegaCon

Billy Graham was fervent in anticommunism and supported of the Vietnam War, while denying his daughter a college education because she was a woman. All the while teetering on the brink of anti-Semitism while fully engaged in political sycophancy.

Oral Roberts evangelized "prosperity gospel" and "divine healing," claiming a nine-hundred-foot-tall Jesus spoke to him. Further, he intimated that he had raised a child from the dead. In his "seed-faith" universe, God bestowed wealth and health on those he favored.

Jim Bakker and Tammy Faye preached biblical prophecy but were also convicted of accounting fraud while selling emergency survival product on their PTL Club broadcasts and at their Heritage USA theme park.

Jerry Falwell's "Moral Majority" turned political action lobby that was anti-gay, anti-feminist, anti-civil rights, and supporting conservative politicians. He spent $10 million on a campaign to convince people Jimmy Carter was not a Christian.

Pat Robertson's 700 Club and Christian Broadcasting Network claimed President Bush was bringing Muslim terrorists into the country to take it over. And he trumpeted that he (Robertson) was providing aid to Rwandan genocide victims when, in fact, he was shipping diamond mining equipment for an investment.

Jimmy Swaggart preached the sins of fornication and the evils of masturbation and dancing while heading a $150-million global television ministry pulling in $500,000 a week. Later, he admitted during a broadcast that he was addicted to prostitutes and pornography. He was, subsequently, defrocked, but not on television.

Joel Osteen sermonized a "happy" theology focused on "prosperity gospel." In other words, those who give him money will make him prosperous. It's part of God's larger plan. He also drives a $300,000 Ferrari with an estimated personal net worth of between $50 to 100 million.

Kenneth Copeland preached "prosperity gospel" and promised if you donate, you will be rewarded a hundredfold. Just not with money. His estimated wealth is $750 million, including several private jets and a $7-million eighteen-thousand-square-foot mansion he calls a parsonage to avoid taxes. He also claims to have cured COVID-19 and is under investigation for federal tax fraud.

Really, there are too many fallen ministers to detail them all here. But let's try with the help of Tom Meisfjord (2018). *Ted Haggard* was caught using meth and hooking up with a male prostitute. *Jesse Duplantis* asked parishioners for $54 million to buy a new jet. God said it had to be a Falcon 7X. *Tony Alamos* put his deceased wife's body on public display for six months, claiming she would be brought back to life. He was also convicted of ten counts of transporting young girls across state lines, asserting, "Consent is puberty." *Robert Tilton* claimed people were impoverished because they had sinned but accepted personal requests for prayers with donations. Turns out the money was banked without prayer. *Marcus Lamb* went on air admitting multiple affairs with women "blackmailing" him for $7.5 million. *Peter Popoff* was engaged in fake faith healing. He would call out strangers' names and identify their health concerns. He also used two-way radios to communicate with staff planted in the audience. He was later busted on national television. *Mike Warnke* claimed he was a reformed Satanist preacher, but also falsely claiming he suffered multiple wounds serving in Vietnam. *Paula White*, President Trump's spiritual adviser, claimed world leaders were in power by the grace of God. *Ernest Angley* claimed he could heal HIV through prayer while preaching against the sins of homosexuality. He turned out to be gay and personally liked to examine the genitals of male parishioners after their vasectomies. *Paul and Jan Couch* with a ministry worth an estimated $750 million. Family members publicly revealed they were helping them engage in tax evasion. (Do you see any patterns here?)

Beginning in the 1970s, conservative evangelical leaders began attacking social change and preaching that Christian values were under assault because that was where the money was hidden. In reality, Christianity was a preexisting model of conspiracy that dovetailed with contemporary conspiracism. At the same time, more Americans than ever (25 percent according to a 2019 Pew survey) identified as Evangelical, of which 80 percent voted for Trump in 2016 (Pew exit poll). In the evangelical world, America had fallen from grace and lost its moral direction. And so ensued a global life and death struggle between secular humanism and Christianity.

Underlying this conflict were any number of conspiratorial notions about the influence of Communism, the Illuminati, a New World Order, but increasingly, a federal government embracing a changing world. And at the center of this conflict was an evolving cultural war over social issues that had pushed aside the teaching of creationism as the primary dogma, including civil rights, gun control, the Equal Rights Amendment, abortion, feminism, and more recently, LGBQT. All captured in the belief that traditional "family values" were under attack.

Evangelical White America

Currently, 65 percent of Americans identify as Christian, down 12 percent from ten years earlier. Approximately 25 percent of Christians identify as Evangelical, the largest religious group in the US, representing 16.5 percent of the US population. Below are some relevant demographics of White evangelicals (edited from the PEW Research Center-Religious Landscape Studies, 2014–2019).

76 percent are White.
57 percent income below $50,000 a year.
14 percent are college educated.
88 percent believe in God.
55 percent take the Word of God literally.
88 percent believe in heaven.
82 percent believe in hell.
56 percent are Republican.
64 percent support smaller government/fewer services.
56 percent believe government aid does more harm than good.
64 percent strongly oppose same-sex marriages.
89 percent oppose theories of evolution.

The truth is, absolutely nothing is curtailing religious freedom in America today. In fact, we are the most religiously polyglot nation on earth. If there's an attack on faith in the US, it's the religious right's mission to save us. And let's not kid ourselves. The court's kowtowing to their mystical demands empowers them to keep returning to heal our sins. The paradox being that the court's upholding of trivial religious claims becomes *de jure* proof that their faith is under assault.

And apparently, only the Christian right feels threatened, not the Scientologists, Catholics, Mormons, or Buddhists. It's really about ceaselessly preaching fear in the name of God to the distrusting, not unlike the strategy used by NRA to raise money. They are coming for your guns. And the absolute-minded fall for it every time. Scroll down Google news in the morning to ads by MDs warning you not to eat something. Fear, like faith, is a form of wealth creation in America. And it is Trump grifting donors for money to help him overturn his false claim of a fraudulent election.

G.

US Supreme Court

Conservative justices share more in common with QAnon Shaman than with US Representative Alexandria Ocasio-Cortez.

At the beating heart of our cultural war resides the Supreme Court. Alarmingly beeping code red year after year. And in all candidness, it is not a council of "poetic champions" brimming with exceptional wisdom and integrity. Today, the Supreme Court is a gerrymandered institution of right-leaning justices with lifetime appointments, propping up an archaic and patrician way of life in America. All saturated in the misbelief that our Founding Fathers would have wanted the twenty-first century to resemble the eighteenth century. Which, if we think about it, is pretty much the un-equalitarian America the court is currently ruling over today. Talk about reality-bending.

Most Supreme Court justices never worked a day in their lives, except in privileged circumstances, whiling away their academic years juiced on conservative ideology rather than experiencing or thinking deeply about the human condition. Here is a simple question: How many Supreme Court justices went to community college or served in the armed forces, as opposed to graduating from an Ivy League university? For them, the law is an abstraction, supported and maintained by ideological notions of how it's supposed to work. As a consequence, money is bending democracy, while a conservative court resides in the detumescent glow of *originalism*, and a nation in tumult.

Dark Money

There are federal election campaign laws in the US, believe it or not (*the Federal Election Campaign Act of 1971 and the Bipartisan Campaign Reform Act of 2002)*. Generally, it's a good idea to "follow the money" when it comes to election integrity, you would think. But leave it to the Supreme Court to defy common sense. In *Buckley v. Valeo* (1975), the court affirmed the government's right to limit campaign contributions but not expenditures. Say what? That sounds like a formula for cheating if there ever was one. The court supported the argument that limiting expenditures potentially constituted a First Amendment "free speech" violation. That is, people with more money get more free speech. Regardless, there are enough loopholes in these laws to make buying a state legislature more anonymous than wearing a hoodie at a crack house.

But the final blow to election integrity came from the Supreme Court in *Citizens United v. FEC* (2010). In a 5–4 decision, the court unleashed unlimited election contributions without having to fully disclose the source of funding, essentially upholding that the government cannot restrict corporations, political action committees, and labor unions from making independent expenditures to support or oppose candidates. Corporations were actually identified as "people" and assured the same inalienable rights as US citizens. The only prohibition on Super Pac spending is they are prohibited from "coordinating" with a campaign (wink, wink). The upshot was to fully unleash dark money on our political system by a court obsessed with the free speech and privacy of the wealthy but apparently unconcerned about election integrity.

According to *Americans for Tax Fairness*, billionaire campaign contributions in 2000 totaled $18.5 million. After *Citizens United* (2010), they increased forty times to $684 million in 2016. The Federal Election Commission reported $100 million in dark money campaign contributions in 2020, but unofficial sources place it closer to $750 million, as money was hidden through opaque shell company contributors. How much of this was foreign money trying to influence election outcomes is unknown, but rest assured, we will never know.

There are many forces at play in the social and political division of America—dark money, social media, conservative cable news, flawed political institutions, globalization, economic and social stratification. But if one had to pick the most powerful among these many competing factors, dark money would be a sound pick for its ability to undermine not just democracy but all forward seeing action. Money invisibly structures our social reality and is the most potent force in it. And dark money, given to us by a conservative Supreme Court in *Citizens United*, is among the most disguised and powerful force operating in our society today. It's wealth serving its own interests at whatever cost to our Republic. As Arendt had assured us earlier, the wealthy have always assumed government covertly represented its interests, so it doesn't believe in democracy.

If one factor could be chosen that would positively alter the future of our cultural war, one that did not default to chance or hoping a broken system will bail us out one more time, it would be how we politically treat "wealth" in America. It would require equitable taxation of the wealthy, limits on campaign financing, and ridding our political system of dark money. We would reveal everyone who donates, how much, and to whom and how. Dark money props up a Congress beholden to donors and not voters, making it primary to our cultural war. It allows those with few concerns about democracy to distort our world.

A divided America is a "broken" America. And cultural war is merely a distraction for the wealthy. And beyond that, if it inhibits social change and poses challenges to a progressive agenda, that's a "win-win" on the right. Yes, a lot of money is all in on denying people a safety net, dismantling environmental protections, and overthrowing elections. And the ultra-wealthy are not particularly concerned if someone gets vaccinated for COVID-19 or not. The worst that can happen is someone dies, another win-win, as red state maps continued lighting up in 2022 with rising COVID-19 infections rates.

Wealth needs to be held more accountable and to pay its fair share. And by wealth, I do not mean just the billionaires but Wall

Street, corporate America, and more generally, a capitalism that is in clear conflict with democratic principles. All the absurd tax loopholes, interest carried forward, estate trust clauses, accounting schemes, offshore accounts, shell corporations, and money laundering operations need to be eliminated. The wealthy have more money than they know what to do with. Their narcissism is distorting the world around them in their belief they earned it, deserve it, have the right to the unending creation of it, and forever get to pass on its privileges. None of which are true. The world needs more and better from them. But just in case, we should be prepared to help them enter the portal to the future, where their drive and vision is more important than their personal wealth.

Less Than We Should Be

The court is also weighing in on a second front in the cultural war, one empowering Evangelical Christians to assert that their beliefs are both universal and constitutionally guaranteed. In this generous reality, America is a Christian nation embedded in messianic prophecy or what is popularly termed "Christian nationalism." The courts appear confused by its duty to affirm the right to practice one's faith, with bending the social order to accommodate everyone's beliefs. A farcical notion that belief in a 2,700-year-old book is a primer for the social reality of America in the twenty-first century. (Let's politely say *originalism* is incestuously engaged in intimacy with *fundamentalism* and leave it there.)

In America, one's beliefs appear to trump civility—no wedding cake or birth control for you. The court is mindlessly and dangerously undermining social civility, tearing at the fabric of who we should aspire to be as a people. While there is nothing in the Constitution about wedding cakes, there is, apparently, a principle that permits bakers to deny wedding cakes to gay couples. There are many factors triggering the absolute-minded, but it all begins with the court empowering magical beliefs and making it everyone's reality. When, ideally, the courts should be a breakwater for all of us, a respite from the craziness of evangelical rantings, vote-slurping money, and media conspiracy campaigns. But the conservative majority on the court has been confusing principle with a severely contracting sphincter in the face of change.

Fomenting Armed Protest in America

The Supreme Court has blood on its hands and is an instrument of violence in America. No court rulings have been more corrosive of our democratic ideals and fostered more continuous violence than those addressing the Second Amendment. It's an amendment clearly written to support the organization of a community to defend itself at the behest of the state has devolved into turning a highly urbanized and populous twenty-first century America into a war zone comparable to a failed narco-state. And, of course, our Founding Fathers had no notion of semiautomatic weapons or the jacketed bullet invented in the 1890s. As a result, gun violence has been endemic in America for decades as the court has prioritized the individual right to "bear arms" over the needs of the community to organize in self-defense "a well-regulated militia." Currently, we are well-organized, which raises a question as to why everyone needs to own a gun. With each ruling, the court has emboldened a violent subculture with a fanatical belief in its right to exercise violence as necessary.

In 2008, the court held in *District of Columbia v. Heller* that:

> The Second Amendment protects an individual right to possess a firearm unconnected with service in a militia and to use that arm for traditionally lawful purposes, such as self-defense within the home.

It would be interesting if the court had enumerated all the other "lawful purposes." But let's start with the obvious. More innocent people die in their homes from gun violence than being protected by a gun. First, it is important to note that consistently reliable data is difficult to attain, but between 2014 and 2020, an estimated 106,000 gun deaths occurred (homicide, murder, and unintentional). From

2006 to 2014, there was an average of seventy-one thousand nonfatal gun injuries each year (EFSGV.org). But perhaps most damning has been the number of mass shootings over the past ten years: 269 in 2014, 335 in 2015, 382 in 2016, 346 in 2017, 336 in 2018, 417 in 2019, 611 in 2020, or 2,696 total (Gun Violence Archive).

Supreme Court—What We Know Now!

In 1771, the British Land Patter Musket (Brown Bess) was the standard military weapon. It was a muzzle-loading, smoothbore rifle weighing 14 lbs. and required twelve steps to load and fire. Muzzle velocity ranged from 940 to 1,330 fps. At its most efficient, a soldier was capable of firing three rounds per minute. During the Civil War, the Sharps carbine was the most utilized weapon and was capable of firing ten rounds per minute at 1,200 fps. Now let's fast forward to 2021. A 9 mm semiautomatic pistol can fire up to forty-five rounds per minute with a muzzle velocity of 1,247 fps. A semiautomatic AR15 rifle is capable of firing forty-five to sixty rounds per minute at 3,300 fps. And a fully automatic AR15 can fire 400 rpm. In short, one individual with a semiautomatic pistol is the equivalent of fifteen soldiers in 1771, and with an automatic AR15, the equivalent firepower of 133 soldiers (but more accurate and lethal).

In the US, there are currently an estimated four hundred million guns, and 3.6 million are manufactured annually, along with 10,258 gun murders in 2019. In 1773, probate records estimate 13 percent of the White male population owned a gun. It is doubtful our Founding Fathers calculated any of this into writing the Second Amendment. Yet constitutional *originalists* keep mindlessly aiming backward, unable to figure out something has changed. But what could that be?

Most of us watching militia groups showing up at public demonstrations with military-style weapons, tactical gear, body armor, and acting as if they are prepared to engage in combat find it bewildering and intimidating. And it is certainly threatening our

First Amendment right to peacefully assemble and express ourselves. In fact, intimidation is key to their showing up to begin with. They can't show up armed at congressional hearings and are forced to walk through metal detectors at our courts, but no problem on the streets of our communities. What two standards are at play here? The continuous presence of guns to threaten and intimidate American citizens and our officials is unprecedented. No other modern nation tolerates this threat of deadly violence as acceptable public norm.

H.

Malicious Constitutional Voting Worm

Stuxnet, first detected in 2010, is malicious computer worm designed to target programmable logic controllers at Iran's nuclear facilities. It was the first known cyberweapon capable of directly taking control of industrial control systems and crippling them.

The first step toward understanding how *command and control* of the American political process has been highjacked is to go back in time. History tells us that right from the convention floor in 1787, the framers allocated each state two US senators, in effect, favoring smaller rural states over larger metropolitan ones. Our founding software programmers were clearly biased in favor of a rural America but also never foresaw urban population centers exploding in the nineteenth century. But more insidiously, they backdoored a Trojan virus into our constitution—the electoral college, whose awaking and full effect would not be known for another 230 years. The result, rural America is overrepresented in the Senate and has been permanently empowered no matter how much the population and size of government grows. And currently, our government's architecture is running slowly and inefficiently with no available software patches or updates in sight.

There is reason to believe that as the nation expanded westward, the Senate immediately began playing "small ball" early in the political game, admitting sparsely populated states west of the Mississippi to further empower a conservative Senate's political influence (and our founders fully believed a patrician Senate would be running the country, and not the executive branch). And here we are today, running inefficiently with unending political glitches. Let's cut to the chase. The fact that each state has two senators, regardless of population size, monumentally empowers small states and diminishes the influence of larger states. This, along with the electoral college, is part of an outdated operating system assuring each state's independence by minimizing the centralization of power in the federal government. Well done. Except we are now the third largest nation in the world with a population of 332 million people. Oops!

So how has this all evolved after forty-six presidents? First, Democrats largely populate the urban-suburban tranche and Republicans exurban-rural communities. But this monumental demographic shift did not fully emerge until the beginning of the twentieth century. In 1920, the national census, for the first time, counted more people residing in urban areas than rural. Okay, no problem. America was less rural. So what? But our electoral system, designed to favor rural over metropolitan, triggered a constitutional Stuxnet virus for the first time. So how does this work, exactly?

The tendency is to view America as divided by regional geography. For example, West, Northeast, Midwest, South, etc. And on election night, many of us are content with red states versus blue states maps. But does any of this reflect political reality? The election map being continually touch screened by an election night analyst looks largely red, with blue dots wildly scattered across the country and clumping along the coasts. But what reality does this reflect? In 2016, Trump won 2,588 counties across the country, and Biden won only 551 counties. But Biden carried the population total of nearly 198 million compared to Trump's 130 million. In short, Biden "won the counties that are home to 60 percent of the total US population." Looking more closely, Biden won the six largest metropolitan areas in Texas, but the majority of Texas's 254 counties, which are largely rural, went for Trump.

Regions and states are not necessarily what divides us. The real divisions are intertwined rural and urban communities that crisscross America. And because Republican voters are more equally dispersed across the country while Democratic voters congregate in apartments, condos, and suburbs, the House retains a rural bias. To further increase this bias, both parties have been taking *active measures* to suppress voters by gerrymandering voting districts. This primarily favors Republican candidates by marginalizing minority urban Democratic voters. In one instance, the district voting line went through the dorm of a Black college campus. The result has been gridlocked government and disenfranchised voters. Look closer. The *New York Times* reported, based on 2020 election results, that there were only forty competitive House seats nationwide. Ten years earlier, that number was seventy-three. And in 1992, that number was 108 congressional districts.

Let's pick on Wyoming, which appears to be every political analyst's default chump for why our operating system sucks. Wyoming has a population of approximately 580,000, compared to California's population of 39.5 million. Presently, the state of Wyoming has less residents than the average California congressional district. So what's the big deal? Wyoming has two senators and one member in the House of Representatives. California has two senators but fifty-three representatives in the House. The real-world outcome is Wyoming exercises "three times more power in the Electoral College than its population would suggest." If California were to have the same voting power as Wyoming, based on its population, it would receive 159 Electoral College votes, compared to its current fifty-five (*NYT* 2020). That, folks, is a problem perpetuated across the entire US at varying scales.

Unbalanced representation in the US Senate has been slowly growing for generations. But recent projections suggest it's only going to worsen. Multiple studies highlight the growing disparity coming our way. By 2040, nine states will account for 50 percent of the population but be represented by fewer than 25 percent of the Senate. Further analysis indicates that 70 percent of the population will reside in the fifteen largest states and be represented by thirty senators. And the twenty-five most populous states will be home to 84.2 percent of the population and only half of Senate seats (*Washington Post* 2017).

As the Senate has drifted politically right, overrepresenting a White rural population, it now skews 6 to 7 percentage points more conservative than the country as a whole. By some projections, "17 percent of the American population can theoretically elect a Republican Senate majority" (Badger 2016). To negate this Republican advantage, Democrats would need to add five additional Democratic leaning states, and dividing California into three states won't do it. Five would be better.

As far as the presidency goes, the Democratic Party presidential candidate has won the popular vote in six of the past seven elections but twice failed to win the presidency. Bottom line, as currently construed, red states have undue influence on deciding which party controls the Senate, House, and an unpopularly elected president. But also, there are arcane filibuster rules governing the Senate, a relic of Southern states proslavery days. So today, there's a high bar of sixty votes to pass legislation through the Senate, once again empowering smaller rural states. As a consequence, a Republican Senate overinfluences Supreme Court nominations, creating the conservative court we have today. It also effectively means Republicans will likely control Supreme Court nominations for years to come. And it was this conservative court that passed *Citizen's United*, bending our political process toward the influence of money. Republicans have correctly calculated this is to their advantage.

So why don't we just upgrade the Constitution and allow it to reflect our changing national demographic? Because the current rural bias favoring Republicans in the Senate and House have not only slowed our operating system but has rendered it obsolete and inoperable. When it comes to amending the Constitution, it requires thirty-eight state legislatures to ratify an amendment after it is proposed by thirty-four states and two-thirds of both houses of Congress (sixty-seven senators and 288 house members of thirty-four states). If you are wondering, this is why there have only been twenty-seven constitutional amendments in total. Today, twelve low-population red states representing fourteen million people can effectively block constitutional amendments supported by two hundred million voters.

So where does that leave us? Our nation is currently being governed by a small gathering of what pollster's term "purple" swing states. Basically, these are states pollsters struggle to predict which party will win the state's Electoral College vote in a presidential election. Between 2000 and 2016, thirty-eight states reliably voted for the same political party, which means twelve states were less predictable, including Arizona, Florida, Ohio, Michigan, Pennsylvania, Iowa, Georgia, New Hampshire, and North Carolina, with Nevada, Georgia, and Arizona recently trending toward the Democratic Party. In swing states, there's a 5 percent or less difference in votes between the two major parties, with moderate voters in these states narrowing the margins of difference between the two parties. A second factor is at play here, forty-eight of fifty states feature winner-takes-all elections in closed two-party primaries, which further acts to polarize issues and vote outcomes.

The process of a highly bimodal electorate seriously began just before the Civil War, as states identified as pro or anti-slavery, but then ebbed until thirty years ago. The broad effect is most of our votes no longer count for anything, except for a 7–10 percent of moderate voters in the swing states, a group that has been attenuating for the past seventy years from nearly 20 percent to hovering closer to 10 percent. In other words, we are becoming increasingly polarized. In *Swing Voters in American Politics* (Mayer 2008), voters rated each presidential candidate 0–100. Not surprisingly, swing voters or moderates generally rated candidates within 15 points of each other. While most other voters are able to clearly differentiate their preference for a candidates by a 30-or 40-point difference. One reason the Republican Party has become obsessed with attacking government and gridlocking the political system is it further polarizes the electorate and empowers a few White conservative voters in rural swing states.

In effect, we are perpetually stalemated until we moderate our opinions of one another. The catch is, there is an enormous amount of dark money invested in stirring up discontent for Republicans to achieve narrow margins of victory in a small subset of White rural areas in a few swing states. That is how presidential elections have come to be decided. Here's what pollsters know. The presidential winner in Florida has won the presidency in every election since 1964 (with the exception of Biden in 2020), and no Republican has won the presidency without winning Ohio. More precisely, no president has won election by more than a single digit since 1988. But the underlying dynamic is even simpler. Republican senators and House members are unwilling to give up untold dark money and sacrifice political power by advocating fair elections and amending our constitution, when all they have to do is appeal to the worst instincts of their political base. Which requires us to ask ourselves, Is America a democracy?

If there's a historical irony here, it's this: The Founding Fathers were horrified by the prospects of the absolute-minded exercising political influence, whom they perceived as an illiterate and landless rabble capable of tanking democracy and crowning a tyrannical king. They envisioned a landed gentry running the country through a powerful Senate, a weak executive branch, a hobbled lower House, and limited voter participation. And no political parties. The Electoral College was a hedge against strong centralized government. The irony being they created the very thing they feared—the political empowerment of a populist, anti-democratic movement in the halls of government. When the true hedge, all along, was the democracy they didn't trust and crippled from the outset.

I.
Rise of Technology and Rapid Social Change

Over the past thirty years, the world has undergone a vast transformation toward a digital reality that had never previously existed. It is founded on the invention of the transistor and computer chip. It infuses every element of our existence, but what is most obvious is the time we spend interacting with it—on our computers, smartphones, video games, internet, and the arising internet of things connecting us seamlessly with our technology. The mainstay of the American way of life, the automobile, now requires 1,400 computer chips so you can drive it to the store (and these are not the self-driving ones). Technology has given rise to the Information Age, in which data rules the world and has transformed our residing in a crude simulation to one increasingly looking like a starship. But also, one in which we are forever being data-harvested, hacked, and tracked for profit, surveilled by tech corporations, law enforcement, and governments. And increasingly, our minds are being entered and influenced.

The impact of technology on human identity is beyond anything we have experienced since encountering Neanderthals. Or at least until we encounter artificial intelligence twenty-five years from now. How we talk and relate to one another has been forever altered. Nothing has had this cultural-wide impact on the world since European colonialism and the four hundred years of conflict and violence that ensued. And it underlies globalization of the economy, a shrinking American middle-class with the loss of manufacturing jobs, and the rise of robotic technologies rendering human labor obsolete. But it also places a premium on education as the driver of our modern world as new centers of wealth and creation flourish (Google, Amazon, Apple, Facebook, Microsoft).

The case could also be made today that there is a new arbiter of social change and conformity in America, one that lies deep in our electronic connectedness and social media platforms and less directly with the direct exercise of authority by government. The reality is, it has become more difficult than ever to hide from the expansive, if not opaque, online norms. Aberrations, which are inevitable and will be profuse, will unfailingly be identified and confronted without the need for history intervening. Cancel culture as a check on our thoughts and actions has morphed into a ruthless and nasty echo chamber distorting reality. We may ultimately want FCC intervention for our own protection. The rise of social media is giving voice to a plague of irrationality that has haunted humans' social life from its earliest beginnings—critical, unreasoning, and subject to violent mass contagion.

Divided Pax Americana

America is politically divided into two thought camps staring across at one another. The fact that America has never lived up to its sense of "exceptionalism" and messianic hype is disturbing to many. "The birthday of a new world is at hand," Tom Paine proclaimed in 1776. But the truth that America was ruthlessly built on various forms of indentured servitude, classism, suppression of voting and labor rights, conservative religious superstition, genocide, slavery, and wealth disparity does not comport with its standing as a beacon of liberty to the world (which it has been for centuries and is still where people want to park their money and immigrate to).

The reality is, no nation, empire, or kingdom has ever been noble. Each defaulted to violence to suppress populations and economically, politically, and militarily dominate the world around them. Destruction and suppression have been the lighted path from the beginning of time. Wake up! We have been violently lighting it up across this country from the beginning. The recently attempted presidential coup and occupation of the Capitol were simply the culmination of violence dating to our founding. Denial of our violent predilection is analogous to a well-tread Hollywood meme—"Strip away the phony tinsel of Hollywood, and you'll find the real tinsel underneath." Besides, how can America be better than we are? So look around. Who are you? Who are we?

There are two parts to how we as a nation have arrived at this moment in our history. The first is as old as politics itself—power. The second has to do with the advent of the internet and social media platforms. Let's explore. The Republican Party has been playing the race and conspiracy cards for decades to hold on to power. And Wall Street and a segment of the billionaire dark money class are funding this strategy. Essentially, they are stirring the fires of hell to hold on to power and assure profits.

Republican leadership and evangelical ministers, in the face of rapid social change and economic uncertainty, have been stoking the fires of conspiracy for the past sixty years (to an audience prone to believing in conspiracies). And no doubt COVID-19 provided the impetus and cover for a rise to prominence once again. And Trump lit the match. Now it is here and is as real as the fears that generated it. An alternative reality has arrived at our doorstep. It is essential to understand we will not be able to reason our way out of our circumstances. The only solution is to relieve the underlying stress and fears that generated it. And the sooner the better!

It is also evident that the internet has hacked a dark pathway to the recesses of human consciousness. That we simultaneously reside in a dual reality, a practical one—recharge the smartphone; take cash; search the internet for QAnon updates; book a flight to Washington, DC; and pack the Trump flag. But also, one that independently confers *meaning* to our actions—hang Mike Pence for helping Democrats steal the election (note to bring rope). These two realities operate independently of one another when we are stressed, creating a dissociative state. Most importantly, social media platforms are designed to cue up distorted emotional states and tap into biases 24-7. E-tech marketing strategies connect us to every self-fulfilling fear and everyone who shares it, siloing us in a *filter bubble.* It is a powerful reinforcement model for triggering *grievance-revenge* and conspiratorial ideation. The media pundits politely describe this as residing in an *alternate fact, post-truth* world.

The notion that the internet is making us all crazier is not crazy when one contemplates how tweets from President Trump (along with help from Republican leadership and QAnon) orchestrated an attempted coup d'état of the US government, all from an underlying premise that was untrue and in practical terms delusional. Welcome to the future in our simulated reality.

Chapter 11
The Rise of Dictators

He articulates and justifies the resentment
damned up in the souls of the frustrated.

—E. Hoffer, *The True Believer*

While each authoritarian leader is unique unto themselves and to a particular time and place, beginning in the twentieth century, they all appear to share a familial DNA. Eric Hoffer was among the first to provide a psychological profile for the one-size-fits-all psychopathology of the modern authoritarian leader. His description was, of course, of Hitler, Mussolini, and Stalin, but seventy years after the fact, it remains descriptive of dictators around the world, including a recent US president.

audacity and joy in defiance
strong willed
fanatical conviction
faith in his destiny and luck
capacity for hatred
contempt for the present
cunning estimate of human nature
delights in symbols
unbounded brazenness
disregard for consistency and fairness

capacity for requiring the utmost loyalty
dominates able men who submit to his will

The question we are confronted with here is pretty obvious. What types of individuals would be enraptured by a leader who exhibits the above characteristics? Why would someone place their trust and hope for the future in an individual most of us wouldn't want as a friend or boss at work? Based on the literature and research, there are two parts to this answer. One is external to each person, to which none of us have control over. Eric Hoffer suggests people adulate someone in a climate of despair and are willing to toss the present away for a redemptive future. Hannah Arendt tells us that tyrants offer a vision of the future that feels more coherent and makes more sense than the complexity, dysfunction, and chaos currently being confronted. Desperate times define desperate responses. For many people, social turmoil and chaos circumscribe their reality. When there are threats to people's social status and economic security and someone is perceived as offering order and hope, they are often adulated.

The second factor at play here is internal to each person. But what would be consistently present in the psyche of so many desperate individuals that an authoritarian leader would be their best hope? Why tether their future to a fanatic and tyrant? Hoffer posits that people who evidence high levels of frustration and disaffection experience self-loathing and a sense of hopelessness from their lack of productivity and are prone to a suspension of disbelief. While Arendt focuses on one's personal sense of isolation and loneliness (*anomie*) because of a loss of community. And in the early 1950s, both were looking back at Nazism and Communism. But as we look forward at authoritarianism and populism today, there are parallels.

Trump's outlandish defiance of established authority and norms, his willingness to double down on every deception he's called out on, to outrageously deny the obvious facts in front of him, and to claim that he is the victim of a conspiracy at every turn makes him a hero to the absolute-minded. His larger-than-life contrarianism and figuratively giving the middle finger to everyone who criticizes him or he believes has been disloyal and betrayed him is literally absolution for the absolute-minded. Attending a Trump rally is more evangelical pilgrimage than a political campaign. It's also a cleansing experience in an America radically divided by status and values. But beneath this veneer of allegiance to Trump lies evidence of an earlier betrayal of trust. And their devotion to Trump is proof of that.

The theory of absolutism proposed here is additive to those of Hoffer and Arendt on the nature of totalitarianism and people's willing subjugation to authoritarian leadership. And this all begins with a betrayal of trust early on, creating a double bind for each child as they become adults. Later in life, this experience is recapitulated with an authoritarian leader. Learning to stay quiet and internalize the dissonance in the face of betrayal is a lifelong survival strategy. This is particularly true when one feels existentially threatened, not unlike the unconscious adaptation of the child. The authoritarian leader becomes the idealized parent who can do no wrong because acknowledging any betrayal is emotionally threatening. And any attack on the idealized parent can be met with violent resistance. Even though one's needs are never going to be fully met, it's better to thrive in the new world to come. This is as true for the child as the adult.

None of the desperation of the 1920s and 1930s is present in the US or Europe today, yet there has been a rise in populism and authoritarian rule. What's going on? Apparently, it does not take much disruption in the status quo to become threatening, portending further instability and chaos to come. Particularly when one's identity is increasingly being challenged and feels under threat. And this is occurring simultaneously with increased economic hardships and social instability for many. While we are nowhere near the catastrophic circumstance giving rise to fascism and communism, the current impact of globalization, internet connectivity on identity, and economic insecurity has been extraordinary. The impact is not just local but global when one adds in continuing worldwide mass migration, rapid social change, climate change, environmental degradation, pandemic, rising economic inequality, and rabid asymmetrical political warfare.

Modern Dictators Require a Modern Understanding

President George W. Bush, after meeting with Russian President Vladimir Putin on June 17, 2001, stated, "I looked the man in the eye. I found him to be very straightforward and trustworthy... I wouldn't have invited him to my ranch if I didn't trust him."

Dark Triad

To understand the modern dictator from a psychological perspective, it is important to understand that they are not psychologically normal, but also that they are not mentally ill. What they primarily exhibit is a "dark triad" of personality traits. This includes malignant narcissism, psychopathy, and Machiavellianism. So let's begin with what is a personality disorder. This is an enduring pattern of inner experiences and behaviors that markedly deviate from the expectations of social norms. It is pervasive and inflexible, with onset in adolescence or early adulthood, per the DSM-5. The key is this is not a mental illness or disease but rather a dysfunctional aspect of personality development (the human equivalent of downloading malicious software). And there are many variants (paranoid, schizoid, schizotypal, antisocial, borderline, histrionic, narcissistic, avoidant, dependent, and obsessive-compulsive).

The origin of a personality disorder is in childhood, typically beginning with a betrayal of trust or other difficult and traumatic life experiences that reinforce maladaptive coping behaviors (learning to lie and act deceptively, excessively demanding, compulsive, or emotionally reactive). Initially, it might provide some limited resolution to issues and struggles, but it becomes increasingly unadaptive and dysfunctional over time. That is unless one becomes a *super-adapter*. This is an individual who turns their norm-shattering adaption into a socially powerful tool, now out in the world successfully wreaking havoc in their own assured way. This is a dictator.

First up is narcissistic personality disorder. It is the most common of the three personality types featured here. Traits include a grandiose sense of self-importance that is forever self-promoting and exaggerating achievements. There is an expectation of being recognized as superior and a preoccupation with fantasies of unlimited success and power. They require excessive admiration to go along with a deep sense of entitlement. Generally, they lack empathy and are exploitive of others, while often envious and arrogant. But hold on, there's an even darker version termed *malignant narcissism*. These are emotionally overreactive individuals who can be exceptionally suspicious and highly aggressive to the point of being sadistic. Paranoia abounds just beneath the surface.

An elder among personality disorders is psychopathy, which is no longer a DSM-5 diagnosis but one with a respectable etiology. These individuals exhibit a general disregard for the welfare of others and are comfortable operating outside social norms and the law. They lack empathy and are incapable of remorse. They tend to be impulsive, highly manipulative, and calculating. And perhaps most significantly, aggressive and predatory. It is important to understand that this is a state of mind as much as it is how they conduct themselves in the world. They are often highly intelligent, financially successful, and they achieve positions of authority. And it goes without saying, they can be exceptionally dangerous. The key difference between malignant narcissism and psychopathy is the former is driven by ego gratification and the latter by self-interest.

This brings us to Machiavellianism. This is not a mental health diagnosis but rather a confluence of personality traits that have gained wide recognition in psychological assessment. Machiavelli was a political philosopher during the Italian Renaissance, well-known, then and now, for his book *The Prince.* Here, Machiavelli outlined his philosophical principles for a "wise ruler." And to be clear, it is a dark treatise on human nature. For example, "A wise ruler ought never to keep faith when by doing so it would be against his interests." Or this, "A prince never lacks good reasons to break his promise." How about "It is much more secure to be feared, than to be loved." His basic insight is if deceit, treachery, and blunt trauma are more expedient than virtue, default to them. In psychological terms, Machiavellianism is descriptive of individuals who are master manipulators, who are naturally calculating and deceptive. And without saying, immoral. They are fixated on power, have a cynical worldview, and are capable of ruthlessly exploiting others. If we were to sum the key traits underlying all three diagnoses, we would discover that dictators are smart, self-absorbed, manipulative, aggressive, amoral, distrusting, and power hungry.

When first encountering the dark triad, most people think, thankfully, that's not me or anyone I know. And there's also the temptation to conclude you would recognize these people coming a mile away. You would be wrong! And lastly, you are certain you would never tolerate them or fall for their games. And you would probably be wrong about this as well. First off, it is never all or nothing with these personality traits. Seldom does anyone possess all these traits in their darkest form. Individuals possess and express these traits both crudely and obviously, but also with subtlety and sophistication. People are much more complicated and nuanced than we want to give them credit for. They are typically less obvious than a checklist of diagnostic criteria.

Too often, this triad of personality disorders succeeds because some of these individuals are smarter than average. They see your vulnerabilities first, then leverage and outmaneuver you before you know there's a game. They are often charming and delightful and can morph into whatever you or the organization requires. This chameleon quality can be whatever is required now. It is easy for them. They know how to play the game. And in an organizational setting, they typically screw you over long before you understand what is happening. They are playing chess while you are enjoying checkers at lunch. Only after the fact does it become obvious to most of us that we have encountered a psychological monster. And those with this cluster of personality traits, the ones that most successfully navigate their social world, are dictators.

Paranoid Personality Disorder

The modern dictator is pupu platter of psychopathology that we cannot fully comprehend without exploring the paranoid personality disorder. This is a distinct disorder hiding in the cluster of dark triad symptoms. *The Diagnostic and Statistical Manual of Mental Disorders* (DSM-5) distinguished between individuals diagnosed with a personality disorder and an individual who may exhibit paranoid *traits*. The key differences are the early age of onset and persistent dysfunction of a personality disorder. But for our purposes, let's peruse a few of the diagnostic criteria for this disorder. (Caution: Do not speculate who may exhibit these "traits." Only a trained professional should do that.)

- They suspect, without sufficient basis, others are exploiting, harming, or deceiving them.
- They are preoccupied with the loyalty and trustworthiness of friends and associates.
- They are reluctant to confide out of a fear that information will be maliciously used against them.
- They read demeaning and threatening messages into benign remarks or events.
- They hold grudges and are unforgiving of perceived slights and insults.
- They see attacks on their character or reputation that are not apparent to others and are quick to react angrily.

Supporting this diagnosis are a number of what are termed "associated features:" *difficult to get along with, argumentative, complaining, hostile aloofness, hypervigilant, lack trust in others, high need for control, rigid and critical, blame others, grandiose fantasies, concerned about power and rank, develop negative stereotypes, attracted to simplistic formulations.* In my clinical estimation, a substantial subset of the absolute-minded exhibits a platter of these *traits* and *associated features*. Not surprisingly, these traits and features appear to describe any number of elected officials, as well as those in the media, at least as they publicly present themselves.

For dictators to succeed, they are required to become increasingly distrusting and paranoid. It is a job requirement. And it seems most of them are fully capable of making this transition. So how do dictators message the world that they are now operationally paranoid? An oligarch mysteriously falls out a window and dies. A princeling is charged with corruption and stripped of his wealth. A general is placed under house arrest for gross insubordination and later executed by firing squad. A family member is confined to a compound and is no longer allowed to shop or drive. A political rival is sentenced to prison for spreading false news. A reporter is kidnapped and imprisoned or, in the worst-case scenario, quartered into small pieces and shipped out in a suitcase. Party members are purged, and their families never hear from them again. Protesters die while being detained in jail or hung in public from a crane. An overseas dissident dies from poisoning. A former political insider is charged with undermining national security and crimes against the state and disappears. Someone publicly suggests the regime could do better and is immediately charged with defaming the political leader and sentenced to death. Basically, lots of people disappear. In the US, the worst that can happen is one's character is publicly maligned. It's a terribly vicious process that most eventually recover from.

The Dictator's Job

> *His Excellency, President for Life, Field Marshal Al Hadji Doctor Idi Amin Dada, VC, DSO, MC, CBE, Lord of All the Beasts of the Earth and Fishes of the Seas and Conqueror of the British Empire in Africa in General and Uganda in Particular.*

Above is the official title of Ugandan dictator Idi Amin before he was chased from power and exiled in Saudi Arabia until his death. And just to be clear, he did not relish this title in its ironic form. And he was not satirizing the declining British Empire (well, maybe just a little). This was no absurdist conjecture about the colonial exploitation of Africa. No, it was a statement to the world of his superiority. In this sense, he represents the unrepentant narcissism and grandiosity of every dictator.

It is impossible to read and write about dictators without wandering into a world of hyperbole, where satire and irony exist alongside mindless violence and human violation, and where despair and dystopia coexist without exaggeration. Dictators appear before us as remarkably hollow human beings. They exercise power pre-logically as emotional tantrums in a moral vacuum. We have no doubts what type of parents they would make or had. One is forced to default to hyperbole and absurdity merely to point out the obvious.

Have you noticed that there are no "happy" dictators? They seldom smile, are stern all the time, and are always issuing threats of some sort. They are never the avuncular type—warm, charming, friendly, and wanting to make you feel welcome. When was the last time you saw a dictator put his arm around someone he wasn't trying to choke out? It takes very little insight to see that beneath whatever social facade they have created is an aloof, ruthless, tightly wound individual with a distrusting edge, who can only smile if they want something or got their way. Being friendly is only a temporary facade to gain what they want. Bottom line, they can never to be trusted.

Really, who wants to be a dictator? Granted, the job comes with lots of perks, but also with plenty of downsides. Dictators are apex political predators, trapped in a hyper *grievance-revenge* mode, to which the only salve is exercising power over others. Consequently, they all possess a dark sadism that drives them to the top of the primate hierarchy. Out of 195 nations today, fifty are ruled by dictators, and none are women. Approximately 3.3 billion people currently reside in a dictatorship, which has been increasing over the past fifteen years. Military juntas last, on average, about 8.5 years, and plain old dictators usually die in office after fifteen years.

It is important to understand that dictators prefer to be perceived as popularly elected to legitimize their political authority. They usually accomplish this under the guise of a corrupted democratic process, which, at best, is a parasitic relationship in which institutions are eaten from the inside out. It's also important to understand that dictators, in a nod to modern sensibilities, prefer to be addressed as Chairman, President or Prime Minister, with a few defaulting to Your Highness. Do not address them as Preeminent Dictator, Giant

Among Kleptocrats, or Enormous Dicts if you do not want to be imprisoned or killed.

The only time dictators are truly honest about how they feel is when they promise retribution and come after you. There are only loyalists in their world, who they never trust and who are fully disposable. What is this ruthlessness about? Where does it come from? The theory of absoluteness presented here mostly explains the psychological dynamics of a dictatorship. But there is one final piece to the psychological puzzle in understanding the sheer ruthlessness of dictators. Dictators suffer from fixated developmental syndrome (FDS). And if you have never heard of this, it's because this is the first time, to my knowledge, it has ever been described. In short, it's the co-optation of the powers of the state to assert the dictator's will over a world he can never trust or feel safe in.

While dictators are developmentally adults, because of FDS, they lead shallow and truncated lives, having failed to fully differentiate as individuals. This actually helps them function as dictators, not having to deal with all the emotional and moral subplots of their decision-making. At some psychological level, they all failed. They failed to learn how to regulate their lives in the face of their parents' failed guardianship. They reside in a state of tantrum, not unlike an infant. Because the parents continually failed to meet the child's physical and emotional needs, dictators are emotionally stuck, recapitulating their trauma in the ruthless and sadistic exercise of power.

Dictators are forever emulating the absent, mindless, indifferent, and abusive parent. This is a reenactment of their parents' failures and an unconscious effort to undo their past hurt, pain, and sense of betrayal. And to be clear, they are not aware of this. This is achieved by exercising the same ruthless indifference to the world they experienced. They desire to control the world and not heal it. As a result, their needs are limitless and can never be met. Hence the continual and unending quest to extend their reach and power. They can never be satisfied. They can never feel safe (or loved). That is why all relationships are cast as tests of loyalty. Because the child had to submit, now everyone in their world is required to submit.

Developmental Regression

Is it possible to pinpoint at what developmental stage a dictator failed to emotionally progress? The answer is yes, but it is also important to understand they were not born dictators but created by the world they were born into. The fundamental dysfunction of dictators resides in their early life experiences. Here, we examine three developmental models focusing on identity, moral reasoning, and emotional IQ. And when these three psychological dimensions overlap, they reach remarkably similar findings. The early life failures to fully differentiate at each developmental stage encodes one's future trajectory. This is as true for dictators as it is for all of us. But the drama of dictatorships suggests a more malignant set of features and characteristics at play. Factors giving rise to resignation, grievance-revenge, a "dark triad" of personality features, and the sadistic attraction to the exercise of authority.

Identity Development

Let's cut to the chase and go directly to Erik Erikson's theory of psychosocial development (*Identity and the Life Cycle*). Only in this context can the emotional dynamic underlying the dictator's ruthless exercise of power be fully explicated.

Erikson posited eight developmental stages of life:

Stage 1. Birth to age one—trust versus mistrust.
Stage 2. Early childhood—autonomy versus shame and doubt.
Stage 3. Preschool years—initiative versus guilt.
Stage 4. Early school years—industry versus inferiority.
Stage 5. Adolescence—identity versus identity confusion.
Stage 6. Early adulthood—intimacy versus isolation.
Stage 7. Adulthood—generativity versus stagnation.
Stage 8. Late life—integrity versus despair.

Successfully advancing through each stage is dependent on adapting to all the social crises one encounters at each stage toward the development of a healthy *ego identity*. Personality develops in a series of stages based on social experiences across a lifetime. A failure to fully master each stage results in a sense of inadequacy instead of mastery and ego strength.

Without going through each stage and the potential consequences of not fully mastering each of them, let's just go straight to the most important stage—the first stage and the development of "trust." It is foundational to mastering all the other stages. This stage powerfully affects the child's mental health. It also shapes and influences a person's personality development and outlook on life. And this is where all dictators remain fixated, at the very first stage of ego development and the inability to trust the world around them. And yes, being a dictator is proof of this initial failure—compulsively reenacting their distrust by having to control the world around them.

As one progresses through each stage, failure takes different forms:

> *Stage 2*—feelings of self-doubt and shame over failing to achieve a sense of autonomy.
> *Stage 3*—a sense of guilt develops over the inability to assert power and control over their world and suffering disapproval for their efforts.
> *Stage 4*—feelings of inferiority.
> *Stage 5*—weak sense of self.

There are obvious perils at every stage. And to varying degrees, all these failures also describe our resident dictator, former President Trump. His trust failures (and to be clear, at the very start, he did not do this to himself; it was done to him) were entirely on display throughout his presidency—a distrusting, insecure, weak sense of self all camouflaged with unending bluster, self-promotion, and denial of his transgressions and the eternal accusing of others.

Moral Development

It is relevant to visit psychologist Lawrence Kohlberg's six stages of moral reasoning (*The Philosophy of Moral Development*). Kohlberg hypothesized there are three levels of moral development, each with two interior stages.

Level 1: Preconventional (up to age nine). Morality is externally controlled. Rules are imposed by authority figures, and conformity of behavior is achieved by avoiding punishment. For many individuals fixated at this stage, rules become fixed and absolute. This can eventually adapt to an overfocus on *reciprocity* as a basis for reward and having one's needs met.

Level 2: Conventional (adolescent and adult). There is a shift from conforming and focusing on individual rewards toward gaining social approval and living up to expectations. An appreciation develops for moral behavior and codes of conduct. At later stages, there develops an understanding of the society as a whole and the role laws and morality play.

Level 3: Postconventional (late life). An individual internalizes a universal perspective of abstract ethical principles and values guiding one's actions (Kohlberg noted that few people achieved this moral state).

A dictator reading this would have no idea what we are discussing and dismiss it as total nonsense. For him, the crux of moral reasoning is to avoid pain and punishment and to do whatever it takes to maximize rewards. He would sense it is hostile, but only because it is about him and appears to assert that there might be something wrong with him (and your life would be in danger). "Totally fake news," he would dismissively claim. Further, he would assert right-wrong, good-bad, moral-immoral are transactional states and have no meaning beyond each person's self-interest (stage 1). And that is how one negotiates with a dictator, understanding their self-interest in the matter. His doing something positive might have a public relations upside, but remember, he is willing to bear unbridled criticism and taunts, which he can do easily, waiting for a chance to kill you (figuratively or literally). Criticisms are always about the person making them and not about him. Now threats, those are different. He understands threats. These are the underlying reality of the dark triad he exists in.

Emotional Development

The notion of *emotional intelligence* had been drifting about academia for nearly forty years, finally crystallizing into research by psychologists Peter Salovey and John Meyers in the 1990s (*Emotional Intelligence*). They described emotional intelligence (EI) as the ability to monitor one's feelings and emotions, as well as others, and to sort them out and utilize them to guide one's thinking and behavior. This research evolved from a realization that measures of general intelligence (*g*) did not fully comport with people's ability to function in the world.

Intelligence is what psychologist David Wechsler (developer of the WAIS IQ test) defined as the "global capacity of an individual to think rationally, act purposely, and deal effectively with their environment." But as it turned out, there were elements of intellectual functioning that did not comport with standardized measures of IQ. Consequently, new theories of intelligence began to evolve, including the notion of emotional intelligence. That is, the ability to use emotions to enhance one's cognitive interaction with the world. As proposed by Salovey and Meyers, emotional intelligence is comprised of four elements.

1. *Emotional perception.* The ability to accurately identify one's emotional state (self-awareness) and express it, but also the ability to recognize the emotional state of others, including the ability to empathize.
2. *Emotional reasoning.* The ability to harness one's emotions toward achieving goals, aims, and objectives in life.
3. *Emotional understanding.* The ability to recognize the origins and cause of one's emotional states.
4. *Emotional management.* The ability to regulate one's emotional life and reflect before one acts.

So what does all this mean in practical terms? It means there is a deep connection between our emotional lives and how well we comport ourselves in life. Our emotional lives not only regulate our cognitively navigating the world but that our decision-making is fully dependent on our emotional awareness and reasoning. But here is the kicker. When trust is disrupted through a loss of object constancy during infancy/childhood, as described earlier, the effect can disrupt a person's ability to regulate their emotions. This can range from highly repressed and overcontrolled emotions to frequent out-of-control outbursts. But always in the context of failing to empathize with others, except to cryptically note they probably got what they deserved.

One can reasonably conclude after examining these stages of development that dictators, by definition, are pretty much stuck at level 1 in all three models.

A. First, there ensues a loss of trust and a struggle to assert dominance and control to heal a fragile and insecure sense of self.
B. As a result, they reside in a transactional world focused on avoiding punishment and maximizing reward. Reciprocity exists only as a negotiating strategy and often a form of extortion. For most absolute-minded individuals, the basic rules of life, whether informal or legal, are fixed and absolute. Shades of gray speak to immorality and untrustworthiness. *Principle and discipline* are the fundamental guidelines to life.
C. Last, there is limited emotional awareness and ability to empathize and emotionally self-regulate. Feelings trigger a sense of weakness and failure to be in control.

Dictators never successfully manage all the developmental stages and remain fixated at the early stages. This plays out in their ruthless attempts to recapitulate their failures/traumas and undo them by manipulating the world around them through the ruthless exercise of power. Distrusting, insecure, and feeling inferior, they are forever trying to prove this is not true (overcompensating). And the proof is in the world they create around themselves, forever demanding respect and adulation to fill the emptiness inside (wearing military uniforms and parades often helps with this).

Looking across the biographies of the modern dictator, one realizes how average they are. Really nothing special here at any stage of their lives. Often a product of low levels of ambition and low expectations, many were simply at the right time and place. Still not special even as a dictator. This is as true for Putin, Xi, Erdogan, and all who will follow. The only things that truly distinguish Donald Trump are his inherited wealth, impressive number of business failures, and his unending efforts to undo his early life failures by publicly flaying his personal demons.

All dictators are entrapped in a looping reality recapitulating unresolved childhood traumas and their failure to fully differentiate as individuals. It is cold and calculating. The exercise of power and control becomes a proxy for their inability to trust. Power acts as a powerful narcotic that anesthetizes them from their actions and shields them from comprehending any higher ethical or moral dimensions. They are time travelers from their past.

Obsequiousness—the Ambrosia of Tyrants

On June 12, 2017, President Trump held his first full cabinet meeting after becoming president. In front of the press and broadcast live on C-SPAN2, one of the most astonishing spectacles in White House history began at the eleven-minute-and-fifty-second mark. First, let's define the word *sycophant*: "self-seeking, servile flatterer; fawning parasite." Each cabinet member was asked by Trump to offer praise for the recent accomplishments of the administration. What ensued was by far the most embarrassing round of tributes any US president had ever received. And as they went around the table, one could not help blush watching them bend the knee and kiss the ring in toady servility. Watching this live on television, one could not help but wonder where self-respect and dignity were. This is America, not North Korea!

However, it was Vice President Mike Pence who most vigorously humped Trump's pant leg: "It is the greatest privilege of my life to serve as vice president to a president who is keeping his word to the American people." (Say what? Don't we generally expect the president to keep his word to the American people? Make no mistake about it. The emphasis was on serving Trump and not the American people.) The eternal question raised by the cabinet's behavior is, Why? Was this set up to be a public spectacle, straight from the dictator's handbook? Probably. Trump wanted a military parade shortly after. Why all the fawning from people who were highly accomplished in their own right? Perhaps most astonishing was Trump taking it all in, content as an inflatable doll bobbing in the breeze, everyone blowing smoke up his ass. There are many aspects to this, and it is complicated.

The primary dynamic is the raw "power" of political hierarchy in the most powerful nation on earth, and the person wielding that power, Trump, is the most powerful person on earth at the time. Trump's personal sense of himself was so grossly inflated and insecure that he required ceaseless glorification of his specialness, and anything less would bring forth his resentment and anger. This often required him to fire someone, but only after rounds of publicly expressing his ire toward them, questioning their commitment, loyalty, and competence. But most importantly, publicly ridiculing them like it was a celebrity roast. Ass-kissing was clearly the way to go in this administration, especially if you want to get a job, keep your job, and make bank on your personal agenda, which is all you really need to know about the people sitting around the conference table that day with Trump.

Let's not dismiss the personal agenda side of this equation. Each cabinet member curtsied or bowed deeply because it furthered their private agenda for recognition, political office, exercising authority, and bending democracy for profit, and all the fringe benefits that accrue from hovering at the vortex of power in Washington, DC. There are infinite numbers of people ready to press your clothes, run errands, delouse you, hose you down, and drive you to the next meeting. People are lined up to curry your favor and shower you with praise and, behind closed doors, make it rain thousand-dollar bills strip-club style. Power is intoxicating to humans, and most of us will do anything for it. Status is the most powerful force in the human social world, next to sex. And that's only because we have to keep reproducing to chase the power (the primate life cycle).

Social status is a primate thing. Among great apes (gorillas, chimpanzees, orangutans, bonobos and, wait for it, humans), alpha male hierarchies are how status is organized. It can be violent upfront, but in the long run, it substantiates rank and one's place in a community (and who gets to mate). Obviously, not many copulate in the president's cabinet as a trust signal, or at least feign celibacy (similar to Catholic priests). But secondarily, the alpha male typically has allies who have his back, a coterie that does his bidding and protects their interests. As embarrassing as the cabinet meeting was to watch, at least they were not sniffing each other's crotches and letting Trump mount them from behind in acts of submission, as is the custom of our primate cousins (but really, public obsequiousness is pretty much the same thing among humans). But deference among primates is typically achieved through violence and fear. But this is what trust looks like for primates. Humans are obviously more complex, but not as much as we would like to believe.

The bottom line, in human relationships, deference is symbolic trust, which is the best you can hope for if you are unable to trust, can't mind read and don't have an agreement in writing. This was on full display watching Trump publicly interact with Putin on the international stage. Here, Trump was smiling, laughing, leaning in, and publicly supporting Putin's initiatives, all the while leaking national security intelligence and, most importantly, accepting Putin's word that he had not interfered in Trump's election, as opposed to believing his own intelligence agencies. I can think of six reasons for this:

1. Putin had *kompromat* on Trump.
2. Trump wanted to brand an even grander Trump Tower in Moscow.
3. Trump wanted to keep Russian oligarch money flowing into his developments.

4. Trump wanted to maintain the fiction that Russian interference did not help him win the election.
5. He admires authoritarian leaders and genuinely wants to be like them in stature and authority.
6. He is a *stooge* being manipulated by Russian intelligence.

The answer is all six are true.

The fact is, most of human history has been about codifying alpha male dominance. Alexander the Great, Julius Caesar, Genghis Khan, Napoleon—the list is endless. And warlords rule throughout the world today as well—Vladimir Putin, Xi Jinping, Recep Erdogan, and on and on. And in the recent past, we had Lenin, Stalin, Hitler, Mussolini, Hirohito, Franco, and Mao. And before this, a never-ending succession of kings, chieftains, and emperors. In other words, power is primarily derived from the top. It is really astounding if you think about it. Every nation on earth today has "one" person either ruling or governing it. Because we are primates and the eternal projection of power is a ruling "strongman" (or woman).

Note: If one were to scrutinize the underlying agenda of nearly every conservative think tank in America, it's to prop up "executive" privilege against the courts, legislative process, and most importantly, the people.

Presidential Military Service

Thirteen US presidents reached the rank of general before becoming President (George Washington, Andrew Jackson, Ulysses S. Grant, Dwight D. Eisenhower, William Harrison, Zachary Taylor, Rutherford B. Hayes, James A. Garfield, William Howard Taft, Franklin Pierce, Chester A. Arthur, Andrew Johnson, Benjamin Harrison). And a near equal number served as high-ranking military officers: Thomas Jefferson, James Madison, James Monroe, James K. Polk, Millard Fillmore, William McKinley, Theodore Roosevelt, Harry S. Truman, Lyndon B. Johnson, Richard Nixon, and Gerald Ford.

The point being, it's not a coincidence that twenty-four US presidents were military officers. Military service projects alpha status. It's also not a coincidence that Trump appointed four generals to serve him—Mattis, Kelly, McMaster, and Flynn—to bolster a fenestrated sense of superiority. Of course, the eternal struggle for democracies is taming this genetic top-down preset—constitutional checks and balances, elected offices, law, norms and tradition, plus a lot of hope and luck.

Let's return to Trump's cabinet meeting on June 12, 2017. Members of his cabinet all understood the terms of service under Trump, given all his earlier public statements, business failures, and lawsuits. And it was not by accident they were all now in parasitic symbiosis with him. They pretty much knew he was an emotional tyrant, likely with the fantasy they could escape his wrath. The case could also be made that their ability to maintain subservience derived from having grown up with a bullying parent, just as Trump had. It was all familiar territory despite the fact each one of them had risen to power before their cabinet appointment and had exercised considerable authority on their own. Their underlying insecurities attracted them to power like moths to a flame.

Each cabinet member likely suffered from a failure of trust in childhood. Petty tyranny was familiar, now an unconscious attractant. That is the only reason they were appointed by Trump and accepted. Based on past experiences, they also believed they knew how to outmaneuver, manipulate, and rise above Trump's antics. Distrusting parents prepared them for what was to come—dancing on a hot skillet. It's the insecurity that comes with rising from distrust. Every petty tyrant in our lives and the world around us begins here, eternally seeking to control the people and the world around them through their distrust.

Trump's attorney generals—Jeff Sessions, Matthew Whitaker, and William Barr—soon discovered they couldn't be obsequious and honorable. The press wouldn't let them. They were forced to choose. However, the more they ping-ponged between these two choices, the more they were clearly obsequious: "Should I screw over the American people or the president?" Clearly a difficult choice for each of them. But they played the cognitive dissonance trick. What is good for the president is good for America. Problem solved. And they get to keep their appointment to high office. Another win-win for everybody. They can whistle *Be Happy* on their way to the White House cafeteria. Besides, the absolute-minded typically default to autocratic solutions and rationalize their decisions. Just ask Senate majority leader Mitch McConnell, trying but unable to smile after each manipulation of Senate rules and demonstration of his power (much like a dungeon master after a deeply satisfying BDSM session). The only thing McConnell is capable of trusting is the power he wields. Most of the power brokers enabling Trump are emotionally afflicted individuals seeking absolution in the halls of power.

Dictatorship—Proxy for Distrust

The Roman Republic lasted 482 years, from 509 BCE to 27 BCE. It was a limited representative democracy with a wealthy patrician class making up the ruling Senate. Over a two-hundred-year period, the lower plebian classes eventually gained a formal voice in the government as well, the *Concilium Plebis*. There were also elected tribal assemblies to govern locally across the empire. Two consuls were elected by the legislative assemblies, serving for one year and presiding over the Roman Senate and commanding the military.

However, in 49 BCE, Julius Caesar, a Roman general and consul returning from the Gallic wars, refused to step down as a general before entering Rome (literally crossed the Rubicon). It was considered treasonous, and a civil war ensued in which Caesar prevailed and was subsequently appointed "dictator" for life. This effectively signaled the end of the Republic as a representative democracy. Caesar was wealthy and popular among the citizens and soldiers of Rome. At the time of his rise to power, the Republic had fallen into partisan violence, growing inequality, and high levels of corruption. Caesar became the popular face of stability in the face of chronic civil unrest.

So why are we talking about the Roman Empire? It's simply this: When Julius Caesar became dictator, Rome ceased to be a Republic, though it would be another 1,500 years before the end of the Roman Empire. It is important to understand that when Donald Trump was elected president in 2016, he effectively became the first American "dictator" in the 246-year history of our country. We need to ask ourselves, Does this herald the end of the American Republic as a democracy, as Julius Caesar did for the Roman Republic?

This is not meant to compare Trump to Julius Caesar, who was a brilliant general, exceptionally intelligent, highly literate, and a profoundly gifted orator and leader. Trump was more SNL clown turned game show host and somehow, no one knows exactly how or why he became elected president of the United States without ever appearing on *Wipeout* or *Love Island*. But more to the point, there is an equivalency here about how Caesar came to power and how Trump came to power. Both events point to potential political turning points for democracies in turmoil. Where Caesar prevailed, Trump is unlikely to. But we should see Trump's election as a meteorite across the night sky, an omen foretelling one possible future. Different times, different places, but an omen nonetheless.

Trump is America's first truly autocratic president. While he never quite gained full "dictator" status, he tried awfully hard with a failed insurrection and attempted coup of the US government. And he plans to try one more time in 2024. Trump's attempted putsch exceeds, for sheer brazenness, the 9/11 aircraft hijacking and its failed attempts to also crash the White House and Pentagon. Equally concerning are the Republican dictator spores dispersing in the political winds.

Note: When Adolf Hitler was appointed German chancellor in 1933, the Nazi Party polled 43 percent of the popular vote as Germany's largest political party. With a population of eighty million, membership in the Nazi Party in 1932 was 11,845; two million in 1933; 5.3 million in 9139; and eight million in 1945. It never reached beyond 10 percent of the German population (Wikipedia). The point being it does not take an overwhelming majority to stage a coup. It is also interesting to note that Hitler had attempted a coup of the German government in 1923. He was subsequently arrested and, while in prison, wrote *Mein Kampf*. What we are witnessing with

Trump may only be the beginning of more to come. As it becomes evident Republicans are ramping up their efforts to suppress voting, break the functioning of government, and delegitimize election results.

Let's see if we can't refine Hoffer's description of the authoritarian leader. We should start by noting that modern dictators all exhibit a shared public persona, one that is required in highly interconnected and media-saturated nation-states. They evolved to become dictators within complex social, political, and economic systems. They are not so much an invading army as a parasitic organism that flips the political switch onto zombie mode and life goes on routinely. That is the minimal requirement for them to succeed.

Hitler, Stalin, and Mao were all radicalized indigenous entities. And equally so, today, with Vladimir Putin, Xi Jinping, Recep Erdogan, and Kim Jong Un. Because social systems have become too large and complex to be messed with, dictators have become more CEO than Vlad the Impaler. Repression is used, but it can't tank the economy or risk losing broad support. It is still required to feign some form of faux legitimacy (voting, courts, press). Arresting and imprisoning opposition leaders is routine. But you still must be able to hold your head up at Davos, the UN, or while summitting with European leaders. It's a deadly public relations job and a tough one. Poisoning people you don't like seems a bit much, as does shooting them and hacking them to pieces. For example, Putin and Mohammed bin Salman, which broadly speaks to their state of fixated developmental syndrome (FDS).

The Dynamics of Dictatorship

They reside in a world without trust. Broken early on and in the place of reason and empathy, the absolute-minded received *principle and discipline*. There was no place for solace here, only feeling emotionally empty and trying to survive the pain and betrayal that can never be acknowledged or spoken. To fall out of *resignation*, there was only *grievance* and *revenge*. They are forever seeking to control and manipulate the world through an intense distrust of it. And if necessary, violence as payback for the betrayal and disloyalty. It is difficult to fully comprehend the narcissistic grandiosity and paranoia required of a dictator seeking to subjugate an entire nation. Russia militarily securing the Crimea, for what? China pacifying the Uighurs people, because of what? And then threatening to invade Taiwan because it is nearby and rejected them? It's not possible to imagine why! A Belarusian dictator hijacks an airliner to kidnap an antagonistic journalist and then pretends he didn't hijack the plane. Brilliant! The only threats they are suffering are in their minds—a fearful loss of power and control until everyone is operating in zombie mode.

Manipulating one's image is the single most important aspect of being a modern dictator. Legitimacy comes from unwavering institutional support from the big four—political party, military, internal security apparatus, and oligarchs. These are not revolutionaries but rather masters of the game. And the key feature is a deep overriding sense of one's exceptionalness—master of the universe, not unlike some fourteen-year-old in his parents' basement ruling the cyber universe in an online multiplayer game, but in real-world time. Here, one is pulling the levers of power and forever manipulating the surrounding world from a deep distrust that is so overwhelming one must try to control the entire universe. For all of them, as they become encased in power and unable to escape, their distrust erupts in paranoid projections. So Russia and China forever see the US as the hidden source of their citizens' discontent, as stirring political opposition, the abject cause of policy failures, and a threat to invade or attack them.

But what truly animates all this is a lifelong underlying emotional insecurity and profound distrust that continually requires tests of fealty, oaths of loyalty, and the perpetual surveillance of everyone? For a dictator, there is not enough subservience in the world. No amount of flattery is satisfactory, no matter how many of their giant posters hang in the halls of government. All the saber-rattling hubris—"Don't tread on me. I am dangerous and will attack and destroy you if provoked"—truly conveys what they don't feel. In the same way billionaires never have enough money, dictators never have enough power.

A dictator can never relax. They require endless proof and reassurance of loyalty and their ability to exercise power in all its forms. They are required to be ruthless to the very end. Kings never trust the food tasters or the ambitions of their closest ally or eldest son. They need leverage over everyone, whether it's economic, popular adulation, kompromat, or fear. It is best when you have all four. Everyone and everything will be sacrificed to hold on to power. Who can be more pathetic than Bashar al-Assad, with nearly five hundred thousand deaths during Syria's ten-year civil war. One cannot be more desperate or more controlling than this. It is all about power.

Dictators seldom get to retire. They know they will be hunted down and tried before a tribunal and killed. This is one of the reasons they desperately hold onto power. But mostly because power is an intoxicating salve to all their underlying grievances and desire for revenge. To quote former Brazilian President Jair Bolsonaro, "I have three alternatives for my future: being arrested, killed or victory" (*Time*, 9/21). What is impressive about this quote is not its insight but rather his blatant statement that he plans to win at all costs. As it turned out, Bolsonaro lost the election in 2022 and peacefully stepped down from office. It also appears he did not attempt to suppress or manipulate the vote count and accepted the election results without attempting a military takeover or arresting his opponent (this is highly unusual). And he was neither arrested nor killed as he predicted. But this is not the end of the story. As violence by his supporters continues to break out, he vacationed in Miami, Florida, plotting his return to power.

Always a Monster

In 2015, a six-foot, 270-pound man beat his six-year-old stepson then grabbed him by the leg and swung his head against a kitchen cabinet, killing the child. He was upset the young boy had taken a cookie (*Miami Herald*). If you can comprehend the mindlessness of this violent act, then you know all there is about dictators. *Just don't ever forget!*

Being in control means everyone has to believe the lies, all of them, whatever they are, for any reason. The lies hide the inner fears, doubts, and most notably, the feeling of weakness and vulnerability. There is only continual self-promotion and aggrandizement. Even if it means being reduced to military parades in Red Square or Tiananmen Square and propaganda news broadcast every evening. Everyone knows the information is being controlled, suppressed, distorted, and that nothing the state says can be trusted. Modern dictators are all emotionally bent early in life, now trying to wipe the slate clean, where only anger and frustration reside. Still, beyond that, there is only being in control to avoid any feelings that connotate pain and loss, and most fearfully, a child's vulnerability. This is the source of needing to invade the world around them. Incapable of emotional intimacy, they have learned to feign it at appropriate times with smirks, half smiles, hand clasps, and bro hugs.

Dictator Magic—Right Place, Right Time, Right Words

Beyond all the psychology, sociology, and political science, there is an even darker reality undergirding the rise of a dictator. It begins in a nascent area of neuroscience research called *collective neuroscience* (Denworth 2023). At its core, it examines brain wave synchrony between individuals and among groups of people to better understand patterns in human social behavior. At a neuronal level, people's brains begin to coordinate in what is termed interbrain synchrony or brain-to-brain synchrony (Kingsbury 2019; Omar 2019). And yes, it is the usual brain suspect—the medial prefrontal cortex. This type of pattern alignment is apparently evidenced in most social mammals, with laboratory researchers particularly excited by the observed brain synchrony among bats (Zang 2019).

Interbrain synchrony goes far beyond two people sharing a common experience and then having similar brain wave patterns, but to the specific alignment of brain wave patterns between two or more people. That is, the brain has specific neurons that map patterns of other people's behavior. And this is now being demonstrated through brain imaging technology such as functional magnetic resonance imaging (fMRI), functional near-infrared spectroscopy (fNIRS), electroencephalography (EEG), and optogenetics. This latter technology features LED lights implanted into a brain to activate discrete groups of neurons after a light-sensitive protein is inserted into the neurons. (And you would be correct in surmising this is not being done to people, yet.)

Currently, these researchers appear exclusively focused on the positive aspects of human social interaction. For example, between teachers and students or how friendships and romances begin, and more generally cooperative interactions at work or in problem-solving settings (you can rest assured this does not hold true for townhome association meetings). But in one interesting experiment with mice (Hong 2015), researchers demonstrated a high level of brain synchrony between dominant mice and submissive mice or what we might think of as between leaders and followers. This was later supported by research on social hierarchy in mice (Fan 2019). (Shout-out to John Steinbeck's *Of Mice and Men.*)

These mice studies have now been replicated with human test subjects (Liang 2023). In a small-scale study of individuals randomly assigned to problem-solving groups, it became evident through fNIRS that that interpersonal neural synchronization emerged from leaders synchronizing their brain activity with that of their followers. It was the "leader-initiated communications" that induced raised levels of synchronization. And significantly, the quality of the communications was prominent in a leader's emergence. In essence, the researchers concluded that leaders are "able to say the right things at the right times." However inadvertently, these researchers may have also opened the door to what we are trying to better understand here—mobs, cults, populism, and the rise of dictators.

If one were to speculate about this at the metaphysical level, you could not do better than Victor Müller at the Max Planck Institute for Human Development in Germany. Müller speculatively connects neural synchrony and dynamic social networks. He makes the case that brain neurology and social behavior are continuously interacting and influencing one another in what he terms *circular causation*. To quote:

> This principle of circular causation works not only within individual brains but also in a hyper-brain network or assembly binding two or more brains together that function as a superordinate system or superorganism.

An example he provided was the complex neuro synchrony of symphonic orchestras. And yes, the idea of any individual being subordinate to a superorganism is as ominous as it sounds and points to the bio-evolutionary tribal nature of *Homo sapiens*.

When one watches the grainy documentary films of Hitler mesmerizing huge audiences of followers and how they all shout and salute in unison and appear saturated in adulation, one might also be observing leadership-induced interbrain synchrony in causal circularity, only with millions of acolytes. It is also likely we are observing this in the militia movement and with proselytizers of conspiracism. And we are clearly seeing a bifurcated brain-to-brain synchrony in the Congress, as Democrats and Republicans struggle to pass something as simple as an appropriation's bill.

Perhaps more to the point, across the country, we can observe how Republican leadership has tapped into the *hyper-brain cell assembly* of the absolute-minded. Individuals who have been neurologically rewired from childhood to navigate betrayal-resignation and grievance-revenge, the predicates to self-deception and conspiracism, now being manipulated through the casual loop of interbrain synchrony or what we know to be a Republican superorganism.

Political Sadism

Sadism—deriving pleasure from inflicting pain, suffering, and humiliation on others.

Masochism—deriving pleasure or satisfaction from one's own pain and humiliation.

Highly driven individuals who are emotionally insecure and distrusting, with an underlying sadistic impulse, have all the core elements of a narcissistic personality and are fully prepared to be dictators for life. They are also capable of wielding power as if it is Thor's hammer.

Initially, they are ambitious and power-thirsting, seeking out all forms of authority to overcome an inner sense of feeling aggrieved and wanting revenge. And to be clear, all they experience are opportunities and people to exploit. But once empowered, they attack any perceived weaknesses in those close to them, e.g., wasn't early to the meeting, equivocated about supporting a policy, failed to mention them at a press conference. All projections of the tyrant's underlying insecurity. It is their paranoia triggering disgust and instigating an aggressive response to punish the disloyal. And to be clear, all failure is disloyalty (not a good time to be a Russian commander in Ukraine). It is also vital to continually identify and further subjugate the weakest and the most suspected so everyone can see that the leader is strong and someone to be feared.

Let's get real. If you seriously fear an exceptionally powerful person in your life, you are unlikely to confront them or expose them for their weaknesses. Dictators know this. They surround themselves with people who give them unflinching loyalty because they are fearfully subservient and making a lot of money at the same time. The people dictators surround themselves with are a public display of their power and sadism on a day-to-day basis. That's why Trump required so many generals to hang around the oval office, so he could continually humiliate respected figures by getting them to say and do his bidding. Basically, he was ordering them around as in *March of the Wooden Soldiers* to demonstrate how powerful he is and how weak they are (the definition of sadism). Later, he publicly humiliates them in a dismissive tone as phony and weak when they stand up to him, now delightfully able to demonstrate his superiority and prove that these generals weren't so powerful after all, firing them game show style.

And Trump was entirely able to rely on the bureaucratic "institutionalists" in the Department of Justice and State Department. Individuals who are proud that they never step outside the lines, quietly going about their business, professionally, of course, troubled by Trump's norm violations but assured of their pensions and that they were following the rules (the *useful idiots* of any coup). No need to worry. The institutionalist will ensure the bureaucracy runs as smoothly after the takeover as before the takeover. They learned long ago that submissiveness and obsequiousness are honorable and will be respected as dignified and principled. They are well adapted to sadism (being managing by authority) and have been for many years. That has been one of the secrets to their success. (Just to be clear, in good time, they do good. And in bad times, they follow the rules.)

Unable to trust, dictators despise what they perceive as weakness. It is an unconscious response to their own harsh discipline and abandonment growing up and the feeling of helplessness in the face of the discipline they experienced. They seek to punish what they perceive as a weakness in others as a means of excising their own demons. This is the underlying sadism of the authoritarian model. Essentially, they are engaged in controlling and humiliating others as an unconscious means of recapitulating and redeeming their childhood traumas. All dictators and the petty tyrants in our lives suffer this underlying dynamic. Trump derives satisfaction from publicly humiliating people who worked for him—a warning sign, not unlike a brightly colored insect warning predators to stand down or suffer the consequences.

Those who submit and stay close to the dynamics of dictatorships have a masochistic relationship to authority ongoing in their own lives. They become enablers of power. And there are always a few trusted weaklings behind the scenes whispering in Trump's ear, believing they are puppeteering him. Each one believes they are smarter. Trump publicly humiliating others is an unconscious signal to his base that he knows what they know and have experienced, making his sadistic demonstrations of power attractive to them, whether they serve in his administration or voted for him. They are all locked into an unconscious redemption of one another.

Parasitic Leaders Are Eating Infected Bird Feces

For years, entomologists have been reporting on parasitic relationships in the insect world. Recently, they have observed an ant species–eating tapeworm eggs from infected bird feces. The tapeworms thrive in the host ants but also appear to significantly extend the host's life. However, noninfected ants became overworked and stressed over time because of resources diverted to the parasitic hosts (who never work). One researcher commented that in ant colonies, "no ant can act alone" and that parasites in these communities "automatically extend their reach" to other ants, creating a "rippling mind-control effect that spreads and amplifies the consequence of infection puppeteering the entire society." Another noted, "The worm's MO is subtle and ingenious. They are not agents of disaster, but an insidious social sickness that sets reality only slightly askew" while "infected workers get a taste of invincibility and status" (Wu, *The Atlantic*). This is the same basic effect authoritarian leaders have on a nation. They divert resources to extend their comfort and safety while puppeteering the political process and stressing the entire community. Obviously, one political party in the US is eating way too much conspiracy-infected bird feces.

Narcissistic Impulse versus Psychopathic Calculation

The two most prominent flashpoints for large-scale military conflict in the world today are remarkably similar, aligning with the historical precedent of invading armies seeking territory and the spoils of war for thousands of years. They include China's President Xi Jinping's threatening to invade the Republic of China or what most of us think of as Taiwan and Russian President Putin's recent invasion of Ukraine. The Chinese Communist Party has insisted, since 1949, that Taiwan is a renegade province and not an independent nation. Asserting the "One-China principle," the CCP is unambiguous that unification is inevitable and if necessary by military force. And Putin, in a word salad public address that appeared remarkably delusional (rife with *alternative facts* about denazification and military biolabs), asserted the Ukraine is not a nation and represents a military threat to Russia. To most of the world, looking on these assertions were bizarre and confabulated nonsense.

So why has Putin plunged Russia into both an unnecessary and unwinnable war, and why is Xi seriously considering the same? Both are confronted with the same inner demons all dictators are acid-etched from—the conflict between *narcissism* or grandiose sense of self and *psychopathy* or the violent, paranoid calculation of how to retain power and maintain political control. These are the unresolved conflicts of failed developmental identities. Both crave a grand legacy (the narcissistic sense of being special and in control and overcoming the helplessness of growing up) that puts them on pedestals next to Stalin and Mao as a masters of their nations' rise from ashes. Xi has already walked to the ledge of the cliff and is peering down while Putin has jumped into the abyss. If there's a paradox here, it's that both have successfully tightened the reins on their political parties and nations as a whole. So why the unending scheming for greater power and control? (This is similar to trying to understand why billionaires always want more money and eternally avoid taxes.) They all experience the insatiable grind for more and fear losing the inflated sense of self that comes with power.

Dictators live in a world in which their perception of threats never diminishes but only exponentially increase in number and ferocity over time. This is not unlike the myth of King Midas, but instead of turning everything they touch into gold, it turns into betrayal. This reality derives from two unresolved dynamics beyond the universal principle of entropy:

1. A chaotic and unresolvable sense of emotional betrayal that hardwires them to a chronic sense of *grievance-revenge*, one that is continuously *recapitulated* onto the world around them.
2. Their successful rise to power and subjugation of nearly everyone around them creates the very threat they fear.

In this sense, every dictator initiates a self-fulfilling threat to themselves. They are driven by distorted emotional lives they cannot escape and can only temporarily suppress by overcontrolling the world around them.

The only trepidation Xi is likely to experience regarding the invasion of Taiwan is calculating the cost of an invasion to him personally. Policy analysts have no doubt that China would prevail, but the question is at what cost militarily, economically, and politically. The consensus is it would be high. If the Chinese economy falters and his economic and political forays across the globe crater, there should be no question he will act militarily. What confronts him at the moment are two unknowns in his psychopathic calculation: (1) do it now and risk the uncertainty of staying in power or (2) wait until his status feels precarious and use it as a pretext for holding on to power. His narcissistic impulse is unyielding—go for the grandest historical legacy now.

It is not a coincidence that from the beginning of recorded history, kings, emperors, rajahs, and sultans have identified with grandiose omnipotence. Many believed they were gods or directly descended from the gods. Next best option was they were anointed by the gods to rule. In time, many settled for a shaman or priest or oracle to consult the gods to guide their actions. But the best fallback was ascending to an afterlife and fulfilling their destiny to become gods. Today, they claim to have been elected by popular mandate and, best of all, have nuclear weapons (which pretty much makes them godlike). It is probably not coincidental that Putin turned sixty-nine when he invaded Ukraine. Denial of his mortality is now being propped up by a violent assertion of his will, as his aging coil falters. (It is not a coincidence he remains bizarrely sheltered and isolated during the COVID-19 pandemic.) His violently striking out from isolation no doubt recapitulates developmental traumas and reflects his growing sense of impotence and mortality.

A recent *NY Times* article (Meyers and Buckley) offers this quote by a "Chinese scholar":

> Strongman politics is again ascendant. Countries are brimming with ambition, like tigers eyeing their prey, keen to find every opportunity among the ruins of the old order.

This is a realist's understanding of dictatorships. Everyone is prey to those without a conscience. This, of course, was a crude hack of William Blake's "The Tyger" (1794) and his erudition of a "fearful symmetry," now enjoying a contemporary update in light of Putin's invasion of Ukraine.

The irony is that as dictators consolidate political power and exercise greater control over the peoples of a nation, it only serves to scale up their underlying paranoid fears and distrust of the world around them. The more they control, the more they fear and worry about—the crucible of their paranoia. But there is also the unconscious realization that there is never enough power to ultimately control their world, and in the end, encoded in their limbic stems is the unremitting fear they are going to be betrayed. Not invading Taiwan is the real threat to Xi as was not invading Ukraine the primary threat to Putin. They chronically simmer in states of grievance-revenge with an incessant need to expand power and control. They have learned that violence is the safest option when residing in an indeterminate world.

A democratic Ukraine on the doorstep of Russia, one that broadly shares a history, language, and culture, became an existential threat to Putin's authority because it recapitulates his childhood sense of familial betrayal. In essence, reconstituting the Soviet empire is tantamount to remaking his childhood emotionally whole, but never having to acknowledge his underlying distrust and the betrayal he endured, now projected on the betrayal he believes the Russian people have suffered. But no amount of empire building can undo his distrust. Next it will be the Baltic states, then Finland, Sweden, Poland, and Moldavia. And inevitably, his paranoia will shift focus to the central Asian nations getting too close to China. But a democratic NATO is the forever parental threat, particularly with US backing.

There is only inner madness in the world of dictators. They do not trust putting a gun to your head, only pulling the trigger. This is how they momentarily anesthetize any sense of vulnerability. As Putin steps into his armored motorcade with anti-tank grenade launchers, portable anti-aircraft missiles, and electronic jamming devices surveilling for improvised roadside explosives. His bodyguards set up their "four rings" of security anticipating the long ride ahead for the next few blocks.

There Are No Ironic Dictatorships

To nuance interacting with a dictator, it's helpful to watch the "Funny Guy Scene" in Martin Scorsese's *Goodfellas*, featuring a brilliant performance by Joe Pesci as a made man. After the Pesci character assaults the club manager with a wine bottle for asking him to make good on his tab, he jokingly shoves a gun at the head of an associate and feigns shooting him for a supposed insult, as the wise guys at the table lean back laughing and enjoying drinks. His insecure need to jokingly intimidate and threaten violence, along with his raging impulsivity, captures the underlying double bind dictators create for everyone around them.

When it comes to dictators, you can never know the *right* answer because you have to answer before fully understanding the question. And simply agreeing may be seen as a provocation. Did you use the right words, the appropriate tone, body language, facial expression? Too causal, too distant? Was the timing off? Was that too much eye contact? Did you hold the smile too long? Was the handshake too weak? Did you laugh too hard? Should you grovel more as you piss your pants and collapse to your knees sobbing and pleading for your children's lives? Suddenly, everyone breaks into laughter. The joke is on you! Having to undergo this emotional waterboarding is a relentless test of loyalty until betrayal is finally revealed.

And if it isn't obvious to you by now, don't try to cleverly interject irony. People who attempt this are among the first dictators go after. Why? Because irony presupposes multiple levels of meaning, hinting the dictator doesn't know what he's talking about, has a hidden agenda, or isn't very smart. And pointing this out publicly comes with considerable risk. On the other hand, satire is too obvious and will immediately get you killed (shout-out to Jonathan Swift). Really, if you are irony-satire prone, avoid contact with dictators. The irony is the ironic class can't stop trying to be cleverer than everyone else. Much like the game of whack-a-mole, they keep popping up with another ironic take because it is so obvious to them that dictatorships are premised on lies and deception, literally a recapitulation of the parental lie that angers the absolute-minded when pointed out to them.

The unpredictable *edge* created by unconstrained power propped up by obvious self-deception is what makes Putin's nuclear threat so frightening to the rest of the world. And as the battle for Ukraine rages, it's also the most dangerous time for everyone in his political circle. Under high levels of stress, a chronic state of *grievance-revenge* plays itself out in a sadistic exercise of threats and violence—assassinate, poison, imprison, demote, sack, exile, and humiliate all of them. Their failures are proof of their disloyalty and corruption, and they are no longer able to maintain the lie.

While Trump admired Putin's ability to play the power game, he was completely envious of the unconstrained power Putin exercised. Putin represented Trump's unrepentant wet dreams (the father figure he is forever seeking approval from). Putin not only affirmed Trump's narcissistic and psychopathic impulses, but he also assured Trump he was always right and never wrong. From this perspective, it's easy to understand the influence Putin exercised over Trump. A Trump who couldn't stop whispering state secrets into Putin's ear just to see him approvingly smile. In fact, there is remarkably little difference between Putin's invasion of Ukraine and Trump's seditious acts against the United States. Put simply, Trump had greater constraints on his exercise of power, this time.

This is Not an Ironic Take on Dictatorships

> I am the only thing standing between the American dream and total anarchy, madness and chaos.
>
> —D. Trump

If one could conceptualize a timeline of the last two hundred years bisected by a quality-of-life measure, we would see something quite remarkable. Two hundred years ago, the world's aristocracy lived in great physical splendor, enjoyed conspicuous consumption, and the benefits of an enormous surplus of labor to do their bidding. And overall, they lived in greater safety and in better health than the average citizen. But over time, this equation has begun to shift.

By the time we reached post-WWII, one could make the case that the upper middle class and upper classes lived lives equal to those of aristocrats and wealthy elites of the world. And far superior to the wealthiest and most privileged people who lived only a hundred years earlier. Turning on lights, watching TV in the comfort of one's home, running water and flushing toilets, getting in the car to go grocery shopping, that's better than having three hundred people working every day with nothing better to do than make you comfortable.

Granted the wealthy and aristocratic class today have more of everything—expensive cars, castles and estates, great jewelry, private jets, and certainly better jet-setting parties on 250-foot yachts in the Mediterranean. But are their lives better? Did their children study exceptionally hard and become molecular biologists, architects, and data research scientists? Did they develop their own inner life fully and explore the world more deeply? Did they ever experience the satisfaction of a job well done or of a long and satisfying career as a lawyer or doctor or teacher?

Today, the wealthy and the aristocratic elite do not live longer or enjoy healthier lives. No, we commoners can go to the same Mayo Clinics, heart centers, and cancer institutes the wealthy jet to. And we know they lack the day-to-day freedom to move about the world. Yes, that private jet is convenient, but it only saves a few hours here and there for $300 million. This is to simply note that the quality-of-life gap has closed, in most instances, between the elite and Middle America. The modern life—extended by unlimited energy, overflowing food production, and dramatic advances in manufacturing, transportation, education, and computer technology—has mostly rendered the extravagances of the wealthy irrelevant and even ridiculously redundant and excessive. And here is the point: more is not necessarily better. That's a nineteenth-century understanding of the world. And at some point, more is just more, which carries its own burden—not better and likely an impediment to a full and meaningful life, but also an emptiness that the extremely wealthy pass on to their children.

Our contemporary reality raises an important question: What are dictators getting out of life that many of us are not already enjoying? Okay, besides an insane amount of power! But something is truly different about them, as with any gang, cartel, or mob boss. We know they're trapped in privilege and leveraged with violence, continually having to deal with heavily armed security details, stepping into the limo and reclining on posh leather seats, and for a moment, quietly contemplating the forty-two plotted assassination attempts on Hitler. The door closes quietly. A quiet sigh of relief, wondering, "Why am I endlessly taking meetings and on phone conferences for hours negotiating kickbacks?" But always with the implicit "I want this payoff, or I will have someone cut off your balls and shove them down your throat." The princeling, oligarchs, and "big shot" CEOs will be charged with "corruption" and as traitors to the state and imprisoned, with dictators eternally fretting to themselves, "Here I am trying to hold everything together, every day. Who would do this if it weren't for me? How thankless this job is and underappreciated I am!"

They have more wealth than anyone can enjoy, and the only real perks are how often people treat them with deference, but mostly out of envy and dread. All that groveling does feel good to dictators though. But how much is too much? Unable to remember the last honest and sincere interaction they had with another human being, because they have never had one for years and no longer even know what they are. And if they believe it was recently, they are deluded and will end up murdering even more people than necessary.

They are more palace dog than free-ranging wolf. The only feral left in a dictator is a ruthless need to murder people who have threatened and betrayed them. But they are never free to go outside, drive the car, or jog alone. And they are never unconstrained to explore the world and life itself. (When was the last time a dictator needed pocket change for an impulse buy at a deli?) No time for that. They need to crush someone who talks back or challenges their directives. In fact, they have no idea what they have lost or what freedom is, which is why they are so good at denying it to everyone else. Who can a dictator trust? How many times have they glanced around the room and pondered, *Who is the leaker? Who is betraying me? Who will it be this time?*

It's a lonely job at the top, given all the people wishing them dead and having to be constantly fearful of someone popping two rounds in the back of their head while they sleep. When was the last time they went to a club with friends or spontaneously stopped at a coffee shop on a Sunday afternoon or took a solitary walk along a creek trail? They are in truly dead-end jobs. And no one loves a dictator. They just fake it for the lifestyle or are afraid to leave. The only way out of a dictatorship is by natural causes or assassination. Making a clean shot likely preoccupies many of them, hoping it won't be an explosive. There will never be a late-life second chance on that world class mega yacht or exclusive lakeside villa on Lake Como or the Black Sea and having friends over for the weekend. They were never exceptionally bright or talented but were in the right place at the right time and had just the right connections and nerve and aggression to make it to the top of a heap of dead bodies. There is the satisfaction of having ascended far beyond their dreams of being an enforcer. Yes, they are ruling everything as far as they can effectively threaten. How glorious is that! Okay, they get the large color posters lining the streets on days the Party celebrates. They always wonder who comes after them, literally and figuratively. Who is on the next poster display, and will they be forgotten? (To better grasp a dictator's preoccupation with his mortality, give a listen to "Just in Case" feat.

Swizz Beats, Rick Ross, and DMX, a rap song from the television series *Godfather of Harlem.*)

Damn meetings all day long, always talking strategy, unending problems, and the chronic dissatisfaction of so many leaves him disgusted with people, always lamenting, "What the hell does everyone want all the time?" That damn foreign press and journalists never stop poking around and asking uncomfortable questions. Any competent dictator knows how to shut up reporters better than that Saudi idiot. It looks like it's time to threaten another nation or leader today. Still pondering which one. Why is someone always trying to invade his county or foment discontent? Those laughs that seemed off and leave him distracted and wondering, "Were they implying I was wrong?" He wants to clarify. He would only threaten a nuclear war that would end the world if it was justified.

When it comes to wealth and quality of life, dictators will claim they earned everything they have stolen, confiscated, or violently reallocated, and the nation is better off for it. What else could explain all the respect and adulation they receive? And giving up power is nonsensical and wishful thinking. Power is wonderful and healing. All dictators want to be clear about this—there is no ironic opt out to being a dictator! The belief by the "ironic class" of thought influencers, that wealth and power are empty experiences, simply makes them easy targets, compulsively trying to change what they don't understand. In fact, every probe into a dictator's integrity is simply a matter of them providing the appropriate counterfactual response. For example, "Why did you militarily intervene in Ukraine?"

"Because it is a corrupt Nazi-infested state preparing to assault Mother Russia." With fifteen to twenty well-rehearsed memes, every dictator can thoughtfully and easily lead a nation.

When dictators die, many will rejoice. Many more will forget them, and most importantly, the truth about them will be revealed, and it will never be pretty. History tells us the last good dictators (the ancient ones) are over a thousand years old. Today, the contemporary idea of the heroic dictator is only being propped up by corrupt party officials that once lived in fear of them. Now near the end of history, there is no peace on earth or in death for dictators. And they could give a shit and hope you keep believing that.

Let's Summarize

As a forensic psychologist, I have spent a career evaluating criminal defendants for the courts. It was easy to become exasperated in knowing all the details of a case and then explaining a defendant's behavior to the court or a jury. How much do they need to know before they can reach a finding on competency to stand trial, not guilty because of insanity, or the risks posed by releasing a violent offender? Is a diagnosis satisfactory (dark triad), or does it require an underlying narrative of what motivated someone to act criminally and violently (e.g., a theory of mind)? And the court would always request that you lay out the defendant's story in detail, so it all adds up and makes sense. Thereby allowing everyone to decode the trajectory? I have tried to do all three when it comes to dictators.

A dictator is a dictator. They all pretty much conduct themselves similarly. Does it really matter why? They rise in times of social chaos and conflict. They all offer a false sense of order and stability. In return, they get to exercise an enormous amount of authority over a nation. They propagate lies and become prophets to people prone to believing them—the absolute-minded. Those who resist are treated aggressively and often violently. As leaders of nations, dictators are habitually intimidating others to hold onto power, which is the only driving force in their lives. They live out their days recapitulating childhood traumas, forever trying to undo the hidden dynamic of abuse and loss of trust.

A ruling strongman (typically a man) came from circumstances in which they were traumatized early in life. The way out of their state of resignation is inevitably finding expression for their grievances by seeking revenge. And when they encounter the power embedded in institutional authority, they find the perfect expression for their grievances and anger. Power knows no bounds and can bend reality around it—manipulations, lies, threats, intimidation, and the continual testing of loyalties. And ultimately, a sadistic expression of the dictator's underlying fear of being exposed as weak and vulnerable (as they were as a child). And there is the powerful ability to manipulate all the adoring and obsequious while surrounding themselves with flattering sycophants who eternally struggle to appease authority.

For the dictator, power redeems the loss of trust and innocence. That is all there is to really know. They have become the embodiment of the parents who abused them and made them suffer, which underlies their sadism. This plays out over and over in human society. This is why human history has been so violent and why survival often required dictators. The underlying psychopathology is less worrying than the reasons for its emergence at this time in US history.

And yes, Donald Trump is an authoritarian figure who is a dangerous threat to this nation, based on diagnoses, underlying theories, personal history, and actions. But he only exists because of dark money, the semi-fascist agenda of the MAGA wing of the Republican Party, and the overzealous support of Christian fundamentalists. The real story here is not Trump but the Republican Party. Herein lies our problem as a nation. It is the dark forces of our nation encountering the dark triad of leadership. These are dangerous times for democracy. To focus on Trump is to miss the real story and the dangers we face. Trump is simply symbolic for what aggrieves our nation and not the cause. America has never been the democracy we mythologized, and it is going to be even less than we hoped for soon. There are forces we have never fully encountered before—pandemic, climate change, and reality-altering technologies rapidly changing our world. It is best to hold on. We know the problems, but the solutions are less obvious.

Chapter 12

The Nine Lessons of v45.0

Each presidential administration is a history lesson in democracy.

The scale of Donald Trump's norm-shattering malfeasance as president is breathtaking. The highlights include Russian election interference, public extortion of the Ukrainian president, two impeachment convictions, a public campaign of lying and disinformation, violation of the Constitution's emolument clause, evading the presidential tax audit, orchestrating a violent insurrection in an act of seditious conspiracy against the US government, and the theft of over ten thousand classified government documents.

However, for all of us who were watching, what truly stood out was how constitutional checks and balances, federal law, internal watchdog agencies, and arcane institutional rules and norms of governance were rendered completely ineffective by Trump. A president with no political experience, no agenda beyond personal wealth creation and self-aggrandizement, with a potpourri of self-serving advisers, ran roughshod over the US government. And this shameless spectacle has continued since Trump has been out of office. What follows are the hard lessons of absolutism.

Lesson v45.1: The United States is no longer a model of democracy. It is important as a nation that we fully grasp the absurdity and dangerousness of what has taken place with the rise of Trumpism and the MAGA capture of the Republican Party. These two events pressure tested our democracy and revealed serious institutional flaws at every level of the government. In effect, we learned that our *Democracy Software Program v46.0* (number of presidents) is no longer backward compatible with our *Governmental Operating System v1.27* (Constitution plus amendments). The two no longer sync, and we are well beyond the occasional operating glitch. What was once proudly exhorted as the "messy" process of democracy has devolved into a corrupted operating system.

Two hundred and fifty years of political compromise has produced an operating system that is blinking the "blue screen of death," or what most of us think of as illiberalism and the decline of democratic norms. More specifically, we are operating in a state of denial and need to stop rebooting a dated operating system held together by patches and updates. The time has come for us to reinvest in new hardware and software. More bluntly, the government requires a serious teardown and rebuild.

Today, a case is being publicly made that the US is no longer a full-fledged democracy but rather a clash of the two elected political parties, one of which is an ideological extremist movement mimicking a political party. The distinctions between them are no longer related to policy differences but to the foundational role of government. We as a nation are debating whether or not we should be a liberal democracy or a semi-autocratic state. And it appears that the money and "we the people" are divided on this matter, which is the only reason we have arrived at this time and place in our history.

What former President Trump and his administration revealed to us is that the rule of law can be manipulated and gamed at the highest levels and across the broadest expanse of the democratic process. Every federal agency can be compromised with limited consequences, including those entrusted with primary oversight, such as the attorney general, inspector general, Department of Justice, and FBI.

The Trump team operated outside political norms and with limited concern for legal blowback. While the Republican Party, acting under the cover of legislative deniability, limited the checks and balances on executive authority. In this fashion, the federal government was reduced to operating as an illiberal administration. Here is the real lesson: If one party in a two-party system does not support the democratic norms, we are no longer a fully functioning democracy.

The internal erosion of norms is what political scientists term as the "politics of legality," with the goal of creating a "managed democracy" untethered from internal and external checks and balances. This is exactly what Hitler did after coming to power in Germany in 1933. Today, we are watching this formula play out around the world in Hungary, Turkey, Belarus, Romania, and India. Essentially, democracy is hollowed out from within. In the US, the first illiberal threshold was crossed when the Republican Party's MAGA caucus committed unwaveringly to a conspiratorial lie—that the 2020 election of Joe Biden was a fraudulent hoax perpetrated on the American people by the Democratic Party, broadly making the case that our government is forever illegitimate if the Democrats win.

Lesson v45.2: Indifference to political norms is the shadow of a political coup. Thanks to the Trump presidency, we gained considerable insight into how incompetently the most powerful nation in the world could be governed. The president watched Fox News every morning and gathered QAnon tips on subreddit threads for policy direction. We also learned that Trump refused to read the classified President's Daily Brief (PDB) or be advised on policy matters because he was easily bored and distracted. But when given the opportunity, he was fully capable of leaking classified information before the camera or confidentially to Russian president Vladimir Putin.

How is it that politics and game shows share so much in common? The president was recorded recapitulating an episode of *The Apprentice: Special Edition Mob-Style* for the entire world to watch. In this special episode, he attempted to extort the Ukrainian president by offering military aid in exchange for help to incriminate the son of his political opponent. He was puzzled by the controversy, claiming he was trying to "save America," and besides, this is how diplomacy operates in the real world. Just ask "real" leaders like Putin or the Saudi king MBS. Trump correctly surmised not much would happen.

It turns out, repeatedly lying is an effective political strategy in a divided democracy. Trump surrounded himself with sycophants who spouted "alternative facts" and disinformation 24-7 from the most important bully pulpit in the world. The goal was to distort the truth of what he was saying. The record reflects that Trump issued over thirty thousand "false or misleading statements" during his time in office. But not to worry. There was a social media check that may or may not have canceled a few misleading statements suggesting violence against members of the Democratic Party.

Three years after the 2020 election, deniers continue to adhere to the MAGA conspiracy that Biden was not legitimately elected. Holding on to this lie has become sacred text and a protective aura for the absolute-minded. As president, Trump could tweet, text, or stand before a national television audience and dog-whistle his tacit political grift. It was as if publicly admitting his shame and deception made him more honest but also free of any significant repercussions. Similar to a child confessing to a wrongdoing to avoid punishment and then being praised for his honesty. Trump faithfully recapitulates this strategy every day, publicly telling lies and falsehoods as proclamations of his honesty and trustworthiness. His brazenness insulated him among the absolute-minded. And yes, this works.

The White House chief of staff, national security officers and intelligence chiefs, and foreign policy advisers were all terrified that Trump might impulsively authorize a nuclear strike. This was an impulsivity that he had demonstrated throughout life and every day he was in office. They took every precaution to keep the briefcase with the nuclear launch codes out of his reach. Please check first with the chairman of the Joint Chiefs of Staff before any formal launch. That was America's failsafe plan to prevent a nuclear war.

Many are still puzzled about how Trump's cabinet never seriously considered invoking the Twenty-Fifth Amendment to remove the POTUS for being "unable to discharge the powers and duties of his office." How administratively incompetent and dangerous can a president of the US be before they are no longer allowed to hold office? The bar is so low that the Twenty-Fifth Amendment only appears relevant if the president dies in office. However, we did learn that a general incompetence and indifference to governing, impulsive psychopathy, and seditious intent are acceptable norms for an American president.

Lesson v45.3: Impeachment and the special counsel are always late to the game. Russian oligarchs and Russian intelligence services were able to financially back Trump's presidential bid and, with the help of social media, manipulate his election win. Robert Mueller, former head of the FBI, was appointed as the special counsel to investigate the possible Russian interference in Trump's election. He was unable to prove that the Trump election campaign and Russian intelligence collaborated, an important lesson from Russia to Trump. In retrospect, it became obvious that Mueller was an "institutionalist" who was terrified of operating outside the bounds of the obvious. Having spent his career carefully assaying power, he spent $32 million over two years to conclude he couldn't rule out Trump's involvement. This will hopefully be his epitaph.

Two years after a violent and seditious conspiracy to topple the US government, not a single person at the top has been indicted, charged, tried, found guilty, or sentenced. The Justice Department has mostly sat on its collective derriere, dotting all the i's and crossing all the t's in an exercise of discretion rather than justice, while a pittance of Capitol rioters received reduced sentences for their remorse and claims of having been tricked. What does it mean when the Justice Department, after watching the televised House Select Committee on the January 6 attack, discovered there had been an attempted coup? And yes, the House symbolically impeached Trump twice (or what Republicans characterized as Soviet-style show trials), which was of marginal consequence to Trump. Each time, he simply retired to playing golf, entertaining foreign money at his Mar-a-Lago resort, and luxuriating in gold-plated bathroom fixture elegance.

Now comes the bureaucratic endgame, nearly two and half years after Trump's attempted coup. US Attorney General Merrick Garland decided to appoint a special counsel to determine if criminal charges are to be filed, a finding he will ultimately have to approve, making this entire process redundant and irrelevant but with improved optics. Basically, Garland stretched the decision time line to infinity or his retirement, whichever comes first.

Let's put the actions of the Justice Department in perspective. In what can only be described as an embarrassing waste of public money, the FBI and Justice Department went after sixty financially well-off families for bribing universities to admit their children in Operation Varsity Blues. It would have been more in the public interest if they had taken the money they spent prosecuting these families and offered student scholarships.

Then in 2022, the FBI and Justice Department brought down minor reality television "terrorists," Todd and Julie Chrisley, who received a combined nineteen years in federal prison for defrauding banks and providing fake financial statements to make it look like they were wealthier than they were. Trump has spent his entire life doing exactly the same thing. Let's cut to the chase. You couldn't make a decent prison toilet wine from these two low-hanging fruit prosecutions. In three significant instances now, the US attorney general and the Justice Department have demonstrated that they are unable to decisively act regarding the deepest interest of the nation, and more relevantly, they are afraid of history.

Sidebar. The Trump organization was charged by the Manhattan district attorney of seventeen counts of criminal tax fraud and found guilty on all seventeen charges. It paid $1.6 million in fines, or what Trump calls chump change. More to the point, Trump, as CEO, was never formally charged, while his CFO fell on his sword for the organization. Another win-win for Trump. And another small bag of money prosecution for a politically minded DA.

Lesson v45.4: It is possible to grift government to a standstill. Trump claimed that he daydreamed about declassifying thousands of US government documents in the detumescent glow of a Diet Coke six-pack, which he later claimed was an official presidential act. Upon leaving office, Trump packed dozens of U-Haul boxes with top secret documents and stored them in his basement. Two years after Trump left office, the government still doesn't fully know what was taken after recovering thirteen thousand documents. And the strong likelihood is the government will never know. And we might reasonably assume that Trump has no idea how many documents he stole, which ones, or where they are. From the government's perspective, this is another Trump shit show that has rendered it consequentially ineffective. The seriousness of his actions might not be known for years, given the extreme sensitivity of what has already been recovered. (Conspiracists are convinced that Trump has classified documents proving, once and for all, that the deep state is run by shape-shifting lizards and aliens.)

Why Trump took any classified documents is unknown, but there is speculation that it was about gaining political leverage to extort the government in case he was charged with a federal crime once out of office. Others conjectured that it was straight out of his book *The Art of Deal* to bribe foreign leaders for a cash payout or put the fix in for another Trump brand licensing deal. He will have to return most of the documents, but without real consequences (except for having disrupted his golf game).

All Trump requires to hold the government forever at bay financially, legally, and politically are overpaid and marginally competent attorneys filing petitions with the federal appeals court and a *writ of certiorari* to the Supreme Court. While everyone else who enabled him will have to wait patiently for a favorable administration or Congress to take power, turn state's evidence, or serve six months in jail and become a social media hero. (History will show Trump could do whatever he wanted as a businessman or a political leader so long as he could afford to pay the fine.)

The ability to flummox the government will allow Trump the opportunity to run for the presidency in 2024. Already, thousands are stepping up and investing in future pardons hedge fund style. While others are exploring how he can govern the country from prison. Once he is back in office, the agenda will be to reset the presidency with what was learned the first time around. Which has pundits openly discussing whether or not presidents could pardon themselves. Why not? The very first act of every administration after taking office should be for the president to pardon themselves and all members of their administration from any and all future federal charges. We may be seeing this soon, rendering the corruption of government criminally untouchable. The fact is, the federal government has been rendered completely feckless against the reality of Trump, and this is just as true now that he is out of office.

Lesson v45.5: Bureaucracy is corrupted top down, inside out. The most obvious reveal of the Trump administration is when sycophancy courses deep throughout a presidential administration, it inevitably corrupts the bureaucracy below. Civil servants bend under the weight of political pressure, and few are capable of speaking truth to power. And to state the obvious, those who don't go along aren't going to make much difference because they will be quietly demoted or fired "for cause" (wink, wink).

When under pressure, career administrators come to believe that they have too much to lose or too much to gain to not compromise and ignore the slippery slope in front of them. An important lesson learned from the Trump administration is that it's always better to compromise a little and play the game. This was as disappointing as it was to learn that many at the Pentagon are much slicker than anyone anticipated.

The first act of a president who wants to operate outside the legal and political norms is understanding that everyone above civil servants in the chain of command—for instance, the fifteen appointed cabinet officers—operate on nothing more than a "pinky promise." This starts with appointing an attorney general who will act as the president's personal Roy Cohn mob-style attorney, one who will conduct the president's bidding by writing Justice Department memos clearing the president of any criminal wrongdoing. Better yet, wrap the president's criminal conduct in Justice Departmental guidelines, cloaking him from either the law or justice. This is closer to a "get out of jail free" card than any mob lawyer has ever dreamed of and smoother and more efficient than a hit job or a payoff.

Ask John Kelly, Trump's second chief of staff, how power corrupts the political process. When the president tasked him with prodding the IRS into opening investigations into his political enemies, including former FBI Director James Comey; his deputy, Andrew McCabe; former CIA director John Brennan; and, just for fun, Hillary Clinton and Jeff Bezos (founder of Amazon and owner of the *Washington Post*). The point being, in Trump's mind, it was "his" IRS and "his" Department of Justice to do "his" bidding. Kelly claimed that he thwarted this effort. However, both Comey and McCabe were "randomly" investigated after Kelly was dismissed.

When government operates without the rigid enforcement of ethical guidelines and departmental policy and procedures, it is an unlimited perk gift shop and an insider stock portfolio investment opportunity for the politically appointed. Once the ethical guardrails are unhinged, inclining public policy toward a corrupt agenda becomes the casual normal. What's the complaint? If someone doesn't like the way the game is played, they can always resign in quiet protest, retire, and write a book. Or finally, for the first time, make a serious bag of money at a public policy institute or political nonprofit.

Civil servants, who work for years and are underpaid and suffer oppressive oversight, are what Trump called "losers," and he treated them as fully disposable. This included his chiefs of staff, heads of the Justice Department, FBI, and Centers for Disease Control (really, everyone). When ethics were eroded, we discovered the helplessness of government to monitor and police itself at every level. Watching the leaders of the CDC, the nation's best and brightest, standing silently on stage with their head bowed as Trump continually misled the nation on the COVID-19 policy was truly a melancholy moment in our nation's history.

Lesson v45.6: The more desperate to acquire power, the more dangerous. As one surveys the Republican Party, it is fairly easy to identity the most absolute-minded among them. They are continually making and endorsing the most outrageous claims and demands, unable to control their underlying mistrust and anger. A cursory survey of the suspected coconspirators in the attempted congressional coup makes it obvious that they were not particularly smart or competent as events and evidence are backward chained, but they were always blunt and persistent, unable intellectually or emotionally to differentiate the world in front of them.

Donald Trump, sitting in the Oval Office, assisted by members of his staff and outside coconspirators, planned and conducted an attempted violent overthrow of the US government. The Justice

Department reluctantly termed this as a potential "seditious conspiracy," or a legal bar too high for them to prosecute. (Apparently, having to stretch is uncomfortable for them.) All the usual suspects associated with this coup are currently without criminal charges. It also appears that Trump may have delegated coordinating much of this coup to the White House chief of staff, working with White supremacist militias and thirty-four unindicted congressional Republican coconspirators.

The president was angry and disappointed over having to watch the riots on TV, particularly after the Secret Service refused to drive him to the Capitol on January 6. He desperately wanted to be out front and lead the charge he fantasized about and, if necessary, order a hit on Vice President Mike Pence if he failed to cooperate. (Mustering all the outrage he could, Pence would later express his disappointment, noting this was not a good idea.)

All alone in the Oval Office, with only a McDonald's Quarter Pounder and fries, Trump cheered the rioters on. He was so pleased by their show of loyalty that he was unwilling to call in the National Guard or immediately make a "stand down" plea before the nation. For the record, he has suffered no serious consequences for his actions (if one excludes a symbolic House impeachment three weeks after he reluctantly left office without remorse).

Because the coup didn't succeed, Trump retired to play golf at his palatial resort in Florida, where he has been grifting hundreds of millions of donation dollars from fraudulent political action committee (PAC) schemes. (He had to reimburse some loose change after paying out millions in political favors and bribes.) One lesson here is there are fewer legal consequences if you can scale up your crimes. And no, Trump will not have to appear in court and will never serve time, not even after fifteen years of engaging in reported "tax dodging schemes." A small fine of a few million dollars should cover all the "mistakes" that were made because he followed the advice of his incompetent accountants (no doubt as part of the IRS deal, he will not have to admit any wrongdoing).

Lesson v45.7: If you are subpoenaed to testify before Congress, show up and assert your Fifth Amendment rights. All of us would have a better chance of riding a golden unicorn to the House Select Committee on the January 6 attack than serving jail time for lying under oath to Congress. How humiliating and inconvenient that the Justice Department became frustrated with a couple of witnesses and obtained warrants so the FBI could search their phones. (The odds were they were using burner phones, making these search warrants a waste of time.) And if someone failed to cooperate and didn't have enough political juice, a grand jury was convened. And if you really "have the goods" and are pushing the limits of noncooperation, you may be handcuffed and perp-walked to a waiting Cadillac Escalade. But not to worry. You will be home for dinner and can call your staff to download an encryption app for your new cell phone.

The only real punishment for being potentially complicit in an attempted coup of the US government was having to pay for legal counsel. Exorbitant legal fees leveraged many into cooperating, which is fairly reflective of how money works in our legal system. Having observed all this up close and personal, the Secret Service and Department of Homeland Security (DHS) deleted their text messages for the days leading up to and including the January 6 riot, claiming it was a scheduled "agency-wide technology migration." With these magic words, the DHS was somehow able to cast a technology spell and make reality disappear Hogwarts style. This is how a really competent federal agency nuances its incompetence or outright malfeasance! Why should they be the only ones to take the fall and go to prison? It didn't seem fair, given their salary range and the dirt they could spill at a congressional hearing. Best to lawyer up and take the Fifth if subpoenaed to testify before a congressional subcommittee. You will be fine because your case is never going to criminal trial anyway.

All of us got to watch the malfeasance of the Trump administration and the failure of consequences playout nightly on MSNBC and CNN. But for the pundit class, it was a *Waiting for Godot* experience, suffering the fatalism and futility of hoping that the arc of justice didn't have to bend across the entire universe before it reached them. Millions of Americans simply gave up watching the nightly news as a senseless experience and waited for the light of the next day to find out nothing had happened. But somehow, everything was worse.

Lesson v45.8: "Money makes the world go round—a mark, a buck, or a pound. That clinking clanking sound can make the world go round." (It has been reported that Trump often hums this show tune from *Cabaret* after consulting with his White House assistant, Hope Hicks, on important policy matters.) The emoluments clause of the US Constitution prohibits federal officeholders from receiving gifts, payments, or other valuable items from foreign states or their rulers or representatives.

During his time in office, President Trump allegedly collected millions of dollars in income from over a dozen foreign nations, including China, Panama, Philippines, Ireland, and the United Arab Emirates, while denying the existence of such accounts. Apparently, Trump forgot to report his indebtedness to a potential foreign influence operation while running for office and five months into his presidency. For example, his $19.8 million loan from a North Korean company with ties to President Kim Jong Un. This was merely a failure to abide by what is basically an "honor system." It turns out that the US Office of Government Ethics does not have the means to investigate these matters and had no knowledge of Trump's outstanding foreign debt (Forbes).

It has been estimated that the Trump Organization saw $2.4 billion in revenues during his four years in office, including from real estate, licensing, hotels, and golf properties. Trump also directed government business toward his own real estate holdings in the US and Scotland. While his sons, who ran the Trump Organization from a blind trust, continued to make financial deals with nations impacted by the Trump administration. In 2017 and 2018, Trump paid $750 in federal taxes, and none in 2020.

After leaving office, Trump's former senior White House adviser and son-in-law, Jared Kushner, brokered a $2 billion investment by the Saudi Arabian sovereign wealth fund in his private equity venture, which some have seen as a payoff for Trump's favorable policies toward the country. Ivanka Trump had multiple clothing brand licensing deals with Chinese manufacturers while serving as a White

House consultant, and these businesses reportedly received Chinese government subsidies, potentially boosting her profits. At the same time, Kushner served as a significant point of contact for Chinese officials in Washington. Tax records also suggest that Russian elites purchased $100 million in Trump-branded properties and continued to invest during his presidency, which could explain his friendly relationship with Russian President Vladimir Putin's foreign policy agenda while in office. In addition to these financial dealings, Trump lied about not having an open business account in China. When, in fact, he paid more business taxes to China than the US in 2020. He also falsely claimed to have donated his $400,000 a year presidential salary to charity, instead keeping it for himself. Perhaps most confusing was not Trump's refusal to turn over his tax returns to Congress while president but the IRS's failure to review his returns, making the case they were too complicated and they didn't have the time or resources to bother with them. Say what?

Since leaving office, Trump has faced limited legal consequences regarding his finances, with the exception of a few fines. During his presidency, he was able to engage in questionable financial activities with ease, often resorting to lies and refusal to cooperate. The emoluments clause, which was meant to prevent foreign financial entanglements, has proven to be an exhausted firewall because of the many loopholes and gray areas that can be exploited in today's financial world. One of Trump's biggest financial disappointments since leaving office has been the sharp decline in the value of his NTF trading cards, which fell by 80 percent within ten days of their release. Additionally, he was not successful in trademarking the phrase "rigged election!" But ten months out of office, he did close a multibillion-dollar name branding deal for a luxury housing and golf complex in Oman. Guess what? It was financed by a Saudi real estate firm betting on his reelection in 2024.

Lesson v45.9: Coup or marketing strategy? Seriously, Donald Trump never thought for a moment that he was overthrowing the US government. He was simply trying to negotiate an extended stay at the White House Airbnb because he was having such a great time, and more power and adulation than any human being could bear except for someone with his specialness. It was all about the great new friends and business contacts he was making (his bros Putin, Jong Un, and Erdogan). In his darkest moments of caffeine withdrawal, and on the advice of his legal team, he couldn't resist exploiting the legal loopholes in a shaky and poorly written contract (federal election law) to get the deal he deserves. He was using basic marketing tactics to apply negotiating pressure, the same as any successful businessman.

Trump believed it was important to begin negotiations by making his case before the public. In this instance, a simple statement of fact was at the heart of a product development rollout—election fraud kept Trump from being a two-term president. This required the intense promotion of a credible story justifying his extended stay. In this instance, he played the respected "victim" card, that the Democrats had stolen the election from him. He knew this wasn't true but wanted to soften the market with some negative advertising about how the "fake" press and Democrats had wronged him. This is what marketing is all about. Bring in some powerful influencers to promote his claims. He wanted Republican leaders with serious name recognition. (Not Marie Osmond or Tom Selleck. Okay, maybe William Shatner.) He wanted Mitch McConnell and Kevin McCarthy as his showrunners and a chorus of thirty-four Republican members of Congress emailing their support for his cause. This added real credibility and a remarkable chain of evidence.

It is also important to create some confusion about your competitor's character. Better to promote dozens of conspiracy claims rather than just one. This gives greater credibility to a stolen election theory and highlights your opponent's duplicity. Really, sixty postelection legal challenges are better than one lame one in rural Wisconsin. Besides, it is vital to stick close to your customer base in closely contested states. And every negotiation requires applying pressure and the occasional threat of a consequence. For example, having the military seize voting machine on the pretext they had been tampered with. It is important to test the Democrats' will and to see if they had the balls to push back. This is basic misdirection or business gamesmanship 101. Everybody does it.

The Capitol riot was just your standard runup to a hostile hedge fund takeover. All those so-called conspiracies about a rigged election were simply Team Trump attempting to short the market and make a little profit on the downside. Everyone knows there are going to be a few unanticipated consequences and sacrifices to be made (not unlike Elon Musk buying Twitter). It was time to move beyond Fox News and Twitter and field test a sample product in a live market to determine the appetite for it. Of course, people were unhappy when they discovered the Trump bobblehead doll had sold out. Seeking to hang Mike Pence was minor but reasonable compensation (no harm, no foul).

Let's be honest, Trump had zero understanding of how government works. As president, it was his government, and everyone in the government worked for him. If he wanted ten thousand National Guardsmen to escort him to the Capital on J6, it was his army, and he could do whatever he wanted. That is what leadership is all about, adding further proof that he deserved stay in office. These troops would perfectly line the hallways of the Capitol Building, making sure everyone was safe from the Capitol police, and then safely escort him to the White House.

And all this "alternative slates of electors" nonsense. Really, who would fall for that silly diversion? Democrats were all up in arms as if it were real. It was all just political theater. Some people were stupid enough to try it, and others were stupid enough to take this effort seriously. Everyone knew nothing was going to come of it. Just trying to pump up the base and motivate support on the ground.

Putting pressure on someone to close a negotiation is the art of the deal. Everyone knows this. The fact that Pence didn't understand this made him a fool and same with that Georgia election official. Apparently, there is no cure for over-worrying about little things like 11,780 votes. They couldn't handle the pressure or the rewards of a rent-free Trump penthouse. Come on! The Justice Department was the Trump USA legal team, working all the negative spaces, finding loopholes, and applying pressure to your competitors. Real negotiations require a few legal threats to soften up the other side and make them come to their senses and agree to the deal you want. Let them know your pockets are deeper than theirs and you have twenty-seven state votes if push comes to shove. Heck, Trump had the Federal Reserve and C-PACs coming out his ass. What conspiracy? What coup attempt? What is sedition? This is all crazy talk by the Democrats who simply don't understand the transactional nature of business in America. This was Trump keeping his campaign promise to run America as successfully as his businesses.

Chapter 13

Will Cultural War Become Civil War?

America's cultural war is a continuation of five hundred years of intergenerational conflict that has played itself forward in unending social and political clashes. But it's important to understand that this was neither inevitable nor an aberration. The underlying cultural divide between the *differentiated* and *undifferentiated* has been a staple of the human drama for thousands of years and was well adapted to European arrival on the North American continent. Besides, a serious disengagement between the rationally minded and the absolute-minded did not begin to seriously take place until the European Enlightenment. Going forward, it's important for us to account for absolutism's stress-induced and fear-driven adaptation to a complex, differentiated, and psychologically oriented reality. In the long-term, our evolving networked simulation is likely to require a generalized readaptation of the human condition.

It's all fine and good to understand the problem, but what are the solutions? The immediate answer is there are not many and certainly nothing as efficient as mRNA COVID-19 vaccines. For one, being absolutist has been a proven adaptation for thousands of years. The problem is, it's less adaptable to a rapidly changing modern world. And beyond the differentiated world, technology and civilizations are colliding. Our paradox is we don't have time for a five-hundred-year conflict because we are all in this together in the here and now as never before. The future is here, and too many of us don't know, don't care, or are trapped trying to escape it.

The way astrophysicists study near space and contemplate how to alter the course of a meteorite from striking earth is how we should contemplate nudging the trajectory of the human drama. It doesn't really seem possible, just yet. But consciousness has been altered in remarkable ways over these past millennia. The reality is, there are no big interventions, and the small ones will leave us feeling helpless and vulnerable. What we have to do is stay the course. We can readily observe how the changing parent-child relationship has altered our world, furthered along by rethinking our assumptions about child-rearing practices, developmental stages of life, health care and education, ultimately reorganizing human life around these evolving and adaptive realities. What is required now is the continued amplification of these revelations.

Here is our dilemma in game theory terms. Behavioral researchers (Rand and Nowak et al. 2021) developed a game titled the "Intergenerational Goods Game." Five volunteer teams were formed and identified as "generations." The object was for each generation to pass along enough resources for the next generation to survive for up to five generations. It didn't happen, and here's why. The key dynamic in this simulation was self-interest or earning money by consuming resources. It proved to be highly rewarding. And there was no immediate gain in self-sacrifice and assuring the future. After eighteen rounds, the first generation had failed to pass on enough resources. While two-thirds of the players were "cooperators," a minority of "defectors" essentially tanked the future for the present. In our present circumstances, we should think of our market economy as generating unending "defectors." But the more generalizable finding of this research was that "voting" can trump self-interest if it is binding on everyone. Score one for democracy securing long-term regeneration of the species.

Unfortunately, the results of this game generally confirm what we already know about ourselves. We are not very good at preparing for what researchers call "long-term risk governance." We casually go about our business until a catastrophe crushes us. And if we survived, we might act against the next iteration of disaster, but probably not, because they are exceedingly rare. Short-term, we are better prepared.

Our simulated reality is redundantly premised on mitigating foreseeable risk—car and airplane safety, disease prevention, bridge and building construction safety specs, clinical trials, insurance, civil law, and nuclear arms treaty. This preparation is certainly truer for civil engineers than gun manufactures (though guns do reliably kill).

Long term, we are always trying to squeak by, hoping that problems will be incidental or coincidental but not devastating when the risks are unknown or not obvious. For example, we are always cutting down trees and draining aquifers. People keep rebuilding their homes and businesses along the flooding Mississippi, as San Francisco sits beautifully waiting for the "big one." And "climate change" dramatically fits the description of a looming catastrophe we are pretty much ignoring, no matter how fast the ice sheets keep melting. In the end, it's a question of how a majority of "cooperators" can overcome the minority of "resisters." And who are the resisters exactly? As presented here, they are the absolute-minded acting out in the world—Republican authoritarianism, wealth inequality, dark money, conservative media, and religious fundamentalism. And here in the US, the majority of "resisters" are extremely recalcitrant and heavily backed financially. Our work is cut out for us.

American Endgame—*Coup d'état?*

Essentially, we have a significant number of citizens attacking a political system they don't trust and fear betrayal by and are at war with it to ensure its correction (principle) and punishment (discipline). And yes, this is self-defeating. But they would rather side with the "lie" that can't be spoken than be on the right side of a history that leaves them feeling irrelevant. And the lie being there was never a betrayal of trust growing up. Besides, any government that supports abortion rights can't be trusted. Harming the innocent is something they unconsciously know all about. They will redeem themselves and the country no matter what the cost.

As long as our goal as a nation is to grudgingly provide the minimum, we will forever be at war with each other. (Think "Ultimatum Game"—if the winner doesn't share, the loser will default their marginal gains to screw the winner.) You cannot demonstrate to millions of people how little they are worth, economically reduce them, and send their children off to war for decades and not expect blowback. Our cultural war begins in infancy and plays out over each generational lifetime. We are still teaching many, at an early age, the unwritten rules of *life* in America—you are on your own. Good luck. Just like Mom and Dad taught them. And nothing brings this reality to the fore faster than unending social change unsettling identity.

If there is a coming American political coup in 2024, it will likely come from the inside. As we recently saw, an authoritarian president was able to run roughshod over executive norms with impunity with the backing of the Republican Party. More likely, we will go under by an overturned or manipulated vote count than a civil war. And if you want to know the outcome, you just need to know where the military stands—with the Constitution or with America's fascist impulse.

Of course, the way to break our current cycle of cultural war is, you know, become socialist, but that requires a level of trust America does not appear capable of. But why do the absolute-minded shrink in fear and rage at this word as if it is the secular equivalent of the antichrist? You cannot trust the government to assist you with your personal struggles or solve societal problems, in general, when you have known since infancy that you cannot trust any powerful force beyond your control, operating with hidden motives and with interests that are continually at odds with yours (say, for example, one's parents). But also, when those you trust are cueing your distrust 24-7 and shouting at you that the struggle is between good and evil? How do you trust authority when survival is premised on an anger-fueled revenge as the norm for interacting with the world outside one's narrow circle of trust?

But herein lies the greatest conundrum of this entire discourse on absolute-mindedness. The government can never be trusted! Why should anyone trust it, whether differentiated or undifferentiated, Democrat or Republican? And the more powerful the government, the less it can be trusted—"absolute power, corrupts absolutely." And while, in general, it might be safe to conjecture democratic governments are more trustworthy than authoritarian regimes, we still want to know in what ways and certainly not in all ways. And no matter what the government does, the interests of some will always be benefited and that of others sacrificed.

When talking about the government as party to our social contract, we should be discussing the degree of corruption, not the absence. The interests of the monied and influential will prevail over that of everyone else the majority of the time, but not in all instances. And let's not quibble. When the government fails, the consequences can be catastrophic. So how do we keep reassuring those who struggle with trust, even though all governments are corrupt to varying degrees, that one must learn to broker trust in all relationships, including with government?

Our dilemma is that a large segment of America is distrusting and has no interest in recalibrating for it. For them, their struggle with trust is not unlike going to a casino and desperately pushing one's chips all in, hoping to break even. While those calibrating their trust can accept their losses but haven't bet the paycheck or rent. The absolute-minded are all in with their faith and political beliefs. No fine-tuning of trust here. Their struggle is a zero-state affair. Because they are undifferentiated internally, they are undifferentiated externally. Quietly residing in grievance, they are all in on the biggest, brashest, loudest campaigns, the biggest lie, the most outrageous claims. "Step right up, ladies and gentlemen!" Being fleeced by a carnie-grifting dictator is no different from attending a televangelist mega-service on Sunday morning, and being all in for eternity. This is where many of the absolute-minded reside as they struggle with distrust—all in.

The rise of populism in the US is just the beginning of more disruptions to come. And those individuals most susceptible and attentive to betrayal are at the forefront of disaffection with the world around them. As social disruption and economic insecurity continues to grow, it will envelop people higher up on the trust double bind continuum. And the only way to prevent this is to tame social disruption by identifying and creating a greater sense of economic security, but also of community. And no matter how well this appears resolved, guaranteed there will remain many aggrieved parties. In other words, we need to be cautious because it can rapidly escalate out of control.

The first thing that needs to be done once government has pulled all the usual levers is to decapitate radicalized news and social media platforms. The prohibition against crying fire in a crowded theater is no longer true today. We are now in a larger theater with more people. And more people are screaming fire in a crowded theater than ever before. One could make the case that there is no such thing as a conservative news media, only arsonists claiming the freedom to play with fire. It is conspiratorial and political theater poisoning America. They will argue, "Don't kill the messenger," but the messenger is harming us.

The liberal naivete that "reason" ultimately prevails in the marketplace of ideas no longer squares with the contagion effect of modern media radicalizing people through their fears and distrust. And the left's nonstop shouting about the evils of the modern world at the gene editing level of reality needs to shrink back, for it does not know what assuaging their "superego" demands is setting loose on the world, forever championing causes and righting wrongs. Really, America is not working for many people and never really has. Discontent is coursing through our nation 24-7 like an arcing high voltage transmission line (really, the entire world). Our slice of the world is never going to be perfect and is never returning to its nostalgic past. The scale of dysfunction and economic corruption has become overwhelmingly self-evident to everyone, and now the entire planet is electronically wired, all of us watching and listening in real time.

In our more immediate future, we have a problem! We have to find a congruent First Amendment means by which to tamp down media provocation in all its diverse forms. We are going to have to eliminate dark money entirely and reverse the Supreme Court delusion that money is free speech. Money, like people, needs to be held accountable. We have to go forward with assuring a social safety net and taxing the wealthy and closing "all" the loopholes. And we need to get a handle on a religious revival that is predicated on asserting its morality on the political process in America. It simply does not belong there, acting as our morality police. Much like the Mullahs of the Islamic world trying to hold on to power through rigid faith, the evangelical world is being held together with fear about the future. Our greatest dilemma is we need the courts now more than ever to structure the future and set limits on wealth, power, and hyperbole, just like our forward-thinking Founding Fathers would if they were alive today. The same ones with all those deep flaws and foibles facing "cancellation" by the overly woke.

What Level of Conflagration Can We Endure?

What if blue states refused to pay federal income tax to stop supporting red states? The five states most dependent on federal funding are all red (South Carolina, Alabama, Arkansas, Mississippi, and West Virginia). This would be the modern equivalent of seceding from the Union.

On December 17, 2021, three retired Army generals (Eaton, Taguba, and Anderson) published an article in the *Washington Post* sharing their concerns over the upcoming 2024 presidential election and the "potential for lethal chaos inside our military." Adding, "We are chilled to our bones at the thought of a coup succeeding next time." (This is in light of the January 6 riot and attempted presidential coup in 2020.) Chief among their fears is the idea of "competing commanders in chief" giving orders—the legally elected president and the "head of a shadow government."

But what triggered these officers to go public with their concerns and violate long-standing norms of political nonpartisanship by the military? It's simple. In May 2021, 124 retired generals and admirals signed an open letter titled "Flag Officers 4 America." They advocated a false conspiracy theory that the 2020 election of President Biden was the result of a rigged election. It went on to warn that the US was "in deep peril" from "a full-blown assault on our Constitutional rights." They went even further, asserting that "Under a Democratic Congress and Current Administration our Country has taken a hard left turn toward Socialism and a Marxist form of tyrannical government." It also raised questions about "the mental and physical condition of the Commander and Chief" (*Politico*).

Any simplistic notion anyone might be entertaining that the military is a staunch supporter of democratic norms has been shattered. It turns out our military leaders are not an ironclad breakwater against a coup by a Republican Party with an authoritarian agenda. Clearly, many military officers, who operated day-to-day with a grinding sense of reality, are histrionic and bordering on delusional when having to operate outside the confines of military order. The most positive spin possible here is that these retired officers, having thrived in a world of principle and discipline, are struggling with their irrelevance in retirement.

We should all be taking notice and have been warned. In the event of an attempted coup, as recently orchestrated by Trump and Republicans, we cannot depend on the military to stand up for our Constitution and the rule of law. The real question we need to ask ourselves is this: What would the military have done if Trump had refused to step down from office and was supported by Republicans in overturning the electoral vote count? I suspect they would define it as a jurisdictional dispute between coequal branches of government and stand on the sidelines. There next most likely action would be to support the sitting president (whoever they decide that might be).

Let's explore. What if the next election outcome is thrown into confusion on January 6, and six Republican-controlled swing states ignore the popular vote and install a slate of legislatively appointed electors, claiming the popular election outcomes were fraudulent. Their *certificates of ascertainment* of approved College Electors are then challenged in both the House and Senate by Democrats. When put to a vote, the two houses split, the Senate rejecting it and the House approving it. Let's "game theory" this out. Republican leadership, at the federal and state levels, claim the election was stolen from them and mobilize violent demonstrations across the nation and in Washington, DC. Republican state governors then declare martial law and deploy the National Guard, claiming they are solely under the state's jurisdiction.

And instead of a few thousand protestors showing up in Washington, DC, what if hundreds of thousand show up to violently take back the presidency? What if federal troops stand down and refuse to deploy at the order of the whoever claims to be president? Or in a national emergency, assert military rule and effectively take control of the federal government to stabilize the political process. Who do they support? That is, where do their biases lie in this matter? And what if in a series of lawsuits filed by Republican states, the Supreme Court sides with them in this matter and confirms "independent state legislative doctrine"? Then how and when does the Army stand down and concede control to civilian authority? Do they cede authority to the popularly elected government or the Supreme Court's ruling that the Republican-appointed slates of electors stand?

The claim of a fraudulent election outcome now has legal credibility, regardless of how the Senate or House voted. And maybe it's not clear who is the truly elected government. Will all the brigades in the Army align or divide based on red state versus blue state affiliation? Will different branches of the military agree or conflict? At the state level, whom will National Guard units take orders from, the governor or the chief of the Army? Will units support the electoral outcome or the court-backed states' attempt to overthrow the election? Will rogue militia units enter the fray? And how will the many state law enforcement agencies respond? Here, the generals' fear of a "civil war" do not seem all that outlandish in light of all the competing claims of legitimacy and a potentially corrupted Supreme Court. But if the Army, the Supreme Court, and the state's claim of independently appointed slates of electors all align, the government will have been effectively overthrown. How would blue states respond to an overthrown election? Could our Union hold? What if the Army stands as the only barrier between democracy and autocracy? Then what?

Martial Law

Martial law is the "displacement of civilian authority by the military." To better understand how a civil war or political coup might play out, it is important to examine the concept of martial law and how federal troops can be deployed in an emergency. Martial law has been declared sixty-eight time in US history, both by federal and state authorities, but primarily by military generals and states. It is important to note that it is not mentioned in the Constitution, and there are no existing federal statues authorizing the president to declare martial law. It appears, under current law, the president lacks the authority to declare martial law, except as authorized by Congress. The only exception being a foreign invasion of the US. However, state officials have authority to declare martial law under state constitutions but must abide by the US Constitution. In these instances, the president has the authority to deploy federal troops to assist civilian law enforcement and civilian authorities in times of emergency.

The only instance in which the military supplanted state government was in Hawaii after the Japanese attack on Pearl Harbor in 1941. Before the nineteenth century, US law did not recognize martial law when, in December 1814, General Andrew Jackson imposed martial law on the city of New Orleans in an upcoming battle with the British. The second declaration of martial law was in 1842, in an event that uncomfortably parallels today. Rhode Islanders were involved in a dispute over the state's constitution. Led by Thomas Dorr, they organized their own convention, adopted a new constitution, held elections, and declared itself the government of Rhode Island (in what became known as Dorr's War). When they attempted to use force to take control of government, martial laws were declared by the state's general assembly, and the militia was called upon to quell the rebellion. Later, throughout the American Civil War, martial law was frequently declared.

The *Posse Comitatus Act* (1878) asserts that it is unlawful for military forces to undertake civilian law enforcement activities except as expressly authorized by Congress. But as always, there are workarounds. The *Insurrection Act* of 1792 and subsequent modifying statutes grant the president the power to deploy troops domestically in instances of insurrection in a state, but only if the state's legislature or governor request federal assistance. This was later modified so the president, without a state's request, could enforce the laws of the United States to suppress rebellion, insurrection, domestic violence, or conspiracy (Sections 251, 252, and 253). In this latter instance, the military might supplant the civilian government and conduct law enforcement activities. Title 32 of the USC permits the use of state National Guard under state command to conduct a federal agenda. But in all instances, law enforcement remains subject to civilian authority.

The real conundrum that is beggared here is what happens when the executive branch exercises its emergency authorities before the court reviews its legality or before Congressional authorization. Which, in a declared emergency, makes some sense. A conservative court might later agree with the president's action, and the Congress might pass legislation authorizing it *ex post facto*. But more likely, a successful coup will have taken place and a corrupt court and Congress legally legitimize it. And that is how democracies tragically end, hollowed from the inside out as norms are chipped away and the law is distorted for political ends. The only civil war of scale that's likely to occur is if military loyalties are divided. In practical terms, we are talking about the Army. All totaled, there are approximately 1,346,400 active-duty military personnel and 799,500 military reservists.

Reframing America's Cultural War

Let's add one final dimension to the American "experiment" in democracy—the American Cultural Wars (1650 to 2023). If one were to review a list of the longest wars in history, something quite astonishing emerges. Throughout recorded history, there have been at least fifty wars exceeding 150 years in length, with the longest lasting 781 years. This latter war was a series of military campaigns by Christian knights attempting to retake the Iberian Peninsula, or what we call Spain and Portugal today, from Muslim control. This was termed the Reconquista (711–1492). Then there are the American Indian wars, which lasted 315 years (1609–1924). The Viking invasion of England lasted 273 years (793–1066). And the Russo-Swedish wars lasted 315 years (1495–1809). (This last one caught me by surprise until I contemplated the current Russian invasion of Ukraine.)

Perhaps it would make more sense to understand the American cultural wars as an ongoing six-hundred-year conflict episodically flaring into violence throughout our history. And this war has had many iterations: French-English War, Indian Wars, Revolutionary War, War with Mexico, slave-sovereignty war, western vigilante land wars, labor suppression wars, and currently, the war between rationalists and absolutists or what we colloquially call Democrats and Republicans. And over the past seventy years, there have been numerous internal conflicts (anti-war movement, civil rights, women's rights, market turbulence, LBGQT rights, militia movement, debates over school curriculums, abortion-immigration, voter suppression, police violence. America is the nation that never rests).

Today, the hot zone of conflict is the unending arbitration of our social, economic, and political prerogatives around the ethnic, racial, class, and religious character of the Republic. And the defining elements of the current conflict are seven unprecedented events all simultaneously coalescing early in the twenty-first century:

1. The election of American's first autocratic president
2. The first attempted political coup to thwart the peaceful transfer of power
3. The curation of a conservative Supreme Court
4. The evolution of an authoritarian-minded Republican Party
5. Unprecedented wealth financially backing an anti-democratic agenda
6. The rise of Christian fundamentalism as a politicized force
7. The unprecedent role of modern technology and social media to surveil and influence public opinion

We are truly in a brave new world.

The reality is the forces at play are primarily a continuation of America's cultural conflict over the same issues eternally at play throughout our history—money and identity. The confusion here is our looking back and not recognizing how limited our democracy has always been. In reality, the most democratic era in American history (1945 to 1973) was recent and exceedingly brief. What is occurring today is as much about our limited democracy as it is about expanding the bounds of democracy to fit our aspirational vision of America. Not everyone in America today is luxuriating in democracy and many have not throughout our history. But the orderly transition of power has always prevailed—an inviolate condition for democracy.

As we race toward the future, it is important to understand that absolutism is relatively impervious to reason, so we should stop trying to over-reason with it. It will not understand or appreciate much of what the left does to reconcile differences and grievances. It is absolute and issues are primarily zero-sum for them. (We saw this fully play out in the aftermath of the Civil War and the gross violation of civil rights that prevailed.) All that can be done in the short-term is to unfailingly enforce the law, starting from the top down, and tamp down the social triggers cueing discontent, hoping to drain the energy out of populist angst. Which means it is time to institute a more equitable distribution of wealth and begin to limit social media's ability to set our world on fire. Running the source code back, it is evident that the antecedents for cultural war have been ever present in an America that is forever at war. One of the current catalysts lies deep in the Clinton administration's financialization of Wall Street and globalization of the economy. The time has come to walk both of these back.

The real flashpoint we are facing is that a large percentage of White Americans (about 39 percent) do not support the democratic process in the face of a radically changing economic and social world, even expressing an inclination toward violence when it comes to resolving differences. And in the past few years, independent voters have pushed these poll numbers as high as 48 percent at times. Given the norm violating political reality we currently face, two to three percentage points is a small margin of error to sustain democracy. And given our constitution was designed to inhibit majority rule, these distorted numbers will often prevail against the will of the majority. And this bias also filters down to the state and local levels as well, where the Republican party has effectively gerrymandered elections to empower radical conservativism in red states. Not to get overly "dialectical" here, while our Founding Fathers were clever at crafting an eighteenth-century democracy, their biases and fears may have inadvertently planted the seeds for its destruction in the twenty-first century.

Epilogue

21st Century Reenvisioning of America

To prevent another coup attempt, our democracy requires a serious overhaul after 250 years of devolving into political dysfunction. It is also important to understand that this has occurred with the tacit approval of the Supreme Court. The court, the final arbiter of the law, has been able to reside in eighteenth-century stasis without oversight or consequence, while a corrupted political process manipulated appointments to the bench. Here is an archaic institution that requires optimization for the twenty-first century. (Really, who would construct the current court's dystopian reality except as part of a bundled package of used video games?)

Let's stop pretending. The American electoral process is embedded in an outdated operating system. To recap, Trump did not win the popular vote but was still elected president. Highly populated areas across the US continue to be grossly underrepresented in the House and Senate, skewing both chambers more ideologically conservative than the country as a whole. The result has been a corruptly configured Supreme Court for generations to come. The reality is that the Trump administration did not represent the majority of American people and ended up empowering a minority populist movement that attempted a violent overthrow of the government.

Our democracy is bug infested with archaic malware that requires a serious upgrade. It is not only being manipulated for financial gain and power but is now being actively wielded to suppress democratic norms. This is the real struggle of our times. What

Trump revealed is that our democracy is not safe standing still. The Constitution, rule of law, and political norms, at all levels of government, can be bent toward a nondemocratic agenda. And here is the most important caveat of all. This can be done without significant legal blowback when our house is divided. Below is a call to reconfigure a modern democracy for the twenty-first century, one that guarantees our elections are inviolate. Once again, the time has come for us as a nation to double down and ensure that our actions are commensurate with our beliefs.

American Democracy Reenvisioned

- Immediately begin the reindustrialization of America as an act of "economic patriotism." Through targeted trade tariffs, trade pacts, tax incentives, and direct federal investment, the US needs to begin protecting supply chains and make America the world's manufacturing powerhouse. We need to move beyond inventing the modern world to building it.
- Prohibit foreign ownership (or investment) of all radio, television, or online media.
- Prohibit foreign ownership (or investment) of all print news media.
- Reinstitute the FCC "fairness doctrine" requiring broadcast licensees to cover controversial issues in a fair and balanced manner (with oversight and enforcement).
- Provide the FCC the regulatory authority to license local and national broadcast networks, cable networks, social media, digital platforms, and internet: To monitor "truth in advertising" and to provide oversight and accountability for "false information" harmful to the public.
- Clearly set forth the terms by which the Supreme Court can be expanded or contracted, as well as term and age limits for justices.

- Implement a judicial code of ethics for personal and professional conduct across all federal courts. Currently, ethical standards for Supreme Court justices are largely optional, with the court standing above the law and without real oversight or accountability.
- The time has come to end the practice of "shopping" for federal judges to assure a favorable judicial outcome.
- Grant statehood to the District of Columbia and Puerto Rico.
- Eliminate the Electoral College and the January 6 Senate confirmation of election results. Create a higher threshold for formal objections to results.
- Allow a more open process for proposing Constitutional amendments, with a popular vote on their ratification and sunsetting for future re-ratification.
- Constitutional amendment that allows for national referendums on important legislation. This process can be initiated by a minimal congressional voting threshold.
- Recalibrate the number of Representatives in Congress to proportionally reflect population imbalances among states.
- Pass legislation voiding the "independent state legislature doctrine" and asserting the federal integrity of the popular vote.
- Pass federal voting rights legislation independent of the states, federalizing the election process at the state level.
- Charter federal agencies with greater independence from the executive branch, particularly the Justice Department and Inspector General.
- Place limits on expanding presidential war powers.
- Place clear and well-defined Constitutional limits on the President's pardon powers.
- Implement term limits of twelve years for the Senate and eight years for the House of Representatives. Term limits should also apply to all state offices as well.
- Create a population-based formula for states to have up to three senators.

- Consider dividing large states like California and Texas into multiple states.
- Create a national panel to qualify federal judges to be appointed by the Justice Department.
- Eliminate the Senate filibuster rule.
- Eliminate the Congressional vote on the "debt ceiling limit" as the money has already been allocated, and it has become a partisan tool for disrupting government.
- Remove the tax-exempt status of churches and religious groups.
- Pass a constitutional amendment preventing the elevation of religious rights over civil rights.
- Fully control the southern border to prevent all unauthorized entry into the US. Authorized entry and granting of provisional status to reside and work in the US should be done administratively and outside the jurisdiction of state and federal courts.
- Build a southern border wall for its symbolic value, even if it has little impact on unauthorized entry.
- Require the full disclosure of all political donations and campaign contributions.
- Rewrite the "emoluments clause" in the Constitution to reflect twenty-first-century financial realities.
- Prohibit all individuals who have held federal office or been appointed to a federal position from acting as lobbyists or agents of foreign governments after leaving office.
- Prohibit all retired military personnel from consulting with or acting as agents of foreign governments that the US is not in military alliance, treaty, or pact with.
- Eliminate gerrymandering of election districts at the state level and create a federal commission to oversee fair redistricting.
- Implement "substantial" minimum taxes on wealth, capital gains, and inheritances.
- Require all large corporations to pay a mandatory minimum tax rate without exceptions.

- Revitalize the IRS to primary audit the wealthy.
- Address the earning disparities between executives and workers.
- Excessive corporate profits should be capped and tapped by the tax code.
- All Social Security benefits should be nontaxable and denied to those with significant retirement incomes.
- Cap the amount of wealth that any "dinosaur" can possess.
- Prevent elected federal officials and family members from insider trading by restricting the trading of individual stocks. Required to place all investments in blind trusts while serving in office.
- Implement a national health care system/account that provides insurance to every American beginning prenatally.
- Prohibit self-carry of guns in public unless authorized by the state for militia action. Ban the ownership of modified military weapons such as the AR15 (this should include regulating caliber and magazine size). Note that most state legislatures, courts, and the federal government prohibit guns, but not the stores we shop in. Why is that?
- Prohibit all nonstate-authorized militia activity in the United States.
- Prohibit all law enforcement and military personnel from engaging in private militia or anti-constitutional activity.
- Provide humanitarian options for the homeless, but under no circumstances are they allowed to camp, sleep, or loiter in public areas, parks, streets, or in front of homes and businesses.
- Prohibit US technology companies from having manufacturing facilities in any authoritarian nation.
- Prohibit US companies from selling technology or software to authoritarian nations.
- Decouple the American economy from the Chinese economy.
- No authoritarian state can have it industries listed on American stock exchanges.

- Regulate, break up, or shut down financial institutions deemed "too big to fail." Tax dollars should not be used to indemnify large corporations and financial institutions against risk.
- Prevent states from manipulating the federal election process for political advantage. Require greater federal authority to evaluate and approve districting within states, as well as standardized voting procedures across all state jurisdictions.
- Remove primary elections from party control and standardize the process. Replace "all or nothing" voting with "ranked choice voting" and a more proportional representation.
- Prevent foreign citizens who arrive in the US giving birth from gaining citizenship.
- Abolish civil forfeiture laws that allow law enforcement to confiscate personal property except for investigation of a crime (subject to court oversight). At no time should law enforcement agencies gain materially or financially from asset forfeiture laws.
- The time has come to do away with archaic common law practices such as adverse possession or squatter's right and the riparian doctrine of giving water rights (public resource) to landowners.
- Federal legislation to tightly regulate how all personal data can be used, monitored, or stored.
- The Presidential Medal of Freedom should be awarded to Anthony S. Fauci, MD, and to Lieutenant Colonel Alexander Vindman for speaking truth to power.

References

Acosta, R. M., and M. Hutchinson. 2017. "Dutch kids aren't stressed out: What Americans can learn from how the Netherlands raises children." *Salon*, March 26, 2017. https://www.salon.com/2017/03/26/dutch-kids-arent-stressed-out-what-americans-can-learnfrom-how-the-netherlands-raises-children/.

ACLED US Crisis Monitor. Acleddata.com

ADL. 2020. "The militia movement." https://www.adl.org/resources/backgrounders/the-militia-movement-2020.

Akhtar, S. 1994. "Object constancy and adult psychopathology." *International Journal of Psychoanalysis* 75(3): 441–455. https://psycnet.apa.org/record/1995-02740-001.

Altemeyer, B. 2004. "The Other 'Authoritarian Personality.'" Taylor and Francis Group, Psychology Press, ISBN: 9780203505984.

Alter, C. 2020. "Down the Rabbit Hole." *Time*, September 2020.

Amblard, F., and G. Deffuant. 2004. "The role of network topology on extremism propagation with the relative agreement opinion dynamics." In *Physica A: Statistical Mechanics and its Application. Elsevier.* ScienceDirect.com.

Ambroziak, K. et al. 2022. "Non-political anger shifts political preferences towards stronger leadership." *Scientific Reports*. europepmc.org.

American SPCC. 2019. "Child maltreatment statistics." https://americanspcc.org/child-abuse-statistics/.

Anderson, Kurt. 2017. *Fantasyland: How America Went Haywire.* New York: Random House.

Aunger, R. 2013. *The Electric Meme: A New Theory of How We Think.* The Free Press.

Axelrod, R. 1997. "The dissemination of culture: A model with local convergence and global polarization." *Journal of Conflict Resolution* 41(2): 203–226. Jstor.org.

Azarian-Ceccato, N. et al. 2010. "Reverberations of the Armenian genocide: narrative intergenerational transmission and the task of not forgetting." *Narrative Inquiry* 20: 106–123. Google Scholar.

Badger, E. 2016. "As American as Apple Pie? The Rural Vote's Disproportionate Slice of Power." *The New York Times*, November 20, 2016.

Bender, B. 2021. "'Disturbing and reckless': Retired brass spread election lie in attack on Biden, Democrats." *Politico*. https://www.politico.com/news/2021/05/11/retired-brass-biden-election-487374.

Blackmore, S. 1999. *The Meme Machine*. Oxford University Press.

Brand, S. et al. 2010. "The impact of maternal childhood abuse on maternal and infant HPA axis function in the postpartum period." *Psychoneuroendocrinology* 35: 686–693. PubMed, Google Scholar.

Bretherton, I. 1992. "The origins of attachment theory: John Bowlby and Mary Ainsworth." *Developmental Psychology, 28*, 759775. http://www.psychology.sunysb.edu/attachment/online/inge_origins.pdf.

Bump, P. 2017. "By 2040, two-thirds of Americans will be represented by 30 percent of the Senate." *The Washington Post*, November 28, 2017.

Burani, K. et al. 2022. "Corporal Punishment is Uniquely Associated with a Greater Neural Response to Errors and Blunted Neural Response to Rewards in Adolescence." *Biological Psychiatry Cognitive Neuroscience and Neuroimaging*.

Cameron, D. 2022. "Homeland Security Admits It Tried to Manufacture Fake Terrorists for Trump." Gizmodo.

Chaudhari, D., and A. Pawar. 2021. "Propaganda analysis in social media: a bibliometric review. Information and Discovery." Emerald Insight. Emerald.com.

Cherry, K. 2021. "What is object permanence?" Very Well Mind. https://www.verywellmind.com/what-is-object-permanence.

Conway, L. G. et al. 2017. "Finding the Lock Ness Monster: Left-Wing Authoritarianism in the United States." *Political Psychology* xx. doi: 10.1111/pops.

Cordero, M. I. et al. 2017. "Effects of interpersonal violence-related post-traumatic stress disorder (PTSD) on mother and child diurnal cortisol rhythm and cortisol reactivity to a laboratory stressor involving separation." *Hormonal Behavior* 90: 15–24. PubMed, Google Scholar.

Costa, D. et al. 2018. "Intergenerational transmission of paternal trauma among U.S. Civil War ex-POWs." *Proceeding of the National Academy of the Sciences.*

Costa, G. M. 2016. "New insights into cortisol levels in PTSD." *Brazilian Journal of Psychiatry* 38(2).

Costello, T. H. et al. 2021. "Clarifying the Structure and Nature of Left-Wing Authoritarianism." *Journal of Personality and Social Psychology*, APA. doi: 10.1037/pspp0000341.

Davila, J. et al. 2005. "Attachment as Vulnerability to the Development of Psychopathology." APA PsycNet.

Davis, J. W. 2014. "The Johnson County War: 1892 invasion of northern Wyoming." https://www.wyohistory.org/encyclopedia/johnson-county-war-1892-invasion-northern-wyoming.

Dawkins, R. 1976. "The Selfish Gene." *Oxford Landmark Science.*

Dennett, D. 1992. *Consciousness Explained.* Back Bay Books, Little, Brown and Company.

Denworth, L. 2023. "Synchronized Minds." *Scientific American* 329 (1).

Dodgson, L. 2017. "Narcissists aren't capable of something called object constancy—and it helps explain why they are so cruel to the people they date." Business Insider. https://www.businessinsider.com/narcissism-object-constancy-2017-8.

"Domestic violent extremism poses heightened threat in 2021." (2021). *Homeland Security.* https://www.dhs.gov/publication/domestic-violent-extremism-poses-heightened-threat-2021.

Drutman, L. 2020. "The Senate has Always Favored Smaller States. It Just Didn't Help Republicans Until Now." *Politics.*

Eaton, P., Tagkuba, A., and S. Anderson. 2021. "3 retired generals: The military must prepare now for a 2024 insurrection." *The Washington Post*, December 12, 2021.

Elving, R. 2022). "Imagine another American Civil War, but this time in every state." NPR: Politics.

Epstein and Corasaniti. 2022. "Taking the Voters Out of the Equation: How the Parties are Killing Competition." *The New York Times*, February 6, 2022.

Ethnic groups in Europe. n.d. Owlapps. https://www.owlapps.net/owlapps_apps/articles?id=13279542&land=en.

Ethnicity and race by countries. 2020. Infoplease. https://www.infoplease.com/world/social-statistics/ethnicity-and-race-countries.

Fan, Z. et al. 2019. "Using the test tube test to measure social hierarchy in mice." *Nature Protocols* 14: 819–831.

Farris, E., and M. Holman. 2022. "We Surveyed U.S. Sheriffs. See Their Views on Power, Race and Immigration." The Marshall Project.

Frank, A. 2020. "Facebook is a Doomsday Machine." *The Atlantic.*

Franks, D. et al. 2008. "Extremism Propagation in Social Networks with Hubs." *Adaptive Behavior* 16(4): 264-274. Digital Library. di.acm.org.

Frankel, S. 2016. "How Ideas Spread: The Role of Social Networks." TEDxSydney.com.

Feral Jundi. n.d. "History: The Range Wars of the old American West." https://feraljundi.com/history-the-range-wars-of-the-old-american-west/.

Field, N. P. et al. 2013. "Parental styles in the intergenerational transmission of trauma stemming from the Khmer Rouge regime in Cambodia." *American Journal of Orthopsychiatry* 83: 483–94. PubMed, Google Scholar.

Finkelhor, D. et al. 2019. "Corporal Punishment: Current Rates from a National Survey." *Journal of Child and Family Studies* 28: 1991–1997.

Follman, M. 2022. *Trigger Points: Inside the Mission to Stop Mass Shootings in America.* HarperCollins.

Freitas, G. 2022. *The Coming Singularity: The Rapid Evolution of Human Identity.* Austin McCauley.

Fukuyama, F. 1992. *The End of History and the Last Man.* Avon Books.

Garstein, M. 2015. "Infant temperaments may reflect parents' cultural values." Washington State University. https://cas.wsu.edu/news/2015/01/28/infant-temperaments-may-reflect-parents-cultural-values/.

Gelfand, M. 2018. *Rule Maker, Rule Breaker.* New York: Scribner.

Golshan, T. 2021. "Sen. Ron Johnson says he sees 'no reason' for COVID-19 mass vaccination." HuffPost. https://www.huffpost.com/entry/ron-johnson-covid-19-vaccine_n_6082ec86e4b0ccb91c23aa51.

Golding, B. 2022. "Here's how Putin protects himself from assassins and coup plots." NYPost.com.

Goldsmith, J., and A. K. Woods. 2020. "Internet speech will never go back to normal." *The Atlantic*, April 2020. https://www.theatlantic.com/ideas/archive/2020/04/what-covid-revealed-about-internet/610549/.

Graham, C. 2017. "Myths and misunderstanding: Slaveholding and the confederate soldier." The American Civil War Museum. https://acwm.org/blog/myths-and-misunderstandings-slaveholding-and-confederate-soldier/.

Hanson, T. 2018. "Central Oregon Range Wars: Century-old sheep shootings offer glimpse into the Old West." *The Bulletin*, July 7, 2018. https://www.bendbulletin.com/sp/central-oregon-range-wars/article_b43e1097-f7d0-52f2-b8c2-9fa4aa0114cb.html.

Hallett, K. 2020. "What is your attachment style? Attachment theory, explained." https://www.mindbodygreen.com/articles/attachment-theory-and-the-4-attachment-styles.

Heylighen, F. 2001. "Memetics." *Principia Cybernetica Web*. Pespmc1.vub.ac.be.

Hirst, K. 2018. "Understanding Mass Media and Mass Communications." ThoughtCo.com.
Hoffer, E. 1951. *The True Believer: Thoughts on the Nature of Mass Movements*. Harper & Row Publishers, Inc.
Hofstadter, R. 1964. "The paranoid style in American politics." *Harper's Magazine*, November 1964. https://harpers.org/archive/1964/11/the-paranoid-style-in-american-politics/.
Hofstadter, R. 1965. *The Paranoid Style in American Politics*. Random House, Inc.
Hong, W. 2019. "The brains of pairs of animals synchronize during social interaction." UCLA Research Brief. https://newsroom.ucla.edu/releases.
Honig, E. 2021. *Hatchet Man: How Bill Barr Broke the Prosecutor's Code and Corrupted the Justice Department.* New York: Harper Collins.
Huntington, S. P. 1996. *The Clash of Civilizations and the Remaking of World Order*. Simon & Schuster.
Inglehart, R. 2020. "Giving Up God." *Foreign Affairs*.
Israel, J. 2010. *A Revolution of the Mind: Radical Enlightenment and the Intellectual Origins of Modern Democracy.* Princeton University Press.
Jost, J. et al. 2003. "Political Conservatism as Motivated Social Cognition." *Psychological Bulletin* 129 no. 3: 339–375.
Kamal, R., Hudman, J., and D. McDermott. 2019. "What do we know about infant mortality in the U.S. and comparable countries?" Peterson-KFF Health System Tracker. https://www.healthsystemtracker.org/chart-collection/infant-mortality-u-s-compare-countries/#item-start.
Katsnelson, A. 2021. "A novel effort to see how poverty affects young brains." *The New York Times*, April 7, 2021. https://www.nytimes.com/2021/04/07/upshot/stimulus-children-poverty-brain.html.
Kauk, J. et al. 2021. "Understanding and countering the spread of conspiracy theories in social networks: Evidence from epidemiological models of Twitter data." *PLOS Digital Health*. https:-doi.org/10.1371/journal.pone, 0256179.

King, C. 2021. "The Fulbright Paradox: Race and the Road to a New American Internationalism." *Foreign Affairs.*

King, J. et al. 2001. "Early Sexual Abuse and low cortisol." *Psychiatry Clinical Neuroscience* 55:71–74. Pub Med, Google Scholar.

Kingsbury, L. et al. 2019. "Correlated neural activity and encoding behavior across brains of socially interacting individuals." *Cell* 178: 429–446.

Konda, T. M. 2019. "How did conspiracy theories come to dominate American culture?" University of Chicago Press. https://lithub.com/how-did-conspiracy-theories-come-to-dominate-american-culture/.

Kumar, K., and G. Geethakumari. 2014. "Detecting misinformation in online social networks using cognitive psychology." *Human-centric Computing and Information Sciences* 4 (14). hcis-journal.springeropen.com.

LaFantasie, G. W. 2004. "Civil War soldier's information and articles about soldiers from the Civil War." *MHQ.* https://www.historynet.com/civil-war-soldiers.

Liang, L. et al. 2015. "Leader emergence through interpersonal neural synchronization." *PNAS* 112 (14). https://doi.org/10.1073/pnas.

Lee, A., and B. L. Hankin. 2009. "Insecure attachment, dysfunctional attitudes, and low self-esteem predicting prospective symptoms of depression and anxiety during adolescence." *Journal of Clinical Adolescent Psychology 38*(2): 219–231. doi: 10.1080/15374410802698396.

Lehrner, A. et al. 2014. "Maternal PTSD associates with greater glucocorticoid sensitivity in offspring of Holocaust survivors." *Psychoneuroendocrinology* 40: 213–20. PMC free article, PubMed, Google Scholar.

Lindzey, G. et al. 1966. "Social dominance in the mouse." *Psychon. Sci.* 5: 451–452.

Lo, I. 2018. "Are your loved ones 'out of sight, out of mind?'" *Psychology Today*, August 16, 2018. https://www.psychologytoday.com/us/blog/living-emotional-intensity/201808/are-your-loved-ones-out-sight-out-mind.

Lowe, R. 2009. "Childhood through the ages." In T. Maynard & T. Nigel (eds.), "An introduction to early childhood studies." SAGE Publications.

Lynch, A. 1996. *Thought Contagion: How Belief Spreads through Society—The New Science of Memes*. New York: Basic Books.

Mahony, C., Brassil, M., Murphy, G., and C. Linehan. 2023. "The efficacy of interventions in reducing belief in conspiracy theories: A systematic review." *PLOS One*. https://doi.org/10.1371/journal.pone. 0280902.

Manson, J. H. 2020. "Right-Wing Authoritarianism, Left-Wing Authoritarianism, and Pandemic-Mitigation Authoritarianism." Department of Anthropology, UCLA. jmaanson@anthro.ucla.edu.

Mayer, W. 2008. *The Swing Voter in American Politics*. Brooking Institute Press.

McLeod, S. 2018. "Mary Ainsworth." *Simply Psychology*. https://www.simplypsychology.org/mary-ainsworth.html.

Menczer, F., and T. Hills. 2020. "The Attention Economy." *Scientific American*.

Meisfjord, T. 2018. https://www.grunge.com/128935/televangilists-who-were-anything-but-holy/?utm_campaign=clip.

Meyers, M. C., and E. Buckley. 2022. "China Sees at Least One Winner Emerging from Ukraine War: China." *The New York Times*, March 14, 2022.

Mondak, J. J. 2010. *Personality and the Foundations of Political Behavior*. Cambridge University Press.

Mooney, C. 2021. "The U.S. Senate: The Most Unrepresentative Body." NPR Illinois.

Muller, V. 2022. "Neural Synchrony and Network Dynamics in Social Interactions: A Hyper-Brain Cell Assembly Hypothesis." *Frontiers Cognitive Neuroscience* 16 (April). Frontiersin.org.

Murphy, T. 2014. "The meltdown of the anti-immigration minuteman militia." *Mother Jones*, August 4, 2012. https://www.motherjones.com/politics/2014/08/minuteman-movement-border-crisis-simcox/.

Myhre, M. et al. 2014. "Maternal childhood abuse predicts externalizing behavior in toddlers: a prospective cohort study." *Scandinavian Journal of Public Health* 42: 263–269. PubMed, Google Scholar.

New World Encyclopedia. n.d. "Margaret Mahler." https://www.newworldencyclopedia.org/entry/Margaret_Mahler.

Nicas, J., Zhong, R., and D. Wakabayashi. 2021. "Censorship, surveillance and profits: a hard bargain for apple in China." *The New York Times*, May 17, 2021. https://www.nytimes.com/2021/05/17/technology/apple-china-censorship-data.html.

Oliver. J., and T. Wood. 2014. "Conspiracy Theories and the Paranoid Style(s) of Mass Opinion." *American Journal of Political Science* 58 no. 4.

Omer, D. B. et al. 2019. "Social Minds Sync Alike." *Cell* 178 (July): 272–274.

O'Neill, A. 2021. "Child mortality in the United States 1800–2020." Statista. https://www.statista.com/statistics/1041693/united-states-all-time-child-mortality-rate.

Owens, J., and S. McLanahan. 2020. "Unpacking the Drivers of Racial Disparities in School Suspension and Expulsion." www.ncbi.nim.gov/pmc/articles/PMC8133760/).

Packer, G. 2021. *The Last Best Hope: America in Crisis and Renewal.* New York: Farrar, Straus and Giroux.

PBS. n.d. "Labor Wars in the U.S." https://www.pbs.org/wgbh/americanexperience/features/theminewars-labor-wars-us/.

Peterson, J., and J. Densley. 2021. *The Violence Project: How to Stop a Mass Shooting Epidemic.* Abrams Press.

Pei, L., and C. Xi. 2015. "An Overview on Opinion Spreading Model. Journal of Applied Mathematics and Physics." *Scientific Research* 3, no. 4. Scirp.org.

Recchiuti, J. L. n.d. "Labor battles in the gilded age." Khan Academy. https://www.khanacademy.org/humanities/us-history/the-gilded-age/gilded-age/a/labor-battles-in-the-gilded-age.

Rosenblum, N. and R. Muirhead. 2019. *A Lot of People Are Saying: The New Conspiracism and the Assault on Democracy.* Princeton University Press.

Roser, M., Ritchie, H., and B. Dadonaite. 2019. "Child and infant mortality." Our World in Data. https://ourworldindata.org/child-mortality.

Sayer, W., and P. Wagner. 2020. "Mass Incarceration: The Whole Pie 2020." Prison Policy Initiative. Prisonpolicy.org.

Schweit, K. 2021. *Stop the Killing: How to End the Mass Shooting Crisis.* Rowman and Littlefield.

Sharp, D. 2021. "Penobscot's don't want ancestors' scalping to be whitewashed." YahooNews.org.

Shermer, M. 2010. "The Conspiracy Theory Detector." *Scientific American.*

Sieck, W. and S. Mueller. 2009. "Cultural variations in collaborative decision making: Driven by beliefs or social norms?" ResearchGate.net.

Silver, N. 2020. "The Senate's Rural Skew Makes It Very Hard for Democrats to Win the Supreme Court." FiveThirtyEight.com.

Simpkins, B. et al. 2010. "Idea Propagation in Social Networks: The Role of 'Cognitive Advantage.'" Eprints.soton.ac.uk.

Soeiro, L. 2020. "What does it mean to have an insecure attachment style?" *Psychology Today* (January). https://www.psychologytoday.com/us/blog/i-hear-you/202001/what-does-it-mean-have-insecure-attachment-style.

Spadoni, A. et al. 2022. "Contributions of early-life unpredictability to neuropsychiatric patterns in adulthood." *Journal of Anxiety and Depression* (July).

Stano, S. 2020. "The Internet and the Spread of Conspiracy Content." In *Routledge Handbook of Conspiracy Theories, Butter-Knight,* 483–496. www.routledge.com. Iris.unito.it.

Stanton, Z. 2021. "How the 'Culture War' could break democracy." *Politico,* May 20, 2021. https://www.politico.com/news/magazine/2021/05/20/culture-war-politics-2021-democracy-analysis-489900.

Stenner, K. 2005. *The Authoritarian Dynamic.* Cambridge University Press.

Stillwell, B. 2019. "These states have their own armies not under the control of the Commander in Chief." Wearethemighty.com.

Stunson, M. 2021. "Tucker Carlson compares kids wearing masks outside to child abuse. 'Call the police.'" *Miami Herald*, April 27, 2021. https://www.miamiherald.com/news/nation-world/national/article250971964.html.

Sung, J., Beijers, R., Garstein, M. A., de Weerth, C., and S. P. Putnman. 2015. "Exploring temperamental differences in infants from the United States of America (US) and the Netherlands." doi: 10.1080/17405629.2014.937700.

SUNY. n.d. "Chapter 2: Social Contagion Theory. Social Network of Conspiracy." sociology@morrisville.edu.

Tetlcok, P. E. et al. 1983. "Cognitive Style and political ideology." *Journal of Personality and Social Psychology* 45: 118–126.

——. 1984. "Stability and change in the complexity of senatorial debate: Testing the cognitive versus rhetorical style hypothesis." *Journal of Personality and Social Psychology* 46: 979–990.

——. 1985. "Supreme Court Decision Making: Cognitive style as a predictor of ideological consistency of voting." *Journal of Personality and Social Psychology* 48: 1227–1239.

Tocqueville, de Alexis. 1835. *Democracy in America*. New York: Bantam Classics.

Trump, M. 2020. *Too Much and Never Enough: How My Family Created the World's Most Dangerous Man*. Simon & Schuster.

Van Prooijen, J, and K. Douglas. 2018. "Belief in conspiracy theories: Basic principles of an emerging research domain." NIH National Library of Medicine, National Center of Biotechnology Information. Ncbi.nih.gov.

Wellness Mastership. 2021. "Despite critics, researchers investigate possible new mental health disorder." https://wellness-mastership.com/despite-critics-researchers-investigate-possible-new-mental-health-disorder.

Wikipedia. n.d. "American militia movement." https://en.wikipedia.org/wiki/American_militia_movement.

Wikipedia. n.d. "History of childhood." https://en.wikipedia.org/wiki/History_of_childhood.

Wikipedia. n.d. "Lincoln country war." https://en.wikipedia.org/wiki/Lincoln_County_War.

Wikipedia. n.d. "List of conspiracy theories. https://en.wikipedia.org/wiki/.

Wikipedia. n.d. "List of countries by infant and under-five mortality rates." https://en.wikipedia.org/wiki/List_of_countries_by_infant_and_under-five_mortality_rates.

Wikipedia. n.d. "Margaret Mahler." https://en.wikipedia.org/wiki/Margaret_Mahler.

Wikipedia. n.d. "Mass shooting in the United States since 1949." https://en.wikipedia.org/wiki/Mass_shootings_in_the_United_States#Deadliest_mass_shootings_since_1949.

Wikipedia. n.d. "Militia." https://en.wikipedia.org/wiki/Militia.

Wikipedia. n.d. "Posse comitatus." https://en.wikipedia.org/wiki/Posse_Comitatus_(organization).

Wikipedia. n.d. "Self-constancy." https://en.wikipedia.org/wiki/Self-constancy.

Whitcomb, D. 2021. "Idaho lawmakers pass bill to kill most of state's wolf population." Reuters, April 28, 2021. https://www.reuters.com/business/environment/idaho-lawmakers-pass-bill-kill-most-states-wolf-population-2021-04-28/.

Wordsworth, W. 1798. "Patterns of childhood death in America." NCBI. https://www.ncbi.nlm.nih.gov/books/NBK220806/.

Wu, K. J. 2021. "The never-aging ants with a terrible secret." *The Atlantic*, May 18, 2021. https://www.theatlantic.com/science/archive/2021/05/ant-tapeworm/618919/.

Yahyavi, S. T. et al. 2015. "Relationship of cortisol, norepinephrine levels with war-induced posttraumatic stress disorder in fathers and their offspring." *Rev Bras Psiquiatr* 37: 93–98. PubMed, Google Scholar.

Yehuda, R., and L. Bierer. 2008. "Transgenerational transmission of cortisol and PTSD risk." *Progress in Brain Research* 167: 121–135. PubMed, Google Scholar.

Yehuda, R., and A. Lehrner. 2018. "Intergenerational transmission of trauma effects: putative role of epigenetic mechanisms." *World Psychiatry*: 243–257.

Yehuda, R. 2022. "Trauma in the Family Tree." *Scientific American*.

Zaidi, L., and D. Foy. 1994. "Childhood abuse experiences and combat-related PTSD. Journal of Traumatic Stress." Wiley Online Library.

Zang, W., and M. Yartsev. 2019. "Correlated neural activity across the brains of socially interacting bats." *Cell* 178: 413–428.

About the Author

Gary A. Freitas, PhD, has been a practicing forensic psychologist and consultant to the courts for the past thirty years. Professionally, he has written on the topics of involuntary commitment, workplace violence, and malingering incompetency to stand trial. He is also an artist and has been creating 3D sculptures from computers and electronic components titled *Singularity: Arising Electronic Consciousness—the Art of Electric Dreaming* (singularityartworks.com). He has authored three books, including *Relationship Realities, War Movies*, and recently, *The Coming Singularity: The Rapid Evolution of Human Identity.*

Printed in the USA
CPSIA information can be obtained
at www.ICGtesting.com
CBHW020353300324
6000CB00001B/2

9 798889 826651